Data Management

For On-Line Systems

Data Management
For On-Line Systems

DAVID LEFKOVITZ

Associate Professor
Moore School of Electrical Engineering
University of Pennsylvania

Staff Consultant
Computer Command and Control Company

HAYDEN BOOK COMPANY, INC.
Rochelle Park, New Jersey

To my wife, Norma

Library of Congress Cataloging in Publication Data

Lefkovitz, David, 1936-
   Data management for on-line systems.

   Bibliography: p.
   1. On-line data processing. 2. Electronic digital
computers—Programming. I. Title.
QA76.6.L42   001.6'4   74-4017
ISBN 0-8104-5100-X

2	3	4	5	6	7	8	9	PRINTING
75	76	77	78	79	80	81	82	YEAR

CONTENTS

INTRODUCTION

The digital computer was originally developed as a high speed calculator for solving ballistic trajectories, differential equations, and systems of algebraic equations. With the attachment of high-density magnetic tape for mass data storage, it was immediately transformed into an information processor, which significantly broadened its area of application. By 1960, more computer hardware was dedicated to information processing than to solving mathematical problems by numerical analysis, although the balance for programmers was not yet tipped so preponderantly. This can readily be understood when one considers that with a few days' effort a programmer can produce a report program of a sort that might easily consume hundreds of computer hours over the report's lifetime, particularly if the files that it processes are very large. Three related events of the 1960s have led to the current situation in which the overwhelming majority of hardware usage *and* programming personnel are dedicated to information processing. These events were: (1) the development of relatively low-cost random-access mass storage; (2) the development of compilers oriented toward data manipulation; and (3) the development of techniques for effectively and efficiently handling a large variety of data formating and organizational requirements in file and record structures.

Of course, the agency for synergizing these developments has been the industry and world-wide demand for a product—large-scale batched and interactive off- and on-line data processing. An enormous number of governmental, commercial, and industrial services came to be based upon the systematic accumulation of data and their rapid, low-unit-cost, repetitive processing. The demand for new systems utilizing these three developments has come both from the natural evolution of existing systems and from the development of new ones whose feasibility has depended entirely on the new technology.

The operational mode of these new systems falls broadly into four classes, derived by combining two dimensions of the problem environment, *turnaround* and *storage medium*, as shown in the table.

Turnaround	Storage mode	Predominant System Characteristic
Slow batch	Serial	Turnaround requirements are sufficiently long for large batches of file update and report transactions to be tolerated.
	Random	Normally not used.
Fast batch	Serial	Turnaround requirements are short, but files are relatively small.
	Random	Turnaround requirements are short, and both file and batch size may vary greatly.
Interactive	Serial	Normally not used.
	Random	File transactions—inquiries or updates—must be effected immediately.

As long as the cost of *random* or *on-line* storage was prohibitively high for megabyte file requirements, severe file size restrictions were imposed on its usage *vis à vis serial* or magnetic tape storage. Although these costs still prohibit its use under certain budgetary constraints and for extremely large data bases (whose processing by serial methods might also be questionable), it is not considered necessary to list file size limitation as a predominant characteristic for *random* systems in this table. Consequently, the major advantages for system development have now shifted toward the use of on-line files; and in the case of interactive systems, their use is mandatory. This fact is amply reflected in numerous large-scale system configurations that typically include 200 to 1,000 megabytes of random access storage.

Since the applications and the file-structuring techniques can vary so widely, and since the analysis, design, and programming of these systems have turned out to be so expensive, the industry is currently faced with a dilemma. Packaged data management systems can reduce development cost for a particular application but may not provide either the flexibility or the efficiency of operation required in many systems. Furthermore, even if a packaged data management system is used, it may still save only a fraction of the total application programming cost.

One may conclude, therefore, that if great numbers of system designers and programmers cannot use packaged data management systems, or indeed if packages must be developed in the profusion required to satisfy the variety of applications for them, it would be wise to look upon the subject of *data management* as a scientific subdiscipline within the technology generically called *data processing*, so that standards for training, development, documentation, and compability can be established. As is traditional with any science, the subject matter can be classified for the purposes of communication and operational utility; premises, axioms, and theorems can be developed that serve as the fundamental building blocks of the science, and, as an engineering discipline, measures of performances and design criteria can be established.

One purpose of this book is to view the subject of *data management* both as a science and as an engineering discipline, and to examine the basic concepts with the intent to classify them and to identify the more fundamental elements of theory and design. A second purpose is to propose and illustrate design principles based upon these concepts that may be useful, either in their presented form or in a readily modified form, to analysts and system designers in a broad spectrum of applications. These principles can also be applied to the design of generalized data management systems themselves.

The question whether it is better to use a DMS package or to custom-design and program whatever data management facilities are required for a specific application is not addressed directly in this book. This decision is a complex function of implementation and operational budget, time frame, availability of a suitable package, availability of talent, and the operational environment. What system analysts and designers will gain from this book is an understanding of the various functions of data management, the means of implementing them, and the role that they play in handling the data manipulation needs of application programs. These functions include data representation, record structure, file structure, file processing, data security, file back-up and recovery, file space allocation, and interaction with operating systems.

This book is a sequel to *File Structures for On-Line Systems*, published in 1969. Its subject, *data management*, broadens the area of discussion; *file structures* is but one subject within such a discussion. A single chapter in this book covers *file structures* and should be used in conjunction with the previous book and cited references for a more complete treatment of this specialized topic. The style of this book is also similar to that of *File Structures for On-Line Systems* inasmuch as heavy use is made of graphic illustrations because verbal description of design technique is difficult, space-consuming, and tedious for the reader.

David Lefkovitz

Philadelphia, Pennsylvania

1
Data Management

1.1 INTRODUCTION

Computer applications divide into two broad categories, numerical computation and data processing. The first is characterized by the computation of functions and by numerical methods for solution of differential equations; it is used largely for scientific and engineering purposes. Data processing, on the other hand, is characterized by the aggregation of data into records and files that are processed by sorting, editing, and formating for printing, and by simple calculations. It is used in commercial, managerial, and bibliographic applications. Some applications, such as discrete simulation, combine the two; queues in the simulation are maintained by data processing techniques, and statistical random variables are generated by methods of numerical computation.

This book, as well as an earlier one entitled *File Structures for On-Line Systems,*[1] attempts to view a part of data processing commonly called *data management* as a science. A number of fundamental definitions and principles will be proposed to serve as basic building blocks for the further expansion and development of the discipline. These principles are presented as techniques so that they can be applied directly, or adapted as required, to a variety of design problems. *File Structures for On-Line Systems* was concerned with storage and retrieval strategies for data in large-scale direct-access storage devices. This book broadens the scope to include the meaning and construction of data elements themselves and their hierarchic arrangement into structures of increasing complexity, such as the field, record, file, and multiple file. It analyzes data structure

---

[1] See Bibliography for all numbered references.

as a general concept and relates it to implementation in compilers like FOR-TRAN, COBOL, and PL/1. The book examines methods of processing data at the record and file levels and also inquires into the complex nature of how the data management system (DMS) is designed to protect the integrity of these data structures.

The rapid growth of computer science and technology in the last 30 years has made it difficult to organize this discipline into a classical science. Furthermore, one cannot readily establish a position of perspective from which to view the significance of the past, the meaning and true state of the present, and, perhaps most importantly, the requirements and dimensions of the future, when development is so rapid. But however tenuous the view may be, it is important for us to establish better foundations out of past works so that present and future scientists can systematically continue to develop the computer information science.[2]

In summary, this book is concerned with data processing applications of computers rather than numerical computation. Within the scope of data processing it is concerned with management of data in the sense of generating and maintaining complex data organizations. The DMS performs these functions as a service to user or application programs.

The automated *information system*, or information storage and retrieval system as it is often called, is effectively a combination of data management system and application programs that are designed to generate and process new data organizations, produce data summaries and reports, and permit file update and inquiry into a variety of processing modes such as interactive fast-batch turnaround and slow-batch turnaround. Chapters 1 through 6 discuss the software concepts of data management, relating them first to data structure itself, then to file structure and processing, and finally to the operating system and the various controls that must be exercised for the protection of data. Chapter 7 is concerned with the analysis of transaction throughput, with regard to both hardware and software, and Chapter 8 discusses some principal applications of data management.

Consider an analogy between the vacuum tube and information system technology, as illustrated in Fig. 1-1. The two are viewed in three steps. Step 1 is characterized as energy conversion. In the case of the vacuum tube, an electric current resistively heats a wire to convert electric energy into thermal energy, which in turn increases the energy state of loosely bound electrons in the metal of the cathode, thereby converting the thermal energy into kinetic energy, the latter manifest as free electrons in motion through a vacuum. The analogy to the information system is the conversion of a data base from one format, say hard copy, to another, say punched cards, in which form it can be read directly into a computer memory. The purpose of the conversion in both cases is to make the converted material (electrons or data) more suitable for subsequent processing.

Historically, the active period in the development of data conversion tech-

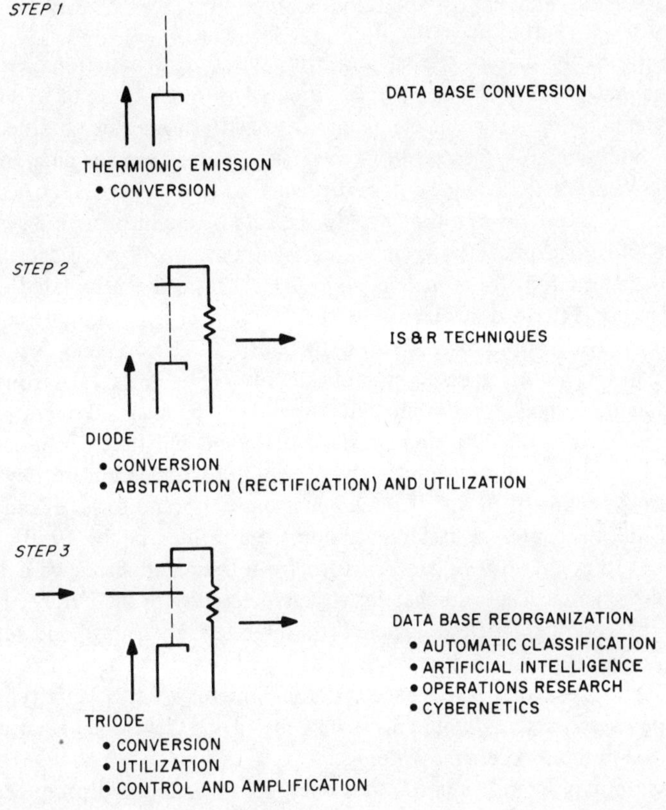

Figure 1-1 Comparison between vacuum tube and information system technology (step 3 is thought amplification)

nology started with the invention of the punched card by Hollerith in 1884,* gained impetus and real operational status in the 1930's and 1940's with a proliferation of tabulating equipment, and crested with the adaptation of high-density magnetic tape for digital data recording in the early 1950's. Developments in data conversion beyond this time have only involved higher recording densities, more convenient mechanisms such as key-to-tape and key-to-disk, and more efficient input and output converters such as OCR and COM. Thus, the perspective of 1972 sees the technology associated with step 1, data conversion,

*Prior digital encoding devices of Jacquard for loom control, and of Babbage and Pascal, should also be noted, but operational utility for large-scale data processing began with Hollerith's punched-card system.

as having peaked in the years 1950 to 1960, with activity since that time being devoted to increasing the efficiency of conversion rather than to the ultimate format of the converted material.

Step 2 in the case of the vacuum tube was the introduction of the anode, which enabled the free electrons to be directed through a circuit in such a way that a meaningful or coherent electronic flow pattern may be obtained. This is called a diode and represents both conversion and a form of data abstraction called *rectification* that may be discerned in the flow pattern; rectification permits a useful output to be obtained. In the case of the information system, the process of abstraction relates to indexing, abstracting, and codification of large bodies of information for storage in and retrieval from the automated data base. In neither case is there amplification in the mechanical sense of more coming out than going in or in the sense of gating or control. There is only a process that reduces or filters a homogeneous stream of converted material (electrons or data) to one that has certain discernible patterns and can be assigned operational roles within the context of a "system." The diode vacuum tube can rectify an a-c signal and produce a d-c current; the information storage and retrieval system can locate a document or set of documents based upon a series of index terms.

As the mechanics of data conversion were refined in the 1950's the techniques of storing and retrieving information from these data bases were developed in the subsequent decade, so that activity associated with the purely mechanical function of creating efficient logical structures for the storage and retrieval of indexed information crested in the decade 1960 to 1970. The introduction of the DASD in the late 1950's gave specific impetus to this activity, although serial tape-based systems would have become highly developed even in the absence of the random-access mass storage.

In summary, step 2 incorporates energy conversion and produces a useful output. In the information system, data are converted into a machine-readable input format, and programs store these data records on tape or disk, using assigned index terms or abstracts in such a way that other programs can selectively extract desired information. This purely mechanical function of storage and retrieval has become most highly developed in the last decade.

Step 3 in the vacuum tube analogy is the triode. With the introduction of a grid, one gets *control* and *amplification*, which means that an auxiliary low energy input to the system can be amplified through the controlling action of the grid. To what is this analogous in the information system? In step 2 the converted data were processed only to allow the retrieval mechanisms to function. The user of the system can expect to get out no more than is put in. The archetypal request is, "Give me every document or record that contains the characteristics A and B." These characteristics were first attributed to the documents either through assignment of index terms or through usage of these terms in a converted abstract of the document that was subsequently examined by a text scanning program; then the files were so organized as to permit retrieval of *all* records to which these assigned characteristics pertained. Hence, a machine is being described in step 2 with an intellect or concept amplification of, at most, unity.

In step 3, however, the human applies his own intellect to an input port of the system, and the data will then be operated upon by the system in some way that will generate an amplified (intellectual) response to the input. Qualities that are normally associated with the higher cognitive and intellectual functions of man are now attributed to the machine, which can assist man in the making of decisions through a reorganization of the data base in such a way that meaningful data patterns present themselves, where previously these patterns were not discernible.

Thus, step 3 represents true "thought amplification," and whereas step 2 was characterized by data base organization, step 3 is essentially a process of data base *reorganization* on a scale in time and space that the human brain cannot achieve. The techniques are only incipient, including automatic classification and automatic abstracting of documents, artificial intelligence, cybernetics, and operations reserach. In certain limited and restricted applications the computer-based information system has either outperformed or has amplified human judgment and decision-making power, such as in game playing or in the optimization of logistics routing, but these accomplishments are either of limited practical value or pertain to very unique situations and cannot readily be generalized.

The future of information processing systems is to be found in the development of step 3—data base reorganization for the purpose of human thought amplification. It is difficult to know at this time when such activity will begin to mature and still more difficult to predict its crest. From the present perspective it must be viewed as being several orders of magnitude more difficult than either conversion (step 1) or IS&R (step 2). One can speculate, therefore, that we are possibly a few generations away from maturation.

In summary, step 1, the methodology of data conversion, clearly represents a period of development that began actively in the 1930's, reached its peak of significant development in the 1950's, and although it remains an area of intense interest and development today through OCR and COM, only certain experimental forms of ultrahigh density storage techniques other than magnetic can have a revolutionary impact upon data processing in the future. Step 2, the implementation of large-scale information storage and retrieval techniques, received its impetus from step 1 developments, and both the theory and the practice have largely been promulgated in the decade of 1960 to the present. We are on the threshold of step 3, which is undoubtedly the most exciting frontier of computer science and technology, the actual realization of human thought amplification with as much generality of application as exhibited by the human brain, and with amplification factors like 10^6, or greater, as have been obtained in other physical sciences.

Assuming that this perspective is reasonably accurate, what obligation does it place upon us? Returning to the theme of the opening statement in this chapter, it would seem that it is incumbent upon us to organize step 2 into a body of knowledge that one can regard as a science. The fundamentals and the most basic and useful design concepts become steadfast and reliable once the crest of significant development is past. One can then more clearly enunciate, classify, and build them into a framework for design engineering and general utilization. They also become the basic building blocks for further extension of the science.

This book has as its primary purposes (1) the organization of data management, viewed as a science, into a more coherent schema of knowledge, and (2) the development of analytic and design principles that can serve as a basis for converting the science into an engineering methodology. This means that methods of analysis and design techniques for data management systems are to be investigated. The methodologies will generally be oriented toward on-line systems, although most of the techniques are equally applicable to batched processing. It will first be necessary to arrive at an understanding of the concept of *data* in its most general sense within the context of automatic data processing. The executive functions of management in a computer environment can then be superimposed upon these concepts in order to develop a discipline that can be called *data management*.

The book is organized in the following way:

1. An operational or functional definition of data is made in this chapter. If one is to design data management systems, he must understand the essence of data. He must know how it is aggregated into increasingly complex structures and the way in which these structures can be formulated and implemented so as to make them as independent as possible from a particular machine environment as well as from certain aspects of data processing. These subjects constitute the material in Chap. 2.

2. The special aggregation of data called the *file* is discussed in Chaps. 3 and 4. Being a very complex and high-level organ within the system, one of the most important aspects of the file is its *structure* or *organization*, the subject of Chap. 3. There are seven basic structures that have thus far been identified and implemented, and a number of multiple file structures that represent variations of certain basic structures. The second important aspect of the file is *processing*, the subject of Chap. 4. Files must be generated, accessed, and updated, and memory space must be maintained for future file growth or contraction.

3. The data management system can also be functionally described through the language that is made available to programmers or users; the principles, techniques, and descriptions of Chaps. 1 through 4 are summarized and more succinctly expressed by an illustrative data management language in Chap. 5.

4. Data management is not viewed here as a total computing system, but rather as a systems component within a larger operational environment. It must interact with other correlative and hierarchically superior elements of the system, such as programming language compilers and executive or operating systems. Chapter 6 is primarily concerned with interactions of the data management

system with certain global or executive functions of the total system environment. In particular, it examines operation of the data management system within a time-shared or multiprogrammed system, maintenance of data base integrity, security, backup, and recovery.

5. Chapters 2 through 6 lay the groundwork for understanding the nature of data itself, how it is structured or built into larger functional aggregates, how the latter are manipulated and processed, and finally, how they interact with executive systems.

6. Chapter 7 takes yet another view of the system regarding the hardware and software as a black box with some transfer function that describes the transaction-processing throughput of the box. A three-step approach is developed to this throughput or processing capacity analysis. First the system must be defined and configured and a model constructed. Then a simple worst case analysis can be developed that enables the designer to estimate very quickly the capacity and dynamic throughput of the system under the assumptions of the model and certain operational parameters and conditions. This analysis of the model enables the design to be roughed out. The model can then be simulated on a computer in order to ascertain more precisely its performance characteristics, and in order to enable certain parameters or components of the system to be varied in such a way that levels of performance that fall within the worst case analysis can be more accurately examined.

Computer simulation is relatively easy for persons without extensive mathematical background to perform. Virtually any combination of techniques described in Chapters 2 through 6 can be modeled and simulated. Furthermore, the simulation may have continued value even after the system has been implemented in hardware or software, since the effect on system performance of newly planned functions can be ascertained from the simulator by grafting the new functions onto the model. If it turns out, as is sometimes the case, that the model and hence the simulation have not accurately describe the system performance, after its implementation, there is obviously an error in either the model or the simulation, or both. Examination of actual system operating conditions and performance will usually uncover the original errors. Of course the damage from misjudgment will already have been done, and hopefully it will not be too severe, but with the added corrections to the model and the simulation, one should then be able to measure the simulation against the actual implementation and determine the amount of trust that can be placed in the simulation.

Having reestablished confidence in it (and given the fact that actual system performance has fallen short of expectation), one can then use the simulation to consider various economically feasible modifications to the system that will restore expected performance levels. In effect, after an initial system has been generally configured that meets the functional requirements at hand, the methodology is essentially "cut-and-try." The cut-and-try procedures are not carried out in the expensive arena of actual implementation, of course, but rather within a computer simulation of the design.

7. In Chap. 8 the book turns from fundamental design principles to applications. Two broad areas of application are examined both from a systems and a techniques viewpoint. These are information storage and retrieval systems and commercial transaction systems. General models are described for each application and the special problems of very large-scale data bases, mode of processing (on-line interactive, off-line small batch and off-line large batch), multiple access, time-sharing operating systems, backup, and recovery are examined in some detail.

1.2 WHAT IS DATA MANAGEMENT?

The answer to this question is multifaceted. First, there are two levels of discussion, one oriented toward the system in the larger sense, the other toward computer programs. Second, there are the major disciplines of data management at the program level. Third, there are the essence and nature of *data* itself. Finally, there is the notion of the *management* of data.

1.2.1 Levels of Discussion

One can identify two levels of discussion within the total context of the data processing system. The first and higher level is called the *user system*. By this is meant a system that is conceived for the purposes of a specific application. It involves the computer largely as a tool. Other major components of the system may be document, voice or video recording devices, data flow procedures, people and their organizational structure, and the like. Design, therefore, in the sense of the user system must encompass all of these components.

The second and lower level of discussion is to be called the *data management system*. This is regarded as software at the user level. It is concerned largely with the design of programs that will provide service facilities for the manipulation of data coming from and going to user written application programs. These programs will usually be written in a compiler language such as COBOL, PL/1, or FORTRAN, and one could conceive of the facilities of the data management system being provided to these languages either as subroutines to be link-edited into the user's program, or as augmentations of the compiler itself, being fully supported within the environment of the operating system.

Chapters 2 through 7 deal mainly with the lower level of discussion, namely the data management system, whereas Chap. 8 is oriented toward the higher level context, the user system.

There is, of course, a very important interface between the two, which involves language, and a model language is developed in Chap. 5 for illustrative purposes. Certain other examples are developed also in the application oriented chapter.

The first answer to the question, "What is data management?," is that it spans two levels of context: one is a lower, software level, where data are symbolically manipulated by computer programs; the other is the higher level of the user and is concerned with the function and role of the data, and to what ends it is being put.

1.2.2 The Disciplines of Data Management

The second answer to this question looks further into the detail of data management systems at the lower level. In response, one finds three major disciplines:

1. The essence of data must in some way be represented for the purpose of computer manipulation and then be susceptive of structure or organization into other and usually more complex aggregates of information, these aggregates being the basic components of human cognition, information handling, and, ultimately, decision making.

2. The larger or more complex aggregates of information are organized into records and files, and these must be processed in order that higher level functions may be performed on the data in the system.

3. Since there is a variety of functions to be performed on data and files, all involving management of various forms, there must be executive control that knows when and how to apply these functions. This discipline may be called the executive component of the data management system.

The three disciplines of data management are thus *data representation and structure*, *file structure and processing*, and *executive controls*. The second response to the question, "What is data management?," is that it involves these basic disciplines.

1.2.3 The Five Facets of Data

Looking now even further into the description and the essential nature of data, one may identify five facets. Each has a role, and the design of the DMS will be affected in various ways depending upon the particular role of data within a given element of design. Hence, the designer's viewpoint changes as he looks upon data from each of these five facets.

Facet 1: *Semantics*—The semantics of data are their meaning, where two interpretations of meaning can be made. One is called the *extent* of meaning, and the other the *intent* of the meaning. The *extent* is a specific definition or denotation of a data item. It is a linguistic or symbolic statement that commonly interprets what the data is to mean. It is analogous to a dictionary definition of a word. It therefore serves as a standard or reference for all other components of the system. Anyone speaking a particular language who wants to know the (extensive) meaning of a word can consult a dictionary and find the standard or common definition of this word.

The second interpretation, *intent*, is sometimes called *connotation* and refers to various nuances or subtle interpretations that often depend upon context for their ultimate understanding or intended meaning. An example is given in Chap. 2 of how the five facets of data are applied within the context of a data management system.

Borrowing from that example in order to illustrate here the difference between extent and intent, consider the data item, "balance" of a customer's account record. We are interested in the extent and intent of *balance*. In the example it is indicated that balance is algorithmically represented in the machine by two subcomponents, one being the generic name of the item, BAL; the other being a symbol that represents the value to be assigned to the data item, B2. The definition or *extent* of balance to the data management system, therefore, is BAL coupled with B2, and the definition is made more precise by indicating how B2 is computed. The *intent* is the interpretation that bears upon the specific context of usage in the application, and in this example it is given as "an amount of money, B2, owed by an individual, who is represented in the system by a record." This same extent could be interpreted differently in other contexts but has been here given one particular connotation.

Facet 2: *Syntax*—The syntax of data, within the framework of this discussion, means its association or relationship to other data in the system. Together or in combination, various data elements and their associations or syntactic relations form data structure, and ultimately the more complex file structures; hence, one may liken the data to very elemental components like atoms, and the structures that they form through a myriad of relations among the highly differentiated atomic matter may be likened to molecules.

Facet 3: *Representation* (format)—The representation of data within the computing system can also be viewed in two ways. One is *explicit* and the other *implicit*. An explicit representation is a specific sequence of digital symbols, usually, but not necessarily, arranged contiguously in computer storage. An example is BAL/$5.35. The implicit representation of data carries the notion of a process that is performed either upon explicit data or other implicit data that have been made explicit through subprocesses. For example, one may assume that the balance values are never recorded in a customer's record, but rather that individual transactions against the customer's account are stored, and that the sum of these transactions constitutes his balance. Hence the data item defined above as balance could be represented implicitly as the sum of all transaction quantities and could be made explicit by performing the indicated processing.

Facet 4: *Hierarchy of Data Aggregates*—The fourth facet of data relates somewhat to the second in that it concerns a specific relationship among data elements. In particular it is recognized that data have a hierarchic property in that they are successively built up into increasingly more complex forms of data.

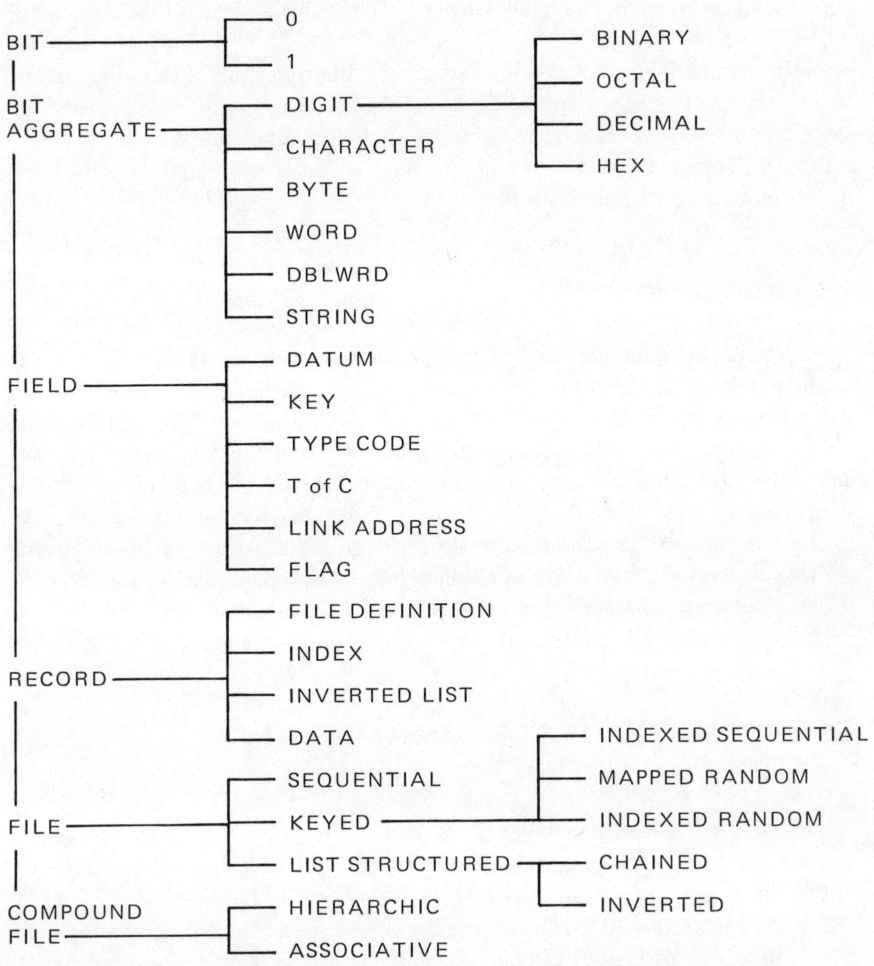

Figure 1-2 Hierarchy of data aggregates

Figure 1-2 illustrates this hierarchy with specific reference to data structure in the data management system. At each level of the hierarchy there exist data with all of the above three facets.

Facet 5: *Function*—Recalling the two contextual levels of the discussion in this book, the user system and the data management system, the fifth facet differentiates the functional nature of the data itself; namely, whether it is user derived and maintained, hence visible to the user, or data management system derived and maintained, and hence (in general) invisible as data per se to the user.

In summary, data have five facets: (1) their meaning, (2) their relation to other data, (3) their representation within the system for the purposes of storage, retrieval, processing, or display, (4) their composition and organization into more complex structures, and (5) their intended use, whether outside or inside the data management system.

1.2.4 Management of Data

Management implies control, and the management of data in the context of these discussions means (1) control over the generation of data and all of the structures to which the data pertain, (2) maintenance of these structures in terms of adding new data, and modifying and deleting existing data, (3) access and storage of data from and into these structures, and (4) control of the flow of data into and out of these structures, control of translation and processing that is performed upon these data, control of integrity and privacy of the data, and control over priorities of usage of the data base. Thus, management is conceived of as *generation*, *maintenance*, *access*, and *control*. These are the services that are performed by the data management system for the user system.

1.3 THE CONTEXT OF DATA MANAGEMENT AS COMPUTER SOFTWARE

Figure 1-3 presents a block diagram description of the operating system and its relation to the data management system. The operating system looks in two directions, one toward software, the other toward hardware.

The operating system controls the compilers. The data management system is a facility provided either through the compiler as commands or subroutines of the compiler language itself or as a direct subsystem to the operating system. The DMS will use the I/O handlers to perform I/O services through the operating system. The scheduler is responsible for the allocation of all computer resources including core, CPU, channels, and peripherals. It schedules the execution time for programs waiting to be run or for programs that are currently rolled out in the case of a time-sharing system. The loader locates a binary object program in core by assigning absolute core addresses to all relocatable addresses in the assembled program and by linking each subroutine into a single program run. The accounting system maintains usage statistics for all chargeable system resources; these are usually limited to the system hardware, although charges for software usage are sometimes also made.

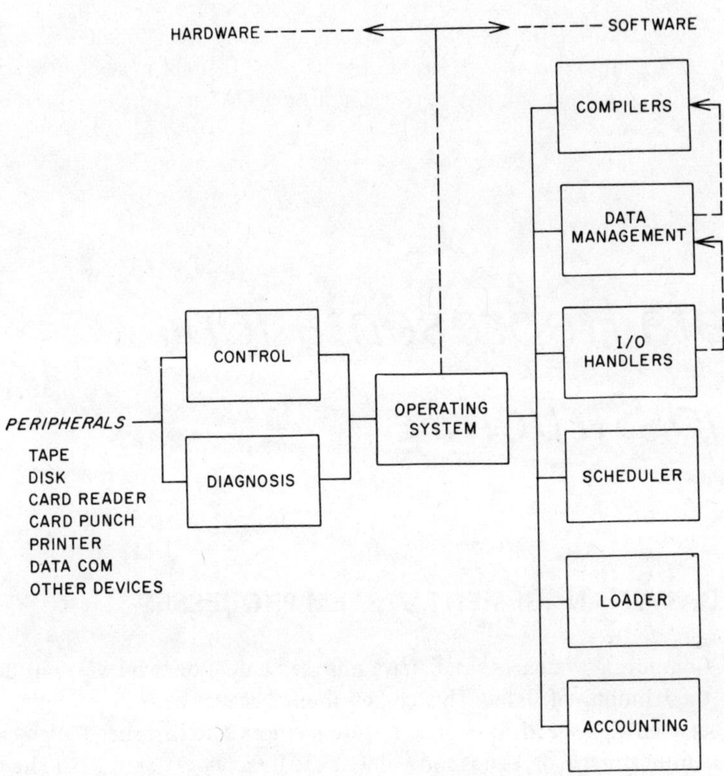

Figure 1-3 The operating system

In the direction of hardware, the operating system exercises physical control of peripheral devices through its I/O handlers. That is, it causes tapes to spin, disks to seek, cards to read, and the like. It controls the reading and writing of data over the channels to core memory and will handle diagnostic interrupts such as those for parity errors, causing necessary command repetitions to be executed.

2

Data Representation and Structure

2.1 DATA MANAGEMENT SYSTEM PROCESSES

Computing systems to date have imposed a dual or two-level consideration upon the handling of data. This comes about because of the mechanical difference between high-speed, low-capacity core memory and low-speed, high-capacity disk or drum storage, or, as it is sometimes called, *secondary storage.* (The generic name to be used for this latter type of electromechanical secondary memory is the Direct Access Storage Device or DASD.) A consequence of this constraint is a unit of information called the *record*, or more precisely, the *physical record*, which is a quantity of information that is transferred as a unit from DASD to core storage.

The block of information transferred in the physical record is generally unrelated in size to the unit of information requested by the program from the DASD. This latter unit of information transfer is called either a *stream* or a *logical record*, and many data streams or logical records can be packed into a single physical record, or *block* as it will be referred to in this book. The DASD is not truly a random access memory like the core memory, since there is a period of time during which it is occupied with mechanical positioning preparatory to transmission. This time is relatively long compared with the duration of the transmission itself. Hence, it would be uneconomic to transmit arbitrarily small amounts of information, since the overhead of mechanical positioning and/ or rotational latency must be sustained regardless of the length of transmission.

The user program, on the other hand, is uninterested in the optimization process involved in data access and transfer between the DASD and core memory. It is concerned only with units of information that have logical significance. Such a unit of information may lie anywhere along the spectrum of data aggregate hierarchy indicated in Chap. 1. It is categorized in two general ways by compilers and data-handling software today. One is called the *logical data record*, and the other is called the *data stream*.

The logical data record, hereafter referred to simply as the record, is a set or collection of individual fields concatenated or contiguous in core memory that is transferred to the user program. The data items may or may not be individually identified and interpreted within the record for the user, depending upon the construction of the compiler. For example, the FORTRAN binary record is unformated while the COBOL record may be formated per data item or may be unformated (called FILLER).

In the case of stream data each unit of transmission is extracted from a block by the compiler or data management system, interpreted according to a specified format and transferred into a core memory location that has been indicated by the user program. An example of stream data transmission is the FORTRAN formated I/O. The statement,

$$\text{READ (5, 100)A, B, I}$$
$$\text{100 FORMAT (2F10.4, 13)}$$

will read from a file named 5 (an internal compiler assigned name). A physical record will be deblocked by I/O routines of the compiler into three individual data elements. The first two data elements will be interpreted as floating point numbers, with a maximum of four significant digits following the decimal point and up to five integer digits preceding the decimal point; the first of these two numbers will be loaded into location A and the second into location B. The third number, interpreted as a three-digit integer, is loaded into the location I.

An example of record transmission in PL/1 is the following:

```
DECLARE 1   TASK
         2   NAME CHARACTER (24),
         2   STATIONS (5),
            3   TIME FIXED DECIMAL (10, 2),
            3   COST FIXED DECIMAL (10, 2);
```

The three data items—NAME, TIME, and COST—are transmitted as a record containing 24 characters plus two words. If the machine uses an eight-bit byte with four bytes per word, the record would contain eight words. The essential difference to the data management system between stream and record data transfer is that the former is structurally monolithic, having a single data item and format per unit of data transfer, whereas the latter usually has multiple data items and formats within each data transmission unit (the record).

This chapter is largely concerned with the field and record levels of the data hierarchy depicted in Fig. 1-2. It delves deeply into the variety of field types and uses and how they are organized into four specific record types to effect data management control. These records are examined, and intrarecord

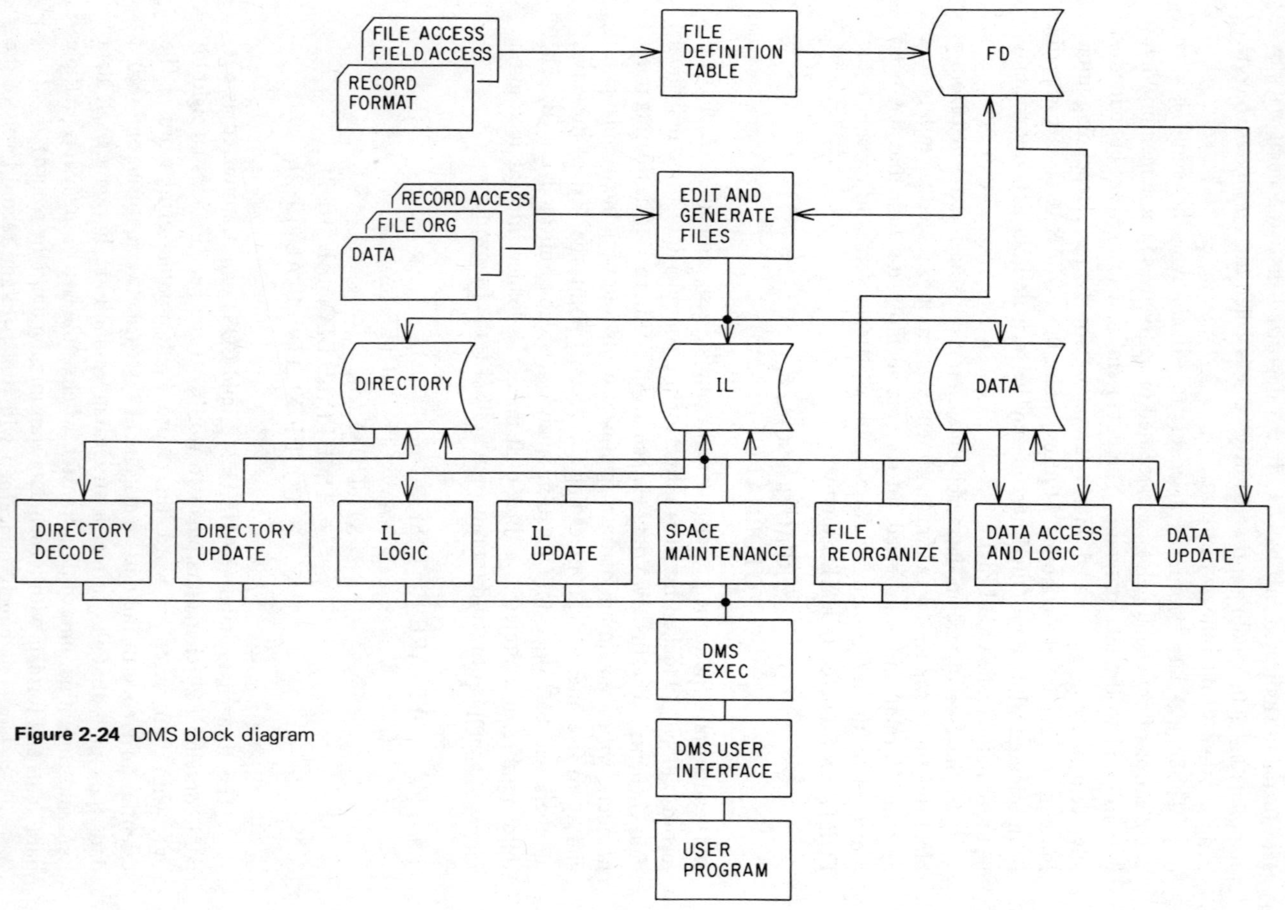

Figure 2-24 DMS block diagram

data structure is then discussed, since most information processing systems will utilize record data transfer rather than stream transfer. Record structure is thus one of the most vital concerns of a data management system. Some general principles of record structure are enunciated, and the record structures of COBOL and PL/1 are compared with a new structure that one could project from the general principles. It is of interest to see how far the designers of COBOL and PL/1 have carried data management (with respect to record structure) and yet how much further one might go, given the need.

It is worthwhile at this point to back off from a detailed discussion and to take a rather large overview of the domain of the data management system. This overview will identify large functional components that will serve as focal points of discussion throughout the remainder of the book.

Figure 2-4 illustrates the DMS purview as a block diagram. There are four file types identified within the DASD (disk or drum) symbols. The symbol is used simply to indicate that these are all random access files. The first is called the *file definition* (FD) *file*; its purpose is to define the record structure for each user data file in the system. Deriving the DMS from a table gives greater generality to the system in terms of enabling dynamic file reorganizations and redefinitions without requiring program recompilations. As it turns out, it is not always possible to make this definition entirely outside the data file itself, since there may be elements of variability within the data file that preclude a common level of description external to the file, as is implied by the FD file. (If one were to look upon a compiler like COBOL or PL/1 as a DMS, however, the FD, though it appears explicitly in source code as DATA DIVISION or PL/1 declarations, would not appear explicitly in compiled object code. It has been translated into addresses or indirect address references called *dope vectors* in the case of PL/1 based structures.)

The second file indicated in the illustration is called a *directory*. Its function is to translate from data item names and/or values into addresses or pointers to either data records in the data file or to records in the inverted list file. It is not necessary, however, that this translation be performed by a file. There are two general methods used to make the translation. One is by means of an algorithm and is called *mapping* or *randomizing*; the other is by means of a table look-up and is called an *index*. Generically, this function of translation is called a directory in Fig. 2-4, but only in the case of an index will there actually be a file.

The third file is the *inverted list file*, the function of which is to enumerate all the data records containing a given data item and value. The records are uniquely indicated in the enumeration either by their address or by means of a unique key of the record. The fourth file shown in the illustration is the *data file*, which contains the user's data. It is by means of the first three of these files that the data management system performs all its essential functions relating to the access or storage of user records in the data file and to the unpacking of data items from the records found in the data file.

The rectangular blocks of the diagram indicate procedures that are executed upon the data contained in the four files. In the case of the two procedures at the top of the diagram, external data must be processed. and these are represented as being entered by punched cards, although any medium of data entry is obviously acceptable. At the bottom of the diagram the user program is identified as a process that interfaces with the DMS executive via a user interface, which is some language or language subset that communicates commands from the user program to the DMS executive. At a very simple level, the FORTRAN formated READ command is a statement in such a language, since it requires data management service in stream data transmission. Sometimes the DMS interacts directly with a person rather than a program, in which case the user interface is called a *command* or *inquiry language*. A complete illustration of DMS user language will be given in Chap. 5 as a demonstration of how the user must communicate with the DMS executive in order to effect those functions, the design of which is the primary concern of this book.

The first task of data management as shown at the top of the illustration is file generation. The required data are provided at two levels to the system. First is that information necessary to describe the file globally (in the sense of common record definition) that is put into the FD and control information, such as the protection for READ and/or WRITE access to the entire file or to a given field within each record of the file. The file definition table is constructed with the record format specification of the file and field access codes. At the second level the actual data that comprise each individual record are introduced along with the organization of the file and, if required, and access code for each individual record. These are used in conjunction with the file definition to edit and generate the three remaining files. The file organization is required in order to determine the manner in which directories and inverted lists (if needed) are to be constructed, as well as to determine certain structural features of the data file itself, such as linkage pointers.

Access and maintenance of the files is performed by the eight procedural blocks shown in the middle of the diagram. The directory decoder reads the index file or computes an address reference from the mapping algorithm, and the directory update processor modifies the index file. The inverted list logic processor reads the inverted list file, and the inverted list update processor modifies or updates the inverted list file. An important internal function of data management is space maintenance—the allocation of physical space in the DASD for new blocks of index, inverted list, data storage, and new FD's. A user may sometimes desire to reorganize the structure of a file or set of files after the original generation. Reorganization can be accomplished within certain constraints without regenerating the files, and therefore a file reorganization processor will have access to all four files. The data access and logic processor reads from the data file and the FD file in order to be able to properly qualify data records that are accessed and to be able to format individual data items for transmission to user programs or for use in other subsystems that may be ancillary or part of the data management system, such as a report generator. Finally, the data update processor must have read/write access to the data file and read access to the file definition. All these processes are under the control of a data management systems executive, which communicates with the user program through a user interface or language.

This chapter examines the function and structure of the various records in these four files. Collectively they represent the total data base of the system, although they really represent two sub-data bases, one that serves the user and the other that serves the data management system. It must be emphasized that this book does not constitute the design of a data management system but rather presents the concepts and principles of data management system design. Towards this end the salient elements of a data management system are identified, their purpose and interrelation are described, and certain techniques for their implementation are given. These concepts and system elements provide design building blocks for the reader to use within his own frame of reference. However, these concepts and system elements will be illustrated by specific examples so that it may appear that parts of an acutal system design based upon these concepts are being presented as well. This impression is intentional, so that the reader, after having gone through Chaps. 2, 3, and 4 will be better able to envision the total assembly of a system. The descriptions of these chapters, however, cannot substitute for detailed design documentation, since all of the design parameters implied by equipment and programming language will not have been specified.

2.2   DATA REPRESENTATION

Figure 2-5 illustrates the five facets of data discussed in Chap. 1. The figure schematically portrays three record types within the DMS control. One is the index record, which is used to translate the data item name and value into an address reference that points to a particular data record containing that data item and value. The second record type shown is a data record, which contains the user's data; two of these are illustrated as record 1 and record 2. The third record type is the FD table, the function of which is to translate a data item name to an internal identifier code of the data item that can be used to locate and interpret a specific data item value within the record.

The figure is intended to illustrate the representation of a data item named "BAL" with a current value symbolically represented as "B2" The data "BAL B2" is identified with at least two records, called record 1 and record 2 in the figure. The illustration shows that (1) an entry is made into the index for a data item BAL with value B2; the index has two levels, the first of which translates the BAL pointing to the second level index of all values of BAL, which may be symbolically represented as B1, B2, etc.

The value index is then translated and (2) points to record 1, which is the

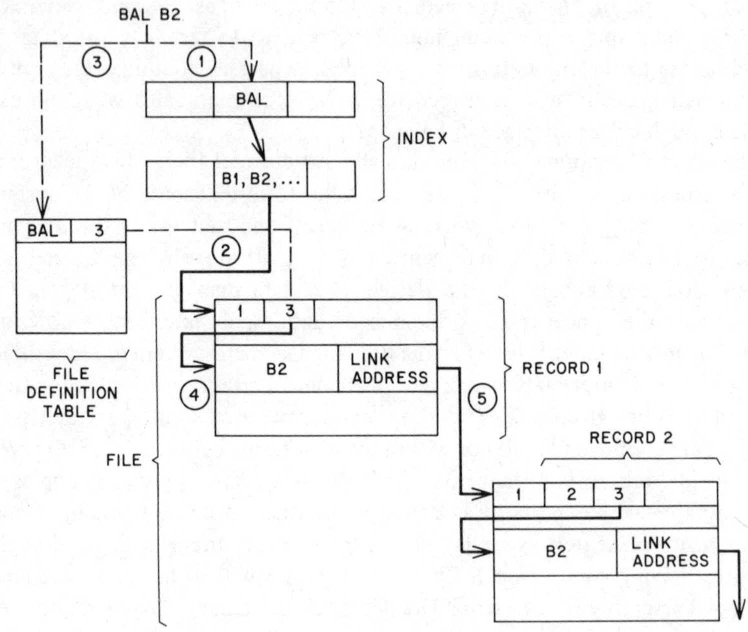

Figure 2-5 An example of the five facets of data

first record of the data file containing the value B2 associated with the data item BAL. Record 1 is what has been previously called a logical record. When it has been deblocked and turned over to a DMS record handler, the latter (3) must consult the file definition table in order to suitably unpack the record. The table indicates that BAL is identified as data item 3; a table of contents at the beginning of the record indicates that the record does in fact contain a data item 3, and the table of contents (4) points or "offsets" to the particular data item where the value B2 can be accessed. Associated with this value is a link address that (5) points from record 1 to record 2, which is similarly decoded.

The purpose of this illustration is to further amplify the various facets of data and to show how they are variously represented and interpreted for usage by the data management system.

The data item in this example is the balance with value B2. The first facet of data is *semantic*. The *extent* or definition of the data item is BAL/B2, where BAL is the name of the data item and B2 is a symbolic representation of the value. The *intent* of BAL/B2 is "an amount of money, B2, owed by a customer, represented in the system by a record."

The second facet is *syntactic*. The *syntactic* relations of the data item that are apparent within this illustration are as follows: (1) The amount of money (balance) represents a class of values, B1, B2, ... This syntactic relation is expressed as the two-level index, where BAL points to a set of values in the second level index, B1, B2, ... (2) The values, B1, B2 . . ., have relations to one another such as $>$, $<$, $=$. This relationship is utilized in the formation of the index and is relied upon as part of the search strategy in the index processing. (3) Several records may share the same balance value. This is illustrated by the address pointers that link record 1, which contains B2, to record 2, which also contains B2. It is said that record 2 has been *associated* with record 1 by virtue of the common data item value B2 of data item BAL. (4) The shared or associated records may themselves be ordered, for example, by time of assignment of BAL/B2. Thus as the chain of associated records is accessed, not only is the association B2 manifest, but also the time order by which these records were assigned the value B2 is also manifest. Note also that the syntactic relation (3) is explicit in the sense that the value B2 is explicitly represented within each record, but that the syntactic relation (4), the time sequence assignment of these values, is not explicit, but rather implied by the order in which the records are accessed. (5) The data item that has been referred to here as "balance" within a single record may be a component within a larger aggregate such as *accounts receivable*; the total collection of all balance values then has another meaning, apart from the meaning of each individual component (i.e., balance), and that is the sum total of money owed on account by all customers. Thus, from this simple example, five syntactic relations have been identified, all based upon the single data item of balance and balance value.

The third facet of data is *representation*. The *explicit representation* is shown to be BAL, appearing both in the index and in the table, and a particular value B2, that might be represented as 195.50, appearing in the index and in the records. The format of BAL is "three alphabetics," and the format of the value is a "fixed point number with two places of decimal precision and a total of, say, up to eight significant digits." An *implicit representation* based upon this data item is the representation of the fifth syntactic relation, namely, the total accounts receivable, which equals the sum of all record balances.

The fourth facet is the *hierarchy of data aggregates*, which is illustrated by the diagram in Fig. 2-6 for the explicit representation of BAL, 195.50. The hierarchy starts with the most primitive symbols of the computer, binary 0 and 1; these aggregate into six-, seven-, or eight-bit characters to form the letters BAL, and the numbers 1, 9, 5, etc. The individual characters then aggregate themselves into two separate fields, BAL and 195.50, which in turn are used in the table, the index, and the data records.

Finally, there is the fifth facet, which is the *functional* aspect of these data. The user-derived data are BAL and 195.50; the system-derived data are index pointers, table entries, and record pointers. The latter, which are invisible, are of no direct concern to the user but are of vital importance inasmuch as they reconstruct for him all of the other attributes, of the data, particularly the syntactic attributes, which are not explicitly evident within the data base that

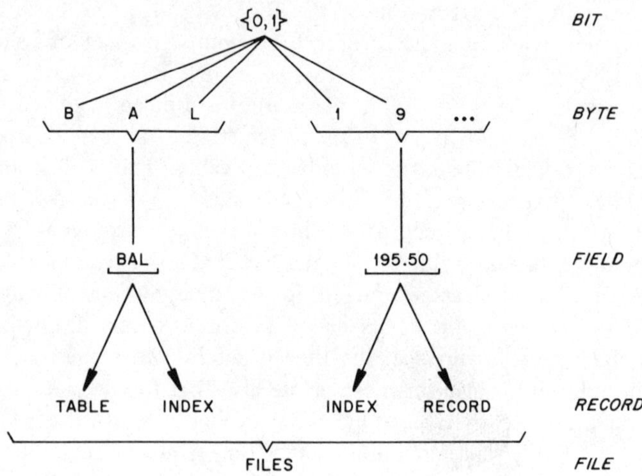

Figure 2-6   Hierarchy of data aggregates for BAL 195.50

the user himself has provided. In addition, the data that he has provided, namely BAL and 195.50, are only accessible through the mechanisms of these pointers and tables.

It is hoped that through this simple illustration the meaning of data and the role of data management have become somewhat more clear. One might say that a major function of data management is continual interpretation; interpretation of data that the user has explicitly placed within its care, and interpretation and manifestation of data constructs within superstructures that are built upon the data and which constitute in themselves data, though in implicit and highly complex format. In addition, as will be shown later in this chapter, it is important to establish certain fundamental and universal properties of data that transcend the mechanics of the type of data processing illustrated by this example, so that the very important notion of *data processing independence* can be established.

2.3   CONTROL FIELDS

It is of interest to note that the level of the hierarchy at which real concern for data aggregation begins in the data management system is the *field*. Data management systems design is primarily concerned with fields of data, records, files, and compound files. An understanding of the roles and specific differentiation of various kinds of data fields is important, because these are the most basic building blocks of the data management system. They are analogous to blood vessels in the human body, carrying nourishment to the vital organs. It is by means of these carriers that the DMS executive extends its control throughout the system. The process of data management system design is largely one of specifying in a precise and comprehensive way a variety of data fields that are responsible for creating data structure like that illustrated in Fig. 2-5 and for communicating among the major system components illustrated in Fig. 2-4. Figure 2-7 enumerates the more significant data fields at the data management system level, and Fig. 2-8 contains the fields generated at the user system

RECORD TYPE CODE

FILE ID

ITEM NO.

CANONICAL NO.

ITEM NAME

ITEM LENGTH

MODE

ACCESS CODE

RETRIEVAL CONTROL

LIST LENTH

LINK ADDRESS

FLAG

COUNTER

DISPLACEMENT (POINTERS)

Figure 2-7 System control fields

KEY (UNIQUE)

KEY (GENERIC)

DATUM

Figure 2-8 User generated fields

level. As can be seen from this illustration, the user's view of his system is a very simplistic one, there actually being only three differentiable types of fields for him to be concerned with, whereas the variety of field types under control of the data management system is far more extensive.

The most complex operational environment for a data management system today, and one that is becoming increasingly more common, is the multiuser multiprogrammed operating system. The records of the four files described in

Fig. 2-4 are frequently intermixed and distributed throughout the mass storage medium in these systems, and a system of directories and pointers is relied upon to locate the appropriate record for a particular user and a particular function to be performed for that user. In all such systems, where physical separation of data among users is not employed, it is good practice to label every record as to type and file so that each processor can examine a given record before processing it in order to determine first whether it is the proper type of record and second whether it correctly identifies with the file for which the intended processing is being performed. Two fields of system control data are defined for this purpose; one is the record type code, which identifies the record by type (four such types have been identified in Fig. 2-4.) The other control field, appearing within every record, is file ID, which is an identification of the data file name that the given record services. For example, the record may belong to an FD file, and index file, or an inverted list file, but there is always presumed to be a data file being served by each of the respective record types.

Another class of control field is that which enables the identification and location of data items within a records. For this purpose each data item may be tagged with a serial number for look-up in the record table of contents, where variable format records are employed. The serial item number is not necessary for fixed format records. For records that have a hierarchic or tree-like data structure, a canonical number, indicating either the precise node in the tree or the level in the tree, is a required control field. For example, COBOL[3] and PL/1,[4] which enable one to construct hierarchic data structures within records, both use the level number. The item name is the normal means of communication between the user or user program and the DMS, although, as will be shown in the illustrative language of Chap. 5, this communication can also be effected via the canonical number and may have to be augmented by an index whenever an item is dimensioned. The item length and mode are designations of precisely how the field has been aggregated from subfield data components such as characters and bits. The mode will indicate, for example, whether the field is comprised of an integer number that can be computed from a binary string of a given length of zeroes and ones; or it may indicate that it is alphanumeric information, wherein the field is to be sliced up into eight-bit strings, each of which (called a *byte*) represents one character of a predetermined set of up to 128 characters (with one bit reserved for parity control).

The access code field performs a gating function. It contains a code that is to be compared with another, external code that is presented to the data management system with a data access or storage request. The purpose of the access code is to permit or deny access or storage of data based upon its comparison with the external code. These codes can be applied at basically three levels of the data hierarchy—the field, the record, and the file. The field access code is normally applied on a file-wide basis. For example, a field of a personnel file may contain *salary*, and it may be desired to deny access to the salary information in all records of the file to a certain class of system users but to allow access to other fields in these records to these same persons. Similarly, one may permit READ access to certain fields but deny WRITE access to these same fields. The record access code applies selectively to various records within the file and can also be applied on a READ and/or WRITE basis. The file access code is applied against the entire file. Other combinations can of course be conceived to suit individual design requirements, such as the conditioning of access based upon the algorithmic processing of data within a record, in which case the system control would reference the particular algorithms and the conditions upon which they are applied.

The next control field indicated in Fig. 2-7 is called retrieval control. This refers to the manner in which lists of records or data items are to be accessed or stored. A list is a set of records that is associated on a record-to-record basis, so that the entire set can be accessed in sequence without having to access any other records that are not in the set. The association among the records in the list is usually based upon equality of the value of a given data item or combination of items common to all the records in a file. In the case where the list is based upon equality of a single data item, this item is said to be a *generic key*, since an access mechanism (that is, a key) is implied by the existence of the list, and it is generic, as distinguished from *unique*, in the sense that the key will access a series of records in the former case and only a single record in the latter case. An example of a list based upon a generic key would be the set of all records in a personnel file with the same value of salary. An example of a list based upon a combination of data items is the set of all records that constitute debits or credits to a given account number within a given time period. This particular list is called a *customer statement* in an accounting system.

There are two general methods of list implementation. One is by means of a forward *link address*, stored within the record, that points from the record to its successor in the list. (There may also be a backward link address that points from a record to its predecessor). This method is called *chaining*. The other method is by means of a separately stored list of addresses (or other unique record identification such as a unique key) in the same sequence as that of the list. This method is called an *inverted list*. At any given moment in time the chain verted lists are discussed in Chap. 4. At any given moment in time the chain or the list is a static structure; access from or storage into the chain creates a dynamic, and it is the function of the retrieval control to determine the exact nature of the dynamic.

There are three usual ways to access or store information on a list. One is to access the first record on the list, where "first" may mean the first record placed there in time or the first record implied by the ordering process of the chain if other than chronological. The second method is to access from the last record on the chain, and the third method is to access a specifically identified record on the chain. If accession is on a time basis from the first or last record, it is called first-in first-out (FIFO) and last-in first-out (LIFO), respectively. If the list is to be maintained in a particular sequence other than a chronological one, it will be according to the values of one or more specifically designated fields within the record. Flexibility in the establishment of retrieval control can vary according to design requirement. It may be a fixed property of the system; it may be variable across files but must be declared at the time of file generation; or it may be completely variable in that it can be modified by the user program at any time.

The list length is a count of the number of records in the list. It is normally used in conjunction with the chain method of list implementation, since data access strategies involving multiple list accesses often depend upon a knowledge of the shortest list. The link address is a pointer from one records in the DASD to another, wherein the records need not be located contiguously. One use of the link address was given above in the chain method of list implementation. Others are to link different levels of an index, to logically extend records, and to interconnect files.

Counters and flags are applied in various ways throughout the system. For example, counters are used within a record table of contents to indicate the number of occurrences of a given data field that may exist in that record; the counter may be used in an index record to indicate the number of occurrences of a given key length in the index. In general, counters are used wherever variable length attributes of the system appear. Flags are usually interpreted as on-off switches, and indicate status. For example, a record delete flag is normally employed in a chained list structure to indicate that although the record may physically be part of the chain, it has logically been deleted from the list.

The displacement is an intrarecord pointer; it is a character or word count that designates the beginning of a field with respect to some reference point in the record. It may be used within a logical record as a table of contents pointer to a field. Displacements are also used at the beginning of a physical record or block to indicate the next available location for storing a logical record within the block. In this way variable length logical records are readily accommodated.

The control fields shown in Fig. 2-7 are not necessarily exhaustive, but they indicate the principal types of fields that the data management system must use to exercise its control.

The user will initially specify data parameters that the system thereafter uses as a control, such as the item name, canonical number, mode, and retrieval control. Having done so, the user is primarily concerned with two types of data fields, as shown in Fig. 2-8. These are the key and the datum. A datum field represents any type of user data, and the key is a special type of data field, being a means of random access to the record. It is represented by a data name in the FD and value within a record. Access to the record by the key is made via a mechanism called the directory, which may be implemented either as an alphabetic or otherwise ordered index or as an algorithmic transformation or mapping upon the key values themselves. Directories and their method of construction are discussed in detail in Chap. 3. If a particular key is permitted to exist in only one record of a file, then it is said to be *unique*, but if a series of records can have the same key, then it is said to be *generic*. Also, a file is said to be a *single key* file if each record has only one key and therefore can be accessed in only one way, whereas a file is said to be *multikey* if any record of the file can have several keys and hence as many access points.

2.4   RECORD TYPES

Figure 2-4 indicates that the design of a data management system is built around four types of files, each of which is to be examined here somewhat more closely in terms of its record content. The four record types under consideration are (1) file definition, (2) index, (3) inverted list, and (4) data.

The purpose of file definition (FD) is to describe all necessary attributes of a file that are common to all records in the file and hence can be abstracted into a single record and stored as such in a single file of file definitions. Any information that is specific to a particular record and which may vary from one record to another within a file is called record definition (RD) and must appear in a header of or elsewhere within the record itself.

The distribution of file control information between these two levels, file and record definition, is entirely a function of the format control of the record itself. It is useful to identify two such types of format control as a basic design concept of the data management system: *field length* and *record format*. These can be considered two dimensions of record control, each of which has a two-valued component. The field length may be *fixed* or *variable*, as may the format, thus producing four different record types within the two-dimensional space. A fixed field length means that the length of a given data item is the same within every record of the file in which it appears; a variable field length means that the length of the field may vary from one record to another. The fixed record format means that every field that is declared to be in the file appears within every record of the file; a variable record format means that all fields do not have to appear within every record, although all fields that are representable in records of the file must be declared initially.

Six of the system control fields given in Fig. 2-7 are required to describe item-oriented characteristics of the file, and, depending upon the record type, may be constant throughout the file or may vary from one record to another. Figure 2-9 presents a matrix in which it is indicated at which level, FD or RD, each of these six control fields must function with respect to the four record types. The matrix indicates that for the FF type record (fixed field length, fixed format) five of the control fields can appear at the file definition level, that the item number need not be indicated explicitly, and that the access code must have a split control, where file and field access is always controlled at the file definition level and the record access at the record definition level. This type of record actually corresponds to the COBOL record, in which all of the fields will appear within a given record and the lengths of each field are fixed with respect

NOTE: F = fixed; V = variable; FD = file definition; RD = record definition

TYPE		ITEM NO.	ITEM NO. (CANONICAL)	ITEM NAME	LENGTH	MODE	ACCESS CODE	
FIELD LENGTH	FORMAT						FILE/ FIELD	RECORD
F	F	(FD)	FD	FD	FD	FD	FD	RD
F	V	RD	FD	FD	FD	FD	FD	RD
V	F	(FD)	FD	FD	RD	FD	FD	RD
V	V	RD	FD	FD	RD	FD	FD	RD

Figure 2-9 Distribution of record format control

to their initial definition. The fact that one may redefine the format or interpretation of a record once it has been placed in working storage does not alter either the format or the length type under the above definition, since the record size accommodates to the largest definition, and with respect to each description of the record in COBOL, the field lengths remain fixed throughout the interpretation of that description. Also, in COBOL, the level number of the tree is used rather than a canonical number, because data can only be stored at an elementary item level, not at a group or higher node level of the tree. COBOL does not use a file, field, or record access code and hence would not require an access control field.

The other three types of records introduce variability either into field length or format. In principle, the VF type could be considered to be functionally equivalent to the VV type since a field can be omitted from a record by letting its field length become zero. However, one may want to retain the distinction in an implementation since a small amount of storage space can be saved in the record table of contents by use of the VV record type. This is particularly true if the percentage of fields appearing in the average record is low compared with the total number of fields defined in the file. PL/1 can represent any of the variable type recorders using either the VARYING attribute for a data item or the REFER option for an array. In the former case, the data item will only be stored in a record as a variable length if it is the last item; otherwise the maximum declared space is reserved. In the case of the REFER option, the array assumes the size of the REFER object variable, although in PL/1 version F only one REFER option may be used per structure and in the optimizer version they cannot be nested.

The content of each record within the four principal system files is now considered. Figure 2-10 presents the content of the file definition record. It is divided into two parts, a header plus item enumerations. In the header are contained the type code of the record, which in this case is file definition, the file ID associated with this particular record, and the file access code, which may indicate READ and/or WRITE access and may be so constructed as to key to various categories of users. For example, one may designate categories of users among those eligible to use this file, and the access codes can be constructed so as to control the use of the files and records by various combinations of these groups or classes of users. Within the item enumeration section the item name must be given for all record types, the item length must be given for fixed-length record types, and the canonical or level number must be given for all record types that have a hierarchic data structure. This is a structure in which a given data item may be conceptually subordinate to another and a formal denotation is to be made of this subordinacy. For example, consider the data item "examination" with subordinate items, "data, examiner, and grade."

	FIELD	USE
HEADER	TYPE CODE	
	FILE ID	HEADER DATA
	FILE ACCESS CODE	
ITEM ENUMERATION (ONE PER ITEM)	ITEM NAME	ALL RECORD TYPES
	ITEM LENGTH	FF, FV
	(CANONICAL NO.)	ALL RECORD TYPES WITH HIERARCHIC DATA STRUCTURE
	MODE	ALL RECORD TYPES
	KEY/INDEX ADDRESS	ALL RECORD TYPES
	ITEM ACCESS CODE	ALL RECORD TYPES

Figure 2-10   File definition record

In COBOL and PL/1, languages that use level numbers to describe hierarchies, only data item names at the lowest or terminal level of the hierarchy actually reference stored data; in COBOL they are called *elementary data items*. All items at higher levels of the hierarchy, called *group data items*, are dummy names, used only to reference or distinguish elementary items. The level numbers in COBOL and PL/1 start at the highest hierarchic level with 01 and increase in value as the hierarchic level decreases. The *mode* specifies the representation of a data item and is required for all record types. The commonly used modes

Table 2-1   Modes and Internal Representation

Mode	Internal representation
Signed integer number	An "N−1" bit binary number plus one sign bit
Fixed point number	Same as a signed integer plus an additional byte or word indicating position of the decimal point.
Floating point number	An "m" bit mantissa which represents the significant digits of the number, a "c" bit characteristic which represents a power to a base (usually 2, 4, 8, or 16) by which the mantissa is multiplied, and one sign bit each for the mantissa and characteristic. For a single-precision floating point number, $m + c + 2 = N$. For a multiple-precision number, additional bits for the mantissa (normally not the characteristic) are available from additional words.
Six-bit (alphanumeric) characters	A 64-character set can be comprised from six bits which are packed into the "N" bit word. The length of the character string is indefinite, utilizing as many words as necessary.
Eight-bit (alphanumeric) bytes	A 256-character set (or 128-character set, where one bit is reserved for parity) can be comprised from eight bits which are packed into the "N" bit word. The length of the byte string is indefinite, utilizing as many words as necessary.
Packed binary coded decimal	Each decimal digit is coded into four bits and packed into the "N" bit word. One digit (four bits) position must be retained for the sign. The number of digits in the string may exceed that which can be packed into one word but will be limited by the hardware or the algorithm that performs the decimal arithmetic. Thirty-two digits is a common (but arbitrary) limit for such numbers.

for data management and their internal representations are given by Table 2-1, where it is assumed that a computer word in core memory contains N bits.

An indication is made in the next field whether the data item is a key; if it is, a link address is provided to the index in which the key values are decoded. If the directory is mapped rather than indexed, the index link is either omitted or is a code that selects a mapping algorithm in the case where multiple algorithms are used. Finally, the item access code, if it is to be used, must be given for all record types. The above set of five or six pieces of information must be repeated for every item in the data record.

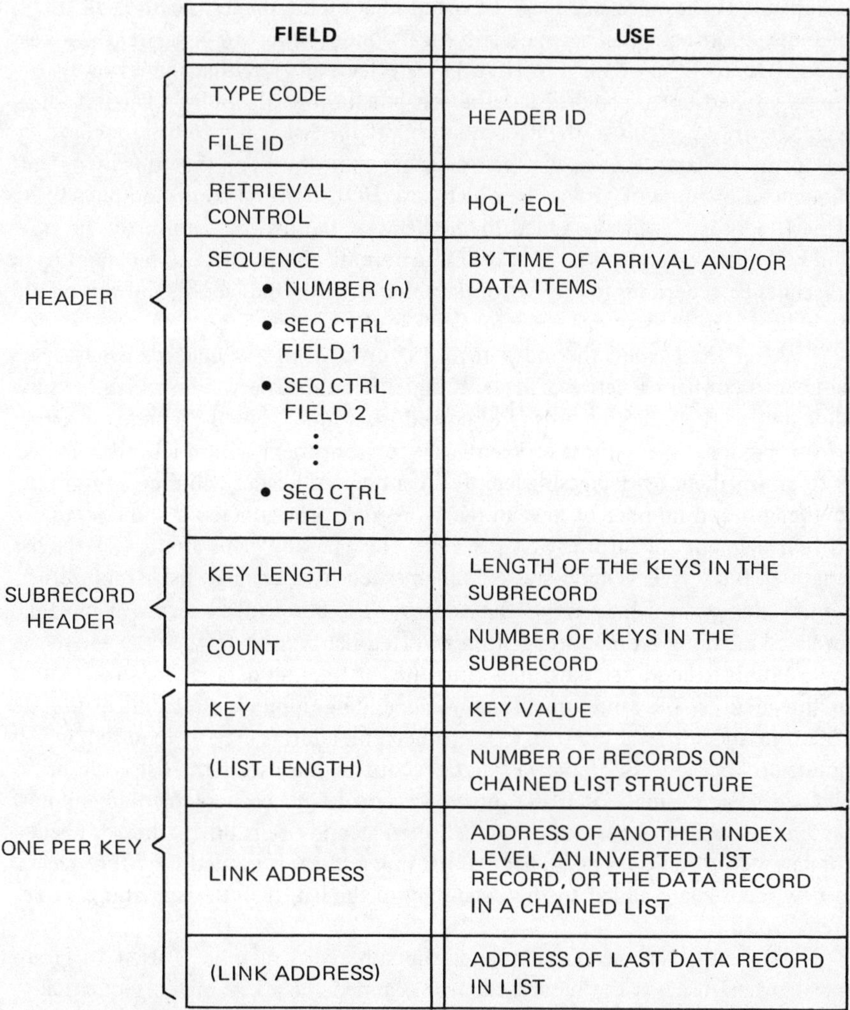

FIELD	USE
HEADER — TYPE CODE	HEADER ID
HEADER — FILE ID	
HEADER — RETRIEVAL CONTROL	HOL, EOL
HEADER — SEQUENCE • NUMBER (n) • SEQ CTRL FIELD 1 • SEQ CTRL FIELD 2 ⋮ • SEQ CTRL FIELD n	BY TIME OF ARRIVAL AND/OR DATA ITEMS
SUBRECORD HEADER — KEY LENGTH	LENGTH OF THE KEYS IN THE SUBRECORD
SUBRECORD HEADER — COUNT	NUMBER OF KEYS IN THE SUBRECORD
ONE PER KEY — KEY	KEY VALUE
ONE PER KEY — (LIST LENGTH)	NUMBER OF RECORDS ON CHAINED LIST STRUCTURE
ONE PER KEY — LINK ADDRESS	ADDRESS OF ANOTHER INDEX LEVEL, AN INVERTED LIST RECORD, OR THE DATA RECORD IN A CHAINED LIST
ONE PER KEY — (LINK ADDRESS)	ADDRESS OF LAST DATA RECORD IN LIST

Figure 2-11 Index record

Figure 2-11 illustrates the content of an index record. It contains either two or three sections, depending upon whether the keys within the index are variable in length. If they do not vary in length, only two sections are needed, and the length of the key is indicated along with the index address in the file definition record. If the length of the key field is variable, the three-part construction of the index record would be required, as indicated in Fig. 2-11. The first part contains the header with the type code, file ID, and the retrieval control, which indicates whether records are to be accessed from the head of the list (HOL) or end of the list (EOL). It is not necessary, however, that this control be indicated in advance, and it can be overridden by the program with HOL, EOL, or indexed or sequential access, a specifically indexed record or sequential access from HOL to EOL or EOL to HOL being effected. Note that the retrieval control is applied not through file definition but through the index. The last set of header entries pertains to the list sequence. If the list is not to be sequenced by one or more data items in the record (other than the key), then it is by default sequenced by time of arrival, in which case HOL retrieval control implies LIFO if new records are always added to the head of the list, as is normally the case, and EOL retrieval control implies FIFO. Alternatively, the list can be maintained in sequence according to any set of data items within the record, and this would be indicated as the sequence control fields in the header.

After the header, the index record is divided into subrecords, where each subrecord contains a series of keys of equal length. The way in which keys are allocated to the index records is discussed in Chap. 3, but if the index has keys of varying length, the most efficient way to store them within an index record is to group them by decreasing length. A subrecord header will then contain the key length and number of keys in the subrecord. The subrecord will contain up to four elements of information per key: (1) The key value itself; (2) the list length if the key is generic and is implemented by a chained list structure; (3) a link address, which is either the address of another index record if multiple levels of indexing are required, or an inverted list address in the case where the index points to an inverted list files structure, or the first data record in a chained or threaded list file structure. Finally, depending upon requirements of the file structure and retrieval control, (4) another link address may be required, which points to the address of the last data record in the list, if the list structure is chained. For example, if FIFO retrieval control is to be implemented and new records are added to the end of the list, then an end-of-list link address is needed for new record addition, and a head-of-list link address is needed for FIFO access. If new records are added to the beginning of the list, then the link address roles are reversed.

It should also be noted that if the subrecord method is used to group variable length keys, the record must be scanned for a key match sequentially, and since the key groupings are arranged in descending order by key length, there is no danger of picking up a truncated form of an existing key. That is, assume that two key values are 68A-253 and 68A-2. Since 68A-253 is stored first, there can be no confusion between the two. This mode of storage, however, precludes a binary search of keys within the record, since the original lexicographic order has not been preserved, at least locally, within the index record. Little, however, is lost by this, since the greater proportion of time is usually spent in the access of the record from the DASD, and the scan of the record within core is several orders of magnitude faster.

If the index contains fixed-length keys, the length of the key is declared outside of the index (that is, in the file definition record), and the entire index record excepting the header can be occupied by the key quadruplets.

FIELD	USE
TYPE CODE FILE ID KEY VALUE	HEADER DATA

LINK ADDRESS
 	
   OR PRIMARY KEYS
	SEQUENCED LIST OF
	
	   ADDRESSES OR KEYS OF RECORDS

SPACE	RESERVED SPACE FOR UPDATE

Figure 2-12 Inverted list record

Figure 2-12 presents the inverted list record. It may contain up to three sections. The first is the header containing the record type code, file ID, and the key value for which the list is being constructed. The second section contains either the link addresses or primary keys of records on the list. The addresses or keys are normally stored in sequence in order to facilitate list intersections or merges as a part of the Boolean search strategy. The primary key is a specifically designated, unique key in the record that serves as the unique record identifier. The reasons for using addresses versus primary keys relate to tradeoffs in the efficiency of processing inquiries versus updates, where address storage favors inquiry and primary key storage favors update. If the list is subject to dynamic update (that is, the insertion of individual addresses or keys as a result of on-line record updating), a certain amount of reserve space should be left at the end of the record to enable new addresses or keys to be inserted in sequence without having to push the highest addresses or keys into the next record. Since inverted lists can vary greatly in size, it is possible that an inverted list record may span two or more blocks; the controls relating to the access of such a multiple block record are not an internal function of the logical record, as depicted in Fig. 2-12, but rather of the I/O management that unblocks records and loads program I/O buffers. This level of control is discussed in Chap. 4. In large data base systems it is not unusual for an inverted list to span many blocks.

Figure 2-13 illustrates a variant of the inverted list record that is used in inverted list pushdown processing. The purpose and algorithm of this processing are described in Chap. 4. The header again contains the type code and file ID, and a section containing sequenced link addresses or primary keys is provided as in the inverted list record. Note that an assumption is made here that the primary keys are fixed in length or are padded to a fixed length, and since it is desirable to optimize the speed of processing of these lists, it is useful to impose this restriction. The pushdown processor record actually contains a series of lists, called pushdown elements, each of which must be separately identifiable. Each pushdown element (which is a list) is assigned to a separate record and identified by an element ID in the header. In the third section of the record there is a forward link to the next element (list) in the pushdown, and in the fourth section there is a backward link to the preceding element.

FIELD	USE
TYPE CODE FILE ID PUSHDOWN ELEMENT ID	HEADER DATA
LINK ADDRESSES OR PRIMARY KEYS	SEQUENCED LIST OF ADDRESSES OR KEYS OF RECORDS
FORWARD LINK ADDRESS	ADDRESS OF NEXT LIST-IN PUSHDOWN
BACKWARD LINK ADDRESS	ADDRESS OF PRECEDING LIST IN PUSHDOWN

Figure 2-13 Inverted list pushdown processor record

Figure 2-14 illustrates a prototype data record. The header contains the record type code, file ID, record access code (if required), and the item count for the FV and VV type of record. If there is variability either in the format or length of data items, the record must contain a table of contents, which has been referred to as record definition control. There must be one entry in the table of contents for each field in the record. If the record is of variable format, the item numbers must be given. If it is of fixed format, it is understood that every item appears within the record, and the item numbers need not appear. If the record type has variable length fields, the lengths of every item must appear in the table of contents. If a data item has multiple occurrences, it is assumed that each occurrence of the data item in that particular record will have the same length; hence both the length of the data item must be given and the number of occurrences of the data item if these occurrences are permitted to vary from one record to another.

It is occurrence variability control in the DASD that is prominently lacking in COBOL; such control is useful in conserving space in random-access storages. The **OCCURS DEPENDING** clause of COBOL does not actually perform this function, since it is only active as a limiter on SEARCH once the record is in core. The REFER option of PL/1, however, does provide such variable occurrence control.

The third section of the record would contain the link addresses or logical links in the form of a file and a key for associative or network file structure linkages. These are discussed in Chap. 3 and represent a linkage or interconnection from one file to another, thus forming a compound file structure. These links do not represent list linkages within the subject data file, but rather they reference a record in another file, which in turn may spin off a chain that is wholly contained within the other file. This record, which starts the chain, is called a *master* or *owner record*.[5] The chained records in the other file(s) are called *detail* or *member records*.[5]

There are two methods of implementing the chain in the other file(s). One is to enable each record in the chain to point to its successor. The other is to store *all* member record links in an array within the owner record. This array is called a *pointer array*. Since the number of chains that can be spun from any owner record (and an owner record may itself be a member to some other owner) is indefinite and the pointer array sizes (if used) are variable, the associative file

FIELD	USE
TYPE CODE FILE ID RECORD ACCESS CODE ITEM COUNT (FV, VV)	HEADER DATA
ITEM NO. (FV, VV) LENGTH (VF,VV) OCCURRENCES	TABLE OF CONTENTS
LINK ADDRESSES OR FILE/KEY	ASSOCIATIVE FILE STRUCTURE LINKS
DATA ITEMS (KEY LINK ADDRESS)	DATA (LINKS FOR CHAINED FILE STRUCTURES)

ONE ENTRY PER ITEM applies to the rows ITEM NO. (FV, VV), LENGTH (VF,VV), and OCCURRENCES.

Figure 2-14 Data record

structure link section must contain its own size control and table of contents from which each chain can be identified (by name) and controlled. The fourth section of the data record contains the data items themselves, and a data item designated as a key in a chained list structure would also contain a link address.

The syntactic organization of data within this section is a principal concern of the user of the system and is commonly referred to as *data structure*.

2.5 DATA STRUCTURE

Attention has thus far been focused upon the field and the specific roles of various types of fields within the four predominant record types defined in Fig. 2-4. It has also been noted that within the hierarchy of data aggregates the field is the smallest aggregate of particular interest in data management system design, and that interest proceeds upward through record, file, and compound file. It is of course true that when one deals at a detailed design level and conceives of the processing associated with the mode of a field, a consideration below the level of field aggregation is certainly required, but these details of design are beyond the concern of this book. Design here centers on the question of how data are to be structured at the field level of aggregation and higher, or perhaps more properly, of how they are most usefully structured. For example, one could in concept imagine a structure in which every data field of every record of every file is related or associated with every other field within the data base. The implementation would require some kind of linkage revealing these associations among all of the associated data fields. In mathematical terms, this structure could be represented as a graph or network, where the nodes of the graph are all of the data fields in the data base, and the associations are branches that connect the nodes. One could then impose specialized branch types upon the graph such as directionality and strength of associativity; this would represent the most generalized concept of data organization possible. The implementation for such a strucutre, given a reasonably large number of data fields in the data base, would of course be exceedingly expensive in terms of memory utilization, since a very large number of link addresses and link descriptor fields would have to be provided. Furthermore, experience has shown that there is little or no practical use for such a structure. The problem therefore comes down to defining *practical* structure at the field aggregation level (and later, in Chap. 3, at the file aggregation level).

The two most common data-handling compiler languages at the field aggregation or intrarecord handling level are COBOL and PL/1.[3,4] Each of these languages has implemented a data structure that is no more complex than the tree shown in Figs. 2-15 and 2-16. There are two concepts of structure that are illustrated in these figures. One is that of the graphical representation of the tree, where the nodes of the graph are represented by white and black circles and the branches that connect the nodes are represented as solid lines. Each node is also labeled with a tree level number and a letter representing its name. The second structural concept is that of *dimensionality*, associated with a particular node; it gives the illustrative appearance of further ramification of the tree at a particular node such as node E, but dimensionality is a totally independent structural description from that of the graph. The dimensionality of a given node represents repetitions in memory space of the *same* kind (mode) of information, in contradistinction to the subdivision or ramification of information implied by the (graphical) solid line tree structure. It is important to distinguish these two structural concepts.

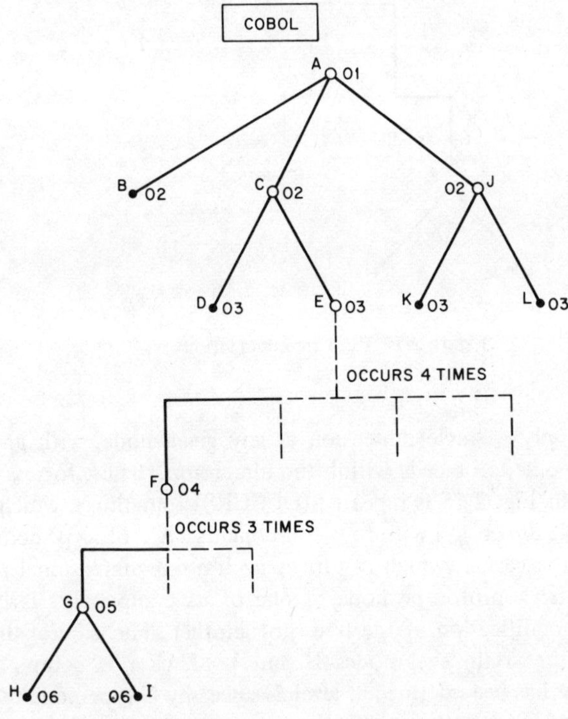

Figure 2-15 Cobol tree data structure

Figures 2-15 and 2-16 present the same data structure as it may be represented in either COBOL or PL/1. PL/1 has the capability of representing any data structure that COBOL can represent, but it can do it in more varied and concise ways. As an illustration, Fig. 2-16 shows how PL/1 would represent the same data structure as is represented by COBOL, but with a different syntax.

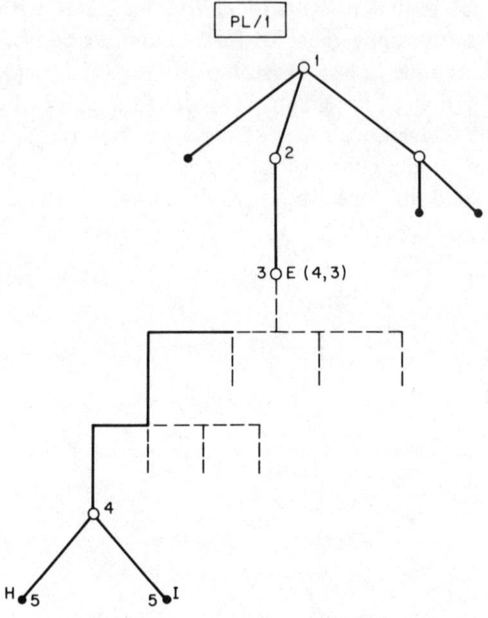

Figure 2-16 PL/1 tree data structure

COBOL allows only a single dimension at any given node, with an arbitrary number of components or cells within the dimension. Thus, for example, the node labeled E in Fig. 2-15 is repeated (OCCURS) four times, which is to say that it has a single dimension with four components. A prototype component is labeled node F at level 04, which in turn is itself a one-dimensional array with three components; a prototype node of one of its components is labeled G, which continues ramification of the tree (not another dimension of the EF substructure) with the sixth level nodes H and I. Thus a 12-component, two-dimensional array has been defined at level 5, since any G type node may be one of three within at F type node, which in turn is one of four within an E type node. By comparison, PL/1 allows multidimensional arrays at a single node. This does not mean that it can therefore represent a larger class of data structures than COBOL, but merely that it represents data structure more concisely; hence it is simply a syntactic difference, not a functional difference of a difference in capability of structural representation.

In the PL/1 illustration, the four-by-three array that subtends node E is represented in the PL/1 syntax as an E of dimension four-by-three, and the original tree data structure (solid lines) takes up at level 4 in the PL/1 diagram. The restriction in COBOL and PL/1 that the data items may be stored only in locations referenced by *terminal* nodes does not limit the representation of data

```
FD   01   A    B    PIC
          02   C
          02   03   D
               03   E      OCCURS 4 TIMES
                    04   F    OCCURS 3 TIMES
                         05  G
                             06   H    PIC
                             06   I    PIC
          02   J
               03   K   PIC
               03   L   PIC
```

Figure 2-17 COBOL file definition

in either the sense of a tree structure as described above or the sense of multi-dimensionality.   There is, however, additional representational capability and certain efficiencies that can accrue from enabling data item storage to be referenced by any node of the graph, although these capabilities go beyond those of tree representation and will be discussed later. COBOL calls the terminal nodes *elementary data items*; nonterminals it calls *group data items*.

In Fig. 2-15 and 2-16 the elementary data items are represented by solid (black) nodes and group data items by open nodes.

Figures 2-17 and 2-18 illustrate the syntax of COBOL and PL/1 representations, respectively, of the graphical structures shown in Figs. 2-15 and 2-16. In

```
DECLARE   1    A;
               2    B    CHAR;
               2    C;
                    3    D    CHAR;
                    3    E    (4,3);
                         4    G;
                              5    H    CHAR;
                              5    I    CHAR;
               2    J;
                    3    K    CHAR;
                    3    L    CHAR;
```

Figure 2-18 PL/1 file definition

Fig. 2-17 the declaration is initiated by the letters FD followed by the first level node, labeled A in the illustration. The first second level node, labeled B, is followed by the word "PIC," which is shorthand for "PICTURE" and is used in the illustration to designate that a specific format can be given for this data item, because it is an elementary or terminal node item.* The remainder of the illustration depicts on a one-to-one basis the information shown in Fig. 2-15. Similarly, Fig. 2-18 illustrates the PL/1 syntax for its corresponding graphical structure in Fig. 2-16, where CHAR (short for CHARACTER) indicates the elementary item.

It should be noted that COBOL and PL/1 do not assign the FD to a file as suggested for generalized file management in Fig. 2-4, but rather use the FD to specifically cross-reference data items in the procedure division to their appearance in working storage buffers. That is, the compiler assigns specific locations in a storage area to these data items.

Figure 2-19 presents a slightly more complex illustration of a hierarchic or tree data structure. COBOL syntax has been used as a vehicle for the example.

```
01    GEOGRAPHY

    02    TIME-ZONE OCCURS 5 TIMES.

        03    NAME PIC X (24).

        03    TEMP-RANGE COMP.

            05    HI.

            05    LO.

        03    COUNTRY OCCURS 10 TIMES.

            05    NAME PIC X (24).

            05    CAPITAL PIC X (24).

            05    POPULATION COMP.

            05    MAJOR-PRODUCTS PIC X (24) OCCURS 8 TIMES.
```

Figure 2-19 COBOL data structure with dimensions

In Fig. 2-20 the group data items are designated by oval enclosures, and the elementary data items are indicated by rectangular enclosures. Consider first the transformation from a level number and positional citation notation for describing the tree, as shown in Fig. 2-19, to a truly canonical notation, as shown in Fig. 2-21, in which each data item is uniquely positioned in the tree by a decimal number; each succeeding decimal position represents a successively lower level of the tree, and the value of the digit in a given position represents a branch at

---

*COBOL allows other declarations of formating and mode of data, but it is beyond the purpose of this discussion to elaborate on these; hence the display clause representation "PIC" is used here simply to signify an elementary data item.

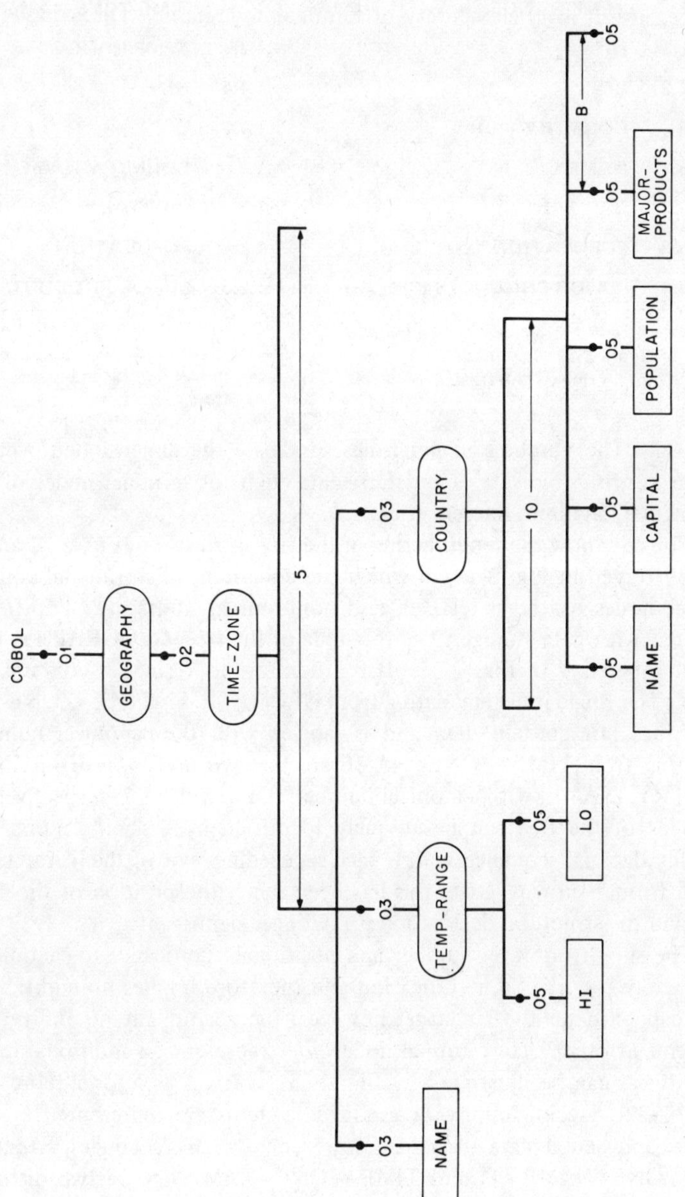

Figure 2-20 Dimensional tree of Fig. 2-19

1.	**GEOGRAPHY**
1.1	**TIME-ZONE (5)**
1.1.1	**NAME***
1.1.2	**TEMP-RANGE**
1.1.2.1	**HI***
1.1.2.2	**LO***
1.1.3	**COUNTRY (10)**
1.1.3.1	**NAME***
1.1.3.2	**CAPITAL***
1.1.3.3	**POPULATION***
1.1.3.4	**MAJOR-PRODUCTS (8)***

1.	**GEOGRAPHY**
1.1	**TIME-ZONE-NAME (5)***
1.1.1	**TEMP-RANGE**
1.1.1.1	**HI***
1.1.1.2	**LO***
1.1.2	**COUNTRY-NAME (10)***
1.1.2.1	**CAPITAL***
1.1.2.2	**POPULATION***
1.1.2.3	**MAJOR-PRODUCTS (8)***

Figure 2-21 Canonical numbering of the tree

Figure 2-22 Another canonical numbering of the tree

that level. The numbers in parentheses indicate the dimensioned occurrences, and the asterisks indicate elementary data items or terminal nodes of the tree where actual data item references exist.

Consider now the renumbering of the tree as shown in Fig. 2-22 and graphically portrayed in Fig. 2-23, in which the constraint of storing data only at the terminal nodes has been relaxed, and nonterminal nodes are permitted to be associated with data storage. The top node of the tree, GEOGRAPHY, is canonically numbered 1 in Fig. 2-22. It is a dummy node since it contains no data storage. The single node emanating from GEOMETRY is TIME–ZONE–NAME, which does not contain data and is labeled with the canonical number 1.1. Emanating from TIME–ZONE–NAME are the two nodes TEMP–RANGE and COUNTRY–NAME, with canonical numbers 1.1.1 and 1.1.2, respectively. Thus the nodes of the tree can be uniquely identified by assigning numbers in an ascending decimal sequence within each succeeding level of the hierarchy, in the decimal format shown. Once this has been done, the position of the data item citation in the structural declaration is no longer significant.

The shift from level number and positional significance to canonical number is purely a syntactic modification and therefore implies no additional functional capability in the language; however, the accompanying ability to store data items at other than terminal nodes *does* represent an additional functional capability, as can be illustrated by Fig. 2-23, which is a pictorial representation of Fig. 2-22. Again dummy or group data items are represented by oval enclosures, and actual data item names are enclosed in rectangles. Assume that TIME–ZONE–NAME (1) and TIME–ZONE–NAME (2) are two distinct time zone names, being two of the five possible components of the TIME–ZONE–NAME dimension. As indicated in the example, there is a ten-component dimension associated with each COUNTRY–NAME emanating from a given TIME

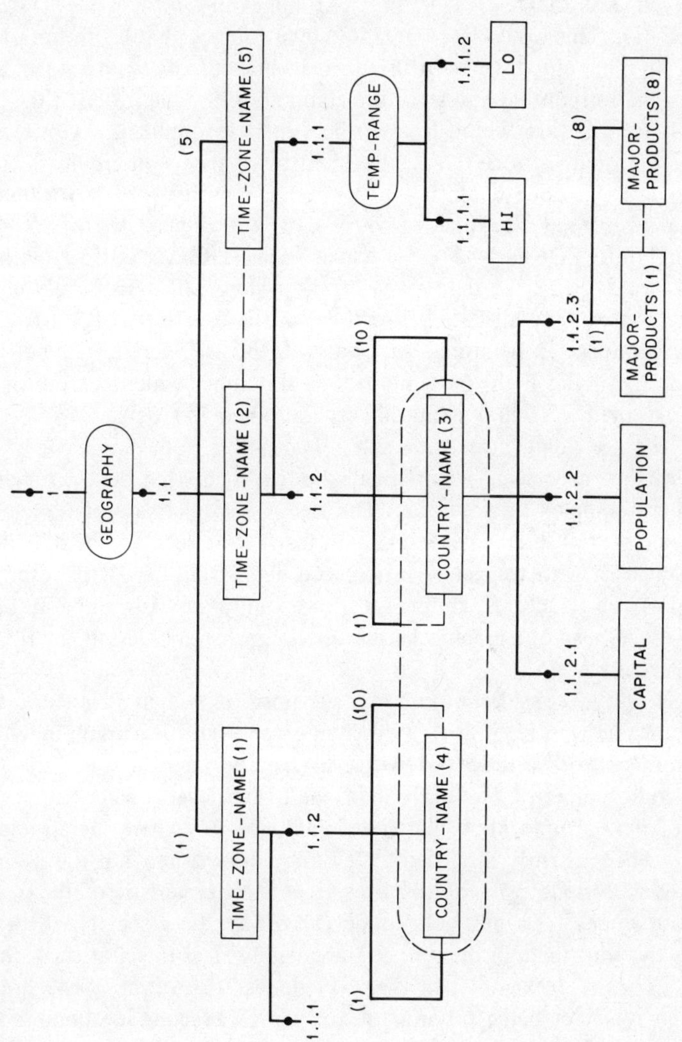

Figure 2-23 Tree structure for diagram of Fig. 2-22

−ZONE−NAME. The record GEOGRAPHY thus far describes ten *countries* within each of five *time zones*.

Assume now, as indicated by the dashed line oval in Fig. 2-23, that COUNTRY−NAME (3), which appears in the array TIME−ZONE−NAME (2), is the same as COUNTRY−NAME (4), appearing in the array TIME−ZONE−NAME (1). This would be represented by a country that lay in both time zones, and from that point downward all information would be identical. If the identity or information content and structure could not be so identified at the level 1.1.2, all this information would have to be stored in duplicate. However, because data are stored at node 1.1.2, the identity of data content in different components of this node could be interpreted as identity of data for the remainder of the subtree (at run time, of course). That is, since COUNTRY−NAME (4) within TIME−ZONE−NAME (1) equals COUNTRY−NAME (3) within TIME−ZONE−NAME (2), the data management system will dynamically equate these two references, and all data below them in the tree (nodes 1.1.2.1, 1.1.2.2, and 1.1.2.3) are also to be stored only once. If the user were to store different data within two nodes with the same canonical number which theretofore has been identical, the DMS will dynamically separate them in storage.

The tree data structure with dimensioned nodes seems to satisfy most practical data processing requirements, but consider what the next higher level of structural complexity would be. The tree is a special case of the graph, and as suggested previously, the general graphical structure seems to be of little practical value, at least with respect to intrarecord data structure. With respect to interrecord or file structures, graphs are more readily applied, probably because the relative overhead of a graphical structure is considerably less at the file level than at the record level.

However, consider an intermediate position, which advances the pure tree structure one step beyond to a directed graph. This is a graph in which a given node can point to a series of lower level (member) nodes, as in a tree, but which can also be pointed to by more than one higher level (owner) node. This concept of data structuring is illustrated in Fig. 2-24, where the structure of Fig. 2-15 has been slightly modified by linking nodes C and J in the second level of the tree with node E in the third level. It is characteristic of the tree that subordinate nodes to a particular node can always be associated with the latter simply by citing them in the syntax immediately after the citation of the superior node. Thus, for example, in Fig. 2-17 nodes D and E at level 3 are indicated unambiguously as being subordinate to level C (a second level node), and not to node J, which is also a second level node by virtue of the positioning of D and E in the syntax immediately following the citation of C.

Thus the combination of level number and position serves to unambiguously represent the intended data structure as a tree. This is no longer possible with a graph, since a node like E in Fig. 2-24 is subordinate to nodes C and J and would have to be cited under each in order to indicate this subordinacy unambiguously. A shift to another notation that appropriately labels and pro-

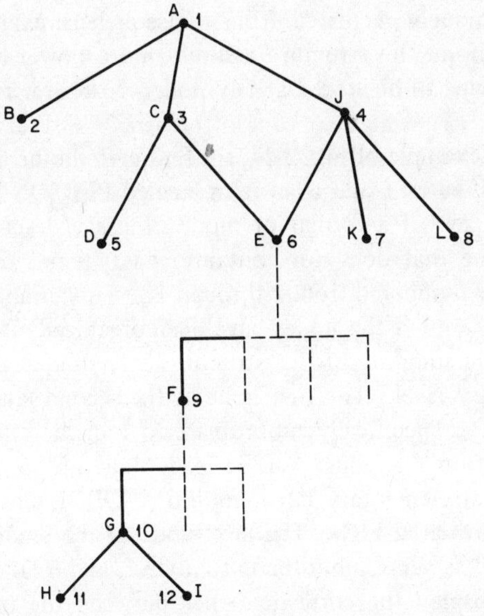

1.	PERSONNEL
1.2	NAME, PIC X (24)
1.3	JOB-ASSIGNMENT PIC X (12)
1.4	PERSONAL DATA
3.5	SALARY COMP-1
3, 4.6	EDUCATION (4)
4.7	MARITAL-STATUS PIC X
4.8	AGE COMP
6.9	LEVEL-OF-EDUCATION (3) PIC X (12)
9.10	MAJOR-SUBJECT PIC X (12)
10.11	GRADE PIC X
10.12	RANK COMP

Figure 2-24 A graphical structure

vides all necessary cross-references to a particular node is more satisfactory. Trees are readily susceptive of a simple canonical notation, but canonical notation for a graph is somewhat more complex. A notation is developed, therefore, to represent the graph of Fig. 2-24 that uniquely describes the structure and at the same time is easy to comprehend and to use. Each node of the tree is not canonically numbered, but the total numbering system is canonical in that the structure can be uniquely recreated from the sequential examination of nodal numbers. Furthermore, the structure assumes more power and significance if one permits data items to be stored at any node of the tree rather than only at terminal nodes.

Following the example of Fig. 2-24, the first node in the canonical numbering scheme is identified as 1 and is an item labeled PERSONNEL. In addition, it is indicated, by lack of a format or mode of usage descriptor, that it is a dummy node or one that does not contain a data item. Every node of the graph is sequentially numbered from 1 through 12. The number assignments are completely arbitrary, but if the nodes have been organized into levels, as shown in the diagram, understanding of this structure is facilitated by numbering the nodes sequentially by level. The first node at the second level is numbered 2, and the fact that it is specifically subordinate to 1 in the directed graph is indicated by the notation 1.2, which can be read "1 points to 2." The data item name is NAME; it is an elementary data item in the COBOL sense and hence has a display picture (abbreviated PIC). The next node of the second level has serial number 3, is denoted as being subordinate to node 1, and is labeled 1.3.

In order to display the correspondence between the modified graph of Fig. 2-24 and the tree of 2-15, the letters that designated the data names in Fig. 2-15 have been retained in the diagram of Fig. 2-24. Node 1.3, a data item, is labeled JOB-ASSIGNMENT. The last node of level 2, a dummy data item, PERSONAL-DATA, is labeled 1.4. The first node of level 3 is canonically identified as 3.5. It is the node with serial number 5 and is subordinate to node 3; hence the path from 1 through 5 can be reconstructed in the syntax by: 1 (PERSONNEL)–1.3 (JOB-ASSIGNMENT)–3.5 (SALARY).

The restriction that the graph be directed is essentially what requires one to cite only successive (or paired) nodes in the canonical node numbering scheme. Note, however, that an individual node number such as 3.5 is not a canonical number, since it does not uniquely represent this node within the structure. It must be coupled with the remainder of the graphical information, namely, 1 and 1.3, in order to be able to reconstruct completely that portion of the graph. The most interesting node of the illustration is, of course, serial number 6, since it is the one that violates the tree structure and is responsible for creating the more general directed graph. Since node 6 is subordinate to both nodes 3 and 4, this multiple subordinacy must be indicated. In general, a node could be subordinate to any number of higher level nodes. This is indicated by the notation 3, 4.6, which reads "3 and 4 point to 6." The name of the data item is EDUCATION, and subtending it is a one-dimensional array with four components. In addition, it is a dummy item, since no data are actually stored in an address associated with the data name, EDUCATION. The last nodes of the third level are identified as 4.7 and 4.8.

Each of the four components under the node EDUCATION (3, 4.6) is of the prototype of node 6.9, LEVEL-OF-EDUCATION. This node is also dimensioned with three components, but, unlike EDUCATION, it is an actual data item with an indicated format of PIC X(12). That is, LEVEL-OF-EDUCATION will actually represent four data items, each up to 12 characters in length. The three components of LEVEL-OF-EDUCATION are given at node 9.10, MAJOR-SUBJECT; each of these data items has, in addition to the major subject name, two subnodes, 10.11 and 10.12.

The structure given in Fig. 2.24 subclassifies all of the information relating to EDUCATION (node 3, 4.6) under both JOB-ASSIGNMENT and PERSONAL-DATA. In order to organize a record in the same way in a pure tree structure, one would have to repeat all the information under EDUCATION, which in this example is the majority of the data in the record, under *both* JOB-ASSIGNMENT and PERSONAL-DATA. This would be an extravagant use of memory both in secondary storage as well as in core storage buffer requirements.

In this chapter an attempt has been made to show that man conceives of data (which is a formalization of information) in a hierarchy of increasingly complex structures. Hierarchy, as classification, implies continual differentiation or fractionalization. In computing systems one starts with the most basic and elemental differentiation of 0 and 1, yes/no, on/off. By assembling two such alternatives in combination, a differentiating power of 4 is achieved; by assembling three, a differentiating power of eight. When an assembly of seven of these so-called bits is made, a differentiating power of 128 is attained, which can represent all of the uppercase and lowercase Roman letters, the ten Arabic numerals, and a variety of other special symbols. For mechanical reasons an eighth bit, called a parity bit, is added in order to assure reliability of transmission of this information unit, called the *byte*.

In natural language man composes words from strings of these characters, and then word sequences, and with these latter two aggregations is able to communicate information. The *field* in the data hierarchy is the analogous minimum unit of information transfer as compared with words or word sequences. As indicated in Chap. 1, data have five facets, one of them being the meaning or interpretation (denotative or cannotative) of the data contained in the field. Another facet is the syntax, which enables a subtle fabric of interpretation to be woven among a manifold of fields. The astronomical quantitative explosion of combinations is a familiar concept, and the attendant power of interpretive capability implied by the syntactic or relational facet of data is actually what gives language its greatest power to communicate information. Hence, in an analogous way we draw upon the syntactic facet of data by conceiving structures of data fields in order to amplify the interpretive power of our information system. These structures have certain basic similarities to those of language but are applied in a more rigid way. From the simple enumeration of data fields we progress to the tree, and then to the graph, so that, for example, as illustrated in Fig. 2-24, GRADE is not simply enumerated along with a series of other data items but rather is indicated as having a special immediate relationship to the data item MAJOR-SUBJECT, which in turn is indicated as having a special immediate relationship to LEVEL-OF-EDUCATION, and such indications communicate a subtle interpretation of information that would have been very laborious to communicate by a simple enumeration of data items plus some kind of descriptive overlay.

It is important at this point to discuss a concept that has been called *data independence*, but which may better be called *data processing independence.* To a compiler writer, data processing independence might carry somewhat the same meaning as machine independence, which is to say that the same source or user language can be translated and run on a variety of machines regardless of particular machine architecture. In the sense of the data management system and the material with which this book is concerned, data processing independence should certainly connote machine independence, but it also has a broader meaning. It means that certain aspects of the five data facets discussed in Chap. 1 should be transparent to the user, in the sense that although he is aware that these aspects or descriptions of the data exist, and although he may be cognizant of the role that they play in the system's interpretation and manipulation of the data, he is nonetheless relieved of certain mechanical functions that are necessary in order to process the data by virtue of these particular aspects.

Consider, for example, the simple aspect of the length of a data item within the representation facet. When the human brain processes data, the amount of brain cell storage required for a given data item is not associated with the manipulation of the data item. In the conception of a sentence, we are cognizant of the meaning of the words, the syntax of the sentence, possibly the grammar of the sentence, but usually not the length of the sentence or even less so the length of the individual words in the sentence. This is not to say that the length of the sentence would never be a particular object of human data processing. In fact, it may at times become a primary object of the processing, as for example, when you read some of the sentences of this book and comment to yourself on their length, but this concern with the length of the items or quantity of data storage is usually not a concern for the capacity or limitations in brain cell storage but rather derives from a consideration of the impact of the length of a sentence upon its intended meaning and on its effectiveness as a vehicle for transfer of information. Analogously, the user of a data management system would usually prefer that any aspect of data description within any of the five facets that does not relate directly to his particular use of the data at that moment be handled in an automatic, though consistent way. Length of data items is a simple example of an aspect of data facet (namely representation) that should be made *independent* of the usage of the data.

A second and more complex example is also related to data storage but at a higher level, namely, the tracking of the number of components in a particular dimension of a data array. In COBOL and even more so in FORTRAN, as well as in PL/1, there is a requirement upon the user to indicate how many components of a given dimension in an array are occupied. There are certain mechanisms in which this can be self-indicating, but these have to be constructed by the programmer himself with every usage. That is, a programmer in FORTRAN may declare a one-dimensional array in a dimension statement to have one hundred locations. If he wants to allow data to be read from cards or a file into the array as a variable number of words (up to a limit of 100), then he will provide a counter or control as the first data item read; this will indicate how many subsequent words are to be read. In a sense he programmatically sets up the same kind of control that is utilized in hardware I/O processors of the nonunit record type.

In certain languages such as PL/1 and ALGOL, the maximum extent of array storage does not have to be declared initially, and can be created and released dynamically, but this class of storage allocation and creation is not sufficiently sensitive to the number of array cells actually occupied at a given time within a data structure. The REFER attribute of PL/1 represents an attempt to assist the programmer in making the number of array components self-defining by designating the dimension size as a variable that is controlled from outside the structure and that governs the dimensionality at the time that space is allocated for the data structure. Once allocated, the value of this variable is assigned to an internal variable in the structure for the programmer's use in determining the limit of the array for the duration of the allocation. This type of PL/1 allocation, called a *based structure variable*, is dynamic in the sense that the space for the structure is allocated by the programmer with an ALLOCATE statement and freed with a FREE statement. Furthermore, the programmer may give a series of allocates without freeing the storage, in which case the current instance of the structure is stored in a stack and is available by means of stack pointers. Thus, each ALLOCATE of a structure which internally has an array dimensioned with a REFER statement can be created with a different dimensionality, and its processing can be controlled from within the structure by means of the REFER variable. This capability is limited in terms of using REFER's hierarchically within a given structure, and in addition, it is still the programmer's responsibility to use the REFER variable as the control on the array.

One could conceive of data processing independence in the sense of relieving the programmer of all array and field size considerations within data structures; such independence would exceed the described PL/1 capability. Data management of this sort would control the number of occurrences internally, as well as data item lengths, if it is a variable-length record type, and the programmer would call for data item occurrences either sequentially or selectively by citing the data name or the data name and a subscript. If access were sequential, the next or previous occurrence would be retrieved depending upon the mode of retrieval control. If it were selective, a specific occurrence indicated by the subscript would be retrieved. When a particular data item occurrence is inaccessible by virtue of having been referenced beyond the current dimensionality, the user is returned a special out-of-data indicator instead of the data. This represents an illustration of data processing independence as applied to one aspect of the *representation* data facet, and in particular to *explicit* representation.

Another example of data processing independence can be given for implicit representation. Assume that a number of basic operators exist that can perform functions on designated data items within all records of a particular file or subfile that had been generated by some file process. Such an operator may be the addition function, in which all values of a given field within a set of accessed records is to be summed. The sum thus represents an implicit representation of data within the file or subfile. Given this set of operators and a procedural language for performing the file processing, the user can call for retrieval of these implicitly derived data as though they were explicit data representation. That is, one can conceive of pseudo or phantom records made up partially or entirely of implicit data; these records could be formated, accessed, and manipulated for reports in the same way as records with explicit representations.

The matter of data processing independence comes down to a differentiation between that part of data description or those data facets that the programmer or user of the data management system is expected to control himself and that part which he does not have to control. In addition, generators may be provided which will create new data for the user without any requirement on the part of the user other than that he knows how the data are structured into fields, records, and files.

Figure 2-10 designates the data that must be provided by the user when the record of the file is initially defined. In addition to this information he will have to indicate the organization of the file, as shown in Fig. 2-4, and he may indicate retrieval control (HOL, EOL) with each data item that is a key, if this control is maintained in the Index record of Fig. 2-11. The dynamic control of data that may vary in length and occurrence is maintained in the data record itself, as illustrated in Fig. 2-14. After this information is provided to the system, reference can be made to data items by item name or canonical number. The mode will be determined from the file definition. The item length will be determined either from the file definition or the data record, depending upon whether it is FF, FV, VF, or VV. If the user calls for subscripted data, it will be accessed if available from the data record. If not available, either because the data item is not present in the (variable format) record or because the occurrence does not exist, it will be so reported. If the storage of a data item in an array is required, the number of occurrences will automatically be increased within the table of contents area of the data record.

A user will reference data either by name, in which case it must be unique or made unique by qualification within a data structure, or by canonical number. If the data item is an array, the user must provide suitable subscripts or the next or previous command for the data, if it exists, to be transferred. In Chap. 5 a prototype language will be presented for the purpose of demonstrating more concretely how the user communicates to the data management system his requirements for data definition and description, intrarecord data processing, and intrarecord or file processing. The concept of data processing independence will be further refined in the presentation of this prototype language, where it will be shown how the mechanical aspects of representation and maintenance of data structure are separated as much as possible from the operations being performed upon the data and the data structures under the direction of the user.

3
File Structures

3.1 FILE STRUCTURES

A file is a set of records commonly described by the same file definition in the sense of Fig. 2-10. As such, the file is a logical rather than a physical concept. The way in which records are organized for access from the file and certain kinds of relationships among records in the file are called *file structure*. Again, the definition of structure is logical rather than physical. There are, however, certain file structures that would be inefficient to implement in a particular storage medium, such as magnetic tape, and hence may carry a physical restriction with respect to implementation. There are seven basic file structures in use today, and these are illustrated and described in Figs. 3-25 through 3-32. Each serves a different access and/or update function; the description with each figure illustrates how the file is accessed and how it is updated.

Included in the language prototype for data management of Chap. 5 are five basic file I/O commands: OPEN, GET, SEARCH, PUT, and CLOSE. The OPEN command establishes an input buffer area—and, if required, an output buffer area—in core memory for the transfer of the record from or to secondary storage. It also initializes a table that describes the current status of the file and will bring into memory descriptive information about the file, such as the file definition table and perhaps a part of the index to the file, in the case of an indexed file. Files can be opened in four modes with respect to the ability to read and/or write from and to them. These modes are commonly defined as follows:

Mode	*Meaning*
IN	The file is assumed to exist and can only be read.
IN-OUT	The file is assumed to exist and can be read and written.

OUT   If the file exists, it is deleted and a new one is created.
               Records can then be written to it. If it does not exist,
               a file is created.

OUT-IN   Same as OUT except that records can be written to
               and read from the file after it has been created.

The existence or nonexistence of a disk file is an essential distinction because of a requirement to protect the overwriting of existing files. For a tape file this distinction is less important, because the tape can be physically protected from destruction by the removal of a ring from the tape reel, which activates a switch that inhibits writing to the tape. The GET command will read one record from the file in accordance with parameters provided in the GET calling sequence. These parameters vary from one type of file structure to another and will be described in conjunction with the respective file structure descriptions. The SEARCH command will access all records in a given file that satisfy some condition. The PUT opearation is the counterpart of GET in that it stores a record into the file instead of accessing it. The CLOSE operation is the counterpart of the OPEN in that it releases buffer storage and restores descriptive tables and index blocks in the event that they have been modified.

Each rectangular block in Figs. 3-35 through 3-32 represents a block of logical records; data access or update is always with reference to a single logical record whereas physical device access is with respect to a block.

The sequential file organization is illustrated in Fig. 3-25. It is the only file organization that imposes a strict physical requirement upon the organization, namely, that the records of the file be physically contiguous. Either magnetic tape or random access memories such as disk or drum are therefore suitable media for the storage of a sequential file. Access from the sequential file starts at the first record within the first block, with the first GET after a file OPEN; each succeeding GET will access the next contiguous record in the file. Thus, if records are packed N per block, a device READ is required only for every N successive record GET's. This situation is illustrated in the figure by a dashed line with an arrowhead that begins with the first record and proceeds serially through the file.

The file may be maintained in a particular sequence according to a key filed within each of the records, although this practice is not necessary. If the file is keyed and maintained in key sequence, and if it is desired to update the file with another record, then it must be inserted in its proper key position. The only way to do this and to maintain the physical sequence of the file is to copy the original file down to the point of insertion to insert the new record, and then to copy the reminder of the file thereafter. If the file is not maintained in key sequence, then updates can be added to the end of the file. Most systems will allow a sequential file to be both read and written within the same OPEN although it may be a dangerous practice, because, if the program begins to write prematurely, vital information will be lost. If one were to require the ring pro-

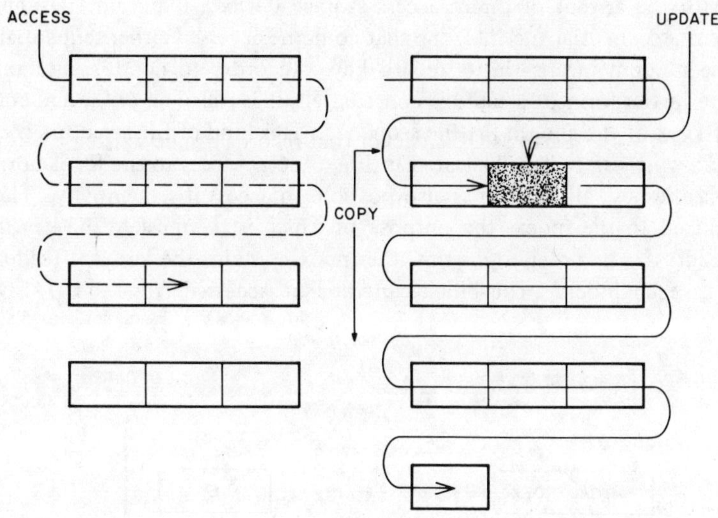

Figure 3-25 Sequential file organization

tection of a magnetic tape when updating a sequential file, the entire tape would have to be copied to another tape, whether or not the updated record were to be inserted in the middle or added at the end; the original tape is opened in a READ only mode and the copy tape is opened in a WRITE only mode.

The principal use of a sequential file is the serial processing of records, that is, when it is desired to begin processing a file with the first record and to process every record thereafter in sequence. In some cases it may not be desired to process the entire file but only to proceed partly through, such as when a search for a particular record is being made. In some systems a sequential file can be read backward, which means that the first record read is the last one in the file, and that with each GET command the next previous one is provided. There is no distinction between these two modes of access insofar as the structure of the file is concerned. The use of sequential files is today largely associated with the use of magnetic tape, since its development and use was governed by the particular nature of that medium. It is used with direct access storage devices in applications where the very high speed of successive record access is a requirement of the processing, since these devices have data transfer rates that are from two to four times faster than tape. Two major applications of sequential files are in sorting and in searching very large volumes of data that, for economic reasons, must be stored on magnetic tape. However, as shown in Chap. 7 of Reference 1, even magnetic tape can be organized for more effective batched search when the cellular partitioned file structure is overlaid upon the sequential structure.

With the advent of direct access storage devices, it became desirable to transform a sequential file into one that could be accessed either sequentially or by some random means via its record key. In order to do this, an auxiliary structure in the form of a table is constructed; it is called an *index* and consists only of keys of the file, in the file sequence. This kind of file structure is called *indexed sequential* and is illustrated in Fig. 3-26. Access to the file is normally made via the key, although it is also possible to access it sequentially. The key is submitted to the index, the purpose of which is to translate the key into a block address. In order to do this, the index contains the last key (called the *range*) in each block. The block can then be accessed from the DASD and

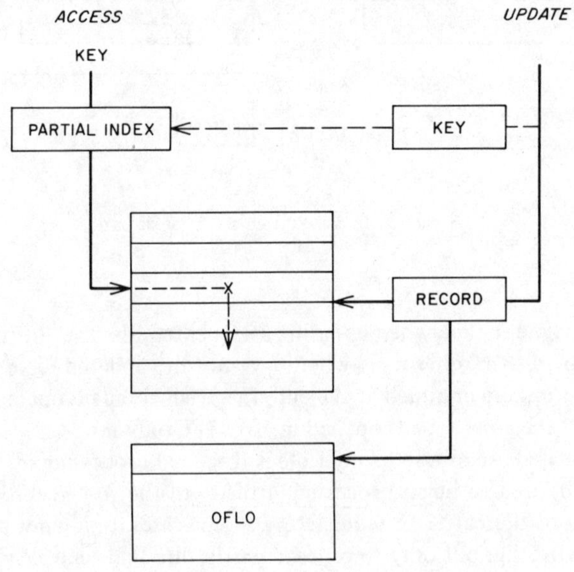

Figure 3-26 Indexed sequential file organization

brought directly into the core memory where it is serially scanned for the logical record containing the access key. The mode of access of the file can be changed from random (that is, indexed) to sequential at any time, as indicated in the diagram, where the output of the index points to a particular block containing the record with the decoded key. This record is designated by the letter X. If the mode were changed to sequential, after access of the record, each successive GET would produce a successive record in the file.

In principle, the key does not have to be unique, although in practice it normally is. Records with duplicate keys could be processed by first accessing the file randomly via the key, an action that will produce the first such record; a sequential read of the file will then produce all subsequent records with the given key. The file may, of course be accessed sequentially for a variety of other reasons.

In order to add a new record to the file, it is not necessary to copy the entire file. The random property of the storage device is utilized in order to minimize update time and the same time to maintain the sequential organization of the file. The block into which the new record must be inserted is found by decoding the index for the first key that is lexicographically higher than the new record key, in order to maintain the file sequence. The indicated block is accessed, and if there is sufficient reserve space within the block, the new record is inserted in its proper position within the block. If the block does not have enough space to accommodate the record, the block is logically extended to an overflow region.

Each block has a control record at the beginning containing a displacement pointer into the block that designates the next available position for record storage and a link address into the overflow region, if required, for logical block extension. When the file is initially generated, any amount of reserved space may be left in order to accommodate these updates without the necessity of a link address, since the links require additional accesses. The distribution of available or free space between the end of block reserve and the overflow region is a function of the expected update dynamics and the desired index size. The details of index construction are discussed later in this chapter, but at this point it may be noted that there is no index entry per block, this being the key of the last record in the block (or in the logically extended block). Thus, fewer records in the initially packed block result in more keys in the index.

In the indexed sequential file organization, new records are usually not added at the end of the block but rather are inserted into their appropriate position within the block, and subsequent records are pushed back in the block. Since these operations are performed in core storage, they are not inefficient. After a series of updates, the logical block extension in the overflow region may also become filled, In this case another overflow block will have to be added to the chain of blocks that comprise the single logical block, where the index entry is still the key of the last record in the chain of blocks. In time, the number of links may become large enough to justify a sequential sort and rewrite of the entire file, re-establishing a one-to-one relation between physical and logical blocks. A new and possibly larger index is also generated, since block terminating records will normally be different. The existence of the overflow region requires a slight modification in the sequential access algorithm, since when a block with such a logical extension is encountered, the physical access must jump to the overflow region in order to continue to provide records in their logical sequence; access returns to the original region of the file when either the overflow block or chain of overflow blocks is completed.

Since the index contains only the last key per logical block, it is called a *partial index*. When implemented on a movable head disk or drum, there is usually a separate partial index for each cylinder, which is stored in a block at the head of the data blocks within a cylinder, called the *block index*. Usually the block is a track, and the block or track index as it may then be called is the top track of the cylinder. If the file contains more than one cylinder, an index of the track indexes, called the cylinder index, is generated, which references the last key of each cylinder. Furthermore, since the file is assumed to be sequentially stored, a one-to-one relation exists between the position of a key reference in the block index and subsequent blocks in the cylinder. For example, the third key in the index is assumed to reference the third block after the index block. The record with the given search key is found by scanning the block until the record with the search key is found. If the block is not hardware addressable, as in the case of the IBM 2314 disk pack system, the index points to a track instead of a block, and each block is preceded by a record containing the range of the block. The channel searches the track for the first range key that is greater than or equal to the search key. The block is then read into core memory and scanned for the existence of the specific search key; in order to facilitate this search, the key of each logical record in a block is extracted and stored in a record immediately preceding the logical record.

The principal use of this file organization is for the random access of records with nonserial keys. There must be a single key designated within each record for file positioning, but the value of this key need not necessarily be unique within the file. If it is, then the access to the file will be unique; if it is not, then the access to the file will be to the first record in the series containing this key, and the other records containing the same key will appear immediately afterward. The key values themselves do not have to be serial since the access mechanism to the records does not use the key itself as a locator, but rather relies upon an index or a look-up in order to point to a particular block containing the indicated record key; hence, the key may be alphanumeric and of varying lengths. The construction of indexes to accommodate these keys is discussed later in this chapter.

Increased update frequency will cause a decrease in record access efficiency since physical access of a chain to one or more blocks is required in the event that the original block will have been logically extended in the manner described above. It would be more efficient to add new records to the end of the file or into whichever block can accommodate them, and to rely entirely upon the index for both the random access of the record as well as its sequential access, particularly if sequential access is required infrequently. Such a file structure, called *index random*, is illustrated in Fig. 3-27. It differs from the indexed sequential organization in two ways. First, all newly added records are put either at the physical end of the file or wherever the space maintenance processor indicates available space. Second, every key of the file must appear in the index because each key in the index points directly to the block in which the record with this key is contained; therefore, it is called a *full index*. The file need not be maintained physically in sequence. It is accessed by translating a key

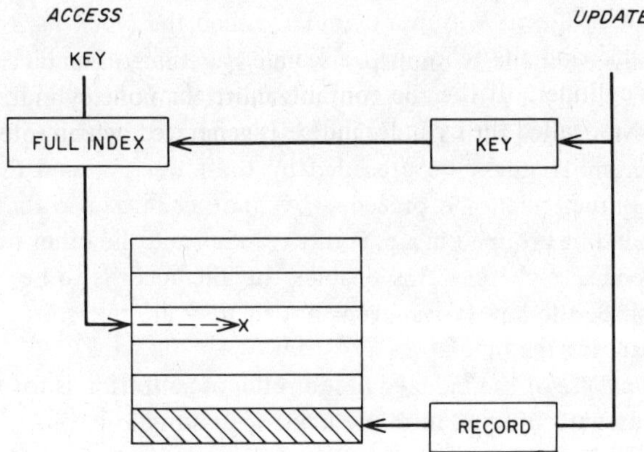

Figure 3-27 Indexed random file organization

via the index into a block address. Within the block will be found the record containing the given key. The key must be unique, because there can be one and only one position for the record in this file, and every record must have at least one such key. Once the record has been located, the subsequent records in the block have keys that are of no particular relation one to another, and the only possible relation among the records is one of chronology. Thus, although it would be possible to read the file sequentially from this point onward, it normally has no particular significance and is therefore not a common mode of access.

The index that is constructed to support an indexed sequential file does not have to contain every key of the file since it only references the last record in a block; hence, it is said to be partially indexed. The indexed random file, on the other hand, is fully indexed, since every key of every record must appear in the index. An indexed random file can be read sequentially only by scanning the index and then reading records randomly from the file as indicated by the index.

Consider now two characteristics of keys and files. One is called the *unique versus generic key*; the other is the *singly versus multiply keyed record*. A unique key is one for which there can be only one record in a file containing the key value; a generic key may represent more than one record. For example, a social security number in a personnel file would be a unique key while a person's age might be a generic key. A singly keyed record is one that contains one and only one key; a multiply keyed record contains more than one key. The indexed sequential file organization permits generic keys but not multiply keyed records, whereas the indexed random file permits multiply keyed records, but only with unique keys. For example, if the records pertained to personnel, and every person had two associated identification numbers such as a social security number and a company identification number, each of which was unique within the total system of such identification numbers, then they could both be entered into the index, each entry pointing to the same record. Thus each record in this file could have two access points instead of one as in the indexed sequential file organization.

It is usually desirable in multiply keyed systems to separate the key indexes either physically by building multiple, distinct indexes or by prefixing each key in a given series with a distinguishing letter. In the above example, the social security number might be preceded by the letter "S" and the company identification number might be preceded by another initial, so that all of one number type would be grouped in a part of the index and the other number type would be grouped elsewhere. This enables the file records to be sequentially accessed by each of the key types, even though they are not stored in physical sequence, by scanning the index.

The principal use of the indexed random file organization is for the random access of records with unique, multiple keys or in situations where the rate of update is so high that excessive chains would develop if an attempt were made to maintain the file in sequence. These chains result in both inefficient access and space utilization since there may be a large number of logically extended blocks where the last block contains only one or two records. The major advantage of the indexed sequential over the indexed random file organization is the ability of the former to provide efficient sequential access starting at any point in the file. Also, the index is smaller because it is partial.

The requirement to maintain an index for the purpose of achieving random access imposes an overhead in both space and time. Separate storage must be provided for the index, and it is usually sufficiently large to require storage in the DASD. Hence, before the actual data record access can be made, one or more index records may have to be randomly accessed. A file structure has been developed that eliminates the additional storage requirement and also attempts to alleviate the additional access problem, but that does not always succeed in doing so, and sometimes makes it worse. This method (Fig. 3-28) is called the *mapped random* file organization. As in the indexed random method, the data records of the file are stored randomly, but the index is replaced by a map, which is an algorithmic transformation from the record key to the block address. The manner in which this is done is described more explicitly further on in this chapter. The map performs the same key-to-address transformation that the index does.

There is one major functional difference between the mapped random and both of the indexed structures. Since there is no indexed enumeration of the keys and since the records are stored randomly, it is not possible to read the mapped file in its sequentially keyed order. Also, since it is not possible to construct a mapping that would assure the translation of two *different* key values to the same block address, a record can have only a single key. It is possible, however, that two different keys will incidentally point to the same block. Since the intended purpose of the block is to store more than one logical record, and to accommodate records of varying length as well, such an incidental many-to-one mapping can be accommodated as long as there is sufficient room within a block. However, there may eventually occur a mapping into a block that has already been filled, in which case a logical extension of this block must be made in much the same way as the indexed sequential block was logically extended. The logical extension of a block in this manner is called a *chain.* The generic key can also be accommodated by this file structure since this is simply another case of many-to-one mapping. The chain block may either be located within the original mapped region of memory or in an overflow region outside of the mapping domain. The former method is used if it is desired to pack the mapped region as tightly as possible at the expense of longer chains; that is, if the new (extended) block can also be reached by another key mapping, then it will contain records from two *different* mappings and hence will fill up faster. By the latter method, all block extensions are made into a region where no key mappings exist. As a result, there tends to be more unutilized space, but with fewer and shorter chains.

The strategy for access of a record starts with the mapping transformation of the key into a block address. The block is accessed and scanned for the record containing the indicated key; if it is not found within the block, the next block in the chain is randomly accessed and again scanned for the indicated key. This process continues until either the record is accessed or is found not be within the file. The file is updated by mapping the key of the new record into a block address. If the block is unoccupied, a record is stored there. If the block is occupied but there is still room within it, the record is also stored there. If there is no room within the block, then it must be logically extended by creating a chained block.

A special case of the mapped random file organization is identity mapping. In this file structure, the keys are serial numbers over a compact range, and the record per block packing must be a constant. This constant can be assured either by requiring the records to be fixed in size or by limiting the maximum record size. In this way, the key itself is the pointer, undergoing a linear transformation that offsets the address in accordance with the block packing. If the packing were N records per block and the key series started at 1, the block address of a record with a key value equal to X would be computed as

$$\text{Block address} = \text{Integral part of} \left(\frac{X-1}{N} \right) + 1$$

The principal use of the mapped random file organization is for the random access of fixed length records with unique serial keys or for the access of fixed or variable length records with generic, nonserial keys, where storage space, such as that which would be required for the index, is at a premium. The access times of the mapped versus the indexed file are comparable since the index access or accesses are offset by the chained block accesses. A disadvantage of mapping is that the file cannot be accessed sequentially via the key values through a serial read of the data file blocks since they are stored randomly, nor can they conveniently be accessed sequentially through the map since all possible keys would have to be generated, mapped, and examined for existence in the accessed records. Also, the technique may not be used with multiply keyed records unless an indirect level of addressing is interposed between the mapping and the data file itself, which translates the many-to-many key address transformations into a many-to-one transformation. Methods for accomplishing this are described in References 1 and 6, but since the interposed level of indirect addressing is tantamount to an index, it is usually more effective to use an indexed method exclusively when dealing with mutliply keyed records.

At the bottom of Fig. 3-28 is a diagram which shows that the indexed random file structure can be constructed from a concatenation of the indexed sequential and the mapped random organizations; the indexed sequential file is used here to translate from the record key to a serial number corresponding to the key. These are then fed to a mapping for translation into block number in the data file. Thus the combination acts like an indexed random file structure, with the exception that the data file addresses cannot be freely assigned. This procedure may have some practical significance if the software with which one is working has an indexed sequential and mapped random file organization and it

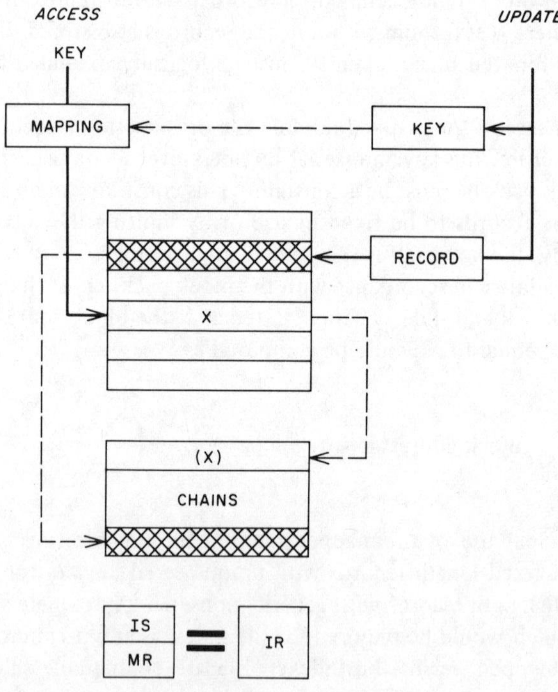

Figure 3-28 Mapped random file organization

is desired to use these without further modification in the construction of an indexed random file structure. For example, OS 360 normally provides an indexed sequential access mechanism (ISAM) and an identity-mapped random structure called the *basic direct access mechanism* (BDAM).[7] Thus, the ISAM and the BDAM can be used in conjunction to define this kind of quasi-indexed random file structure. A useful extension of this dual-structure combination is to provide a series of ISAM's, one per key type, all feeding into the one BDAM-controlled data file. This arrangement will then provide multiply keyed file access as well as generic key access.

The primary use of the three random file structures just described is for the storage and access of records with a single, unique key, although certain of them, as indicated, can be adapted for multiply keyed records and for generic keys. Furthermore, the attributes of generic key and multiply keyed records cannot be employed simultaneously with the same file structure. The indexed sequential structure will handle generic keys but not multiply keyed records; the indexed or mapped random structure will handle the multiply keyed record but not the generic key. Since it is often desirable to manipulate data with both these characteristics, it is necessary to devise yet another kind of file structure specifically intended to handle them or to use the dual structure concept described in Fig. 3-28. Three specific types of file structures have been developed to handle the generic key and the multiply keyed record simultaneously. These are (1) the chained list file structure, (2) the inverted list file structure, and (3) the cellular partitioned file structure.

Figure 3-29 illustrates the chained list file organization. As before, the logical records are assumed to be blocked, but to simplify the diagram only

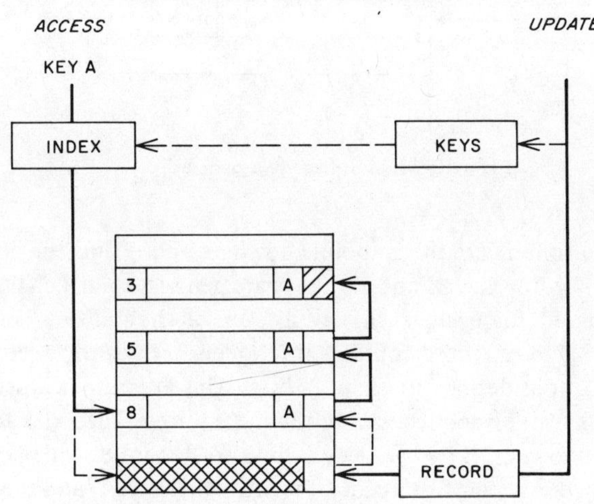

Figure 3-29 Chained list file organization

logical records are displayed. The methodology employed extends the concept of the indexed random file structure to handle generic keys, since this file structure already has the multiply keyed record capability. As shown in Fig. 3-29. there is associated with each generic key *within* the record a link address field, the purpose of which is to point to the next record in the file that contains the same key value.

In the illustration, there are assumed to be three records containing key A. The index translates to the first of these records, which is shown as the lowermost record in the series, with a designated record ID number of 8 (solid line from index to data file). The first record with key A points to another record with key A (Record 5) via the link address field, and the second record with an A points to a third record with an A (Record 3). The link address field in the third

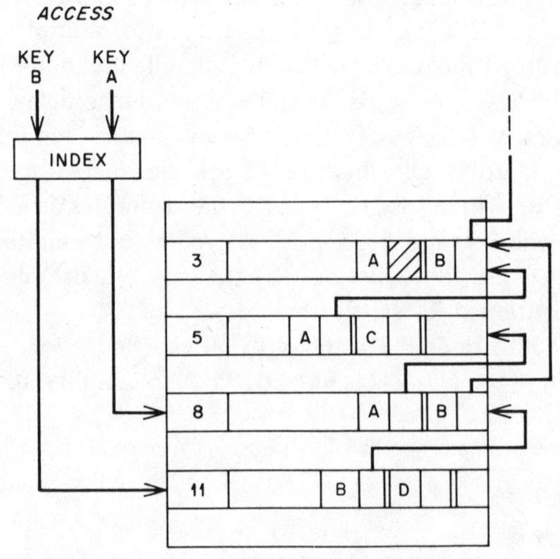

Figure 3-30 Multilist file organization

record is shaded to indicate that it points nowhere and is thus the end of the list. If records are multiply keyed and the keys are generic, then a chain of this type will be constructed for every such key in each of the multiply keyed records. For example, if a given record contains three generic keys, this record will reside on three chains, or as defined in Chap. 2, *lists*. The situation is illustrated in Fig. 3-30, where keys A and B are decoded in the index. Key B decodes to Record 11, which contains two keys, B and D. Key B links to Record 8, which contains keys A and B. Record 8 is the first record that contains key A, and therefore key A decodes through the index directly to Record 8. The next record on the A list after 8 is Record 5, and therefore key A in Record 8 links to Record 5. Key A in Record 5 links to Record 3, and the shaded region in the key A link address indicates that it is the end of the list. Key B links from Record 8 to Record 3, and from there it links out to another record; therefore, Record 3 is the terminal record in the A list but not in the B list.

The schematic of Figs. 3-29 and 3-30 relates specifically to the *data items* segment of the prototype data record shown in Fig. 2-14, where it is indicated that certain items may have link addresses in order to implement the chained file structure. A chained list structure that accommodates both generic keys as well as multiply keyed records, as illustrated in Fig. 3-30, is called a *multilist file organization*; it was originally described by Prywes and Gray.[8] The update procedure for a chained list file is largely a function of how the file is to be accessed. The new record to be added to the chain is normally inserted either at the beginning or the end of the chain. Only in the case where the lists are maintained in a particular key sequence other than that for which the chain is being constructed, say for demand report generation purposes, would it be necessary to insert the record in the middle of the chain. The normal procedure is to add a new record at the beginning of the chain and to maintain only one-directional chain linkages. When the record is added at the beginning of the chain, as indicated in Fig. 3-29, the address of the new record becomes the link address emanating from the index, appearing as the dashed line extension from the index, and the address of the former head of list becomes the link address in the new record; thus, the new record replaces the former as the head of list. In this way only one random access other than that necessary to store the new record is required, namely, that of the index record, and none of the remaining records on the chain need be accessed. When the chain is traversed for the purpose of access or retrieval, the latest record added to the chain will be the first to be retrieved; therefore, this procedure leads naturally to a last-in-first-out (LIFO) method of retrieval control, in the sense described in the discussion of Fig. 2-11. If it is desired to implement first-in-first-out (FIFO) control, and yet, to retain this simple update procedure, then it is necessary to store the end-of-list address in the index record as well as the head-of-list address, as indicated in Fig. 2-11. The new update record is then stored at the end of the list rather than at the head of the list; it will also require an additional access, because the last record in the list must have its link address changed from an end-of-list indicator to the address of the newly added record. The index record would still have to be read in order to find the end of list, and then written back to disk with an updated end-of-list link address. If both LIFO and FIFO control were to be maintained simultaneously, then either head-or end-of-list record insertion could be employed, but both the head- and end-of-list addresses must be maintained in the index and, in addition, bidirectional link addresses must be used within the records so that the list can be traversed in either direction.

Chapter 4 discusses in greater detail the update processes for a list structure, and the implications of one-directional versus bidirectional links is further explored there. When adding a new record to a multilist file, it is necessary to update the index with *every* key of the new record. If the key is unique, it will

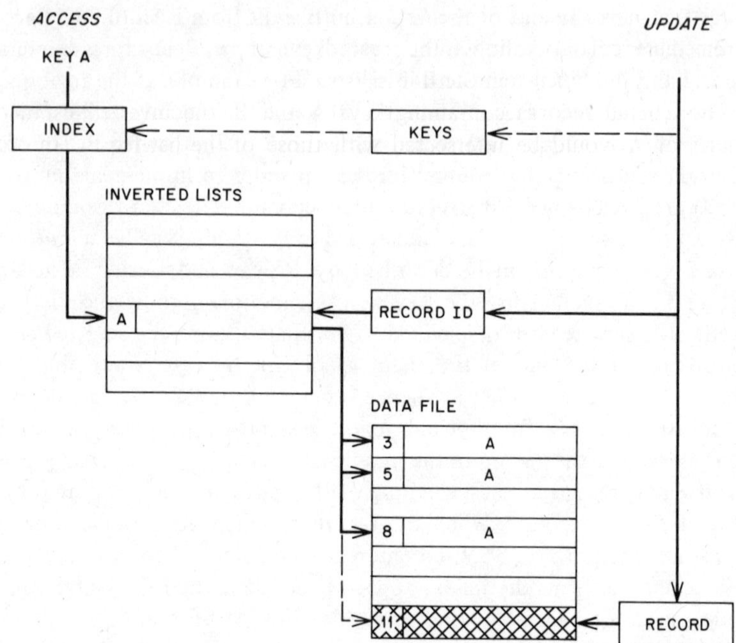

Figure 3-31 Inverted list file organization

require the addition of a new key to the index; if the key is generic, it may be new, in which case it must be added to the index, or it may already exist in the index, in which case it would be necessary only to update its list length indication, as designated in Fig. 2-11, and to add the record to its appropriate list.

The second method of implementing file structures for generic and multiply keyed records is called the *inverted list file organization* and is illustrated in Fig. 3-31. By this method, another file is inserted as an intermediary between the index and the data file. This intermediary file contains records that are simply lists of pointers to the data file records. Every key in the index points to one of these lists, called an *inverted list*, and the list in turn points to all of the records in the data file that contain the given generic key. In Fig. 3-31 key A is translated through the index to point to a particular record in the inverted list. The inverted list record then enumerates and points to three records, namely 3, 5, and 8. The pointer contained in the inverted list may either be a link address or a unique record key. The link address may be a block address, in which case the records of the data file block are scanned for all records containing the given key, or it may be the logical record address, given as a block address plus record number within block. The latter address type is normally used if multikey logic is employed because it precisely co-ordinates the records to be accessed.

The block or record decoding for multikey logic is performed by accessing all inverted lists corresponding to the several keys in the logic expression and then executing the indicated logic on these lists. For example, if the logic required the access of all records containing keys A and B, the inverted list with the addresses of A would be intersected with those of the list for B. In order to expedite this process, the inverted lists are maintained in address sequence. If only a block address were used in the multikey logic application, then each record accessed from the block would have to be tested for satisfaction of the logical condition. It is possible for a block to be indicated for access by the inverted list logic processing without any record in the block to satisfy the logical condition. For example, assume that Record 1 in the block contains key A but not key B, and that Record 2 contains B but not A; then the logic A and B will access this block but neither Record 1 nor 2 will satisfy the request logic. Addressing by record rather than by block is normally practiced, therefore, if the full power of inverted list access is to be obtained. The only advantage of addressing by block lies in the use of inverted lists for systems where multiple-key logic is not employed. Addressing by block is actually a special type of cellular partition, which is the third method of list-structured file organization to be discussed.

The use of a unique record key is an alternative to that of a record address. The key is translated via an index or map into the data record address after being accessed from the inverted lists. Such a key is sometimes referred to as a primary key of the record. The advantage of using a primary key as a pointer is that relocation of a record with a consequent change in its address will not necessitate an update of the inverted lists on which the record appears. Only the primary key to record address index need be updated. Such relocation will occur for all records whenever a file is regenerated in order to remove logical block extensions; it will also occur for individual records in systems that do not utilize logical data block extension when a record increases in size and cannot be restored to the same block. If the pointers were the record or block address, relocation and address modification of the record would require that *all* inverted lists pertaining to keys of the relocated record would have to be updated by removing the record address from each of these lists and replacing it with the new record address.

An alternative approach to the storage of address or key pointers is the generation of a series of bit maps, one per key in the system. Each map holds as many bits as there are records in the file. Thus, either a maximum file size must be established or the programs that generate and maintain these maps must be able to dynamically expand and contract the map size. If record N contains key X, then the map for key X will have its Nth bit set to 1. This implementation is analogous to the peek-a-boo or optical coincidence card system.[9] In order to find all records containing keys X and Y, the maps for X and Y are conjuncted. The resultant bit positions containing a 1 are then translated to record addresses. The advantage of the bit map approach is update speed. A comparison of its processing speed with that of lists is a function of file and list size, where smaller files favor the bit map and smaller lists favor the list approach. The storage requirement comparison turns out to be a function only of the ratio of the average list length to the file size (in records), and the crossover is readily computed as follows: Let B = the number of bits in the computer word; p = the ratio of average list length to file size; and F = the file size. Assume that a record address requires one computer word. Since the number of words required for the average size inverted list equals pF and the number of words required for a bit map equals F/B, the bit map storage will be less than the list storage when

$$F/B < pF$$

or

$$1/B < p$$

That is, when the ratio of the average list length to the file size is greater than the reciprocal of the number of bits per computer word, the bit map storage is less than the list storage. A 32-bit word machine will, therefore, have a crossover at 3 percent. A hybrid inverted list structure could also be constructed in which lists would be bit mapped or address stored according to their length. Logic would be performed exclusively in one or the other mode. For example, if logic were performed as bit maps, all accessed address lists would be converted to bit maps before logic execution.

As indicated on the right side of Fig. 3-31, new records are added to the end of the data file, and the record identification, whether it be an address pointer or a primary key, is inserted in sequence into the inverted list.

As in the case of the multilist, all new keys must be added to the index, but it is normally not necessary to maintain a count of the list length, since this is required to optimize retrieval strategy using the multilist technique only.

When a unique key is designated as an identifier of the record for use as an inverted list pointer or for sequence and access control in an indexed sequential file, it is called the *primary* key of the file; all other keys in multiply-keyed files are called *secondary* keys. The data file in the chained or multilist file organization may be indexed random, with both primary and secondary keys appearing in the same index, or it may be indexed sequential, in which case only the primary key appears in the file index. All secondary keys are then translated by a separate indexed sequential file into the primary key. As indicated previously, it is sometimes desirable in multiply keyed files to define the primary or locator key, as one may think of it, as a record serial number (that may or may not be recorded as data within the record); the secondary indexed sequential indexes then translate to the primary key serial number, which is then decoded to a record address by an identity map.

Although the diagram of Fig. 3-31 illustrates only a single key within each of the records 3, 5, and 8, the inverted list method is also applicable to the multiply keyed file. In the example illustrated in Fig. 3-30, list A would contain records 3, 5, and 8 (as shown in Fig. 3-31); list B would contain records 3 and 8 (and 11 after the update) plus others, since the B list does not terminate; lists would also exist for other keys such as C, D, etc. In fact, the major advantage of the inverted list organization is that access can efficiently be made to the file for multikey inquiries since logical operations like intersection and union can readily be performed on these lists in order to produce a resultant list of access pointers.

The third method for handling generic keys and multiply-keyed records is called the *cellular partitioned file organization*, illustrated in Fig. 3-32. This

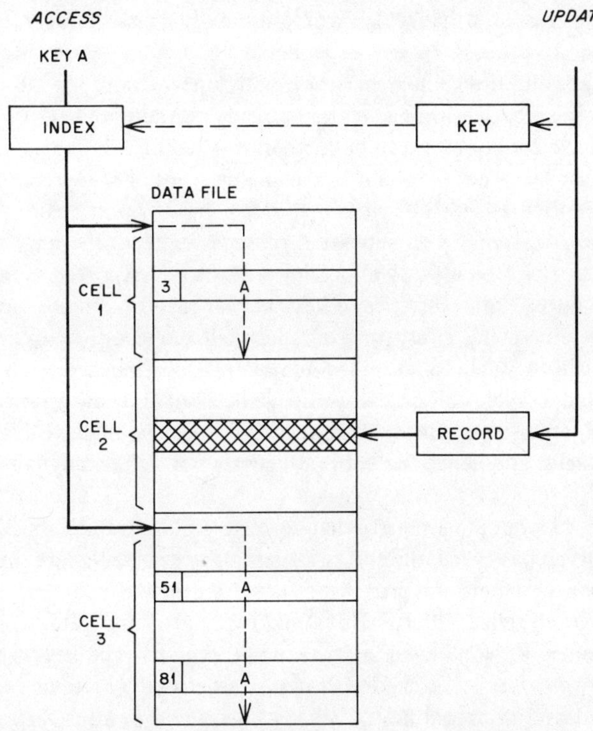

Figure 3-32 Cellular partitioned file organization

method is equivalent to the inverted list method with block address pointers, except that pointers reference larger, contiguous partitions of DASD storage called *cells*. The cells may be of arbitrary size, or they may be related to some physical partition of the device such as a cylinder (or fraction of a cylinder), strip, or card in an IBM data cell or NCR CRAM system, etc. The cell may be internally organized by any of the other file structure mechanisms; it may be sequential, indexed (that is, subindexed), or mapped. The example of Fig. 3-32 shows the cell to be sequentially organized. The index decodes key A to cells

1 and 3. Cell 1 is read sequentially, and a block is retrieved which contains Record 3 having key A; cell 3 has two records, 5 and 8, containing key A. The main purpose of the cellular partition is to reduce the size and maintenance of the index. It relies to a greater extent on processing within the cells and hence can be viewed as a hierarchy of organizations. When the cellular suborganization is sequential, the size of the cell determines a strict space–time tradeoff between the size and processing of the index versus the processing time in the data file itself. Chapter 7 of Reference 1 discusses an application of cellular partitions to batched searching on magnetic tape, wherein it is shown how the batch size can be increased beyond that which would normally cause the operation to pass from tape speed to processor speed dependence.

When updating the cellular partition with a new record, an attempt is first made to place the record within a cell that already contains all keys of the record so that the index does not have to be further updated. Failing this, the record is placed in an available cell containing the majority of the keys of the record. Appendix B of Reference 1 describes a strategy, based upon this principle, that was employed to determine an allocation scheme for record storage that would minimize the size of the index by allocating records to cells based upon the highest degree of mutual co-occurrence of keys in that record with the keys of other records in the same cell. Thus, for example, if all the records with key A could be collected within a single cell, there would be only one index reference to a cell with key A, and a single-cell access would yield all of the key A records. There are, of course, other keys within these records which would have similar attractions to other cells, and hence the entire process is not unlike a dynamic program optimization.

Figure 3-33 presents a matrix that correlates file attribute with file organization. The seven basic structures or organizations discussed above are classified in the chart as five, where the three list structures have been commonly grouped into one category, called LIST. Three major file attribute categories are indicated: (1) Nonkeyed, (2) keyed and (3) record length. The keyed category is subdivided into three subsets, each with two alternatives: (1) unique and generic keys, (2) serial and nonserial keys, and (3) singly- and multiply-keyed records. The record length is indicated as either fixed or variable. In each of the subattributes of the keyed category a weaker and stronger alternative is given, such as unique/generic or serial/nonserial. The stronger subattribute obviously implies the weaker. The table indicates on the right side by an X the most appropriate file organization for a given set of file attributes that are indicated by X's on the left side. The first line of the table indicates that a nonkeyed file is implemented only by a sequential (S) file organization. In the second row, a system with unique, nonserial keys with only a single key per record and a variable record length can be implemented by the indexed sequential (IS), indexed random (IR), and mapped random (MR) organizations. Although the list structure file organization could also be used, it is not indicated in this row of the matrix, because its use in this way would actually be identical to one of the others and would only

| FILE ATTRIBUTE | | | | | | | | | FILE ORGANIZATION | | | | |
| NON KEYED | KEYED | | | | | | RECORD LENGTH | | S | IS | IR | MR | LIST |
	UNIQ	GENERIC	SERIAL	NON SERIAL	SINGLE	MULTIPLE	FXD	VBL					
X								X	X				
	X			X	X			X		X	X	X	
	X			X		X		X			X		
	X		X	X			X					X(IM)	
		X		X	X			X		X		X	
		X		X		X		X					X

Figure 3-33 File attribute compared to file organization

represent a degenerate case of the list structure. On the third line of the table it is indicated that a system with unique and nonserial keys but with multiply-keyed, variable-length records can be implemented by the indexed random file but not the indexed sequential or mapped random. The indexed sequential organization relies upon a unique relative position of the record in the data file based upon the key of the record, and the mapped random method relies upon a unique location of the record in the file, based also upon the key; for this reason these two file structures can accommodate only a single key within the record.

The fourth line of the table indicates that a system with a unique but serial-numbered key and a singly-keyed, fixed-length record (or a fixed number of records per block) can be implemented most appropriately by a mapped random file with identity mapping. This is a special case of line 2 but has the advantage that there is no index to store or decode, and it is guaranteed that there will be only one access in the data file. Line 5 shows that a system with generic, and nonserial keys and singly-keyed, variable-length records can be implemented by the indexed sequential and the mapped random file organizations. The generic key can be accommodated because the key is used to coordinate the position of an initial record within these file structures; as many other records with the same key can then follow in the same block as are required. If the block becomes filled, it can be logically extended by linking it to a spare block in an overflow region. Line 6 represents a system with generic, nonserial keys in multiply-keyed, variable-length records. The list structures are specifically designed to accommodate this entire set of attributes.

These seven basic file structures can be combined and adapted to suit any specific design requirement, and Reference 1 describes a number of such variants and combinations. The purpose here is to portray them simply as elemental building blocks within the total design schema.

Chapter 1 alluded to a *hierarchy of data aggregates* as one of the five facets of data. Chapter 2 concentrated on a particular level of that hierarchy, namely the *data record* and its internal structure. This chapter has to the present point focused upon a higher level of aggregation in the hierarchy, the *file*, which is a data structure that combines and interrelates records. The next higher level of the hierarchy to be considered is the *multiple file structure,* which consists of sets of interrelated files. Again, the tree and graph structures are found to be of both theoretical and practical interest. Figure 2-14 in Chap. 2 designated the third segment of the prototype data record as one that would provide the linkage for interfile associations. In particular, two such relations are to be defined, one called *hierarchic* that is related to the tree structure, and the other called *associative* that is related to the more general graphical structure or, as it is sometimes referred to, the network structure.

The hierarchic multiple file organization is defined as follows. Consider two distinct files, A and B. If any record of file A may be associated with a series of one or more records in file B, and if every record of file B must be a member of one such series, then files A and B are said to have a hierarchic relationship, where A is called the master[1] or owner[5] file and B is called the detail[1] or member[5] file. The internal organizations of A and B are arbitrary except for the fact that some mechanism must be established to implement the hierarchic relationship. There are four ways to construct this mechanism. One is the *chain* linkage, whereby the master record links to the first detail record by an interfile link address, as indicated in Fig. 2-14, and each detail links to the next within the detail file. The interrecord linkage may be constructed as a file name (of the detail file) plus a record key. If the detail file structure were chained, the key could be generic and the list of detail records would automatically be accessed. If the detail file structure were not chained, then the record key should uniquely point to the first detail record and a chaining mechanism built to access the remaining details. In the latter case, the file name-unique key combination could be substituted by the first detail record address within the detail file. This practice eliminates the need to translate the key through an index or map, but requires the master record to be updated whenever the detail is readdressed.

The second method of implementing the master-detail linkage is similar to the first in that the initial interfile link is a file name with generic key appended, but the detail file is organized indexed sequential by the generic keys so that all the details are automatically maintained in sequence. This approach increases the efficiency of producing a detail within master report since the detail file can be read sequentially starting at any point. It is less efficient to update, though, than the indexed random structure that could be used in conjunction with the first method.

The third method of implementing the master-detail linkage is via the *pointer array*, which is a list of the link addresses stored entirely within the master record. In this way no linkages or link access mechanisms are required in the detail file. This method is analogous to the inverted list approach, although it is not normally necessary to maintain the pointers in sequence. The programming of this method is more complex because allowance must be made for variable length pointer arrays.

The fourth method is to use inverted lists instead of the pointer arrays of method 3 or the chained lists of method 1. In this case, the detail interfile link is a file name and a generic key to an inverted list.

A file may be both a master and a detail in a pair of hierarchic relations, but a master file cannot be a detail to any file that is itself in a subordinate chain below it. For example, file A may be a master to file B, and file B may be a master to file C. If, however, file C were to be a master to file A, the multiple file structure would no longer be hierarchic.

It should be noted that there is a direct tradeoff that can be made between the hierarchic arrangement of information through intrarecord structure as described in Chap. 2 and interrecord and interfile structure as described above. It is also possible to define a multiplicity of record formats in the same file, as can be done in COBOL or PL/1, and to establish the master-detail hierarchy within the same file.

An illustration of the hierarchic multiple-file organization is presented in Fig. 3-34. Across the top of the diagram the files are given canonical labels according to the tree structure to which they conform. The files are also given natural names in order to relate them directly to a meaningful example. Consider file 1 to be a customer file. Each record within the file contains customer information, such as account number, name and address, current and aged balances, and sales data. A subordinate body of information that may pertain to any individual customer record is the series of back-orders outstanding against the particular customer. The tree diagram in the middle of Fig. 3-34 indicates this by a connection from the customer file (1) to the back-order (1.1). The file schematic in the upper part of the diagram contains a pointer from the customer record (file 1) to the first of a series of records in file 1.1. Each record within the series in file 1.1 pertains to a specific back-order for the given cus-

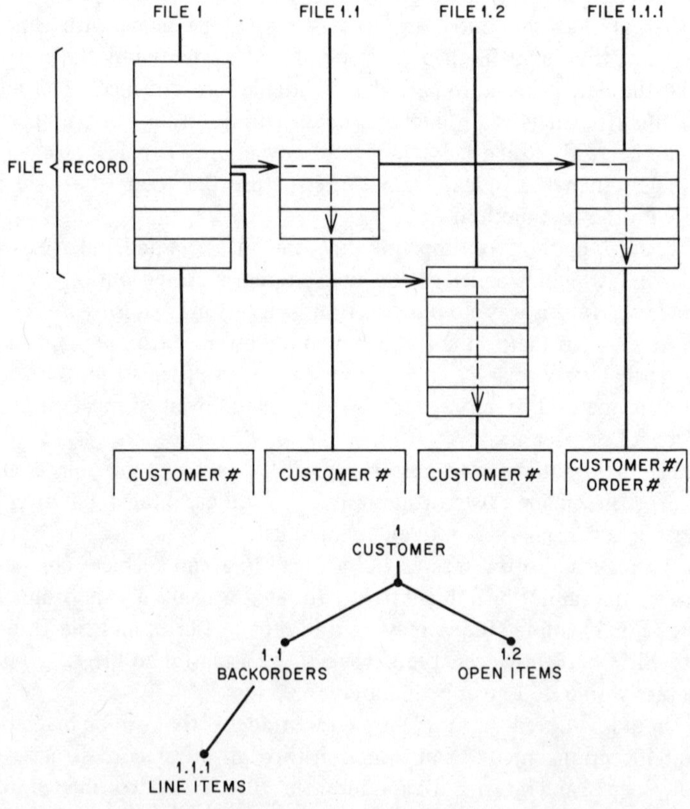

Figure 3-34 Hierarchic multiple file organization

tomer. The backorder record has its own independent intrarecord structure and can be accessed either via the customer file or independently according to the particular file structure of file 1.1, which need not be the same as that of file 1. Each file within the multiple-file organization may have its own independent structure, and groups of records are accessible either via the master file in the multiple-file structure or via its own file structure. File 1 in the illustration is the master file, and 1.1 is the detail file. A file can be both master and detail in the hierarchy, as shown by the third level file 1.1.1.

The key of the customer file is CUSTOMER No., and it is unique. The key of the detail file 1.1 is also CUSTOMER No., but it is generic. This file can be organized as indexed sequential or random, but it has the functional capability of accessing all detail records (back-orders) belonging to a given customer. The schematic of file 1.1 shows the details to be contiguous, but this characteristic only need imply logical contiguity achieved either through the index in the indexed random structure or through the index and file in the indexed sequential structure.

If it were desired to index directly to a specific backorder, the key in file 1.1 would be CUSTOMER No. - ORDER No. It is useful, in this context, to construct index decoders that can recognize concatenated keys and will decode any number of links in the concatenated series. Thus, access could be made either to a specific back order via the full key or to a series of back orders via the partial key CUSTOMER No. The example of Fig. 3-34 is carried one level deeper, where it is shown that the back-order file (1.1), which is a detail to the customer file (1), is also a master file and has a subordinate file, canonically numbered 1.1.1, that contains records with the line items of the order. Thus, each record of file 1.1 may point to a series of records within file 1.1.1, again accessible either from the pointer in the file 1.1 record or independently via the file structure of file 1.1.1, the key of which may be CUSTOMER No. - ORDER No. - LINE No. or CUSTOMER No. - ORDER No. or CUSTOMER No. Where the key is CUSTOMER No. - ORDER No., the line number would be stored as data, and in the last case, where the key is only CUSTOMER No., both the order and line numbers would be data. Another file branching from the customer file is the open-item file (1.2), within which each open item outstanding against a given customer is contained as a record. By an "open item" here is meant an unpaid invoice or a cash receipt that is waiting to be reported in a current statement to the customer. Note that in order to report a statement to a particular customer one need only access the particular customer record in file 1, which in turn points to the series of open-item records within file 1.2. Furthermore, if the open items are recorded in file 1.2 in date sequence, the report is simply generated by printing the record contents, in a suitable format, within the given customer number series, since the customary sequence of such a statement is by date.

It was indicated in Chap. 2 that although a general graphical structure for a record may be of theoretical interest, it would usually be impractical because of the overhead implied by so many linkages. The overhead is relatively less significant at the file level because the extent of the memory medium onto which the graph is being mapped is so much greater, being the DASD in the latter case as compared with core memory in the former. A multiple-file organization in which any given record of any file can point to or associate with one or more records in any other file is called an *associative* or *network* multiple-file organization. The rules of construction are quite open: any file may be of any organization, including list structured, and any file may be linked to any other file. The same four linkage types apply to the network structure, namely chains, indexed sequential, pointer arrays, and inverted lists.

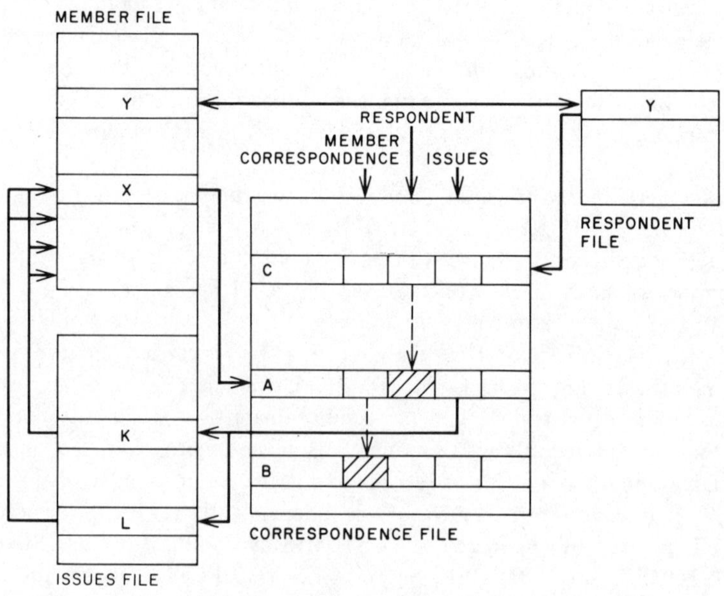

Figure 3-35 An associative multiple file organization

Figure 3-35 presents an example of an associative multiple-file organization. Consider the first file to be one containing the records of members in a political organization; the second file contains correspondence from the members to the organization headquarters; the third file contains records relating to certain personnel within the organization, who are themselves members, and whose job it is to respond to the correspondence; a fourth file is an issues file. A given member file record, Y, is shown pointing to a respondent record and conversely, in consideration of the fact that members are also respondents. Another member file record, X, is pointing to the first in a chain to two correspondence records (A and B) that represent individual correspondences that this member has made to the headquarters. The correspondence file has two internal chains and one associative link to another file. One is the correspondence chain and is linked from the member file; the second is the chain of correspondence that a given respondent has answered or is responsible for answering, and these are linked from the respondent file. The associative link is a pointer array to records in the issues file, which represent issues with which the organization is concerned and to which the particular correspondence pertains.

It should be noted that the pointer array is more powerful in this function that the chain since a many-to-many relationship can be established with the pointer array whereas only a one-to-many relationship can be effected via the chain.   That is, one member can be chained to many correspondences (submitted by this member), but many correspondences can point to many issues, some of which may overlap, by means of the pointer array. The respondent record Y points to a chain of correspondence, the second of which is correspondence A from member X.   This is also the last correspondence in the respondent Y set.   Correspondence A points via the pointer array to records K and L in the issues file, which in turn are associated with the member file by a pointer array. Records K and L will both point to member X and will, of course, also point to other members of the organization which have, because of their correspondence, become associated with these particular issues.

The pointer type illustrated here is that of a pointer array, which designates all records in the member file that are to be associated with particular issues. Thus it is shown that the direction, hierarchic level, and record mappings (one-to-one, one-to-many, many-to-many) in an associative or network multiple-file structure are completely arbitrary.   Any intrafile linkages, such as would be required by a chained-list structure, are still retained with the date items in segment 4 of the prototype data record of Fig. 2-14.

3.2 DIRECTORIES

The preceding discussion has implied a dual substructure within each of the random file organizations, and in the case of the inverted list, a triple substructure.   The dual substructure consists of a key decoding mechanism and the data file.   It is, in fact, the interposition of the key decoder that distinguishes random from sequential file organizations.   Thus, access to records in a random file is divided into two subprocesses; one translates from an external or symbolic key, representing the record to be accessed, to the record address reference, and the second is the access of the data record itself.   To some extent the method of translation from key to address is independent of the way in which the data file is organized, and it is the various combinations of specific data file organization and key translation methodology that actually produces the seven basic file organizations.

There are two general methods of key translation, one being the index or table look-up, in which all or a selected subset of the keys of the file are represented in a table that is normally stored in the same medium as the data file itself; the other method is an algorithmic translation implemented by a computer program that operates upon the key as data and produces an address reference as a result of this operation. In the latter case the keys are mapped into record addresses without the need to store them explicitly in a table. The following discussion pertains to a few of the techniques used to implement indexes and mapping algorithms.

An index can graphically be viewed as a tree[10,11] of one of two types, balanced or unbalanced. In a balanced tree the number of random accessions required to decode any given key of the index is the same as that to decode any other key of the index, plus or minus one accession. The main purpose of the balanced tree is to assure uniformity of decoding time, at least in terms of the number of random accessions, for any key in the index. In an unbalanced tree the number of random accessions required to decode any given key of the index may vary from one key to another by an arbitrary number of accessions. The purpose of the unbalanced tree may be intentionally to give advantage to decoding speed for certain keys over others, or it may be to overcome the particular disadvantage of the unbalanced tree, which is a potentially higher cost in the number of accessions to update the index[10,11,12].

Three techniques for the construction and update of tree indexes are to be described. The first is a balanced tree, the second is an unbalanced tree, and the third is an unbalanced tree by the above definition but one that is graphically balanced. The graphical distinction is of course immaterial, since it is the functional definition that really counts; the third tree acts functionally in every way like an unbalanced tree, and hence would be selected for implementation under any of the considerations for an unbalanced tree.

Figure 3-36 illustrates the construction and update of the balanced tree index.[10] The example assumes that there are 19 keys to be indexed, represented by the letters A through S. It assumes that each key may be variable in length, so that a block will accommodate a varying number of these keys. Each block is represented as a rectangle in the diagram. In graphical terminology, each of these rectangles or blocks is called a node of the tree. The lower most left-hand node of the diagram contains three keys, A, B, and C. In addition, it is indicated that the three keys do not entirely fill the block, and reserve space at the end of block is designated by shaded lines. The tree is generated from left to right in alphabetic ascending key sequence, starting with what is called the *output level* of the tree. Referring to Fig. 2-11 in Chap. 2, it is indicated that for each key in the block there is enumerated the key value, the list length if a chained list structure is being indexed, a link address, and an optional link address which points to the last data record in a chained list for end of list retrieval control. At the output level of the tree, the link address references another file, being either the data file or an inverted list file. At a nonoutput or higher level of the tree, the link address will reference a block within the index file itself; that is, it references a lower level node of the tree.

The header and subrecord header in Fig. 2-11 are not shown explicitly in Fig. 3-36; the header is assumed to exist at the front end of each block, and the subrecord header is assumed to exist at the beginning of each run of keys of a given length. The symbol A in Fig. 3-36 therefore pertains to the two-to four-fold information packet of *key*, (*list length*), *link address*, (*link address*) that is required per key. When a block has been filled at a given level, the last key value (in key not length sequence) of the block becomes a key entry in a higher level node. For example, it is assumed in Fig. 3-36 that keys A, B, and C can be loaded into the first block. Key C is represented as the highest in sequence and becomes an entry in the first node of the second level. This entry is called the *range* of the lower level node.

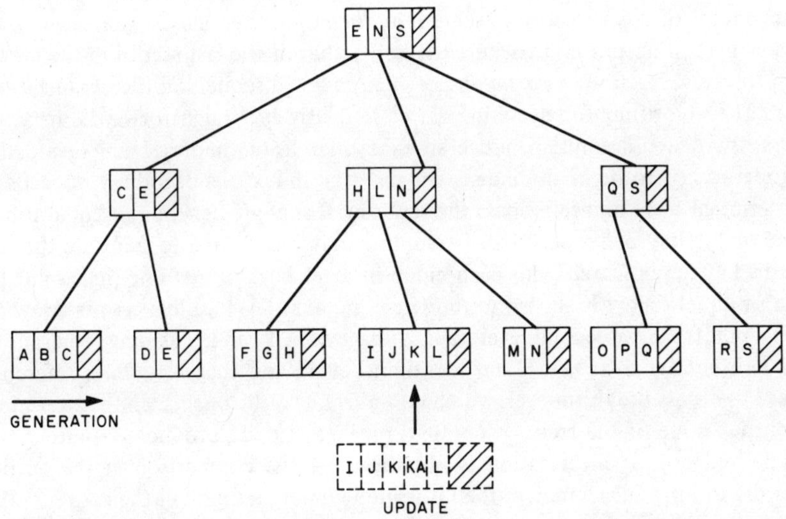

Figure 3-36 The balanced tree index

It is important to note that the range of a node is not necessarily indicated by the last key cited in the node, since, in the case of variable length key indexes, the keys may be grouped and sorted by ascending key length. To simplify the illustration in Fig. 3-36, the last key in the block also defines the range of the block. When a second level block is filled, such as is illustrated by the loading of keys C and E into the first node of level 2, the range of this node is loaded into a next higher level node. If the index is to be updated on-line, it is advisable to leave reserved space at the end of each block, as indicated by the shaded area within each of the blocks in Fig. 3-36. In practice, very large indexes can be constructed on two levels, since a block may hold a considerable number of key references.

Reference 1 contains formulations for computing the storage requirements for an index. For example, if the key/address packet were 16 characters, the block size were 2,000 characters, and 15 percent of the block were allocated for reserve space, header, and subheaders, then a one-level tree could index 106 records, a two-level tree could index around 10,000 records, and a three-level tree could index one million records. If one were to access the first level of an index for a particular file when the file is opened, and if this level were to be retained in core throughout the period during which the file remains open, then the index of a two-level tree could invariably be decoded in no more than one random accession. This is a common practice, used to reduce the number of random accessions through an index by one.

If one assumes that there exists a record for every key in level 3 of the tree in Fig. 3-36, then the tree describes a *full index*. If below the third level (or the output level of any depth tree) there is a *block* of sequentially organized records per key in each output node, where the key is that of the last record in the block, then the tree describes a *partial index* in an indexed sequential file organization.

The algorithm for decoding a tree is relatively straightforward. In a full index, the decoding must produce an exact match, or the key being decoded is considered not to be in the index. In a partial index, the decoding proceeds to the terminal node and references the first key that is greater than or equal to the value of the key being decoded. Assuming that it is desired to translate the key K, this key is compared with each entry in level 1. The first one that is greater than or equal to key K is used to reference the next level; in this case it is key N, which points to the second level node with keys H, L, and N as range references. Key K is greater than key H but less than key L, and therefore the L reference is used to access the third level, which contains keys I through L and is a terminal or output node of the tree. A comparison in this node produces a match, and the desired output information is obtained. If the comparison at the output level did not produce a match, then it is immediately known, in the case of a full index, that the index cannot decode the given key.

In the course of file update it may become necessary to add a new key to the file. In Fig. 3-36 this new key is identified as KA. The first step in index update is to decode the key in order to find its proper position in the index, which in this case will be between keys K and L. If there is sufficient space within the block to insert the new key, then the insertion is made and the block is replaced with no further index maintenance required. If the block is filled and a new key cannot be inserted, then one or more keys at either end (that is, from the I or from the L) must be displaced from this node and put into an adjacent node. The result of such displacement will be to modify the range of one of the output nodes, and hence an update is required in the two affected output nodes as well as in the second level node that points to this output node. If it turns out that the adjacent node cannot accommodate another key, then the next adjacent output node is used, with a consequent rippling effect. As the originally allocated reserved space becomes consumed throughout the index, the extent of ripple will increase. This is one of the undesirable properties of the balanced tree index.

Figure 3-37 illustrates the unbalanced tree index. In contrast to the balanced tree, no reserve space has been deliberately left in any of the blocks, except those at the end of the process that might incidentally have extra space remaining. Keys A, B, C, and D completely fill the first block; the range is D and is placed in the first node of the second level. When the tree is originally built, it is balanced, but since, by design, it does not have to maintain its balance, one may deliberately unbalance the tree when generated in order to reduce the number of accesses required to decode certain keys in perference to others.

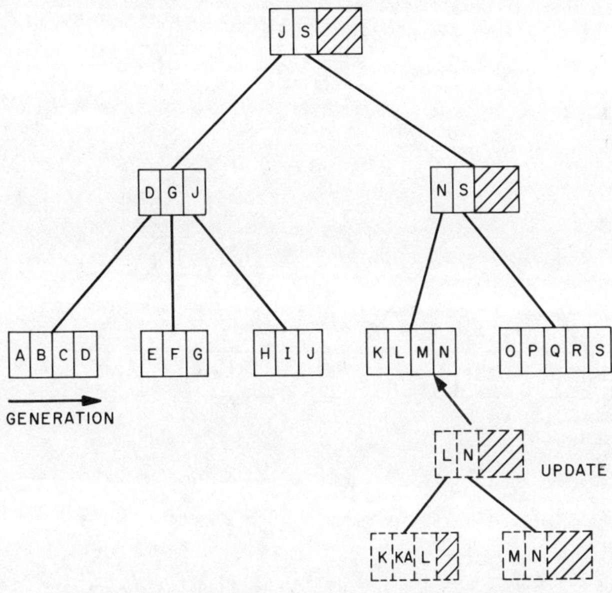

Figure 3-37 The unbalanced tree index, Method 1

The addition of the new key, KA, is examined now in the unbalanced tree. First, it is decoded to find its position in the index. This is found to be between keys K and L within the K, L, M, N node. This node is then split with half the keys, plus the new key, going into one of the nodes, and the other half going into the other node, as indicated in the figure by the two nodes K, KA, L and M, N. Each of these nodes will, of course, have approximately half of its space unused and thus becomes available for future expansion. The original output node (K, L, M, N) is replaced by a nonoutput node that references the two new divided nodes by their new ranges. The single output node K, L, M, N is thus replaced by three nodes, and the range N of the small subtree is preserved at the second level. Whenever a new key cannot be inserted between two existing keys because of insufficient space within the block, the update is invariably limited in scope to three blocks—the splitting of the fully loaded (output) block with its transformation into a nonoutput node and the creation of two new output nodes beneath it in the tree. This limitation in update scope is paid for, at least temporarily, by the creation of a considerable amount of unused space. In time, as updates continue, this space may be utilized; for example, the addition of a key LA to this index would not require any further expansion since it would be accommodated within the M, N, output node.

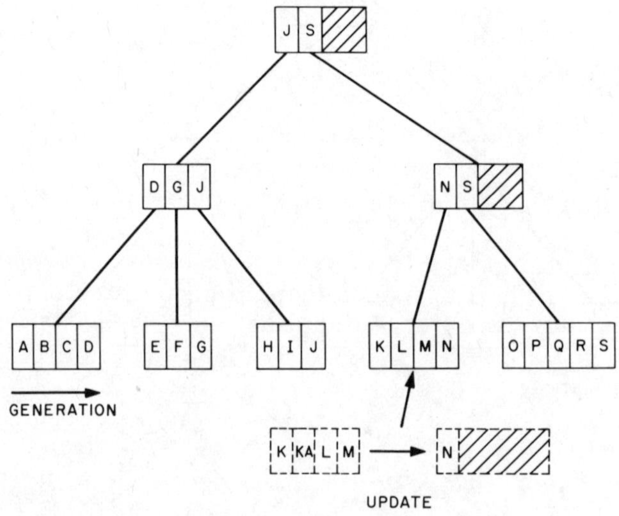

Figure 3-38 The unbalanced tree index, Method 2

Figure 3-38 illustrates another implementation of an unbalanced tree that is more economical in additional space utilization than the former method. The tree is generated in the same way as that of Fig. 3-37, but in order to update it, if the output block is filled, it is logically extended to a double length block by linking it to an empty block. As a graph, it is still balanced, but what was formerely a one-block node is now a two-block node. From an access standpoint, therefore, the tree is unbalanced, because additional accesses must be made within the terminal node if the decoded key is in the extension block. Furthermore, as this process continues, and as additional extensions are added, the search will become increasingly less efficient than the unbalanced tree of Fig. 3-37. One should therefore maintain a statistic on the number of nodal extensions, and when this value exceeds a certain limit, the entire tree should be regenerated. The illustration again shows an update of key KA. The appropriate output node

(K, L, M, N) is first located. Since it is filled, another node is linked to it; keys K, KA, L, and M are loaded into the first block, and key N, which is still the range of the two-block node, is loaded into the second block. Note that the second level node containing N will still reference the first block of the two-block terminal node, so that in order to decode key N, one must first access the initial block containing keys K through M, and then access the extension. It also turns out that this technique is less vulnerable to loss of data in a system crash if an additional modification is made. This will be discussed in Chap. 4, where the problem of file integrity is examined.

The easiest tree to program is the unbalanced tree, because it is not necessary to program for the ripple effect. Of the two balanced tree techniques presented, the latter is a bit simpler, because one is never concerned in the update process with creating new nonterminal nodes. Furthermore, the disadvantage of the unbalanced tree can be controlled by simply recording the degree of imbalance, as represented either by the additional levels of depth of the tree or by the number of nodal extensions. In most system operations there is a lower cost opportunity to regenerate indexes periodically. Only in those systems where the expense of regeneration is exceedingly high would it be necessary to consider both the programming and additional operational complexities of the balanced tree.

The other general method of key-to-address translation is *mapping*. The methodology is basically to extract as many bits from the key, or from some string of bits that is operationally derived from the key, as will define a compact space of addresses into which all of the data records will fit. In order to accommodate variable length in data records, the addresses that are generated by the mapping cannot point to the record directly but should point to a block within which the variable length record is contained. Thus the block can be accessed from DASD, brought into core memory, and scanned for the appropriate data record. The link address that appears in the output node of an index is controlled by the program that allocates space in the data file; this is *not* the case in the transformation of the key to a data block reference. Consider the following set of six-bit characters which in miniature might represent a set of keys:

Seven Key Values	*Values of Least Significant Two Bits*
100110	2
110001	1
100010	2
110000	0
010010	2
000111	3
001010	2

Assume that the records containing these keys are to be loaded into a four-block space. It would then be necessary to extract two of the six bits in order to reference one of the four blocks. Assume further that each block could hold two records so that the total capacity of the storage would be eight records. If the least significant two bits were used for the mapping, four of the seven records would be directed to block 2, which would thereupon overflow. The mapping system must accommodate such an overflow by linking the block (in this case, block 2) to a block extension; thus, five rather than four blocks would be required to store the seven records. Note that only one record has been directed to block 1, one to block 0, and one to block 3. Thus, it is the uneven distribution of the mapping that has caused more storage than is really needed to be allocated.

Ideally, the total set of mappings should be *uniform* in the sense that an equal number of mapped transformation values would be generated for each block. Since it is sometimes the case that bit string regularities can develop within sequences of characters or numerals taken from natural language, the kind of bunching or nonuniform distribution of mappings illustrated by this simple example may commonly occur in the translation of natural language keys. Therefore, it is desirable to perform arithmetic or logical operations upon the bit strings that comprise the character strings in order to wash out or compensate for these regularities. It is a process not unlike that used to generate random numbers, because these also must obey a uniform distribution law; hence, the name that is frequently applied to this technique is *randomizing*. It is common to extract bytes or characters from the input string, to concatenate the bits of the characters, and to extract subsets of bits that cross byte boundaries, in order to eliminate the repetitive effects of the bytes themselves. This procedure is usually sufficient to randomize the transformation, but one may in addition perform some arithmetic operations upon the extracted bits, such as to square the binary number represented by the bits and then to extract again some subset of bits from the squared number. Reference 11 contains some specific algorithms for randomizing.

As indicated in Fig. 3-39 the number of bits ultimately extracted or sampled from the randomized key must be $\log_2 B$, where B is the number of blocks that have been allocated for storage to the data file. An overflow region outside of the compact mapped region of B blocks is normally provided for the block extension, although one can allocate the overflow also within the mapped region if a tighter packing is desired. This is accomplished in the following way. If a block overflows, the next unoccupied block (or any block with available space) within the mapped region is seized as an extension. Keys with two *different* mappings can then be assigned to this block; they can enter directly via the mapping algorithm or indirectly via the other mapping for which this block is an extension.

The result of multiple mapping to a block is to pack the mapped space more tightly and to create longer chains of extensions.

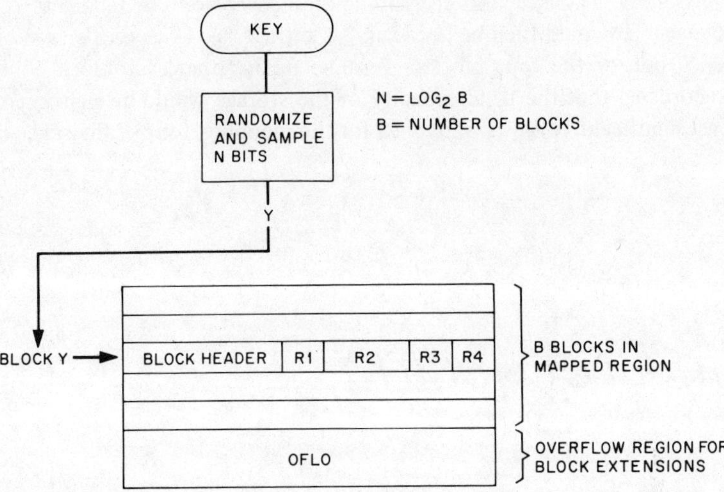

Figure 3-39 The randomizer

In the special case where the data record is fixed in length, or the number of records per block is constant, and the key is a serial number, K, the block number can be obtained by dividing K-1 by the number of records per block, taking the integer part of this ratio and adding one. This is called an *identity* mapping because it serves as a unique identification between the key mapping and the record location; hence, the space is completely packed and there are no chains. The identity mapping is obviously the fastest and most economical key decoder; it is utilized wherever the assignment of keys is under the control of the designer so that he can serialize them.

4

File Processing

In Figure 2-4 of Chap. 2, four major file processing functions were indicated: (1) Space maintenance, (2) file generation, (3) file update, and (4) data access. This chapter examines each in some detail. Also indicated in the figure is a data management system user interface that communicates between the DMS executive and the user program. Its purpose is to enable the user program to call upon each of the services provided by the data management system. To the user this interface must have a linguistic format, and all of the design elements of the system are manifest to the user through this language. In a sense the DMS language can be regarded as a functional description of the system; therefore, an illustrative language of this type is to be developed in Chap. 5 that will make clear how the design concepts of the first four chapters are functionally integrated into a language that effectively interfaces the user with the various operational components of the system.

4.1 SPACE MAINTENANCE

Space maintenance is the dynamic allocation and recovery of file space in the DASD. When a file issues a PUT command such that more disk space is needed than was previously allocated for this file, the DMS must find and allocate sufficient space to satisfy the requirements of the operation. Conversely, a PUT operation may also release space either because of an outright record deletion or because the record being returned to storage is smaller than when it was accessed, in which case space may be returned to the general pool of available DASD storage. The space maintenance function is best performed by two-level control. The first or top level is a systemwide control that may be called *system*

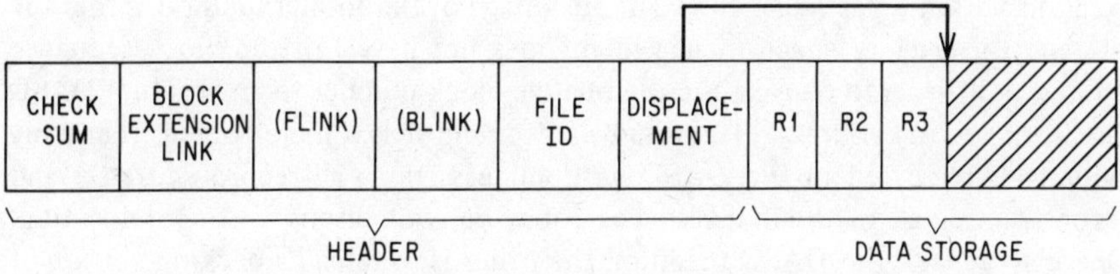

Figure 4-40 Block structure

control; the second and lower level is specific to a particular file and may be called *file control.* Both are components of the DMS executive control and as such are not directly accessible to the user. System control is responsible only for distinguishing the current inventory of in-use and not-in-use DASD storage. File control is responsible for storing into and accessing specific records from each user's files.

Before proceeding to the various methods of implementing these two control systems, it is necessary to look once again at the two most elemental units of storage in the system, the record and the block. The simple block structure that has been assumed in previous chapters is illustrated in Fig. 4-40. The block is a physical record that is transferred from direct-access storage to core memory. Within it are contained logical records that are the actual responses to file GET and PUT operations. In the context of certain languages it may even be specified fields within the records that are the intended responses.

The front of the block contains a leader with a number of control fields. Reading from right to left in the header, there is the displacement pointer which points to the beginning of available space for record storage within the block. Since it is normal, though not necessary, to assign a block exclusively to a file for integrity checking and recovery purposes, the file identification is stored. One of the system control methods for space maintenance is called *list of available space*; it requires that forward and backward links be stored in the header. A link address logically extends the block through the addition of another physical record. Some examples of its use have been given in previous chapters. In Fig. 3-38, it is used in an unbalanced tree to logically extend the size of a node; it is used in the indexed sequential and mapped access methods of Figs. 3-26 and 3-28 to logically extend a block to accommodate additional records; it may also be used to logically extend an inverted list. It will subsequently be shown to have still other uses. When being accessed from the DASD, it is usually the case that the block extension will overlay the original block in the core buffer. Finally, there may be a block check sum that is used for a continuous test of data integrity and also as an aid in recovery.

The unpacking of the block into variable length data records is controlled by means of the file definition and the table of contents within the record itself. The block number may be assigned with respect to two possible kinds of reference points. One is an absolute position in the DASD and the other is a relative position within a particular file. The advantage of the former method is that the file control level of space management does not have to store block sequence references in order to convert the file relative block number to an absolute DASD block (or sector) address. The disadvantage, and it is a major one, is that a file cannot be relocated in the DASD without reassigning all record addresses and reconstructing all of the indexes. There may be two reasons for such relocation. One is to repack the DASD medium; the other is to reload a back-up version of the file. When DASD absolute block addresses are used, records from different files can be mixed within a block, but when the block number is relative to a file, all records within the block must be from the same file.

A specific logical record is accessed either by giving its block number and a key value, which is called *content* addressing, or by giving its *logical* address, which is composed of a block number plus a sequential record number within the block. Once the appropriate block has been transferred from the DASD to core memory, the logical record is unpacked either by scanning for the first record with the indicated key where content addressing is used, or by scanning for the indicated record (within block) sequence number where logical addressing is used. If the record is of the FF type, the individual records are readily delimited by the fixed size that is ascertained from the file definition record; if the record has either format or field length variability, the records are serially delimited by using the record size field in each record's table of contents as illustrated in Fig. 2-14.

The block structure facilitates the handling of variable length logical records. If a record contracts in size as a result of an update, the block is simply rewritten, more reserve space will become available, and the displacement pointer will be decreased by the amount of the record reduction. If a record increases in size such that all of the records can still be written back into the block, then the displacement pointer will increase by the amount of the record increase. The logical address of each record is still the same, because each still occupies the same relative position within the block. Only if a record expands so much in size that a block could not be rewritten without overflow would it be necessary to relocate records physically on the DASD outside of the original block.

A number of approaches to the reallocation may then be taken. One is to extend the block logically by linking another block to the current one, and rewriting all records back into the two blocks. In this way neither the logical nor the content address will change. Since both blocks are not normally buffered in memory at the same time, it is desirable to pack an integral number of records into each block; that is, a record is not split between two blocks unless absolutely necessary, such as in the case where a record exceeds the length of a single block. Another method would be to remove a record from the block and relocate it. This would only be permitted in an indexed random file organization (or a list structure that employed an indexed random organization). Such a relocation would change the record's address and would necessitate an update of all indexes, inverted lists, and chains that reference the relocated record. A third and generally less desirable method is to create a trailer or logical extension of the record itself, in some general overflow space. This approach would again require that either a core buffer overlay or multiple buffers be used in order to bring the entire record into memory at the same time.

The second purpose of blocking is to reduce the number of DASD file I/O operations. Unfortunately the opportunities for such a saving are limited, because the only file organization in which it is always practical to defer the I/O operation is the sequential file organization, which is not normally used for random file access. This step is accomplished by reading a clock of records from the DASD into a core buffer in response either to an OPEN or GET command to the file. Once the block has been read, it may service an entire series of GET's in a sequential file without having a read again from the DASD until the series is complete. Similarly, records can be written into a block by a PUT operation on a sequential file, and the block is not written till full or the file is subjected to CLOSE. Hence, many GET or PUT operations may imply only a single READ or WRITE operation to secondary storage. There is one other instance in which data blocking may be used to defer an I/O operation. Since the indexed random file may select the data record address independently of (1) the key value, (2) the key transformation through a mapping, or (3) the key sequence, it may also choose to pack new records from a succession of PUT operations into a single block that is buffered in core until such a time as the block is full, whereupon it will write the block to secondary storage. Thus the records in the block do not contain sequential keys but rather contain any arbitrary set of keys resulting from a succession of PUT commands for new records.

If the buffer space were needed for another block, such as would be required in response to a GET command to this same file for a key that was not represented in the current block, then the current block would have to be written before another block is read and overlayed. If sufficient core memory were available, two buffers could be allocated to accommodate both the READ and the WRITE. There is, however, a danger inherent in delayed random file record buffering. If the system is operating in an on-line environment, and there were to be a malfunction such that core memory were destroyed, or at least that portion of memory containing the buffer were destroyed, then all records in the delayed buffer would be lost. In the case of the sequential file, recovery from such a situation is facilitated by the fact that the break can be correlated with a time sequence of record updates to the file, and, depending upon the method of recovery, the records after the break could readily be restored to the file. In the case of delayed buffering in the random file, there is no such correlation; the records that are lost are not simply those that would have appeared logically either at the end or at any particular position in the index of the file, and furthermore, there may have been any number of reads and writes between any of the records in the lost buffer, which would greatly complicate the recovery process. The subject of file back-up and recovery is covered in Chap. 6; it is mentioned here to illustrate a drawback in the delayed buffering of indexed random files.

In summary, the entire secondary storage medium is considered to be sub-divided into equal-sized blocks, each having the structure illustrated in Fig. 4-40. System control is concerned with the allocation of complete, empty blocks for new or relocated record storage. File control is concerned with the access and space management of already assigned blocks to a particular file. This latter access may be for the purpose of (1) reading records, in which case no space reallocation is implied; (2) of updating existing records, in which case the modification of the block displacement is implied only if the update changes the size of the record; and (3) of the creation of new records in the file, in which case additional space must be allocated within either an existing block already assigned to the file or from a completely new block.

4.1.1 SYSTEM CONTROL

There are two general methods of system control. One uses a *bit map*, which designates by a zero or one the allocation status of every block in the system. The zero would mean that the block is free to be allocated in its entirety, and a one would mean that a block has already been assigned to a file and is at this moment under file control. The file relinquishes control of a block only when a block becomes completely empty, whereupon the bit corresponding to the position in the map of the given block is changed from a one to a zero. A separate map is usually maintained for each independent memory module such as a disk pack so as to minimize the amount of reconstruction necessary if the map should be destroyed and to reduce the buffer size needed by the system control program for the bit map. In fact, this buffer size may even be further reduced by subdividing the bit map within the DASD module either on a physical basis such as a set of cylinders or on a logical basis such as user (account) ID. If, when a block is returned to the available space pool, the displacement is set to zero, and if, in addition, all or a portion of the block is check summed, then it can be reliably ascertained at a future time whether or not the block is free. If there is spurious writing into the block because of a system or hardware mal-function, the checksum will most likely not tally. Thus, a bit map for a particular module can be reconstructed by reading every block in the module; any block that does not produce a correct check sum tally will be flagged. If this block were under file control, then an indication would be made to the user of the file that its contents are now unreliable; otherwise the bit map is reconstructed according to whether the value of the displacement is zero or nonzero.

Whenever system control must allocate new space in a given module, the bit map for the module must be read into core, the space allocated, and the appropriate bits set to one in the map. The map is then written back to disk so as to permanently record the allocation. The same process is performed with a one-to-zero bit change when space is released from file control.

The second method of system control is called the *list of available space* method. In the case of the bit map, when all space is clear and unoccupied, the

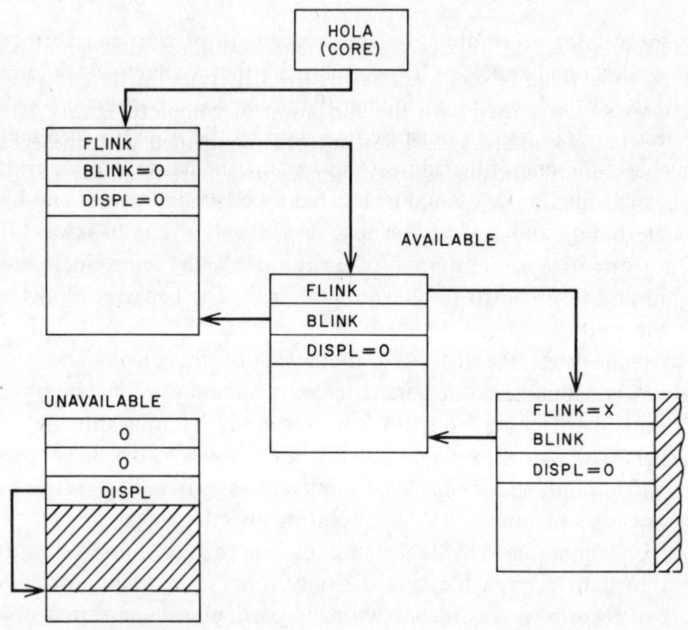

Figure 4-41 Space maintenance by list of available space method

entire memory allocated for file storage is represented as zeros in the bit map. In the list of available space method, the original contiguous clear space is indicated only by the starting block position, which is called the head of the list of available space. Space is issued from and returned to the head of the list. If, after files have been established, an individual block becomes free as an island of space within a region of occupied blocks, this block is linked into the list of available space by becoming the head of the list. As additional blocks become available they in turn become the head of the list, and eventually there will exist a chained list of available space which terminates at the beginning of the bulk reserve space. Figure 4-41 illustrates how this chain might appear. The head of the list of available space is always retained in core and points to the first available block; this block has both a forward and a backward link as indicated by the symbols FLINK and BLINK, respectively. The forward link points to the next available block, and the backward link is zero. The block displacement is also zero. The forward link in the next available block points to a third block that is available and that in turn has a forward link with a special symbol assignment, indicated here as an X, which means that this block begins the contiguous block of available storage. The backward link in the second record points to the first record; the backward link in the third record points to the second record.

   If the head of the list of available space is lost, the chain can be recreated either by examining every block for a displacement of zero and correct checksum tally, as described above, or by accessing the first available block and following the BLINK's back to the beginning of the list. If a particular block in the chain is destroyed, the chain must be recreated by the total file scan method or, alternatively, if the end of list address were maintained as well as the head of list address, a single missing link could be located by chaining forward and backward from the beginning and end of the list, respectively. The backward links are actually not essential to the normal operation of the list since blocks are always issued from and returned to the head of the list. The backward links are there only for the purpose of list reconstruction and can be eliminated if one were willing to reconstruct the list by scanning all of the blocks and testing for displacement equaling zero. A partial recovery of the list could be obtained by scanning until the first available block were found, denoting this the new head of (a partial) list. An unavailable block is also shown in the diagram, wherein both the forward link and the backward link addresses have been set to zero, and displacement is some nonzero number pointing into the block.

If block numbers are DASD absolute references, it is not necessary to assign an entire block to a given file, and the only function of file control would be the access of records in accordance with the particular organization of the file. If, on the other hand, the block numbers are assigned relative to a file, then an entire block will belong to a particular file, and file control must maintain a block inventory per file. There are two basic ways to implement this inventory. One is the nonreusable block method and the other, the reusable block method. The first is a far simpler method; it is easier to design and implement and is less costly in terms of a price paid in disk accesses for the maintenance performed. However, it tends to be more costly in memory utilization, particularly if records are being deleted, relocated, or shortened with a fair frequency. The nonreusable block method makes no attempt to use space that becomes available within a block, by virtue of any of these updates, since it does not keep track of the blocks under its control that have any reserve space available for new record allocation.

For each file a control record is maintained that contains a series of field pairs of triplets depending, respectively, upon whether the nonreusable block or reusable block method of file control is employed. In the case of the former, the pair of fields is a block address and count, where the block address may be relative to a file base address or to the beginning of the memory module, and the count corresponds to a number of subsequent blocks that have been assigned to this file. A third field is added for reusable block control and consists of a series of bit indicators where one bit position is assigned per block in the count of blocks. For example, one 32-bit word could be used for 32 sequential block indicators. A one in bit position "n" would indicate that block "n," in the sequence, is filled, and a zero would indicate that it is not filled, which implies that it has more than a prespecified minimum amount of available space and hence can have new or relocated records assigned to it. Since space can be assigned to a file by system control in noncontiguous blocks or block sequences, as many of these field pairs or triplets is required as there are assignments of noncontiguous block sequences. If a block is updated and its status changes from being filled to non-filled, or conversely, the file control record must be updated under the reusable block method, but it does not have to be updated under the nonreusable block method; hence, the reusable block method sustains additional update overhead when a block status changes, but if files are dynamically updated in the sense that records are being relocated, deleted, and added, then considerable space savings can be achieved by the reusable block method.

In summary, under the nonreusable block method of file control whenever a record is added or relocated, the *last* block indicated in the file control record is accessed for storage; if this block is unable to accommodate the record, a request is made to system control for another block. Any space made available within existing blocks of the file as a result of record deletion, size reduction, or relocation may be reused only incidentally in the event that another record in the same block expands in size, or if the file has an indexed sequential organization, and a record is to be inserted into this block; otherwise this space remains unused until the file is regenerated. Under the reusable block method, all space that becomes available is tracked and is reusable at the file control level.[13]

4.2 FILE GENERATION

The major file generation problem is the creation of the indexes, inverted lists, and multiple list structures given a file definition and a set of data records. Figure 4-42 shows that this process can be performed by a series of sorts upon sequentially organized files. The input and intermediate files in the diagram are represented by means of tape symbols in order to emphasize the serial nature of these files although the file storage medium may, in fact, be a DASD. The input to the process is a set of data records on file F1 following the prototype format of Fig. 2-14. Of principal concern in the figure is the fact that the set of keys in the record, upon which the list structures are to be based, are clearly differentiated from all the remaining data of the record. The square brackets indicate a set or list of items such as keys or addresses. In block 1 each data record is assigned an address in the DASD, as it is blocked into physical records. If a chained list is to be generated, space is allocated for link addresses that will be supplied subsequently in the processing. The address assignments are symbolically labeled AD in the diagram. The input file F1 is written as F2 along with the addresses and in address sequence. The sequence of a file in the diagram is indicated by underlining the field or fields upon which the file is ordered. The process chart of Fig. 4-42 is capable of producing any of three list structures: (1) The chained or multilist, (2) the inverted list by address, and (3) the inverted list by primary key. The chained list (CL) and the inverted list (IL) by address follow the lower path at this point, whereas the inverted list by primary key follows the upper path. In the former case, block 1 writes the file F3A,

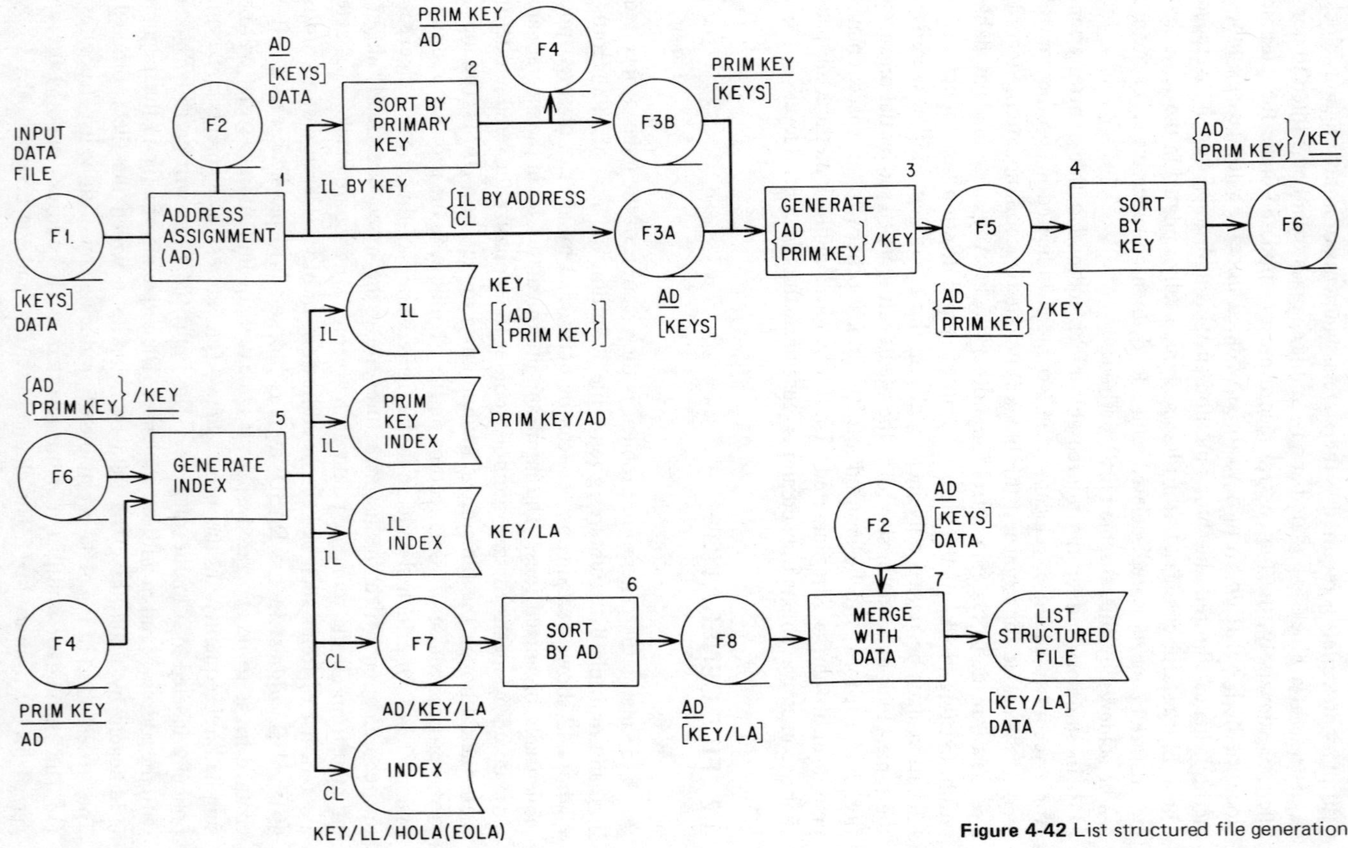

Figure 4-42 List structured file generation

which contains only the address and a set of keys in address sequence. This file is used to generate indexes, inverted lists, and link addresses. Each record on this file consists of an address and a set of keys.

If inverted lists are to be generated and primary keys instead of addresses are to be record pointers, the records of F1 plus the assigned address AD are sorted by the unique primary key in block 2 and written onto files F3B and F4. The inverted lists are generated from F3B, and the primary key to record address index is generated from F4. In block 3 the records of an F3 file are broken into smaller records, each of which contains two fields, an address (or primary key), and a key. That is, each key in the key list of the F3 record is paired with the address or primary key and written to file F5; thus N keys in the input record key list are broken into N records, each with an address (or primary key)/key pair. File F5 is sorted by key in block 4 generating file F6, called the key-to-address file, which is used to generate the indexes.

If an inverted list is to be generated, as indicated by the three files out of block 5 labeled IL, all the addresses or primary keys falling within a given key series become a record in the inverted list file headed by this key. These records will automatically be in address or primary key sequence, since the file that was input to the key sort process (block 4) was in address or primary key sequence. The index is created directly from the key-to-address file, since this file is in key sequence, where the output link addresses (LA) of the index point to inverted lists. A prototype of the index record is shown in Fig. 2-11, and, as shown, an inverted list index need not contain the list length or a link address to the last data record in the list. The index for the inverted list is generated, as shown in Fig. 4-42, directly from the key-to-address file by means of one of the processes described in Chap. 3 (Figs. 3-37 to 3-39), depending upon whether the index is to be a balanced or an unbalanced tree. A randomizer is not recommended because of the widely varying record sizes of inverted lists. Only the keys in the key-to-address file are required to generate the index to the inverted list, since the output of the index points to the inverted list, not to the data file. The address in the key-to-address file (or alternatively the primary keys in lieu of the addresses) are grouped into a record in the inverted list, where one record contains all the addresses (or primary keys) pertaining to a particular key. Since the key-to-address file is already sorted in address (or primary key) within key sequence, the addresses or primary keys in the inverted list record will already be in sequence, as is required for subsequent processing of the inverted list. In the case of an inverted list by primary key, an additional index to translate the primary key to the data record address (AD) is required. This is also generated in block 5 from file F4.

The generation of chained or multilists follows the downward path to the CL, labeled files, out of the index generation block. The first address in a given sequence of addresses under a certain key on the key-to-address file (F6) becomes the head-of-list address and is stored as such in the index record. In addition, the number of addresses under the key on the key-to-address file is stored in the index record as the list length, and, if it is required to point via the index also to the last record in the list, the last address in the sequence is stored in the record as the end of list address. Each address after the head-of-list address becomes the link address for the previous record on the key address file. For example, consider a sub-sequence of records on the key-to-address file all of which have the same key, the addresses being in ascending sequence. Let these records be enumerated within this sub-sequence as records 1, 2, 3, etc. The address of record 1 becomes the head-of-list address in the index record for this particular key. The address of record 2 becomes the link address (LA) for record 1, which is stored as a record in file F7 along with the key and its address AD (that is, the address of record 1 on file F6). Record 2 in the sub-sequence of file F6 is then stored in file F7 with a link address that is the address of record 3. In this way file F7 is generated from file F6, where, for a given key, the address field (AD) of a record on file F7 is the same as the address field of the record for that key on file F6, and the link address field for a record N within a given sub-sequence corresponding to a particular key is the address of record N + 1 in that same sub-sequence on file F6. The link address of the last record in the sub-sequence is set to 0 or to some other list-terminating symbol. File F7 will be in key sequence, because it was generated on a one-to-one basis from the key address file, which is also in key sequence. It is then sorted in block 6 by address (AD), and a new type of record is created, wherein all the keys and their accompanying link addresses having the same address (AD) are grouped within a record, and the address (AD) becomes a header field, represented in Fig. 4-42 as file F8.

In the case of an inverted list, file F2 may be loaded directly to disk according to the indicated address assignments, since link addresses do not have to be inserted into the data records. In the case of a multilist or chained list file structure, the link addresses must be inserted into the records along with the keys prior to loading the data records onto the file. This step is accomplished by merging file F8 with the original data records and their address assignments, which have been created as file F2. The result is a chained list structured file that can be stored on disk according to the address assignments, and in which each key has an associated link address.

Reference 4 discusses a number of variants on the inverted and multilist file structures, which involve partial inversion, and it is recommended that this reference be consulted for variations upon these two basic list structuring themes.

Figure 3-33 indicated that records with single but generic keys can have file structures that use the mapped random access method instead of an indexed access method. This approach is possible but not recommended because it is limited to the case of a single key per record, and its implementation for the inverted list is very awkward. If, however, it were decided to use this method, the following modifications of the file generation process depicted in Fig. 4-42 would have to be considered. First, it would have to be decided at the outset whether the list structuring were to be performed by an inverted or a chained list. If it were to be inverted, the entire process could be carried out exactly as shown in Fig. 4-42 for file F1 through F6, but each record on F1 would have only one key and the addresses in block 1 would be assigned by the mapping algorithm operating upon the record key. There would be no index generation; instead, each key on the key-to-address file would be randomized to generate an inverted list address wherein the list of all address or primary keys (in sequence) would be stored. The major problem here is that the lists may tend to vary greatly in size. Some may be considerably less than a block length, and some may span several blocks. Since the addressing is oriented toward blocks, it follows that some blocks will be greatly under-utilized and others will have to link to an overflow area.

If a chained list structure is to be implemented using the mapped random technique, then addresses cannot be assigned initially; instead, a unique serial number is assigned to each record, and this number is used in lieu of an address in file F3A. File F6 is generated as a key-to-serial number file instead of a key-to-address file. Addresses are assigned in the block to which file F6 is input. The first record in a particular grouping will be assigned an address based upon the randomization of its key. Subsequent records in the list of this key are assigned an address in the nonmapped region; since this link address is a freely assigned pointer (and in fact should not consume an address within the mapped region), the remaining records on the list are located in the overflow region. The utilization of space in the mapped region will be a function of the block size. Furthermore, it becomes inconvenient to add new records to the top of the list, as is normally done in the list structured file, since this would necessitate moving the top record, in the mapped region, to another location outside of the mapped region. Instead, it is more effective to insert a new record onto a list as the second member of the list, since all that one must do to effect this is to transfer the link address from the top record to the new record, and to make the address of the new record the link address in the top record. Alternatively, the address of the last record in the list could be stored in the first record, and new entries to the list could be added to the bottom. Obviously, adding new records into the list at a position other than the top or the bottom destroys the LIFO, FIFO capability discussed in Chap. 3.

Figure 4-43 presents another way of looking at the essential differences among the various basic file structures. It indicates the processing that would be required to reorganize a file from one structure to another, if such restructuring is feasible. For example, to change a sequential file to an indexed sequential file, it is first assumed that a particular field of the record has been designated as a key of the record, upon which the file is sequenced; then only an index need be generated. Of course, subsequent updates to the file must retain the sequential organization of the file while updating the index. In order to change an indexed sequential file into an indexed random file, there is no overt data file reorganization required of the file structure, but the partial index must be converted into a complete index, and the requirement in the file update process to maintain the data file in sequence may be dropped.

	SEG	IS	IR	MR	CL	IL
SEQ		GENERATE INDEX	GENERATE INDEX	REALLOCATE RECORDS ACCORDING TO KEY MAPPING	USE LIST-STRUCTURED FILE GENERATION-CHAINED LISTS	USE LIST-STRUCTURED FILE GENERATION-INVERTED LISTS
IS	DELETE INDEX		NO REORG REQUIRED	↓		↓
IR	(1) DELETE INDEX (2) SORT RECORDS BY KEY	(1) SORT RECORDS BY KEY (2) REBUILD INDEX		↓		
MR	SORT RECORDS BY KEY	(1) SORT RECORDS BY KEY (2) GENERATE INDEX	GENERATE INDEX		↓	
CL	NA	NA	NA	NA		↓
IL	NA	NA	NA	NA	↓	

Figure 4-43 File reorganization

4.3 RANDOM FILE UPDATE

Figure 4-42 implies a batched processing file generation schema. In on-line systems, it is frequently the case that one has the opportunity to generate files by such a method, but from this point onward file updates are performed randomly on a one-at-a-time basis either on-line or in small batches. Alternatively, a file can be generated by bootstrapping with completely on-line update processes such as those to be discussed shortly. A major problem encountered in on-line file update is the sudden interruption of service, sometimes referred to as a "crash," which can leave the files in one of three states:

1. The file has maintained full integrity and exists in a state that it would otherwise have been in had the crash not occurred.

2. The *file integrity* has been lost (or, as is sometimes said, the file is *corrupt*), which means that it is not wholly usable because the index references data are either no longer in the file or never were in the file.

3. The *data integrity* has been lost, which means that all the file that is accessible belongs to the file, but that certain records cannot be accessed that are a part of the file and should be accessible.

In the case of a loss of file integrity the data management system must either restore full integrity automatically or must restore a former version of the file, a "back-up." In the case of a loss of data integrity, the DMS may restore full integrity automatically, restore a back-up, or indicate to the user that data are inaccessible and allow him to decide between his own manual restoration of the data or reversion to a back-up. The discussion of file recovery according to the above requirements is to be divided into two parts. In this chapter, the details of performing updates in such a way as to be able to recover files automatically (wherever possible) will be presented; in Chap. 6 the overall strategies associated with backing up files and methods of total file reconstruction will be presented for use where the specific techniques of automatic recovery discussed in this chapter either fail or are not implemented.

The major consequence of a crash with respect to file manipulation is that core memory containing blocks from indexes, inverted lists, or data files are lost. Since most updates involve two or more write operations to the DASD, the system crash that occurs after the first write operation but before the last may cause the file to be in an uncertain state with respect to the accessibility of one or more records.

The keys to automatic manitenance of file integrity are (1) the order in which update operations are performed and (2) an algorithm that permits one to detect a corrupt file and to either correct it or restore it via back-up. The following set of figures indicates the order in which specific operations are to be performed for each type of file update. In some cases, it is possible to assure no loss of file or data integrity simply by means of the order in which information is written to the DASD. In other cases, although it is possible to formulate such a strategy, it is expensive in terms of the number of DASD reads and writes, and other procedures that recover the list integrity are recommended. Three classes of file organization are discussed: the singly keyed file structure, the chained list file structure, and the inverted list file structure. As shown in Fig. 4-44, each figure has two columns. In the left-hand column the operation is described in steps; in the right-hand column the consequence of a crash after the completion of the given step is indicated.

4.3.1. Singly Keyed Files

Figure 4-44 gives the procedure corresponding to a keyed file update for record addition. It is assumed that the records have a single unique key. It is also assumed that information contained in the file control record that is brought into core and maintained under file control at OPEN time indicates a currently available block into which the next record can be placed. If no such block currently exists under file control, that is, if all currently assigned blocks are filled, then it is assumed that a request can be made to system control for another complete block to be allocated. The first step in the addition of a record to a keyed file is to read the current block and allocate space in that block for the new record. If the current block cannot accommodate the new record, then another block must be obtained. Therefore, by a process in which all available blocks under file control are examined for usable space or by which additional space is obtained from system control, the term *allocate space* in these diagrams means effectively, that a block is brought into core, the displacement indicator at the head of the block is updated, and an address for the record is obtained.

As indicated in the right-hand column of the diagram there is no consequence with respect to file or data integrity if a crash should occur after the allocation of space, because a block has not been written back to the DASD. In the second step the record is added to the block and the block is written to the storage device. If a crash should occur after this step, space will be occupied in secondary storage by a record that has not yet been indexed. This means that logically, in terms of the file structure, the record does not exist, although physically it occupies space. If a crash should occur at this time, the file would still retain its integrity, but the record would not be considered to be a part of the file as yet. In the third step the index is updated. Depending upon the type and size of the index, there may be one or more DASD writes in the process of updating the index. If there is only one write, there is no crash consequence, because at the conclusion of the write, the record will have been added to the file. If, on the other hand, it required more than one write to update the index, then a variety of situations could arise, some of which would leave the file in a corrupt state.

For example, consider the update procedure for the unbalanced tree of Fig. 3-37. Assume that it were required to split the node as illustrated and that the node K, L, M, N is to be replaced by the three nodes shown in dashed lines

STEP	OPERATION	CRASH CONSEQUENCE
1.	READ CURRENT BLOCK ALLOCATE SPACE	NONE
2.	ADD RECORD AND WRITE BLOCK	SPACE RESERVED FOR NON-INDEXED RECORD
3.	UPDATE INDEX	

Figure 4-44 Keyed file update record addition

below in the diagram. Assume further that the node, L, N had just overwritten the node K, L, M, N when the system crashed. In this case, the keys K through N will have been lost. The unbalanced tree procedure of Fig. 3-38 is safer in this respect. In this case the new node K, KA, L, M will replace the node K, L, M, N, and a new node containing a single key N will be written as another block. Since there can only be a single key in this new block, one could leave space in the first block—namely, K, KA, L, M—for the key N and its associated link address, reduntantly, so that if the crash should occur before the node extension record were written, the index, and hence the file, will have maintained its integrity even though the update has not been completed.

In the case of Fig. 3-37, where it is impractical to use such a stratagem, one must consider a technique whereby the index can be reconstructed as a function of the records currently in the data file. The technique entails reading the entire data file sequentially and reconstructing the index based upon the keys within each record of the file. If the file is large, the most effective way to reconstruct the index is by means of the file generation technique described in Fig. 4-42. If the file is small, the index could be randomly (bootstrap) generated by means of successive updates. When the update of the index is completed, there will be no crash consequence with respect to the entire process of record addition, because the procedure will be complete. If, in the execution of step 3, it is found that the key already exists in the index, an appropriate error condition would be returned to the user program, the data block would have to be retrieved, and the space de-allocated by resetting the displacement pointer.

The DMS can be designed to respond in a number of ways when operation is restored after a crash. Since the file cannot have lost integrity at any step, although the update will not have been effected if step 3 is incomplete, the DMS could be designed so as not to respond in any way to a crash during this type of update, leaving it to the user or user program to ascertain the state of data integrity (that is, whether the new record exists or not in the file). A second design option is to reinitiate the update in the stepwise sequence 3, 1, 2, where steps 1 and 2 are performed only if the key does not already appear in the index. This will doubly allocate space for the record if the crash occurred between steps

STEP	OPERATION	CRASH CONSEQUENCE
1.	READ BLOCK CONTAINING RECORD	NONE
2.	UPDATE INDEX	SPACE RESERVED FOR NON INDEXED RECORD
3.	DELETE RECORD RELEASE SPACE WRITE BLOCK	

Figure 4-45 Keyed file update record deletion

2 and 3, but only the second allocation will be referenced from the index. A completely different approach to automatic recovery is to perform the steps initially in the order 1, 3, 2. This would necessitate two buffers or additional reads and writes to the data file; a crash between steps 3 and 2 would then leave the file corrupt. The recovery process would decode the index for the key; if not present, the entire update process would be repeated; if present, it would read the data record and determine whether it contained the correct key; if it did not, steps 1 and 2 would be completed.

It is thus seen that the DMS designer has a number of options with respect to how he will implement update recovery and, based upon his selection, how the basic update algorithm is to be constructed. The remainder of the update procedures to be described assume a particular sequence based upon minimizing the chance of file corruption, although alternative sequences can be devised based upon other approaches to recovery.

Figure 4-45 indicates how a record would be deleted from a keyed file. In the first step the index is decoded and the block containing the record is read. Since nothing has been written yet to the DASD, there is no crash consequence. In the second step, the index is updated. At the conclusion of this step a crash would result in space being reserved for a nonindexed record, which maintains file integrity even though the reserved space is unusable until the file and index are regenerated. In the third step, the record is deleted from the block, the block is repacked, and displacement in the block header is appropriately adjusted, and the block is written back to the DASD. At the conclusion of this step, the record has been logically and physically deleted from the file.

If a record is to be relocated and assigned a new address, the link address in the index must be appropriately updated. In addition, the block from which the record is taken should be repacked and restored if the reusable block method of file control is implemented; if nonreusable block file control is employed, then it would be sufficient to modify only the index in order to remove the record logically from the former block. One can consider the process of record relocation as a concatenation of the process of record deletion followed by record addition, and this will be true for chained and inverted list structures as well.

4.3.2   Chained List Structured Files

Figure 4-46 describes the method of adding records to a chained list structure. In step 1, the current data block is read and sufficient space is allocated to contain the new data record with all of its link addresses. An address is assigned to the record by virtue of this space allocation, although the data block cannot yet be written to the disk, because the link addresses must be transferred from the index.

STEP	OPERATION	CRASH CONSEQUENCE
1.	READ CURRENT DATA BLOCK AND ALLOCATE SPACE	NONE
2.	FOR EACH KEY IN RECORD (a) DECODE AND READ INDEX BLOCK (b) EXTRACT HOLA. IF KEY DOES NOT EXIST, ADD KEY TO INDEX RECORD AND HOLA = ϕ. INSERT HOLA IN NEW DATA RECORD AS THE LINK ADDRESS (c) INSERT NEW RECORD ADDRESS AS NEW HOLA. (d) WRITE BLOCK CONTAINING INDEX RECORD.	LOSS OF FILE INTEGRITY
3.	WRITE DATA BLOCK.	

Figure 4-46 Chained list update record addition

Step 2 is performed repetitively for each key in the record. Its purpose is to update the index and to add new keys to the index that are not already there. For each key in the record four sub-steps must be taken; these are labeled (a) through (d) in the figure. First the index is decoded, and the appropriate index block is read. Second, the head-of-list address (HOLA) is extracted from the index record with the block, if the key exists.   If the key does not exist, this address must be added to the index record, and the head of list is set to a null or special end-of-list sentinel. The HOLA is also inserted as a link address into the data record that is at this time buffered in the data block in core. Third, the data record address assigned in step 1 is inserted into the index record for the key as the new head-of-list link address. Fourth, the block containing the index record is written to the disk. If there are other keys contained within the same block, then one could perform the first three substeps for each of these keys befor writing the block back to disk. These four substeps are performed for every key in the record.

If a crash occurs before the completion of step 2, some index records corresponding to the new record will have been updated and others not. Those that have been updated will point to a nonexistent record as the head of list, and the file will consequentaly have lost its integrity. If all data written to disk prior to the crash has been preserved on the disk but the crash causes destruction of core memory, recovery from this situation is complicated by the fact that vital data, namely, the links to the previous head of list (for the already updated index records) is lost. If core memory is not lost, or at least that part of memory containing the data block from step 1 (which currently contains these links), then recovery can be made either by continuation of the process, if the operating system has maintained program control, or by restarting the update from step 2, reprocessing the index, and looking for a match between the new record address assignment from step 1 and head of list address in each index record. A match indicates an already updated index record; the first mismatch indicates the place where real processing of the index, in accordance with the four substeps of step 2, must continue. In the case where the vital links are lost, there are three possible ways to recover. One is to restore a back-up file and reprocess all transactions against the file from that point in time onward. The second way is to regenerate the index from the data file, which will restore it to its state just prior to the update and then to reinitiate the update. The third way is to record the vital data routinely as a part of the update process. This can be done either by providing an additional field in the index record for this purpose, which will increase the index size but will not incur any additional I/O overhead, or it can be done by executing step 3 after every iteration of step 2, which will increase I/O overhead but not affect file size.

Finally, in step 3 the data block is written to disk. Note that the data file is updated first in the nonchained file structure in order to protect against false access, but that this cannot be done in the case of the chained file structure because the link addresses must first be obtained from the index.

Figure 4-47 presents the sequence for deleting a record from a chained list. The key of the record to be deleted is decoded in the index in step 1, and the block containing the data record is read into core. In the second step a flag

STEP	OPERATION	CRASH CONSEQUENCE
1.	READ BLOCK CONTAINING DATA RECORD	NONE
2.	SET RECORD DELETE FLAG DELETE NONKEY DATA RELEASE SPACE	NONE
3.	WRITE DATA BLOCK	

Figure 4-47 Chained list update record deletion

is set in the record, indicating that the record has been logically deleted from the file. In this way all of the linkages associated with the keys of that record remain in the file; whenever this record is accessed as part of a list search, the delete indicator is interpreted by the search program to mean that the record is actually not in the file and the search continues at the next record on the list being accessed. If the record must be physically removed from the data file, then forward and backward links are normally used so that a bridge can effectively be constructed across the record. That is, the backward link is used to access the previous record in the chain; the link address currently in the record being deleted replaces the link address in the previous record that has been accessed by means of the backward link. The forward link is used to access the next record in the chain, and its backward link is changed to point to the record previous to the one being deleted. In this way there is no further reference to the record that is to be deleted in the chain and the record can therefore be physically deleted from the block. The alternative to backward links is to search the list from the beginning until the record to be deleted along with its predecessor and successor are found, and then to effect the bridge, but this approach may be too costly where lists are long.

At the completion of step 2, the record will have been deleted either logically by the setting of the delete indicator or physically by a modification of link addresses and the actual deletion of the record. If logical deletion of the record is used in step 2, some space can be regained in the block by deleting all of the non-key data from the record, since these are not required to maintain list linkages. If there should be a crash at the conclusion of this step, the file integirty is maintained but the update has not yet been effected. The block is then rewritten to disk in step 3.

It is frequently required to transfer a record from one list to another in list structured files. Figure 4-48 indicates the sequence of operations necessary to perform such an operation. In the first step, the key of the record to be transferred is decoded in the index, and the block containing the record is read into core.

In step 2, a key delete flag is set for the key corresponding to the list from which the record is being transferred, and the key corresponding to the list to which the record is being transferred is added to the record. The key delete flag is used in the same way and for the same reason that the record delete flag was used; it permits the linkage to be retained so that subsequent records on the list (from which the record is being transferred) can still be accessed, but when the access or search program reaches the given record on a search of the list from which the record has been transferred, it will consider the record not to be present on the list as indicated by the key delete flag. If backward links are employed, then, again, the key delete flag does not have to be used, since the linkage of the old list can be bridged over this record. If there is a crash after step 2, there is no consequence because the data block has not yet been written back to disk.

STEP	OPERATION	CRASH CONSEQUENCE
1.	READ BLOCK CONTAINING DATA RECORD	NONE
2.	SET KEY DELETE FLAG FOR OLD KEY AND ADD NEW KEY TO RECORD	NONE
3.	DECODE (NEW) KEY AND READ INDEX BLOCK TRANSFER HOLA IN INDEX TO LA OF NEW KEY IN RECORD AND RECORD ADDRESS TO HOLA IN INDEX	NONE
4.	ALLOCATE SPACE WRITE BLOCK CONTAINING DATA RECORD	LOSS OF DATA INTEGRITY
5.	WRITE BLOCK CONTAINING INDEX RECORD	

Figure 4-48 Chained list update list transfer

In step 3, the new key is decoded in the index and the appropriate index block is read into core. The record is going to be added to the new list at the beginning, in the same way that new records are added to all lists in the file, as described in Fig. 4-46. This is done by transferring the head of list address, found in the index record corresponding to the new key, to the link address field of the new key in the data record and by storing the record address of the record being transferred onto the list in the head-of-list address field of the index record.

In step 4, space is reallocated in the block, and the block containing the data record is written to disk. Since the record is being expanded, it is possible that there will be insufficient space in the block, and the block will have to be logically extended. If the system should crash after step 4, there would be no loss of file integrity since all data that can be accessed belongs to the file, but there *will* be a loss of data integrity since the record will have logically been removed from the former list by virtue of the key delete flag being set (although the list will still be intact), and the record will not yet have been logically added to the new list, although it will contain the new key with a link address to the current first record on the list.

The reason that it will not be on the new list is that there will be no index linkage to this record, since the updated index block is to be written to disk in step 5. The current index record for the new list still points to the previous first record in the list, which will become the second record on the list, after step 5.

In step 5, then, the block containing the updated index record is written to disk, and the list-to-list record transfer will be complete.

As indicated previously, the simplest procedure for relocation of a record, wherein there is an address modification, is first to delete the record and then to add it to the file. This is illustrated in Fig. 4-49.

Similar update strategies are required for the inverted list file structures. These are shown in Figs. 4-50 through 4-52.

RECORD RELOCATE = DELETE + ADD

Figure 4-49 Chained list update record relocate

4.3.3 Inverted List structured Files

Figure 4-50 illustrates the process for adding a new record to an inverted list file. In step 1, the currently available data block is read into core. In step 2, the record is added to the data block if there is sufficient space; if not, another data blcok is obtained from system control. When the record has been added, the block can be rewritten to disk. Note that steps 2 and 3 in the inverted list update for a record addition are performed in the reverse order from the corresponding chained list update. This is because a link address does not have to be inserted into the data record in the case of the inverted list, where such link addresses can be obtained only from the index. Therefore, the data block can be written back to the disk in step 2, as in the case of the (singly) keyed file

STEP	OPERATION	CRASH CONSEQUENCE
1.	READ CURRENT DATA BLOCK	NONE
2.	ADD RECORD TO DATA BLOCK ALLOCATE SPACE WRITE DATA BLOCK	SPACE RESERVED FOR NON-INDEXED RECORD
3.	FOR EACH KEY IN RECORD: (a) DECODE INDEX AND READ INVERTED LIST (b) INSERT RECORD ADDRESS (OR PRIMARY KEY) OF DATA INTO LIST (c) WRITE INVERTED LIST	LOSS OF DATA INTEGRITY

Figure 4-50 Inverted list update record addition

STEP	OPERATION	CRASH CONSEQUENCE
1.	READ BLOCK CONTAINING RECORD	NONE
2A.	FOR EACH KEY IN RECORD: (a) DECODE INDEX AND READ INVERTED LIST (b) REMOVE DATA RECORD ADDRESS (OR PRIMARY KEY) FROM LIST (c) WRITE INVERTED LIST	LOSS OF DATA INTEGRITY
3A.	DELETE RECORD FROM BLOCK RELEASE SPACE WRITE BLOCK	
2B.	SET RECORD DELETE FLAG	NONE
3B.	WRITE BLOCK CONTAINING RECORD	

Figure 4-51 Inverted list record deletion

update of Fig. 4-44. If the system should crash after step 2, the only consequence is that space will have been reserved for a nonindexed record. That is, the record has been physically added to the file, but not logically, and hence is not actually in the file yet. In step 3, the inverted list for every key in the record must be updated with either the address or the primary key of the record, depending upon the mode of construction of the inverted list. This is done by the three sub-steps indicated in the figure under step 3. If there is a crash before all inverted lists have been updated, the file will have lost data integrity, in the sense that the new record will not be accessible by all its keys. The update is completed when step 3 is finished. Recovery from this loss of integrity is comparatively easy, because there is no loss of vital linkage data. The recovery process, in the event of core loss, would repeat steps 1 and 2, and repeat step 3 without inserting the new address a second time.

Records are deleted from an inverted list by the process shown in Fig. 4-51. Two methods, identified as A and B, are available. In step 1 the key of the record to be deleted is decoded in the index, and the block containing the record is read into core. In the A method, indicated by steps 2A and 3A, the record is both logically and physically deleted from the file. In step 2A, three sub-steps are performed for each key in the record. In sub-step (a), the index is decoded for the key and the appropriate inverted list is read. In sub-step (b) the data record address or primary key is removed from the list, and the record containing the list is repacked into its data block and rewritten in sub-step (c) back to disk. If the system should crash before the end of step 2A, there will be loss of data integrity, because the record will not be accessible by all of its keys. In step 3A, the record is deleted from the block, the records in the block are repacked, and the block is written back to disk. By method B, where the record is logically but not physically deleted from the file, a record delete flag is set, and the record can be reduced in size to a header and the delete flag; then, in step 3B the block containing the record is rewritten to disk. No update is made in the index; therefore, method B is faster, but some small amount of usable space is not reclaimed and, more importantly, access will be made somewhat slower by a need to retrieve the records with delete flags. If the system should crash after 2B, there will be no loss of file integrity, because the record will effectively not have been deleted from the file yet. In summary, the advantages of method B are (1) that it is impervious to crash consequences, and (2) it is faster. Its disadvantage is that unnecessary entries are retained in the inverted lists, which makes the inverted list processing less efficient as well as contributing to higher storage costs, and the number of data record access exceeds that which is actually necessary by the number of such deleted records.

Figure 4-52 illustrates the procedure for transfer of a record from one list to another using the inverted list structure. In step 1, the block containing the record to be transferred is read into core. In step 2, the old key is deleted from the record and the new key is added. Since there are no link addresses, the old key is actually deleted from the record, which may result in gain or loss in space, depending upon the relative sizes of the two keys. It should also be noted that it

STEP	OPERATION	CRASH CONSEQUENCES
1.	READ BLOCK CONTAINING DATA RECORD	NONE
2.	DELETE OLD KEY ADD NEW KEY ALLOCATE (OR RELEASE) SPACE WRITE DATA BLOCK	LOSS OF DATA INTEGRITY
3.	DECODE INDEX FOR OLD KEY AND READ INVERTED LIST DELETE RECORD ADDRESS (OR PRIMARY KEY) FROM LIST AND WRITE INVERTED LIST.	LOSS OF DATA INTEGRITY
4.	DECODE INCES FOR NEW KEY AND READ INVERTED LIST INSERT RECORD ADDRESS (OR PRIMARY KEY) INTO LIST AND WRITE INVERTED LIST.	

Figure 4-52 Inverted list update list transfer

is not absolutely necessary to store keys in data records for an inverted list file structure. The keys themselves, if stored in the record, are then in the role of data items and not necessarily in the role of a key. As will be shown later in this chapter, the access mechanisms that utilize keys are completely operative, in the case of inverted list structures, from the inverted lists, and do not depend upon the existence of the keys in the record for their functioning. However, one will usually find the keys in the record, because they are required data items for the purposes of intrarecord computation and data display. When the record has thus been modified and the block repacked, it can be written back to disk. If the system should crash after step 2, the file will have lost date integrity in the sense that the record will not be accessible on the new list and will still be accessible on the old list. In step 3, the inverted list corresponding to the old key is read and the record address or primary key is deleted from that list. The list is then written back to disk. A part of the data integrity will have been restored at this point, but not all of it, since the record will still not be accessible via the new list. In step 4 the inverted list corresponding to the new key will be similarly updated and the list transfer will be complete.

The above descriptions have shown how keyed, chained, and inverted lists files can be updated with respect to record additions, deletions, relocations, and logical list transfers. It is shown in these descriptions that there is a preferred sequence to the update of the index and the data file, respectively, where in some cases the ordering of these operations is such as to protect the file integrity under any operational circumstances, and in other cases, notably in conjunction with the list structures, there may be loss of file or data integrity as the result of a system failure that destroys file information contained in core buffers that have yet to be written to disk. How recovery and restoration of file integrity is accomplished is a subject that is treated more comprehensively in Chap. 6. At this point, it is introduced only to indicate the reason for ordering the operations in each of the respective update procedures. Certain general conclusions with respect to the relative update efficiency of these file structures are drawn at the end of this chapter and presented in Figure 4-60. Chapter 8 of Reference 1 develops a methodology for computing the update timing based upon the algorithms expressed in the form of Figs. 4-44 through 4-52, and quantitative expressions of these conclusions could be obtained by the methods and charts depicted in this reference.

4.3.3   Multiple File Access and Update

Certain system designs require multiple program access to the same file. This presents no problem if the file is only being read, but if it is being updated by more than one program simultaneously, then a block interlock must be imposed. That is, two programs may OPEN the same file in an update mode (IN-OUT, OUT-IN) and may GET and PUT different blocks, but if one attempts to GET a block that is currently buffered in core for another program, then the DMS must terminate the operation and give an interlock status return to the calling program.   The program may continue to issue the GET command until the interlock is removed, which will occur when the first user issues a PUT for the block.   Another DMS service might be to hold and stack the request until the interlock is removed.   This kind of control could be built into the bit map used by file control for reusable block allocation, where one bit would indicate whether a block were filled, and a second bit would indicate whether it were currently interlocked.   There would be no need to write the map to disk with each status change of the interlock bit since this would unnecessarily double the device I/O load on every GET and PUT.   If there were a crash, the interlock map would be reset to zero if buffers were lost since all updates would be reinitiated.

4.4   DATA ACCESS STRATEGIES

In Chap. 1, it was indicated that file processing is one of the three disciplines of data management, the other two being data structure and representtation and executive systems.   This chapter has been wholly dedicated to the subject of file processing, which has been subdivided into the topics of space maintenance, file generation, file update, and data access strategies.   The concluding section of this chapter will therefore deal with the data access strategies.

A data access strategy is a means by which records are selected for retrieval from a file.   It is normally associated with a logic schema, which directs that certain conditions be satisfied by those records that are so selected for retrieval. There are three basic or commonly used such schema, enumerated and defined in Fig. 4-53.   The Boolean logic, as indicated in the diagram, is normally conceived in three sub-forms: (1) the disjunctive normal form (DNF, sometimes called the *sum-of-products*), (2) the conjunctive normal form (CNF, sometimes called the *product-of-sums*), and (3) the factored form, which is a combination of the other two.   The most commonly used is the factored form, since it is the most concise, but certain types of data retrieval fit more specifically into the CNF or DNF format. For example, systems that have large numbers of synonyms or data items whose intensive meaning is the same fall more readily into the CNF category.

In the CNF illustration of Fig. 4-53, it might be the case that data items represented by the letters A, B, and C are synonyms, and hence the retrieval condition on a record is that it should contain either A or B or C, and that this threefold choice be conjuncted with some other set of conditions, which likewise may enumerate other sets of synonyms. Systems in which the data base develops over a long period of time may find CNF logic useful, because within any given discipline new terms are continually being added to the vocabulary, and a retrospective search may require that many terms be disjuncted simply because their usage is dated, and the use of any one of them or any sub-set will not adequately cover the way in which relevant documents have been indexed over the entire time span of the data base development.

The DNF form of a Boolean logic expression is more natural for non-

▶ **BOOLEAN LOGIC**

    DNF $AB\overline{C} + DE$

    CNF $(A + B + C) \cdot (\overline{D} + E + F)$

    FACTORED $A(B + C) + D\overline{E}$

▶ **WEIGHTED LOGIC**

$$w_1A_1, w_2A_2, \ldots w_nA_n, W$$

ACCESS IF $W_1A_1 + w_2A_2 + \ldots + w_nA_n \geqslant W$, WHERE + IS ARITHMETIC PLUS; w_i ARE WEIGHTING COEFFICIENTS; A_i ARE BOOLEAN VARIABLES INTERPRETED AS NUMERIC VALUES 0 (FALSE) AND 1 (TRUE).

▶ **RELATIONAL LOGIC**

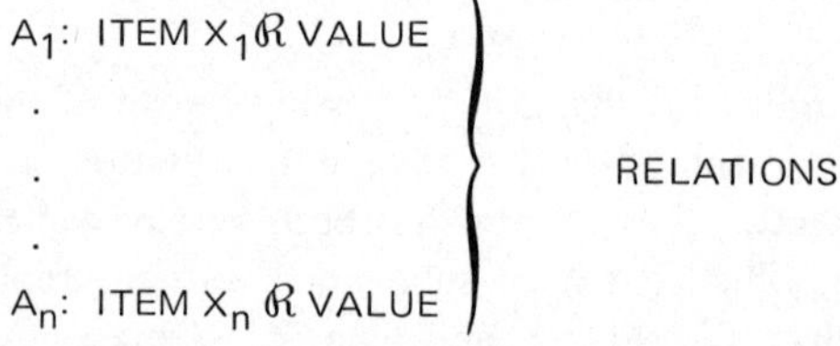

ACCESS $f(A_1, \ldots A_n)$, WHERE f IS A BOOLEAN OR WEIGHTED LOGIC FUNCTION.

Figure 4-53 Data access strategies

synonymic keyword vocabularies, with little literal redundancy in the expression, where a *literal* is interpreted to mean a key (represented in Fig. 4-53 as a letter A, B, C, etc.) or the negation of a key ($\overline{A}$, $\overline{B}$, etc.). If there is likely to be repetition or redundancy of literals, the factored form is usually perferred. In the example in the figure the factored form A (B + C) would be rendered in a DNF format as AB + AC. Processing is more efficient, particularly in the case of inverted lists, if the expression is factored. Also, people more naturally think of logical expressions in factored form. A special case of Boolean logic is the single key access, which would simply be represented as the Boolean logic expression A.

The second logic schema presented in Fig. 4-53 is called weighted logic and is used where varying degrees of importance are to be associated with the individual data items; this importance is based upon the judgment of the inquirer and may change from one inquiry to another. The keys of logic variables in the weighted logic expression are designated as A_1 through A_n. Associated with each variable is a weight, w_i. Both the variables and the weights are assigned by the inquirer, where a variable is considered to be a data item name and value, such as City/New York. If a record has a data item with the given value, the variable is said to be "true" or in the weighted logic expression, to have a value 1; otherwise it is said to be "false" and has a value 0. The arithmetic expression

$w_1 A_1 + w_2 A_2 + \ldots + w_n A_n$ is evaluated, and if the value of this summation is greater than or equal to a user assigned weight, W, the record is qualified for retrieval.

The relational logic is commonly used in information retrieval systems and is somewhat more complex to implement on a real time basis than either of the other two. It has been used as the basis for the SEARCH command in the DMS language presented in Chap. 5. It is actually a two-dimensional logic schema wherein the first dimension is a relational specification for a data item in terms of one or more values that the data item may assume; the second dimension is a logic function of either the Boolean or weighted type, the arguments of which are the conditions established by the relations. For example, a data item may be *age*; the relation, *greater than*; and the value, *25*. A second data item may be *geographic location*; the relation, *equal*, and the value, *United States*. If the logic combining these two relational conditions were the Boolean function AND, then the records for all persons over age 25 and located in the United States would be retrieved.

4.4.1   Implementation of Access Strategies

The *pushdown* is a commonly used programming technique in the manipulation of logical operations with list structures. A pushdown is an ordered list of elements constructed in such a way that when a new element is added to the list, it replaces the first element in the list; elements are accessed or removed from the list starting with the first element. When an element is added to the list, it is said to be "pushed" onto the list; when it is accessed, it is said to be "pulled" or "popped" from the list. Normally when an element is accessed or popped from the list it is also removed, but in some implementations a choice is given upon access as to whether the element will be removed or not. The natural order of storage and access to and from a pushdown is therefore on the basis of last-in first-out (LIFO). The concept of the pushdown is applicable to list processing and particularly to the processing of list structured files in accordance with the above described logic schema. The *elements* of the pushdown become *lists*, so that the pushdown construction is actually a list of lists.

Figure 4-54 illustrates how a factored logic expression is processed by means of a pushdown and also shows schematically how a pushdown can be implemented. At the top of the figure a simple factored expression is given as $(A + B) \cdot C$. This expression is called an *infix notation* because the logic symbols + and · are embedded or fixed within the expression. In order to represent this expression as a pushdown, the logic notation is changed from infix to *postfix*, which means that the designation of the logic operation always follows the variables that are arguments of the operation. The postfix notation of $(A + B) \cdot C$ is as shown in Fig. 4-54, wherein the operation OR is first to be performed upon the variables A and B, and then the operation AND is to be performed upon C and the result of the former operation.

In list processing, the variables A, B, and C would represent three lists of

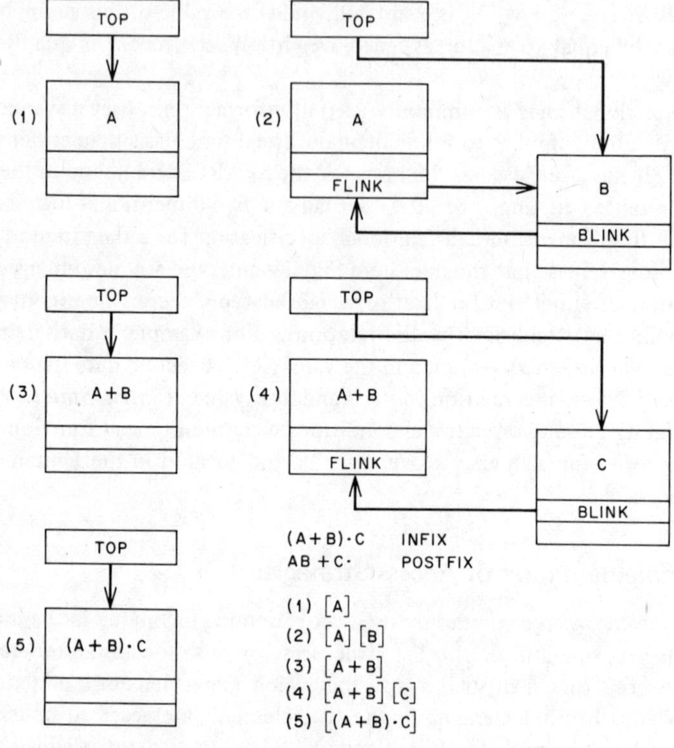

Figure 4-54 File structure of a pushdown

records. For example, A might represent all records with the key data item, NATION, having a value, USA. The three lists of the example are then processed in five steps as shown in the figure. The square brackets enclosing a variable or an expression represent an *element* of the pushdown, where this element is itself a list. Another name for the pushdown is *stack*, and this will be used hereafter in place of the term pushdown.

In Step 1, the list corresponding to A is accessed and "pushed" onto the stack, so that the stack at the end of step 1 contains only the list A. The expression is processed by scanning the postfix notation from left to right. Whenever a variable is encountered, the indicated list is accessed from storage and "pushed" onto the stack. When an operator is encountered, as many elements (lists) of the stack are "popped" as are required to satisfy the operand requirements of the operator. The common Boolean operators used in information retrieval are the binary operators AND, OR, and AND NOT. This means that whenever a binary Boolean operator is encounted in the postfix scan, the preceding *two* lists are "popped" from the stack. The second symbol in the postfix scan of the example is the variable B; the list corresponding to B is therefore "pushed" onto the stack, as represented in step 2. At this point the stack has two distinct lists, A and B. The third symbol encountered in the left-to-right scan of the positive notation is +, which is a binary Boolean operator. This means that the last two elements or lists of the stack are "popped" and operated upon in accordance with the type of operator.

From step 2 the two distinct lists B and A are removed, and a new list A OR B is generated. After step 3 the stack contains a single list, A OR B. The fourth symbol encountered is another variable, C, and the corresponding list is "pushed" onto the stack as shown in step 4. The fifth and last symbol is the Boolean operator, ·; the last two lists on the stack are accessed and intersected, forming the final list $(A + B) \cdot C$. In the lower part of the figure, the file structure for the pushdown is shown schematically. Each rectangle in the figure represents either a chained or an inverted list structure. It is assumed that each list has two pointers associated with it, one called a forward link that can point to another such list following it in the stack and the other a backward link that points to the immediately preceding list in the stack. There is also a pointer that always points to the top or first element in the stack. After step 1 in the postfix scan there appears a list A, which has 0 values for its forward and backward links because it is the only list in the stack. After step 2, the stack contains two lists, A and B; list A contains a forward link to list B, and list B contains a backward link to list A. When the OR operator is encountered in the third step, the top two lists are accessed via the route: top of stack pointer to B, backward link to A. A new list is then generated by merging these two lists as required by the OR operation. The remainder of the example follows steps 3, 4, and 5 shown in the upper part of the diagram.

Figure 4-55 summarizes the steps for processing list structures by a pushdown stack using binary Boolean operators. In theory any of the 16 Boolean functions of two variables could be used, but the most common ones are the AND, OR, and AND NOT functions. The AND function is implemented by intersecting the addresses or primary keys on two lists to form a single intersection list. The OR function is implemented by merging two lists, and the

(1)   TRANSFORM THE KEYLIST LOGIC EXPRESSION TO POSTFIX NOTATION.

(2)   SCAN THE POSTFIX STRING FROM LEFT TO RIGHT.

(3)   WHEN A SYMBOL IS ENCOUNTERED, PUSH THE LIST ONTO THE STACK.

(4)   WHEN AN *OP* IS ENCOUNTERED, POP THE LAST TWO LISTS, APPLY THE OP, AND PUSH THE RESULTING LIST BACK ONTO THE STACK. IF THERE IS ONLY ONE LIST WHEN AN OP IS ENCOUNTERED, THE STRING IS INVALID.

(5)   WHEN THE LAST OP OF THE STRING IS ENCOUNTERED, THERE MUST BE EXACTLY TWO LISTS REMAINING IN THE STACK, WHICH ARE THEN COMBINED TO FORM THE RESULTANT LIST OF THE SEARCH.

Figure 4-55 Pushdown list processing algorithm

$$((A + (B + C) \cdot D\,\overline{E}) \cdot (F + G)$$

POST-FIX	A B C + + D E ↑ · F G + ·
SCAN	1 2 3 4 5 6 7 8 9 10 11 12 13

SCAN	STACK
1	[A]
2	[A] [B]
3	[A] [B] [C]
4	[A] [B + C]
5	[A + B + C]
6	[A + B + C] [D]
7	[A + B + C] [D] [E]
8	[A + B + C] [D · $\overline{D}$]
9	[(A + B + C) · D · $\overline{E}$]
10	[(A + B + C) · D · $\overline{E}$] [F]
11	[(A + B + C) · D · $\overline{E}$] [F] [G]
12	[(A + B + C) · D · $\overline{E}$] [F + G]
13	[(A + B + C) · D · $\overline{E}$ · (F + G)]

Figure 4-56 Pushdown list processing example

AND NOT function is implemented by incorporating all addresses from the second list that are not to be found on the first list. Figure 4-56 presents a more complex example in the processing of what in Fig. 4-53 is called a Boolean logic schema in factored form.

The processing of weighted logic, as defined in Fig. 4-53, is relatively simple conceptually, but can be operationally very expensive. Figure 4-57 presents the two necessary steps in this technique. First the union of lists re-

(1)   ACCESS THE LIST $A_1 + A_2 + \ldots + A_n$, WHERE + IS THE BOOLEAN UNION OPERATOR.

(2)   RETRIEVE EACH RECORD IN THE LIST THAT SATISFIES THE EXPRESSION $w_1A_1 + w_2A_2 + \ldots + w_nA_n \geqslant W$, WHERE + IS THE ARITHMETIC OPERATOR PLUS.

Figure 4-57 Weighted logic list processing

presented by the variables A_1 through A_n will be processed onto a single list. In the second step, each record on the generated list is tested by the weighting expression to determine whether it is a response to the weighted logic request; If examination of a record shows it to contain a key A_i, then A_k is assigned a value of 1 in the weighting expression; if it does not contain key A_i, then A_i is assigned the value of 0.

Relational logic list processing has some special requirements that are enumerated in Fig. 4-58. First, there must be a two-level index hierarchy, where

SPECIAL REQUIREMENTS

ATTRIBUTE–VALUE INDEX HIERARCHY

INVERTED LISTS

QUALIFICATION

THERE MUST BE AT LEAST ONE NON-NEGATED KEY IN EACH DNF DIS-JUNCT, *OR* ALL TERMS OF AT LEAST ONE CNF CONJUNCT MUST BE A KEY (NO TERM IN A CNF MAY BE NEGATED).

FORMULA REDUCTION

DNF: SELECT AS MANY NON-NEGATED TERMS IN EACH DISJUNCT AS THERE ARE KEYS TO FORM A REDUCED DNF.

CNF: SELECT AS MANY CONJUNCTS THAT HAVE ALL OF THEIR DIS-JUNCTED TERMS AS KEYS, TO FORM A REDUCED CNF.

Figure 4-58 Relational logic list processing

the first level contains the data item names or what may be called the attributes of each key, and the second level contains the values of the data items. Second, the processor would be exceedingly inefficient if inverted lists were not used for the list structures. Third, if the file is large, a qualification must be made on the structure of an inquiry in terms of its key and non-key data items. If one were willing to search the file sequentially, this qualification need not be made, but in a real-time or interactive environment, where the data base has a large number of records, the qualification is mandatory. The qualification states that when the inquiry, which is expressed as a Boolean formula F, is viewed as a DNF, there must be at least one nonnegated key in each disjunct of the DNF. If the inquiry is viewed as a CNF, then all terms of at least one CNF conjunct must be a key, and no terms in this conjunct may be negated. In the case of the DNF, all terms in each of the disjuncts may either be keys or non-keys except for the fact that at least one of them must be a nonnegated key. In the case of the CNF, all conjuncts other than the one selected by the qualification may contain keys or non-keys, and they may or may not be negated. In the case of a factored formula, it must obey the above qualification when transformed to either a CNF or DNF. The purpose of this qualification is to assure that there will exist a set of lists (hopefully considerably less than the set of all lists in the data base) that will contain every record in the data base that satisfies the formula F. If an inquiry satisfies this qualification, then a modification of F must be formulated that contains only keys so that an optimal search can be made based only upon list access. This procedure is called *formula reduction* and is the fourth special requirement indicated in Fig. 4-58. In the case of the DNF, formula reduction amounts to selecting as many nonnegated terms in each adjunct as are keys in order to form a reduced DNF. This approach will result in the fewest possible records being transferred to disk. In the CNF case, the objective is to select as many conjuncts that have all of their disjuncted terms as keys in order to form a reduced CNF.

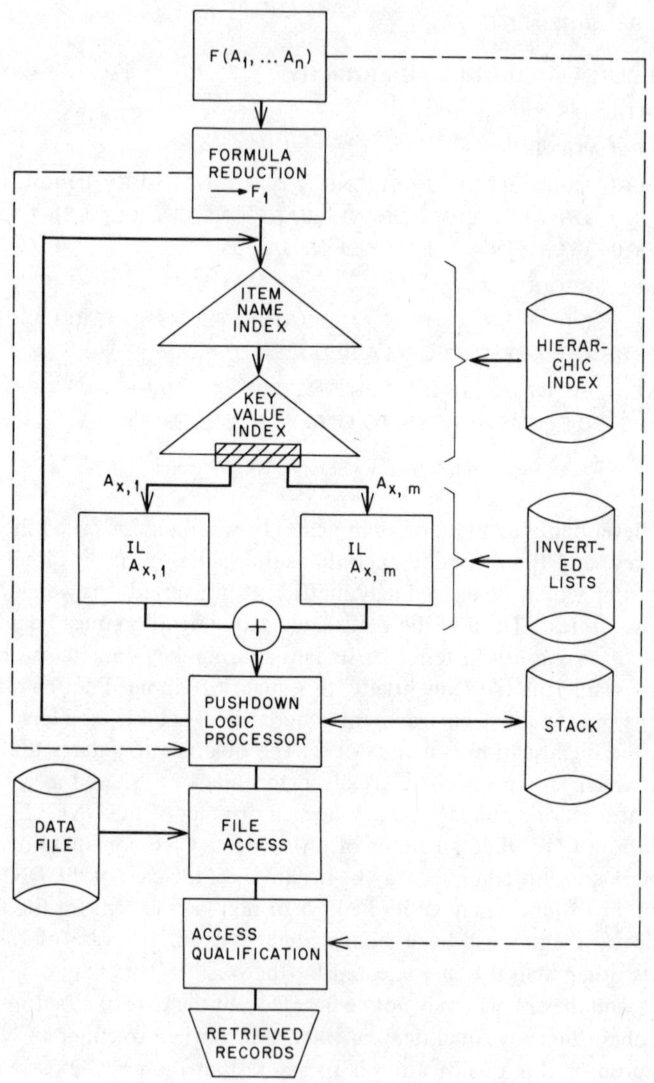

Figure 4-59 Relational logic processor

The alternative to formula reduction is the separation of key and non-key relations into two distinct Boolean expressions.

In Figure 4-59, the relational logic processor is illustrated as a block diagram. The inputs to the processor are the n relations A_1 through A_n and the

Boolean or weighted logic function F, as indicated at the top of the diagram. After determining which data items are keys, a formula reduction is performed resulting in another function F_1, whose arguments are a subset from the original arguments. The following process is carried out for each argument of the function F_1. Let one of these arguments be called A_x. A_x represents a relation, as shown in Fig. 4-53, which contains three parts: An item name, a relation, and one or more values that the relation is to satisfy. The first part, the item name, is decoded in the first level of the hierarchic index in order to find the appropriate value index. The key value index is then decoded and scanned in order to produce a set of values, labeled $A_{x,1}$ through $A_{x,m}$, that will satisfy the relation A_x. For example, if the relation were "between limits" and the limit values were 17 and 25, the key value index would be decoded for 17 and would be read sequentially to find all key value references from 17 to 25; the result would be the m values, indicated as $A_{x,1}$ through $A_{x,m}$ in the diagram. The output of the key value index will be a link address to an inverted list if the data files are structured by inverted lists. If they are structured by multilists, then the outputs of the key value index would be head of list addresses. However, since a series of such lists is to be produced for each of the relations A_1 through A_n, the recommended list structuring technique, as indicated in Fig. 4-58, is inverted lists rather than chained lists or multilists.

Since any of the values that satisfied the relation is acceptable in meeting the condition, the lists represented by $A_{x,1}$ through $A_{x,m}$ must be merged, and it is this merged list that becomes the input list of the pushdown processor corresponding to the argument A_x in the function F_1. This process is repeated for every argument of F_1, and each in turn can be processed by the pushdown logic processor, given that F_1 has been converted to postfixed notation for use by the pushdown logic processor (as indicated by the dashed line from the block containing F_1 to the logic processor). The final result of this operation will be a list of record addresses or primary keys (on the stack) that satisfies the reduced formula F_1. These records are then accessed from the data file, and final qualification is made on each record in accordance with the original formula F.

On the inverted list file structure, a variant that facilitates relational logic is to invert the data file itself instead of abstracting lists of address references. [14] This is done by storing each data item on a separate list *instead* of in a data record as depicted in Fig. 2-14. The order of data items on a respective list corresponds with the order in which the records would have been stored in the data file. Thus, if each record had n data items, A through A_n, and if there were R records in the file, then instead of there being a data file with R records, each of which contains n data items, there would be n files, each with R records containing one data item apiece. File 1 would contain all the A_1 data items in the order in which the R records would have appeared in the uninverted data file; file 2 would contain all of the A_2 data items, etc. This inverted file structure has maximum advantage for small files and relational logic since an entire file $(A_1, A_2, \text{etc.})$ corresponding to a single data item, or a large part of the file, can be brought into core and relationally operated upon for equality, greater than, less than, etc. Another useful characteristic of the approach is that the record structure can be easily modified since new data items are established simply by establishing a new list, and data items can be eliminated by deleting a list. Variable format and variable item length records as well as hierarchic data structures can also be accommodated by this method. A major disadvantage is the inefficiency of displaying all of the data items in a single data record.

Figure 4-60 presents a comparison of three list structured file organizations: the multilist, the inverted list by address, and the inverted list by primary key. The two principal advantages of a multilist file organization are ease of programming and speed of update. Its principal disadvantage is that it is inefficient for logical manipulation of long lists. That is, in order to intersect two lists, the shorter one must be completely traversed, and each record must be examined to determine whether it contains both keys. As frequently occurs, the intersected list is considerably smaller than even the shorter list, and hence many records will have been accessed that do not become a part of the response to the retrieval request. The search strategy, however, is very simple and does not require inverted lists or pushdowns. Updates are effected as indicated in Figs. 4-46 through 4-49 by the simple expedient of record and key delete bits, which have the effect of accessing and altering the fewest possible number of records, but at the expense of leaving additional, unwanted records both in the file as well as in the list structure, though logically deleted as signaled by the delete flag. The condition of usage of the multilist, therefore, is in (1) systems that have relatively short lists of generic keys, (2) systems in which inquiries will have at least one short list within each query conjunct (if this is possible to ascertain), or (3) systems in which updating is relatively more dynamic than inquiry, since the update versus inquiry trade-off in a multilist system favors the former. There may also be a consideration of program design and development cost, in which case the multilist system would again be favored.

The primary advantage of the inverted list structure where the lists contain addresses of the referenced records is that the technique provides for the most efficient logical list manipulation. Its principal disadvantages are that it is more complex to program than the multilist, and the update is the least efficient of the three list structures. Therefore, its principal conditions of usage should be in systems that have long lists and in which inquiry is more prevalent than update. A compromise between the two is the inverted list structure in which primary keys rather than addresses are stored in the lists. This technique represents a good trade-off of the better features of the multilist and inverted list by address. The principal advantages are (1) that it is more efficient than the multilist for logical list manipulation and (2) it is almost as efficient for update as the multilist. Its principal disadvantages are (1) that it is more compelx to program than the multilist and (2) it is not as efficient for inquiry as inverted list by address. Therefore, one may conclude that except for the complexity of programming,

LIST STRUCTURE	ADVANTAGE	CONDITION	DISADVANTAGE
CHAINED (MULTILIST)	(1) PROGRAMMING EASE (2) FAST UPDATE	(1) RELATIVELY SHORT LISTS (2) INQUIRIES WITH AT LEAST ONE SHORT LIST CONJUNCT (3) UPDATE MORE DYNAMIC THAN INQUIRY	(1) INEFFICIENT FOR LOGICAL MANIPULATION OF LONG LISTS
INVERTED BY ADDRESS	(1) MOST EFFICIENT FOR LOGICAL LIST MANIPULATION	(1) LONG LISTS (2) INQUIRY MORE PREVALENT THAN UPDATE	(1) MORE COMPLEX TO PROGRAM THAN MULTILIST (2) UPDATE IS LEAST EFFICIENT
	(1) MORE EFFICIENT THAN MULTILIST FOR LOGICAL LIST MANIPULATION (2) ALMOST AS EFFICIENT FOR UPDATE AS MULTILIST	(1) LONG LISTS (2) HIGH RATE OF UPDATES	(1) MORE COMPLEX TO PROGRAM THAN MULTILIST (2) NOT AS EFFICIENT FOR INQUIRY AS INVERTED LIST BY ADDRESS

Figure 4-60 Comparison of list structured file organizations

the inverted list by primary key is a more efficient list structuring technique overall than the multilist technique, and, except for the sacrifice of a small amount of retrieval efficiency, it is superior as well to the inverted list structure by address.

5

The DMS Language

The linguist studies language and its structure in order to determine its functional and expressive capacity. The etymologist studies language and more particularly its words in order to understand the life of the people whose everyday requirements contributed to the development of the language. To the etymologist, language and words are windows into the superstructure of human development. In this chapter the DMS language is similarly viewed, although the language to be examined here is not one that has had a natural development. It is hypothetical and is intended to reflect both the functional and structural properties of the elemental design theory presented in the previous four chapters.

In Fig. 2-4 of Chap. 2 there is shown an interface between the executive of the data management system and the user program. This implies a language. The functional specification of a language is a complex and lengthy procedure, particularly one that is to interface between a user or user program and the functions of data management. However, in order to illustrate in a more concrete way some of the design concepts that have been presented up to this point, the basic skelton of such a language is presented. Furthermore, only those parts of the language are developed that relate specifically to data management, and in particular to those aspects that will best exemplify and highlight the subject of this book. An attempt is also made through this illustrative language specification to further convey the notion of *data processing independence*, discussed in Chap. 1. Figure 5-61 enumerated in groups the commands of the language. In the first column the name of the command is given and in the second its purpose.

At the top of Fig. 2-4, it is indicated that file definition represents the first step in the generation of a data base. There must therefore be a file definition (FD) declare and a redeclare command for the purposes of file generation and

COMMAND	FUNCTION
DECLARE **REDECLARE**	FILE GENERATION
POINTER	DATA STRUCTURE SELECTION
CONTROL **RESET** **RELEASE**	DATA ACCESS CONTROL
TRANSFER **EDIT** **MOVE**	DATA TRANSFER IN CORE
OPEN **CLOSE**	FILE OPEN, CLOSE
GET **PUT** **DELETE**	FILE TO CORE/CORE TO FILE DATA TRANSFER AND RECORD DELETION
COPY **SORT**	FILE TO FILE DATA TRANSFER AND RECORD SEQUENCING
SEARCH	FILE SEARCH
ADD **SUB** **MULT** **DIV**	ARITHMETIC OPERATIONS
CONVERT	ITEM MODE CONVERSION
DO **FOR** **IF**	FILE PROCESSING AND PROGRAM CONTROL
PRINT	DATA DISPLAY

Figure 5-61 Basic commands of a data management language

regeneration, as given in the first group of Fig. 5-61. The DECLARE command establishes all parameters of the record and file as well as the declaration and format of all data items that comprise the record. It may also be desirable to modify the declaration after the file has been generated, in which case a REDECLARE is required. The second group command is called POINTER; it enables one to focus or point to parts of a data structure after it has been transferred from secondary storage to core memory. It is one of the more important functions leading to data processing independence. The third group of commands provides specific access control both to data in secondary storage as well as to data that are in core storage under pointer control. These commands—CONTROL, RESET, and RELEASE—determine the order in which data are to be accessed either from the file or from a structure in memory. The fourth set of commands enable data to be transferred or moved from one working area in core to another and to be edited. They are called TRANSFER, EDIT, and MOVE.

The next three groups relate more specifically to the manipulation of files themselves. The fifth group contains the file OPEN and CLOSE commands. The OPEN will bring the file definition record into memory if the data record interpretation is via the FD generated table; if the FD is compiled into the program, as in the case of COBOL, then it does not perform such a function. The OPEN may also bring the first level of an index and the file control tables into memory and will call for allocation of data input and/or output buffers. The CLOSE command writes modified tables back to disk and releases space. The sixth group contains the GET, PUT, and DELETE commands, which perform file to core and core to file data transfer and record deletion. The seventh group contains a COPY and SORT command, enabling file-to-file data transfer and record sequencing. The eight group contains a SEARCH command, which enables files or structures to be searched automatically for a variety of conditions.

All of these commands relate to data management per se, but a complete language would have to process data by means of arithmetic and control statements as well. Some of these are included only for the sake of completeness, but their function is analogous, and in some cases identical, to those in a standard compiler language like PL/1 or FORTRAN. There is a set of arithmetic functions to perform the basic operations of addition, subtraction, multiplication and division. A CONVERT command will convert a data item from one mode to another. There are two control statements FOR and IF; the FOR statement is analogous to the DO or loop control statement in FORTRAN or PL/1; however, it controls a loop at the file access level rather than at the compiler statement level. Thus, one record at a time is processed under the control of the FOR statement. There is also a normal program loop control function such as the DO that is defined for PL/1 or FORTRAN. The IF statement as it is defined operates in a slightly more general way than its counterpart in the algebraic compiler. Finally, there is a printing or display capability in the language. The PRINT command contains a series of sub-commands that are used in order to format the data for display.

The DMS language, as it will be called, is described by presenting the syntax for each statement with a semantic description of how the statement is used and the meaning of each parameter. The following conventions are observed in the syntax statements. All command, subcommand, and connector words that have special reserved meaning are presented in capital letters. Command variables are all in lower case. A dummy command variable may be used and then defined below the syntax using the format: *dummy*: = *expanded definition*, where *dummy* is the dummy variable and *expanded definition* is another syntactic expression. Data enclosed in square brackets are optional. Two or more data items enclosed in braces indicate an alternative selection, where one of the items in the list must be selected, unless the braces are enclosed in square brackets, in which case the entry of information contained within the braces is optional. If one of the alternatives is underlined, it is selected automatically upon default of the field whether or not the field is optional. Parentheses are symbols of the DMS language and *not* of the syntax description. Other symbols of puncutation in the DMS language are comma, semicolon, period, colon, slash, and equals sign.

$\begin{Bmatrix} \text{DECLARE} \\ \text{REDECLARE} \end{Bmatrix}$ FD   file name, organization, record type [, file access code]; item description-1;item description-2;. . .;item description-n.

item description-i: =item no-i, item name-i [, dummy indicator], format [,$\begin{Bmatrix} \text{length} \\ \text{magnitude} \end{Bmatrix}$] [,precision] [,display] [key indicator,[item no-sl/item no-s2/ . . . item no-sn/]] [,item access code]

$\begin{Bmatrix} \text{DECLARE} \\ \text{REDECLARE} \end{Bmatrix}$ WS   [area name]; item description-1; . . .; item description-n:
.
.
.
[area name]; item description-1; . . .; item description-n.

The DECLARE statement establishes the file definition record of Fig. 2-10. The REDECLARE statement modifies it and, where necessary, the file structure as well. The first parameter is *file name*, which establishes the field in a directory of all files held under a given account and initializes an FD record that is to be built according to the remaining parameters. Subsequent DMS command references to this file name may refer either to the file itself and its associated index on secondary storage or to a buffer in core that currently holds a record from this file; the context of the command determines the appropriate frame of reference. The second parameter of the DECLARE is *organization*. This may be sequential, indexed sequential, indexed random, mapped random, chained or multilist structured, inverted list structured, or multiple file structured. A file may have two superimposed organizations such as indexed random and multiple file. The third data item is *record type*, being FF, FV, VF, VV, as described in Chap. 2. The fourth item is an optional *file access code*. Referring to Fig. 2-10 in Chap. 2, these data provide all of the information that is required to complete the header and to establish the remainder of the file definition record once the enumerative information per item is provided. It also enables the initialization of the index record as illustrated in Fig. 2-11, the inverted list record of Fig. 2-12 if required, and the data record of Fig. 2-14.

Following the file access code is a series of item descriptions containing one description per item in the record. Since in this type of syntax a particular field of information is accorded a specific position within the string of fields, every field is to be indicated either by appropriate information or by the placement of the indicated punctuation, which is usually a comma. Commas as place holders do not have to appear, however, at the end of a phrase (terminated by a semicolon) or at the end of a complete sentence. Thus if file access codes were to be omitted, for example, a semicolon would follow record type, and no comma would be required as a place holder for the missing file access code.

An *item description* is defined as (designated in the syntax by the symbol,: =) an *item number* followed by an *item name*, as required information. The number would be a serial number in the case of a nonhierarchic data structure and a level of canonical number in the case of a hierarchic or network structure. These two fields are followed by a *dummy indicator* that simply designates whether the item is a dummy within a hierarchic data structure or whether it actually represents a variable that references data. For example, in Fig. 2-21 the item number, item name given by *1.1.2 TEMP-RANGE* is a dummy since no data are to be stored in a location referenced only as 1.1.2. The data in that structure relating to temperature range are stored at nodes 1.1.2.1 and 1.1.2.2. Therefore, in the declaration of the data item 1.1.2, the dummy indicator would be set; in the declaration of 1.1.2.1, HI, the dummy indicator would be omitted and would be replaced in the syntax by a comma.

The next four elements of data description collectively designate the mode of processing. They indicate (1) how the data item is aggregated at the bit and character level into a field, (2) specific numeric properties for the purpose of computation, and, if applicable, (3) how the data item is to be displayed. The first of these four elements in the item description is the *format*. Most data can be managed by five formats:

L	Left-justified alphanumeric
R	Right-justified alphanumeric
I	Integer
n	Fixed point with n decimal places
F	Floating point

No attempt is made in the specification of this langauge for absolute completeness, since its purpose is illustrative. The format, in terms of the hierarchy of data aggregates, is actually describing data at the bit aggregation and field levels. Other data strings might also be formated, such as binary or hexadecimal digits, but the five given here represent the most common in DMS usage. The format is a required field. The next field, which also relates to mode of processing, is not required but is presented as an alternative depending upon the format. It is the *length* or *magnitude* of the data item. *Length* is to be specified if the record type is fixed field length and the format is alphanumeric, in which case the length is interpreted as the number of characters in the alphanumeric string.

If the record type is variable field length, then one could decide upon two methods of implementation. One is to require a length, which would represent a maximum field length, and the other, which would be far more desirable from a data processing independence standpoint, would be to require no length, and to dynamically maintain field length of alphanumeric information, whatever size it may be. The *magnitude* may be specified, if the format is I, n, or F, as the highest (positive or negative) power of 10 of the number. For I, the magnitude specifies the number of digits in the number. For the n format, it specifies the maximum number of integer digits in the number, and in the case of F, it specifies the largest power that the base of the number, which is assumed to be 10, can be raised to, where the power may be positive or negative. It would be desirable to provide default magnitudes for the I, n, and F as well; therefore none of the alternatives is underlined.

The next data item, which is also associated with mode, is called *precision*. Precision is a required specification only of the F format. It is the number of significant digits in a normalized F format number. Precision is also specified in a fixed point format, but it is explicitly given as the number n in the format statement itself. The fixed point format n would normally be implemented by means of decimal arithmetic, since both the magnitude and the precision are independently variable. The implementation of large magnitude integers may be conveniently effected either by multiple precision or decimal arithmetic, although the former would probably result in a more efficient implementation. The implementation of floating point would normally be by means of multiple precision, since the essential design of the floating point number is based upon independence of selection of magnitude and precision. Again, a default precision should be supplied automatically. The last element of modal description is a *display* indication that describes the data item for the purpose of printing. It is not intended here to detail methods of display representation, but the various display formats of either COBOL or PL/1 would suffice. If it were not intended to display the item, or if it were intended to insert display information by means of the REDECLARE or CONVERT, the display field could be omitted.

The next element of item description in the *key indicator*, which simply states whether the data item is to be a key and therefore will require the construction of an index or map. A key implies a list of all records containing the given key value. If the key is unique, the list always has one member, but if it is generic, it may contain many records, in which case it may be ordered according to the major to minor sequence, *item no-sl/item no-s2/ . . . item no-sn* , which reads "item number sn within . . . within item number s2 within item number s1," where the item numbers uniquely identify data items by which the list may be ordered. Alternatively, the sequence may be replaced with the reserved words FIFO or LIFO, which will construct the list according to time of arrival, and if the sequence is omitted altogether, then LIFO is assumed by default. The last element of information is an *item access code,* which provides READ or WRITE security for the given data item within the record on a filewide basis.

A REDECLARE statement is used to modify any of the above elements of descriptive information either about the file (that is, organization, record type, and file access code) or about any of the data items. Redeclaration could have very far-reaching consequences in a data management system, since it effectively enables one to reorganize the file structure; to modify the record type and thus drastically alter the way in which information is stored in the records; and to change the actual record structure itself by deletion, addition, or modification of items within the record. It should also be noted that the present discussion is not concerned with efficiency of operation, since it is obvious that the implications of what is being said here may be very complex and time consuming computationally, but the discussion is at a rather broad functional level and is directed largely at an understanding of the concept underlying *data processing independence.* It is certainly the case that humans, somewhere in the data processing involved with cognition, learning, and problem solving, declare and redeclare data structures continually, and it is therefore not unreasonable to consider the analogue of this processing the data management system. Whether it is to be used in a particular implementation of a data management system is purely a matter of specific requirement. In the general scheme of design and technology, DECLARATION and REDECLARATION of the type here described should not be dismissed simply because of their inherent complexities.

Since it is not always the case that record structures are "for export only" and that it is desired to create structures as completely internal entities within core memory, usually called working storage, a correspondent of the FD DECLARE and REDECLARE for working storage should be provided. In the syntax, an area name can be given to associate a series of item descriptions (1 through n), or individual items can be declared without any collective name. A series of collective names can be entered under a single DECLARE, where each collective area name and its associated item descriptions are terminated by a colon. The final area name in the declaration is terminated by a period.

It is one thing to consider the formulation of a complex data structure. It is another to manipulate and process it. Consider again the human mind as a data processor. It may conceive an aggregate of information in some complex structure, such as a hierarchy or a graph, but when it must manipulate these data, which is to say that it must perform certain abstract arithmetic, logical, or syntactic operations upon the information, the human mind has a focusing mechanism whereby it can extract from the total structure only that part of it that is essential, at a given moment, to the execution of a particular operation. It has some kind of pointer mechanism that can select part of a complex data structure, and which on some repetitive basis, can continue to move the pointer in a way that appropriately scans, reformats, or restructures the data as necessary and in accordance with the ongoing process of cognition. An attempt is made in the pointer command to formalize such a construct. POINTER operates upon a data structure designated by a file name, area name, or another pointer name.

$$
\text{POINTER pointer name-1,} \left\{ \begin{array}{l} \text{file name} \\ \text{area name} \\ \text{pointer name-2} \end{array} \right\} \text{, item select-1; item select-2, ... ; item select-n; [status return]}
$$

$$
\text{item select-i:} = \text{item number-i [index-1, ..., index-k)], [} \left\{ \begin{array}{l} \overline{\text{NEXT}} \\ \text{PREVIOUS} \\ \text{SAME} \\ \text{STEP} \\ \text{TOP } [\{ \overline{\text{POP}} / \text{NOPOP} \}] \\ \text{BOTTOM } [\{ \overline{\text{PULL}} / \text{NOPULL} \} \end{array} \right\}]
$$

The context of file name here is the core buffer that is used to hold a record from the file cited by *file name*. The pointer itself that is operating upon this buffer or area is given a pointer name. Thus, the first two fields of the command are *pointer name-1* and a required alternate selection of *file name*, *area name*, or *pointer name-2*, where *pointer name-1* is the name of the storage area into which the data being pointed to will be transferred, and *file name*, *area name*, or *pointer name-2* is the area in which the pointer operates.

There follow a series of *item selects*, where each item select has the following syntax: The first element of description of an item select is an item number that may be optionally followed by a series of *indices* enclosed in parentheses. The item select represents a selection of a node within the tree or graph of the host data structure that is to be found in file name, area name, or pointer name-2. It is important to understand the composition of the index series and to recall the meaning of a hierarchic data structure with dimensional nodes. The item number is a canonical number that uniquely represents the node of the data item within the tree or graph structure. The series of indices is used to coordinate a specific data item or series of data item within the given node, according to dimensionality. The indexing *must* start at the top of the tree, and it may go not lower than the level of the item number, but it need not reach that level. A specific example will help to illustrate this point. Consider the data structure represented by Fig. 2-23. Assume that we would like to point to COUNTRY-NAME (3) within TIME-ZONE-NAME (2). The topmost dimension of this tree occurs at node 1.1 and has dimensional components 1 to 5; the next level dimension is at 1.1.2 and has components 1 to 10, as indicated in the figure.

COUNTRY-NAME (3) could be pointed to as an item select by the expression 1.1.2 (2, 3). On the other hand, if it were desired to point to all COUNTRY-NAMEs under TIME-ZONE-NAME (2), then the item select specification would be 1.1.2 (2). In the first example, a specific COUNTRY-NAME has been pointed to, and in the second example, a set of COUNTRY-NAMEs has been pointed to. The pointer function or command can legitimately point to either of these structures, that is, it need not point to a unique data item. If in addition it were desired to point not only to COUNTRY-NAME (3) but also to the CAPITAL and all MAJOR PRODUCTs of COUNTRY-NAME (3), then two more item selects could be added to the pointer list, giving an item select listing of 1.1.2 (2, 3); 1.1.2.1; 1.1.2.3. It is assumed that the selection of 1.1.2.3 will be controlled by any other item selects in the series that are superior in the hierarchy, and in this case there is a 1.1.2; hence that 1.1.2.3 is qualified by the pointing of 1.1.2, which in this case is specifically dimensioned at (2, 3). Since no dimensional component has been cited specifically within 1.1.2.3, it is assumed that all eight occurrences are to be included in the pointer. In summary, the above item select list will point to the CAPITAL and the eight MAJOR PRODUCTs of COUNTRY-NAME (3) in TIME-ZONE-NAME (2).

The third element of information that may be associated with an item select corresponds to the method of access control. Given a list of data entities, whether they be data items in an array within core memory or records listed in a file, one must consider the way in which each entity, in turn, will be accessed for processing.

First, the list has a physical or natural ordering, and the items on the list could be accessed, one at a time, in that order. This is the meaning of the NEXT option. When a pointer command for a given pointer name-1 is first executed, if the NEXT option has been specified for a partiuclar item select, or if the option is defaulted, in which case it is automatically interpreted to be NEXT (as indicated by the underline), the pointer will start at the first occurrence of the item number, and with each subsequent execution of this particular pointer command (upon pointer name-1), the next occurrence (in a dimensional sense) of the item will be pointed to. If the indexing of *item number* has been specific to a particular occurrence or if item number is not dimensioned at all, NEXT will have no effect and will simply point to *item number* invariably. The PREVIOUS option will cause the access control to cycle in the reverse direction from NEXT. If the option selected is SAME, then the index will not move. If the option selected is STEP, then the index moves as in NEXT except that it cycles in coordination with the occurrence indexes of all of the other item selections with STEP control, where the higher tree level nodes cycle more slowly than the lower level nodes. Consider, for example, an item selection series in the example of Fig. 2-23 to be:

1.1.2 (2), STEP; 1.1.3, STEP.

The pointer would reference COUNTRY-NAME (1) within TIME-ZONE-NAME (2) and cycle through the eight major products with each execution of the pointer command; then it would reference COUNTRY-NAME (2) within TIME-ZONE-NAME (2) and again cycle through the eight major products of COUNTRY-NAME (2) with each subsequent execution of the pointer command, and so forth, until all ten country names with TIME-ZONE-NAME (2) had been referenced.

If two items at the same tree level are to be stepped, then the latter is cycled faster than the former to produce all combinations. If a one-dimensional list is pointered, a normal mode of access is from the TOP (head) of the list or BOTTOM (end) of the list. Each time the POINTER command is executed, the next item in the list defined by the *item select* will be pointed to, that is, will be transferred to *pointer name-1.* Two subsequently defined commands, CONTROL and RESET, are used to specify the natural order of the list and to reset the pointer to the beginning of the list. The selection TOP means that access is to be from the top of the list (whether it be LIFO or FIFO), and if, in addition, it is qualified by POP, then once the item occurrence has been referenced, it is permanently deleted from the pointer reference; if TOP is qualified by NOPOP, then the top item is referenced but not deleted. The BOTTOM selection operates the same way as TOP, except that access if from the bottom of the list rather than from the top of the list, and the qualifications PULL and NOPULL stand in the same relation to BOTTOM as POP and NOPOP do to TOP.

After all item selects have been made, a status return location may be given if it is desired to obtain a status indication about the pointer reference. This status has only two values. If will be 0 if the pointer command is in fact pointing to data; it will be 1 if the pointer command is not pointing to any information, as would be the case at the conclusion of all possible STEP cycles, or at the end of all lists under NEXT, PREVIOUS, TOP, or BOTTOM control. It is also possible to redefine an already defined *pointer name* by citing the same *pointer name* again in a pointer command as both pointer name-1 and pointer name-2; any item selects that are to be unaltered are defaulted in the redefinition, and new or modified item selects are redefined as desired.

One may note that the concept of "data item" has gradually become increasingly diffuse. It began in the hierarchy of data aggregates as a field, which was a specific aggregation of bits or characters that represented a unique item of data. Then the notion of a tree was introduced such that a given data item, though still unique, was now related to other data items in the intrarecord hierarchy, and this relationship expanded the intensive meaning of the original item. Then the concept of dimensionality was introduced, and the data item could now be extrapolated to multiple instances or values. By analogy to mathematics, what was once a unique function has become a many valued function. At this point, although "data item" still represents a unique point in an intrarecord data hierarchy, it no longer references a character or bit string with unique meaning either intensive or extensive. Yet the precision of computer language requires that a distinction be made between that "data item" which defines a class of items and that which defines a single, uniquely addressable item. Therefore, the generic term *identifier* is to be substituted here for the term *data item*.

An identifier can have two frames of reference, indicated in the box as *identifier* and *identifier**.

Identifier means

$$\left\{ \begin{array}{l} \text{Item name } [(\text{index})] \\ \text{Item number } [(\text{index})] \\ \text{Pointer name } [(\text{relative item no. } [(\text{index})]\,)] \end{array} \right\}$$

in which:

1. *Item name* or *item number* means the first item occurrence.
2. *Item name* (*index*) or *item number* (*index*) means a specifically indexed occurrence.
3. *Pointer name* means the current selection of the highest level item name.
4. *Pointer name* (*relative item no.*) means the first occurrence of the relative item number of pointer name.
5. *Pointer name* [*relative item no.* (*index*)] means the specifically indexed relative item number of pointer name.

*Identifier** means

$$\left\{ \begin{array}{l} \text{Item name } [(\text{index})] \\ \text{Item number } [(\text{index})] \\ \text{Pointer name } [(\text{relative item no. } [(\text{index})]\,)] \end{array} \right\}$$

in which:

1. *Item name* or *item number* means all occurrences.
2. *Pointer name* means the entire current selection.
3. *Pointer name* (*rel. item no.*) means all occurrences of the indicated item.
4. *Indexed items* indicate a specific occurrence.

Identifier refers to a specifically addressable data item designated by (1) an item name or index item name, (2) an item number or indexed item number, or (3) a pointer name. If it is identified by an item name or number, then reference is to the first occurrence only. If it is identified by an item name and an index or item number and an index, then reference is made to the specifically indexed occurrence. Finally, if the identifier is a pointer name, then reference is made to the current selection of the highest level item name, with its indicated selection qualifier, such as NEXT, PREVIOUS, SAME, etc. If there is no qualifier, and all occurrences of the item name are thereby implied, then the identifier references only the first occurrence of the highest level item name.

*Identifier** may reference all components of a dimensioned item name or number and either an entire structure referenced by a pointer name or a suitably described substructure of a pointer name. That is, an item name or item number references all occurrences of the item name or number. A pointer name references the entire current selection of the pointer. A pointer name qualified by a relative item number means all occurrences of the indicated item within the pointer name, where the relative item number is a canonical number of a node in the *subtree* defined by the pointer name data structure. The relative item numbers may also be indexed if they are dimensioned.

The following examples illustrate the meaning of *identifier*. They reference the file definition GEOGRAPHY given in Fig. 2-22 and illustrated in Fig. 2-23.

Identifier	*Meaning*
COUNTRY-NAME	COUNTRY-NAME (1, 1)
COUNTRY-NAME (2)	COUNTRY-NAME (2, 1)
1.1.2.1	CAPITAL (1, 1)
1.1.2.3. (2, 3, 4)	MAJOR PRODUCT (2, 3, 4)

The first example of identifier is COUNTRY-NAME, which means the first occurrence of COUNTRY-NAME within the first occurrence of TIME-ZONE-NAME, since there is no further indexing specification in the identifier. The second example is COUNTRY-NAME (2), which means COUNTRY-NAME (2, 1), since the second component of the first dimension is given. The third example of an identifier is 1.1.2.1, which is an item number, and refers to the CAPITAL (1, 1). The fourth example is 1.1.2.3 (2, 3, 4) and specifically references a data item at the third dimensional level.

As another illustration, let the following POINTER be defined:

POINTER NATION, GEOGRAPHY, 1.1.2 (2), NEXT; 1.1.2.3.

The NATION subtree is illustrated in Fig. 5-62. It contains the eight major products in each country under the second TIME-ZONE. The first time this POINTER is referenced, the eight products of the first country will appear in NATION; the second reference (without an intervening RESET) will place the eight products of the second country in NATION, and so forth.

Examples of identifiers that reference this pointer may then appear as follows:

Identifier	*Meaning*
NATION	1.1.2 (2), NEXT
NATION (1.1. (3))	1.1.2.3 (2, NEXT, 3)

The meaning of the first of these identifiers may be translated as that COUNTRY—NAME within TIME—ZONE—NAME (2) that the NEXT option currently indi-

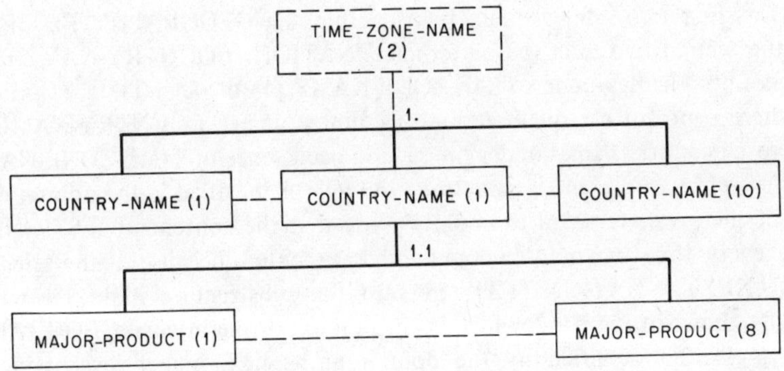

Figure 5-62 The NATION subtree

cates. The meaning of the second is the third MAJOR–PRODUCT within the NEXT COUNTRY–NAME within the second TIME–ZONE–NAME.

The identifier NATION references only the highest level, as it is not qualified. Since a selection control of NEXT is specified in the POINTER command at this level, a specific data item in node 1.1.2 (2) is referenced according to the current position of the pointer as determined by NEXT. The last example is a qualified *pointer name*, NATION [1.1 (3)]. The canonical numbering of a qualified pointer name references a substructure of the original data structure that the *pointer name* itself is referencing. The subtree corresponding to the pointer name NATION, illustrated in Fig. 5-62, has two nodes, COUNTRY-NAME (numbered 1.) and MAJOR PRODUCT (numbered 1.1). The identifier NATION [1.1 (3)] is referencing a specific data item, which is the third component of MAJOR PRODUCT (node 1.1 in NATION) within one of the ten country names at relative node 1. The meaning of NATION [1.1. (3)] with respect to the original structure, GEOGRAPHY, is 1.1.2.3 (2, NEXT, 3); that is, the third component of MAJOR PRODUCT within the NEXT selection of COUNTRY-NAME within TIME-ZONE-NAME (2).

A set of examples for identifier* is given below.

*Identifier**	*Meaning*
COUNTRY-NAME	COUNTRY-NAME (1, 1) through COUNTRY-NAME (5, 10) including all substructures
COUNTRY-NAME (2)	COUNTRY-NAME (2, 1) through COUNTRY-NAME (2, 10) including all substructures
NATION	All of nation as specified in the pointer command
NATION (1.1)	1.1.2.3 (2, NEXT, 1) through 1.1.2.3 (2, NEXT, 8)

The first two refer to data items within the GEOGRAPHY FD of Fig. 2-22; the second two refer to pointer name NATION. COUNTRY-NAME refers to all country names under TIME-ZONE-NAME (1) through TIME-ZONE (5), since there is no further qualification of country name. COUNTRY-NAME (2) refers to all country names under the second occurrence of TIME-ZONE-NAME. NATION refers to the entire structure NATION as specified in the pointer command of the previous set of examples. Note that the content of NATION will change every time the pointer command is executed, because of the selection control NEXT. NATION (1.1) refers to the substructure node 1.1 within NATION, shown in Fig. 5-62, which in the context of the original GEOGRAPHY record is 1.1.2.3 qualified by the pointer at its next higher level, which is COUNTRY-NAME (2) under NEXT selection control. Since the relative item number 1.1 is not indexed, the identifier* of NATION (1.1) refers to all eight components of 1.1.2.3.

In summary, *identifier* always refers to a particular, addressable data item within a data structure; *identifier** may refer to any data structure as defined by an item name, an item number, or a pointer name.

The next set of commands refer to data access control.

<table>
<tr><td>CONTROL</td><td>identifier, retrieval control</td></tr>
<tr><td>RESET</td><td>identifier</td></tr>
<tr><td>RELEASE</td><td>pointer name</td></tr>
</table>

The arguments of CONTROL are an identifier and a mode of retrieval control. The *identifier* must reference a data item that may either be an item select within a *pointer name* or a key within a file definition. In the former case, any item select that is qualified by NEXT, PREVIOUS, TOP, or BOTTOM can have its access established by a CONTROL statement. In the latter case, any list can have its access established or altered either in the DECLARE or REDECLARE statement or a CONTROL statement, but the data item referenced in either of these statement types must be a key.

Retrieval control can have two values: LIFO or FIFO. If it is LIFO, it means that records are put onto the list defined by *identifier* in such a way that the last record entered onto the list appears at the top of the list, and under NEXT or TOP access selection, the access starts from the top of the list; that is, the last record entered onto the list becomes the first one to be accessed or taken off of the list. If the retrieval control is FIFO, then the last record entered onto the list is put at the bottom so that NEXT or TOP access will always retrieve the first record added. Thus, the first record in becomes the first record out.

The second command in this set is RESET. Upon issue of this command, the access control for the list designated by the identifier will reset to the beginning. Note that POP and PULL qualifications remove items from a list, and therefore the reset would be applied in this case to a shorter (and possibly null) list.

The third statement is RELEASE, with an argument *pointer name*. This command will completely erase and release the allocated storage for the pointer reference established by *pointer name* in a POINTER command. Note that *pointer name* can be redefined as often as desired by means of the reuse of *pointer name* in a POINTER command, but the RELEASE command will completly eliminate the reference to the latest structure definition of pointer name and release the name *pointer name* for resuse if desired.

The next set of commands are referred to in Fig. 5-61 as the core-to-core data transfer commands. These enable the transfer of data items and structures from one core-defined area to another.

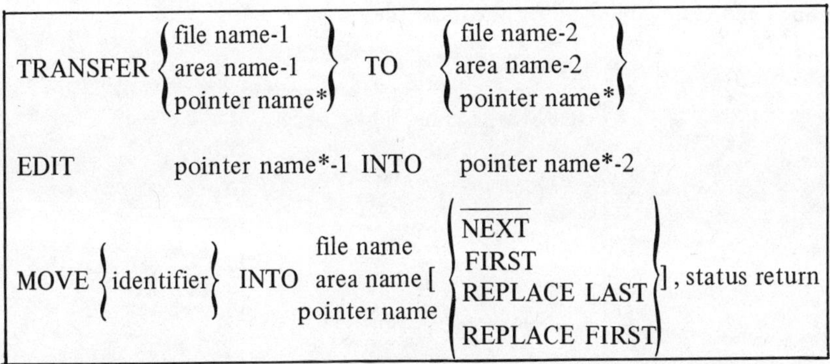

The first command is called TRANSFER. It enables one to transfer from an area defined by *file name, area name,* or *pointer name** to another *file name, area name,* or *pointer name.** File name in this command refers to the core buffer associated with a particular file, and area name refers to working storage in core established in a DECLARE or REDECLARE WS statement. The purpose of file name to file name transfer might be to read a record from one file and write it onto another. The purpose of area name or pointer name transfer to file name might be to write data that had been developed in an area name or a pointer name onto a file. And the purpose of a file name to an area name transfer might be to read a record from a file and to move it into a working storage area.

The second command is called EDIT; its purpose is to move and merge one data structure into another. The rules for merger are based entirely upon the canonical numbers in the respective pointer names. The resultant of *pointer name-2* is the merger of both *pointer name*-1* and *pointer name-2*. All data under a given canonically numbered node of pointer name*-1 is added to the same node in pointer name*-2 if one already exists; if it does not exist, the node is added to the latter structure.

The third command in this category is MOVE. It will move a specific data item referenced by *identifier* into a data structure identified by a file name, an area name, or a pointer name. If the data item does not already exist in the structure into which it is to be moved, a status return of 1 is given and the move does not take place; otherwise, the data item is moved into the data structure in accordance with the indicated qualification. The default is NEXT which means that it becomes the next occurrence of that data item. The qualification FIRST means that it is inserted at the head of the list of occurrences, or becomes the first occurrence. An item moved into a list under NEXT control would result in FIFO access from the TOP of the list; an item moved under FIRST control would result in LIFO access from the TOP of the list. The other two options enable the new data item to replace either the last or the first item.

The next set of commands are file OPEN and CLOSE and are analogous to open and close commands in the most file management systems.

OPEN filename, mode, access

mode

    IN
    IN-OUT
    OUT
    OUT-IN

access

    LOCKED
    LOCKED-W
    UNLOCKED

CLOSE   filename

The OPEN command will allocate a data buffer for *filename*, will bring necessary file control tables into core for DASD space allocation, and, if the file has an index, may bring the top node of the index into core. It will then set indicators in the file control table according to the *mode* of usage and *access* condition. The IN mode means that the file already exists and can only be read. The IN-OUT mode means that the file already exists and that it can be read and written. The OUT mode means that the file does not exist, that one is to be created, and that records are only to be written to it. The OUT-IN mode means that the file does not exist, that one is to be created, and that records are to be written to *and* read from it.

A LOCKED access means that no other user may have any access to *filename* while it is open. The LOCKED-W access means that no other user may write to this file while it is open, although he may read the file. The UNLOCKED access means that anyone else may read or write to this file while it is open. The CLOSE command releases the OPEN mode specification and causes all buffers and control tables to be written from core storage to the DASD.

The next set of commands enable the user to transfer records from file to core and from core to file, as well as to delete records. These are the GET, PUT and DELETE commands.

$$\begin{Bmatrix} \text{GET} \\ \text{PUT} \\ \text{DELETE} \end{Bmatrix} \quad \text{file name [, file access code] [, field access code]} \\ \text{[, record access code] [key identifier:key value]}$$

$$\left[, \begin{Bmatrix} \overline{\text{NEXT}} \\ \text{PREVIOUS} \\ \text{index} \\ \text{TOP } [\begin{Bmatrix} \overline{\text{PULL}} \\ \text{NOPOP} \end{Bmatrix}] \\ \text{BOTTOM } [\begin{Bmatrix} \overline{\text{PULL}} \\ \text{NOPULL} \end{Bmatrix}] \end{Bmatrix} \right], \text{status return}$$

The first argument is the *file name*, which is used to reference both the file on the secondary storage as well as a core buffer assigned to this file. The second, third, and fourth data elements are optional; these are the *file*, *field*, and *record access codes*. The fifth data element is the key *identifier* and the *key value*, which are required if the file is randomly organized and is to be accessed by means of a key. If the file is to be accessed sequentially, the key may be omitted. The *key identifier*, is an identifier, as defined above, but must also have been specified as a key of the record in the DECLARE statement. The key value is a particular value that the identifier is to assume. If the key is generic, the access control is required. If none is provided, NEXT is assumed, and the access control will be determined by the LIFO, FIFO retrieval control currently associated with the key (and stored in the index record). The direction of access can be reversed by inserting PREVIOUS as the access qualification; it can be made specific by an *index,* which means that the n'th record of the list is to be accessed where n is the index value. The TOP/BOTTOM control described previously may also be employed, which means that the records that are accessed can also be deleted automatically from the file (POP and PULL have no meaning for the PUT and DELETE commands), or they can be PUT or DELETED onto or from the top or the bottom of the list, as desired. The status return of these commands is somewhat more complex than in other commands, as indicated by the following schedule:

1. Operation completed satisfactorily.
2. The item named by the key identifier does not exist in the file definition.
3. The item named by the key identifier is a dummy item.
4. The item occurrence of the key identifier does not exist.
5. The key is valid but no records were found.
6. The NEXT or PREVIOUS command is complete and no more records remain on the list.
7. The TOP or BOTTOM command is complete and no more records remain on the list.
8. A system I/O error was encountered of type 8-N.

The next two command types enable file-to-file data transfer and record sequencing.

COPY   filename-1   TO   filename-2

SORT   filename-1   TO   filename-2   BY

identifier-1 [, . . . , identifier-n] ,   status return

The first is a COPY command, which copies all of the records in *filename-1* to *filename-2*.   The second, SORT command will sort all of the records on *file name-1* by *identifier-n* within *identifier-n-1* . . . within *identifier-1*. If *file name-2* is present, the sorted file will be stored in *file name-2*, leaving the original in *file name-1*. If *file name-2* is not present, the sorted file will be put back into *file name-1*. There are two sort return indications. Indication 1 is that the file has been successfully sorted. Indication 2 is that there are one or more records on the file that do not contain one or more of the sort control identifiers.

One of the most complex commands to implement is SEARCH. It enables one to search either files or data structures based upon a variety of data relationships.

SEARCH

$\left\{ \begin{array}{l} \text{filename-A} \\ \text{identifier*-A} \end{array} \right\}$,   label-1 = identifier*-1, relation-1, value-1 [, value-1.1,
. . . , value 1.j] ;
label-N = identifier*-N, relation-N, value-N [, value-N.1,
. . . value-N.j] .

$\left\{ \begin{array}{l} \text{filename-B} \\ \text{identifier *-B} \end{array} \right\}$ = f(label-1, . . . label-N); status return

The first argument is the *file name* or *identifier** that is to be searched. This is followed by a series of phrases, each terminated by a semicolon; the last phrase is terminated by a period. Each phrase has four parts: part 1 is a label which appears to the left of an equals sign: part 2 is an identifier*; part 3 is an arithmetic or logical relation such as greater than, less than, equals, between limits, set inclusion, etc; part 4 is one or more values or item name references to values. Such a phrase sets up a condition for search. The condition is identified by the label for subsequent processing and states that some item value in identifier* (within filename-A or identifier*-A) must satisfy the given relation to the value or values indicated. Allowing the left hand side of the relation to be identifier*-x rather than identifier-x is a further step in the direction of data processing independence since it introduces ambiguity and conceptual imprecision, characteristics of natural language that have utility in some circumstances. For example, consider again the illustration.

POINTER NATION GEOGRAPHY, 1.1.2 (2), NEXT; 1.1.2.3.

The condition NATION CONTAINS 'COFFEE' is conceptually imprecise. but since the logical construction of NATION includes MAJOR PRODUCTS, the intent of the condition is clear, even though a NATION whose CAPITAL was named COFFEE would also satisfy this condition. However, it should be realized that similar ambiguities are inherent in human communication, where it is frequently the case that such inferences are implicity or "understood" components of conversational messages.

After the enumeration of condition phrases, which are terminated by a period, a second file name or identifier* (filename-B or identifier*-B) is given followed by an equals sign, and a functional expression, the arguments of which are the above described phrase labels. For example, a Boolean function would examine the truth or falsity of each phrase as identified by the labels, where the specific values of the N identifiers in the phrases are obtained from records accessed from *filename-A* or from the data structure represented by *identifier*A*. Thus, each record that is brought into core memory can be tested as can any data structure represented by an identifier*, to determine whether the function is satisfied that relates to the N phrases or conditions given in the search specifications. The status return will indicate (1) the number of records appearing in *filename-B* or *identifier*-B*, (2) that the search can only be performed by sequential access of the file, and (3) that one or more of the items referenced in the conditions are dummy items and hence cannot be tested.

The next set of commands performs arithmetic operations, and these commands are analogous to those in an algebraic compiler.

$$\begin{Bmatrix} \text{ADD} \\ \text{SUB} \\ \text{MULT} \\ \text{DIV} \end{Bmatrix} \text{identifier-1} \begin{Bmatrix} \text{TO} \\ \text{FROM} \\ \text{BY} \\ \text{BY} \end{Bmatrix} \text{identifier-2}[\,,\text{identifier-3}]\;[\,,\text{status return}]$$

Identifier-1 is added to, subtracted from, multiplied, or divided by *identifier-2,* and the result is stored in *identifier-2* unless *identifier-3* is present, in which case the result is stored in *identifier-3.* In accordance with the principle of data processing independence, mode adjustments are automatic, and the resultant will follow a set of predetermined rules where the modes of the input arguments of the operation are different. For example, it should be of no concern to the user if identifier-1 were defined as fixed point and identifier-2 as floating point. In general, he need not even be concerned with the mode that the system will automatically determine for identifier-3, because if identifier-3 is used in another arithmetic operation, the operation is again performed regardless of whether it conforms to the mode of the other operand. On the other hand, if the user is concerned with the mode of *identifier-3*, then he can use the CONVERT command to convert it to any desired mode. There may also be certain incompatible modes that will be indicated in a status return. For example, it would normally be meaningless to add alphanumeric information to numeric information.

The CONVERT statement is used to convert the mode of an identifier into another mode.

$$\boxed{\text{CONVERT identifier, format } [, \begin{Bmatrix} \text{length} \\ \text{magnitude} \end{Bmatrix}] \ [, \text{precision}] \ [; \text{display}] , \text{status return}}$$

The first element of the CONVERT statement is the identifier; the second is the format to which the identifier is to be converted; the third element is the length or magnitude, depending upon the format, as described previously with the DECLARE statement; the fourth element is the precision of a floating point format; the fifth element is the display specification; and the last, a required element, is the status return, which will indicate whether the conversion is possible. For example, it should not be possible to convert alphanumeric information that contains alphabetic characters into a numeric format.

The next set of commands controls file and program processing (see top of next page).

The DO-END statement is identical to that defined in PL/1. The FOR-END statement is analogous except that the loop control is applied to a file, where the next record in a given file is accessed with each iteration of the loop. For example, the SEARCH command could be employed to produce a *filename-B*, and iterative processing could be performed on each record of *filename-B* by means of the FOR statement. An IF statement is constructed similar to that of PL/1, but the condition of the IF statement is developed in an identical way to that of the SEARCH command.

The last statement indicated in Fig. 5-61 is a PRINT command, which should readily enable the user to print the current contents of data items or structures. It should also enable him to print free text such as that used for labeling and to register the display horizontally and vertically on the page.

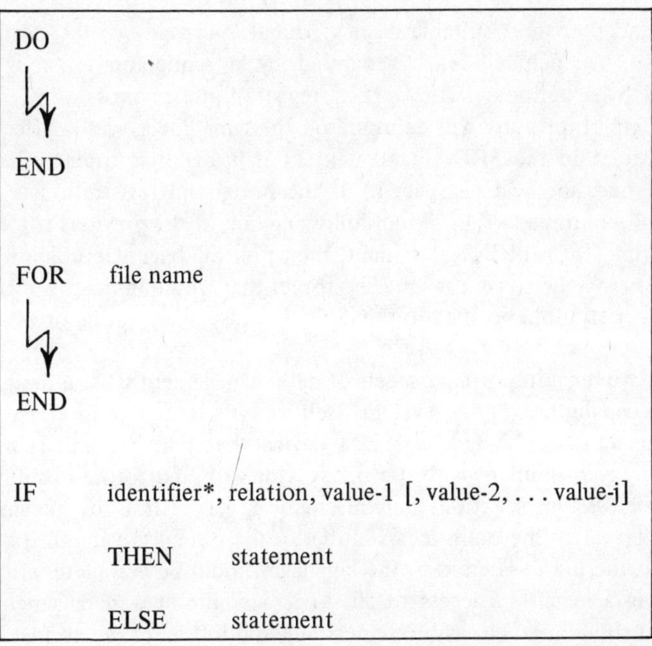

The first element in the PRINT statement permits vertical registration by designating an absolute line number on the page, Lx, or by a vertical tab VTx, which will have the effect of skipping x lines beyond the last printed line or to top of form, wherein x would be assigned a special symbol such as an asterisk.

PRINT [{ Lx / VTx }], [{ Cx / HTx }] { 'text 'string' / identifier / [Fn,] identifier* } ; . . . [status return]

The second element of the print description is horizontal registration by which it can be indicated that printing starts at the specific column Cx, that it tab horizontally x spaces (HTx), or that it skip to the next preassigned tab position, wherein x would be assigned a special symbol. The next and only required element is the information to be printed; it may appear as a text string, in which case it would be enclosed in quotes; it may be an identifier, or it may be an identifier*, in which case a format function, Fn, may be provided that indicates who the data structure is to be formated for display.

The display format of each individual data item in *identifier* or *identifier* * is designated in the DECLARE statement of the data item or in a CONVERT statement, but if it were defaulted, the system should provide a standard display format for each mode of data. In addition, if the display function, Fn of *identifier* * is not given, the system should also be able to analyze the structure and prepare a suitable display format. As many of these triplets as desired can be included, each separated by a semicolon (;) and the last terminated by a period. If the vertical registration element is omitted from a particular triplet, printing will continue on the same line as was in effect for the previous triplet in the PRINT statement; if it is the first triplet of a PRINT statement, one line will be spaced. If the horizontal registration is omitted, printing will continue in the column following that of the previous triplet; if it is the first triplet of a PRINT statement, then printing begins in column one. A status return may be given after the last triplet that would indicate a vertical or a horizontal registration specification that would cause overprinting or off-the-page printing.

The two most important aspects of data management system design are the functional capabilities of the system itself and the language interface. Like a transmission clutch, the language is a device that matches and transmits the thought energy of humans who use the system with and to the machine which merely processes information in a mechanical way. It is by means of the language that all of the built-in capabilities of the sytems are manifest and made available to the user. Therefore, the language should be complete with respect to providing a means of access to all services of the data management system. However, it should also be easy to understand and to use, or the average user will be reluctant to utilize the facilities fully, settling instead for the minimum necessary to get by and to do his job. By limiting himself to only the more primitive or fundamental capabilities of language, such as the FORTRAN subset of PL/1, the programmer or designer limits the scope of his problem-solving ability.

There are always trade-offs to be made in language design between conciseness of expression and range of exposition. Natural language favors the latter, providing highly varied syntactic structures and semantics with numerous connotations for a given denotation. The meaning of information conveyed by natural language is frequently context-dependent. In data management language it appears that the advantage lies in the direction of conciseness and the avoidance, as much as possible, of context-dependence, although an example of context-dependence in the DMS with respect to the user of *identifier** was given above and was indicated in that specific usage as being desirable. The mechanism of the clutch alluded to above will be defeated if the mechanical component of the system, namely the data management system programs, cannot understand precisely what information structure and processing are required.

Data management can be viewed from a usage standpoint within two frameworks. One is that of general-purpose programming; the other is that of a specific information handling system designed for a particular data base or class of data bases and a particular set of processes that are performed upon them. In the former framework the most successful approach to data management language has been the expansion of a general-purpose language to include new statements from the data management language. A notable example of this is the integrated data store (IDS) of General Electric,[15] which extends COBOL in this way. The advantage of this approach is that the complete procedural language with arithmetic, control, and I/O statements need not be developed. This has been called the *host language approach*,[5] where, in this case, COBOL is the host language.

The extension of an existing compiler to accommodate a data management language as illustrated in this chapter might be somewhat more difficult, because mode and display information about data items can be dynamically changed; because data structure can be dynamically created, modified, and destroyed; and because record structure is extremely variable. Therefore, it may require less effort to add arithmetic, control, and input/output statements, a few of which are illustrated in the sample language. In either case it will always be necessary to consider the imbedding of the data management language into a procedural framework that will allow the writing of general purpose computer programs for data base manipulation.

The second framework of data management language is the nonprocedural or what is sometimes called the *self-contained language*,[6] which is specifically designed for the purpose of information storage and retrieval and is not intended for use in the writing of general-purpose programs. Such languages, however, may have some procedural capability that would enable the users to generate reports freely or to specify certain kinds of new processes that may be performed on records that are accessed from files.

6
System Control

6.1 INTRODUCTION

Chapters 2 through 5 have discussed specific functions of the DMS that relate directly to user service—the structure of data within a record, the structure of records within and among files, the processing of records and files, and finally the formulation of a data management language. Certain controls, such as for space maintenance, file back-up and recovery, file and data integrity, and security were also discussed. This chapter is devoted to a discussion of factors that control the operation of the system but which do not involve routine and normally visible data management services. They affect the user inasmuch as his mode of system operation and the way in which his files are backed up is determined by them. In addition, the performance of the system with respect to throughput is largely determined by these system controls, and in Chap.7 a systematic approach to the analysis of system throughput is developed.

In this chapter, control of the principal hardware components is first examined. Then the various methods of program (operating system) control are described so that the concepts of time sharing and interactive and multiple user processing can be properly analyzed. Finally, general methods of file back-up and recovery are discussed in greater detail than previously.

The systems of greatest interest today are those that provide for shared or multiple use of the automatic data processing equipment. Over the past twenty years the hardware architecture of computers has increasingly made use of shared facilities as a simple consequence of interfacing a set of lower speed devices to a single higher speed device. This pattern of interfacing repeats itself throughout the hardware of the computer, so that today the time and use sharing of hardware facilities in a computing system is commonplace. Another principle of modern computer construction is that of asynchronous or autonomous component operation, wherein a subsystem is given a specific task to perform under its own internal control, with a given set of dedicated or possibly shared facilities.   Upon completion of the task, the subsystem interrupts the controlling component for which the task has been performed and appropriately communicates either data and/or control information. Since a number of asynchronous or autonomous tasks may be in process at one time in the service of a particular controlling component of the system, priorities are assigned to these tasks so that the master control can schedule its own processing upon interrupt by the various task completions. It might be said that the modern computing system has an anatomy with a brain as its master control and with various organs, each of which is designed to perform a specialized function upon command from the master control. These organs, in turn, may have their own internal subsystems which are controlled in a similar way. The subsystems contain components or devices that operate upon tasks given to them by the subsystem master control and which report completion by means of an interrupt, just as the subsystem (organ of the computer anatomy) reports its task completions to the master control (brain) by an interrupt. There are two ways in which a device can report task completion to its master control. One is by interruption; the other is by being polled periodically. Thus, the autonomous components in a computing system are said to operate either on an interrupt basis or upon a polling basis, depending upon whether the autonomous component interrupts its master control when it has completed a task or whether it must wait to be polled by its master control before it can indicate task completion and transfer data.

It is important to understand these principles of computer architecture when analzing the total system which includes both hardware and software for the purpose of optimizing data processing throughput. The designer of a data management system should understand the relationships between storage mechanisms like disks and drums and the central processing unit that is responsible for processing the data that are stored on these devices. There are also other interactions that involve the transfer of data that are to be managed and which may impact upon seemingly unrelated data flows and processing because of the fact that they may share certain facilities or resources in the system. The next chapter is exclusively concerned with the analysis of the system as a hardware and software combination, for the purpose of determining whether a given configuration of hardware and software, which includes data and file structure, can sustain a given level of transaction throughput.

A notable extension of the principles of shared facilities and resources in hardware construction has been made to software in recent years. Many operating systems being written today allow for the simultaneous residence in core memory or overlapped execution of more than one user program, and these various programs may be controlling different parts of the computing system on a simultaneous or a turn-taking basis. A generic term, *time sharing*, is applied to these systems. In the next two sections more precise definitions and classifications of the concepts and principles of time sharing will be elaborated. Both the hardware aspects of time sharing, discussed above, and the software aspects are important in the design of the data management system. The hardware is important because it bears directly upon the efficiency and productivity of data management; the software is important because it places very stringent requirements upon the control and integrity of data bases and requires elaborate structures for backup and recovery of information in the event of system malfunction. This is particularly important in on-line or interactive time sharing systems.

Figure 6-63 presents the typical "anatomy" of the computer hardware system, with particular emphasis upon the shared processing facilities. Each device is represented by a differently shaped symbol, and the data transmission paths between the devices are labeled with a number in parentheses indicating the number of parallel bit paths provided. The letter "S" following one of these numbers indicates that the transmission path may be shared by time multiplexing for a number of devices attached to the line. That is, given that a peripheral device requires the use of a line for a unit of transmission (such as a record or a string of characters), the line may not be used exclusively by that device for the duration of its unit of transmission but may be interrupted on a regular basis an arbitrary number of times for other device transmissions. Other kinds of process sharing are also indicated in the diagram and will be explained.

The center of a computing system is usually considered to be the main or high-speed core memory, appearing in the diagram as a rectangular block at the top. Three types of processors, being relatively autonomous computers, usually share the memory either on an interrupt-driven, turn-taking basis or on a parallel basis wherein the memory is actually divided into separate modules, each of which can be simultaneously accessed by a different processor. The first processor type is the *central processing unit* (*CPU*), which may be likened to the master control or brain of the computer, since it controls the sequencing and execution of commands in the user's program and performs all of the arithmetic and logic functions of the program. A typical CPU to memory transmission channel of 32 bits is shown in the diagram. In most computers an aggregation of this number of bits is called a word and represents the amount of information that can be accessed at a single time from a memory module. The word size may, of course, vary from one machine to another, and in some machines the unit of access may be multiple words or subwords.

The other two processor types perform all of the communication between the main memory and data storage, entry, and display devices. In most systems, all of the device-to-device, device-to-processor, processor-to-device, and processor-to-processor data transmission passes through the main memory, and it is one of these two types of processors that controls this transmission. They are, therefore, called *input/output* (*I/O*) *processors*, since they control (through very simple data processing as compared with that of the CPU) the input and output of data

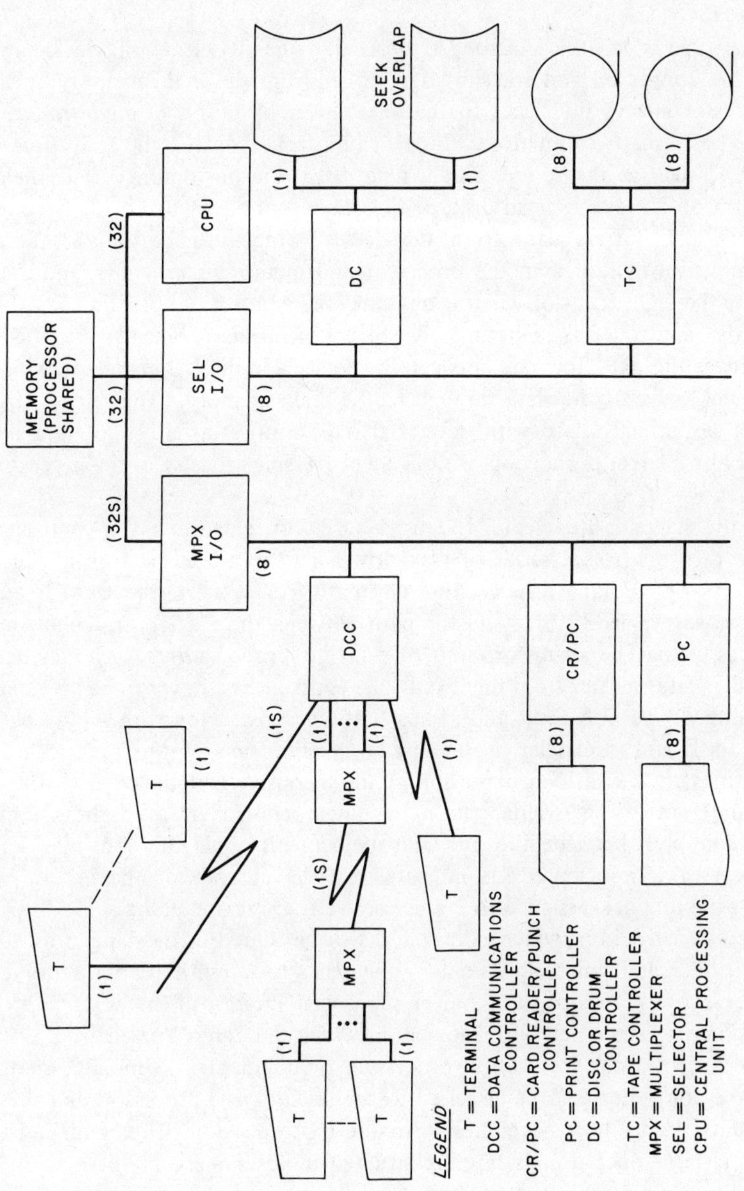

Figure 6-63 Shared processing facilities

to and from the main memory. Some manufacturers prefer to call the I/O processor a *data channel*, although this term somewhat oversimplifies the function of the component; the term *processor*, on the other hand, perhaps overstates it.

One type is called a *selector I/O processor* since it selects one device at a time to be connected and transmit data to or from the main memory. The I/O processor always interfaces to the data device by means of a *controller*, a unit that performs two functions. First, it physically controls the activation of the device, such as the spinning of a tape drive, the positioning of the head mechanism on a movable head disk, or the reading of a punched card. Second, it collects and buffers data from the device, which usually transfers at a considerably lower rate than the processor and memory can handle, and then interrupts the I/O processor when it has collected a buffer full of data. For this reason, the controller is sometimes called a *synchronizer,* since it essentially synchronizes the data flow rate between the device and the I/O processor, which in turn will transmit the data through to the main memory. The selector I/O processor is normally used with devices that transmit at a fairly high rate and hence require a larger proportion of the data processing capacity of the processor or channel.

In the diagram, the selector I/O processor is connected to a disk controller, which in turn controls a series of disk drives, and to a tape controller, which controls a series of tape drives. The data path from the I/O processor to the memory is shown as 32 bits, and the path between the disk controller and the I/O processor may be a subword unit of eight bits, called a *byte*, or it may be a full word. Data transfer from the disk to the controller is shown to be bit serial, although there are also disks and drums that are constructed with a byte path between disk and controller. The disk controller can set the various head mechanisms of the disk into motion simultaneously, and hence *seek* (head positioning) activity is overlapped on a single controller, even though the transmission path between the disk and main memory via the controller and I/O processor is not shared, as indicated by the absence of the letter "S" following the numbers assigned to the respective transmission paths.

This construction, which allows seeks to be shared or overlapped by the same controller, and which allows only a single disk to transmit at a time through the selector I/O processor, is a matter of central interest in the next chapter, which is largely concerned with the way in which data are accessed from disks in response to various transaction processing requirements. Normally, a large number of controllers can be attached to the selector I/O processor, and these attachments simply become addresses to the I/O processor. The command to perform an I/O operation is initially situated in main memory, because it is part of the user's programs, but when the CPU encounters such a command or chain of commands within its control sequence, it automatically assigns them for execution to the appropriate I/O processor, as indicated by the type of device that is being called for within the command. In some computers, like the Burroughs B6500, the I/O processors are not assigned specific device controllers, but are dynamically allocated to a controller at the time service is required. These commands are then executed by the I/O processor, usually directly out of main memory, without any further attention from the CPU. Depending upon the type of I/O command, the CPU will either suspend its activity until the completion of the I/O operation or will continue execution of subsequent commands in parallel with the execution of the I/O operations. In the latter case programmer has some additional options. The CPU can periodically poll the status of the I/O processor for completion and in this way receive an indication of the state of processing of the I/O command or set of comamnds; alternatively, the CPU may rely entirely upon an interrupt by the I/O processor upon its completion. When the CPU continues its control sequence on an overlapped basis, it may again encounter additional I/O commands which may also be directed to the same I/O processor and even to the same device as the previous command; hence, I/O commands can be stacked for the I/O processor and may even be assigned various priorities for execution.

The other type of I/O processor is called a multiplexer. It can attach itself simultaneously to more than one controller and can intermix the respective data flows from these controllers. For this reason, the letter S is attached to the transmission path between the multiplexer and the memory. It can perform this mixing of data flows even if the controllers transmit at different speeds, but it may not mix a combined data flow rate that exceeds the rate at which main memory can be accessed. In practice, the multiplexer operates at some fraction, like 80 percent, of full main memory access rate. The multiplexer normally controls lower speed devices, such as typewriter terminals, card readers, punches, and line printers. In some systems, high-speed devices such as disks and tapes can also be multiplexed.

The DCC block shown in the diagram actually contains a number of components that perform more than the function of a controller; a character is transmitted along the data line (usually a telephone line) as a series of bits that are collected in a one-byte data buffer associated with the data line (a double buffer may be used to increase the turnaround time). When the buffer is full, it sets a flag. The controller scans the flags sequentially and, whenever set, transfers the buffer to its own storage and in turn inserts the byte in to the multiplexed data stream to main memory. The reason that scanning can be used in this way, as well as that the bits arriving from the data communication line do not have to be multiplexed through the DCC, is that the rate of transfer between the DCC and the multiplexer is so much faster than the rate of transmission along a low-speed data communication line that, if required, all data lines—were they to arrive in a filled state simultaneously—could be emptied one after the other in the above described manner without losing a single character from any of the lines.

Typically, a data communication cluster on a single controller may consist of 64 lines. If each line were to transmit at 15 characters per second, the transmission rate for all 64 lines would be only 960 characters per second. Since the multiplexer to memory transfer rate is on the order of 4 million characters per second, it is readily seen how simple a task it is to sequentially scan this number of lines by a single controller and to inject such a data flow into the multiplexer data stream. In fact, a multiplexing I/O processor could support a large number of such data communication controllers. The sharing of hardware facilities, however, extends itself even beyond the controller, in the case of low-speed data communications, as indicated in the upper left-hand part of the diagram. Since the transmission lines that are used for normal low-speed data communication can handle up to around 250 characters per second, the typical low-speed typewriter operating from 10 to 30 characters per second is greatly under-utilizing the line. The line facility can be shared either by multiplexing the terminal transmissions or by attaching a number of terminals in a series to a single line, where each terminal transmits a bit serial stream along the line, but where the DCC acts somewhat like a selector channel, selecting one terminal at a time for single-character transmission. This latter type of connection is called *line dropping*, where the device, which is passive, is activated for transmission by a peripheral subcomponent of the controller that specifically services a particular line.

Figure 6-63 illustrates how processing facilities are shared throughout the entire computer hardware system for the express purpose of maximizing data flow and total system processing capacity. These same principles have only recently been applied to operating system software design, and here they have had a special impact on data management system design. In the next section a number of definitions are made that will clarify the many concepts and techniques that are utilized in the implementation of facility sharing software. In Par. 6.3 the techniques of implementation are further explained and classified. The purpose of Pars. 6.1 through 6.3 is to describe and illustrate briefly the way in which a computer system is assembled for maximum processing efficiency and capacity within the limits of present technology. Two facts then follow from this presentation that bear upon the design of data management systems. One is that very special problems are introduced because of facility sharing; these relate to file access, security, and integrity. The second is that facility sharing control in a computing system will impact the design of data and file structures, particularly with regard to throughput in on-line or interactive systems. Paragraph 6.4 therefore discusses the problems and methods of solution for the recovery of file integrity from system malfunction in this type of operational environment. Chapter 7 will discuss processing efficiency and throughput in a facility sharing computer system.

6.2   DEFINITIONS

Time sharing is an umbrella concept and as such not a very definitive term. It embraces a number of operational modes, and a variety of techniques are employed in its implementation. Time sharing, with respect to hardware construction, has already been discussed, as well as illustrated in Fig. 6-63. With respect to software, it refers to the ability of an operating system to control the execution of more than a single program at one time. Distinction is made in time-sharing systems between *interactive* and *batched* processing. The former is sometimes called on-line or real-time processing, and for some persons it is the only type of computer system that would be called *time sharing.* However, it is considered here more useful to apply the concept of time sharing to both types of processing, because some of the techniques that are used to effect the sharing of computer resources are applied in both interactive and batched systems, the major difference being in the criterion of resource optimization. Interactive time sharing assigns priority to the processing that is required for reacting to terminal input and output, because, by its definition, this processing is interacting in some way with the user, who is sitting at the terminal, providing the input data and expecting output data from a process, usually in order to make another response. Processes such as the editing of data, the debugging of programs, and the execution of relatively short transactions or transaction chains are characteristic of interactive processing. If a trade-off involves the better utilization of disk space versus access speed in order to service a group of users more economically rather than provide fast response to an individual user, the trade-off will normally be made in favor of the latter alternative in interactive systems. In contrast, the batched processing system attempts to minimize overall system cost and thus make the system as economical as possible for each individual user, with secondary regard to individual job completion time.

Multiprogramming is the residence of more than one user program in execution memory at a given time. The system monitor or executive may switch processor control among the jobs without waiting for the completion of any given job. The definition of multiprogramming depends upon both of these factors, namely, simultaneous residency in core and interruptibility of execution by any processor before normal termination of the run.

A program is said to be *reentrant* if it can be interrupted while in control of a given user and placed under the control of another user program (which usually starts at the beginning of the program) before the first user has completed execution and given up ultimate control; furthermore, the interrupted program must be able to regain control and continue to use the program as though the other user had never been given control. This adaptability essentially requires that any modifications of the program or of data areas within the program that a given user will make while in control must not in any way be allowed to affect the operation of the program for the other user. A reentrant program, therefore, is structured in such a way that all modifiable code and data are separable from the program itself and must be preserved in some automatic way for use and reuse by the respective user programs that concurrently share the code at any given time.

Virtual memory is the effective space addressable by a single user program. Usually this space is considered to be equal in size to some portion of the physical core memory that has been dedicated for program execution. There are, however, two ways that the memory space, within which a program is built and executed, can be increased in size beyond a given physical allocation. One way is by means of overlays, wherein blocks of code are executed in series with one block overlaying another at the time at which it is to be executed. The second and considerably more significant way of extending virtual memory beyond physical memory is by means of the virtual memory machine. This is a hardware characteristic and is illustrated in Fig. 6-64. The physical core memory is divided into equal-length subdivisions called *pages*. These are graphically portrayed at the right side of the diagram by a physical memory that is

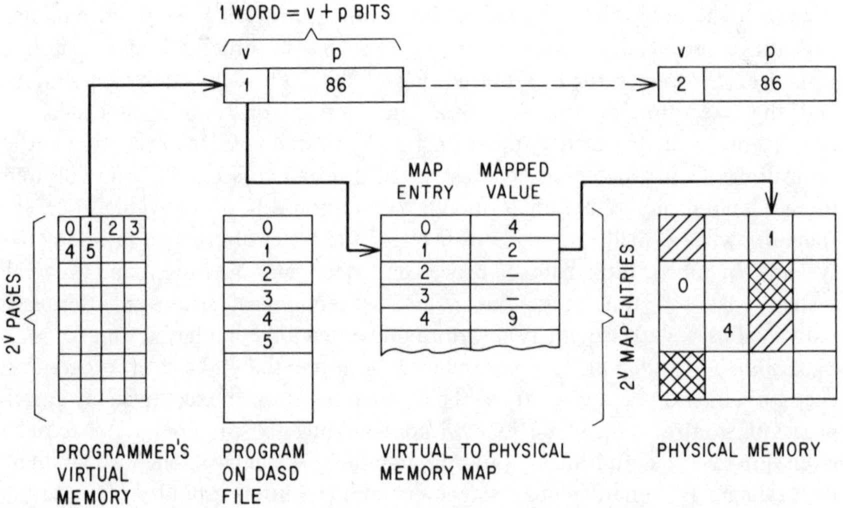

Figure 6-64 The virtual memory machine

subdivided into sixteen pages. Each page contains 2^p words, typically 512. At the left side of the diagram is shown the programmer's virtual memory, which is normally greater than the number of pages in the physical memory. As an example, the physical memory is shown to contain 16 pages, and the programmer's virtual memory, 32 pages. The memory address is composed of v + p bits, where the v and the p parts are separately decoded and processed, as shown at the top of the diagram. The v part designates the page in virtual memory in which the word is contained, and the p part designates the word within the page.

In the illustration, it is shown that a program is contained in six pages (0 through 5), and that this six-page program is also stored in the DASD program file, in page sequence, but randomly accessible by page. When the program is to be executed, all or a part of the program, where a part may be as small as one page, will be loaded into physical memory. If it is the case that the virtual memory is larger than the physical memory, and that a program occupies more space in the virtual memory than exists in the physical memory, then all of the program cannot be loaded into the physical memory at one time. The example shows that three of the six pages are actually loaded into the physical memory (pages 0, 1, and 4), but not contiguously. In principle, the program execution can begin with only the one page with which the program starts being loaded into memory. This loading is controlled by the system monitor, which in a multiprogramming environment looks for an available page or set of pages in the physical memory in which to load the program. In the example, it has loaded page 1 of the program into page 2 of the physical memory; it has loaded page 0 of the program into page 4 of the physical memory, and page 4 of the program into page 9 of the physical memory. The shaded and cross-hatched pages are presumed to be occupied by other programs.

A hardware table called the virtual-to-physical-memory map is used to translate from the program designated page to the physical memory designated page. As indicated in the illustration, page 0 of the program appears in the 0th position of the table and is translated via this table to page 4 of the physical memory; program page 1 is translated to physical memory page 2; and program page 4 is translated to physical memory page 9. Program page 2 is not translated at all into a physical memory address, because at this point in time it has not been loaded. With every memory-address decoding cycle, the v part of the word must be translated via the map and then concatenated with the p part in order to permit its physical access into core memory. The example shows that the virtual memory address, 186, is translated to 286 through the v mapping. Typically this translation is performed in a few tens of nanoseconds and thus adds that many nanoseconds to the basic memory cycle of the machine. For example, the memory cycle may be 800 nanoseconds and the translation 50 nanoseconds, yielding an effective cycle time of 850 nanoseconds. Note that the translation process is a dynamic one; the actual address references in the program are always in terms of the programmer's virtual memory space and are translated into physical memory space only at the time at which the given instruction is being executed. Therefore, a data or instruction access can reference a program word that is not currently located in physical memory.

With reference to the example, it may occur that a word in page 1 will reference a word as data or as an instruction transfer in page 3, and when the hardware translation takes place, it will be seen from the map that page 3 is not currently resident in core; a READ command is immediately issued for record 3 in the program file on the DASD. Program execution, of course, is interrupted at this point, whereupon CPU control would normally pass to another program in physical memory. When control is transferred, the entire map of the former program must be written to a specially designated position in the program (DASD or swapper) file, and the map of the program in current control is read from its program file since there can only be one mapping in execution at any time. When page 3 has been read from the DASD and has been allocated space in the physical memory, execution of the former program can continue in its turn, whereupon its map is restored and updated with an entry in position 3 containing the assigned physical memory page. If no available page space exists in the physical memory for the new page, one of the other pages, either of this program or of another, must be written to the program file and its space thereby released for use by the required page. Pages can also be write-protected by means of a bit appended to each map entry, and a write-protected page need not be written back to the program file since its content cannot have been changed. The nonmodifiable code position of a re-entrant program would be handled in such a way.

It is important to note that virtual memory space is not subdivided among all of the time-sharing system at a given time, but rather is available in its entirety to each user because each user has his own program file on the DASD, which may contain, for a given program, as many pages as are available in the entire virtual memory. It is only at the time of page loading into the physical memory that a scarce resource is encountered, being the physical memory which must be shared by all programs concurrently in execution; by means of the above described swapping of pages, it is possible to enable concurrent execution of many programs, each of which sees the entire virtual memory as its program space.

In the virtual memory machine it is possible for a page to be brought into physical memory, to be swapped out to disk, and then to be brought back into memory again in another page location. All that need be changed is the table entry in the map. In systems that do not have virtual memory hardware, there is still the ability to locate a program anywhere in core. When a program is compiled, all addresses normally reference a fixed location such as address 0, and when it is loaded into core memory for execution, all address references are offset by a constant depending upon the initial loading position of the program. This process is called *relocation*. It is normally performed as a software function by a program called the loader. Since the loader must add the constant off-set to every memory reference in the program, it is a relatively time-consuming process. In such systems, therefore, it would not be desirable to relocate the program continually in different parts of the memory with each roll-out and roll-in. Instead, the program is loaded once and either remains in core during the entire execution of the run, or, if swapped, is reloaded into the same location.

Certain machines have *hardware relocation,* which, like the virtual memory, adds the offset to each address reference at memory access time. The difference, however, is that there is usually one (although sometimes two) offset values. That is, the entire program is offset when loaded, and the single relocation constant is loaded into a register, called the *relocation register*; it is added to every memory reference at the time that it is used to access data or instructions from the memory. The relocation register actually consists of two registers; one contains the lower bound or initial loading position of the program, and the other contains the upper bound. The program must then be loaded contiguously between these two limits, and the hardware address decoder that automatically adds the lower-bound register to every memory access also tests it against the upper-bound register to assure that the program is not addressing a location outside of its allocated boundary.

In some systems two sets of relocation registers are provided so that re-entrant programs can be loaded under the control of one set of registers and the modifiable data areas under the other. In this way the program which is being commonly used does not have to be swapped, and the data areas for the various users can be swapped as required. The relocation register can be implemented as either a paged or nonpaged memory. The register is shorter if it is used with a paged memory because the offset has to be measured only in integral values of pages, whereas if the offset is continuous throughout memory, then the relocation register, like an index register, must have as many bits as required to address the entire memory.

Normally, an entire program is loaded at execution time, although it may be swapped and relocated as required by the time-sharing monitor. When used in this way, the program space seen by the user *cannot* be larger than the physical memory, in contrast with the virtual mapped memory system. It would be inefficient to operate a relocation register system as though it were a mapped virtual memory by segmenting the programs by page or page multiples, because only one set of contiguously loaded pages could be brought into the memory at a time; if the number of pages were too small, the monitor would be continually swapping program segments; if the number of segments were too large, fewer jobs would be multiprogrammed.

The term, *file security*, in contrast to *integrity*, means that access to a file, either for the purpose of reading data from it or writing data into it, may be limited or secured automatically under the control of certain users who have the authority to do so.[16] The security is maintained under program control by the data management system through the use of access codes, the characteristics of which were discussed in Chaps. 2 and 3. Thus, the inhibition of file access as a result of security is a deliberate and intended act on the part of one or more users of the system; the inhibition of access to a file by loss of integrity, on the other hand, is not an intended and deliberate act of the users but is brought about by some system-related failure. Security, as discussed in previous chapters, may be stratified throughout the data base; it may apply to an entire file, to a particular field or set of fields within a file, or on a selective basis to particular records in the file. Security may apply to retrieving data from the file only, to updating and modifying file content, or to both. The access codes can be constructed in a variety of ways in order to create various classes of access. One could liken it to a set of locks for which various keys can be cut to open all of the locks or any desired subset of the locks. In some systems it is required to extend file security beyond the data management system. The bits comprising characters are scrambled prior to transmission over a data communication line by means of a hardware device; a counterpart of the device is placed at the receiving end in order to unscramble the bit patterns. It is very difficult, of course, to provide absolute security to files, because the locks or access codes or the hardware scramblers are in themselves algorithmic structures or devices, which, like any code, can be deciphered. Also, the data files exist in a recorded medium, which, in principle, could be accessed and interpreted by a program operating at an appropriate level of control within the system.

A *system crash* is an interruption of normal service. The effects of the crash will vary in severity according to the resulting state of the system when it is returned to normal operation. The least effect of a crash would be simply to stop the clock that controls the normal program sequence in the CPU and other elements of process synchronization. When restarted, with the possible exception of retransmission from certain I/O devices, the normal program and data control could continue as though the crash had not occurred. The next level of severity would be the loss of data in core memory, which would render invalid any operating program that depended upon this data. In this case, a program restart would be necessary, and particular attention must be given to file integrity, because certain data files may have been updated or may have been in the process of being updated by this program prior to the crash. The next level of serverity would be irrecoverable loss of data in the DASD, which could be caused either by physical damage to the device or by writing incorrect data to the disk. If the data lost are in an index, they can be recovered if the file can be read; otherwise one could not reconstruct the state of the disk prior to the crash by means of analyzing the data existing on the disk at the time when service is restored. Other means of backup must therefore be provided.

File backup is the replication of data that are written to a file; the backup file is used in the event of the third type of crash described above. In a word, it is redundancy. *File recovery* is the process whereby the integrity of a file is restored.

6.3 CLASSES OF TIME-SHARING SYSTEMS

The principal objective of a time-sharing system is to optimize the utilization of as many of the computing system's resources as possible in order to effect either a minimum response time to as many simultaneous interactive users as possible or a minimum cost of processing. The techniques and system characterisitcs defined above are oriented toward these purposes. Figure 6-65 specifically indicates the particular optimization that each of the salient system characteristics is designed to handle. The system characteristic appears in the first column, a requirement for interactive processing is indicated in the second column, and the optimization is indicated in the third column.

Multiprogramming is used in both the interactive and batched processing systems; it is intended to optimize utilization of the CPU, peripheral devices, and core memory. If there is more than one program in core and one of them requires the service of an I/O processor, then the other may be able to use the CPU, whereas if there were only one program in core and it required I/O processing, the CPU would be idle. Similarly, the peripherals and the I/O processors will be more heavily utilized if there are many programs in core, because it is frequently the case that a single program will issue an I/O command and suspend all processing until the data have been transferred. Multiprogramming enables core to be utilized for program execution on a more continual basis than otherwise; without multiprogramming, the memory may be as fully utilized, but as much with swapping as with program execution.

SYSTEM CHARACTERISTIC	INTERACTIVE PROCESSING REQUIREMENT	OPTIMIZATION
MULTIPROGRAMMING	NO	(1) CPU (2) PERIPHERALS (3) CORE
SWAPPING	YES	(1) CORE (2) NUMBER OF TERMINALS
HARDWARE RELOCATION	YES	SWAPPING
MEMORY MAP	YES	(1) SIZE OF VIRTUAL MEMORY SPACE (2) MULTI-PROGRAMMING (3) HARDWARE RELOCATION
RE-ENTRANT CODING	NO	(1) CORE (2) MULTIPROGRAMMING

Figure 6-65 Time-sharing resource optimization

Swapping, the second system characteristic shown in Fig. 6-65, is normally a requirement only of interactive processing. It is inherently inefficient in that input/output processing, over and above the normal requirements of the user's program, is required to roll the program in and out. This inefficiency is largely overcome by the provision of a separate channel or I/O processor and a high-performance swapping disk or drum. In some cases these drums can transfer data at memory speed and have a random access of from 5 to 10 milliseconds. Swapping primarily optimizes the use of core by making it available, albeit on a distributive basis, to a larger number of users within a given time span than is possible without swapping. In this way it also optimizes the number of terminals that can simultaneously process interactively.

The third characteristic—hardware relocation—optimizes swapping and therefore is also a requirement only of interactive processing. It basically enables the time-sharing monitor to roll a program back into memory to a location other than the one it rolled it out of.

The memory map optimizes virtual memory space by enabling the program space to be greater than the size of physical memory. In this way if effectively enlarges core and thereby optimizes multiprogramming. It is also a refinement on hardware relocation, since the memory map can be looked upon as a large series of relocation registers. Therefore, it optimizes hardware relocation, which in turn is an optimization of swapping.

The last characteristic given in the figure is *re-entrant coding*, which optimizes core utilization in that many programs may share the same core via usage of the re-entrant code. Re-entrant coding effectively increases multiprogramming, because more user programs can be considered to be in operation at the same time. Separate memory need be allocated to each program only for its data buffers and modifiable code and working storage. Both interactive and batched processing systems can benefit from re-entrant coding.

Figure 6-66 presents a classification of time-sharing systems according to the first four of the system characteristics given in Fig. 6-65. The fifth characteristic, re-entrant coding, is not a characteristic of the hardware or time-sharing monitor but is rather a function of the way in which code is written or compiled for execution. The systems are divided into three classes, the first two of which are more notable for the characteristics that they lack. Classes 1 and 2 use neither hardware relocation nor the memory map. The division between classes 1 and 2, on the one hand, and class 3, on the other, is considered to be the division between a time-sharing machine (that is, hardware) and a non-time-sharing machine. However, many computers that do not have hardware relocation or a memory map, and therefore fall into classes 1 or 2, are used in time-sharing applications.

Four subclasses of these, labeled 1A, 1B, 2A, and 2B are defined; since two of them are identical, there are only three distinct system configurations. Subclass 1A does not utilize multiprogramming but swapping instead. It is therefore intended for interactive processing in systems with relatively little core, or in the implementation of the simplest type of system where a significant investment in software development is not desired. The subclass 1A system divides memory into two regions. In one region is the time-sharing monitor and data management software; the other region is used to swap the interactive programs on a round robin basis. A program would normally be swapped at one of three events: (1) Its time slice expires, (2) it is waiting for terminal I/O, or (3) the job terminates. A program will not be swapped if it is waiting for disk I/O, because the data buffers are normally part of the program.

A variant would be to make a pool data buffer available within the monitor region, in which case the program could be swapped on disk I/O; however, this would still not be very efficient because there is not multiprogramming.

In subclass 1B systems, multiprogramming can be introduced in two steps. First, a third region can be defined in which nonswappable programs run. The swapping region is usually called the *foreground*, and it is the region in which interactive processing from the terminals takes place. The nonswapping region is normally called the *background* and processes from a batched queue. The efficiency of the system is increased over that of the 1A because during the time that a program is being swapped into or out of the foreground region, the CPU and I/O processors can be functioning in the background. A further refinement

CLASS	SUB CLASS	MULTIPROGRAMMING	SWAPPING	HARDWARE RELOCATION	MEMORY MAP
1	1A	N	Y	N	N
	1B	Y	Y	N	N
2	2A	Y	N	N	N
	2B	Y	Y	N	N
3	3A	Y	Y	Y	N
	3B	Y	Y	Y	Y

Figure 6-66 Classification of time-sharing systems

on the 1B subclass is to add a second foreground partition. In this way the loading of the system and the service to terminal users in terms of interactive response time can be better balanced. When there are a large number of terminals requiring interactive service, the multiprogramming can be directed toward the two foreground regions; when the interactive load is reduced, the background can be activated more frequently. One system that is of the 1B type is the IBM TSO, which allocates an OS partition as foreground and uses the remaining OS partitions as background. Another 1B type is the BTM (batched time-sharing monitor) of Xerox Data Systems which runs on the Sigma 5 and Sigma 7. In addition to the monitor region, it allocates one foreground and one background partition.

The subclass 2A system is not suitable for interactive processing unless the core memory is very large, or unless a special application program is used re-entrantly. The reason is that it does not employ swapping, but it does multiprogram. One notable system in this class is the CPS system that runs on the IBM 360. This is an interpretive PL/1 processor that is re-entrant, and hence every user of the system is operating under the control of the CPS processor and is writing and executing (interpretively) PL/1 code. As a special-purpose system for the writing and debugging of PL/1 code by a large number of simultaneous users, it is very effective, but it is not a general purpose time-sharing system. Another example of this type of system would be a dedicated information storage and retrieval system, written re-entrantly to service a large number of terminals. The only way in which a subclass 2A system could be implemented as a general-purpose time-sharing system would be to provide a large amount of core, such as might be the case with one or two million bytes of main memory or of IBM LCS. This in effect represents a tradeoff between the LCS and a high-performance swapping disk and dedicated channel. The cost at the present time favors the swapping disk and channel.

The subclass 2B system is identical to the 1B system. It should be noted that since there is no hardware relocation, when a particular job is rolled in after a swap, it must be brought back into the same partition and the same location within the partition that it was originally loaded into. To use software relocation with every swap would be impractical.

Class 3 systems, the most advanced, are specifically designed from a hardware as well as software standpoint as time-sharing systems. To date, the software development for these systems has been very expensive. However, they are now proving to be very effective. The basic difference between subclasses 3A and 3B is in the provision of a hardware memory map, providing a virtual memory in user program space that is potentially larger than the physical memory. The PDP-10 of Digital Equipment Corporation system and the Univac 1108 are subclass 3A systems, although DEC is now delivering a PDP-10 with a memory map. A number of computers have been built with memory maps that have been provided with the appropriate software. These include the IBM 360 model 67, the Xerox Data Systems Sigma 7 and Sigma 9, the RCA Spectra model 46, and the GE 636.

6.4   RECOVERY FROM SYSTEM MALFUNCTION

The designer of a data management system must consider levels of file backup and recovery. A basic trade-off underlies each of these levels, where the greatest assurance of recovery is paid for by a considerably greater operational overhead. Regardless of which level is selected, there is a basic minimum of protection that must always be given, and this is the maintenance of complete file integrity with respect to whatever set of files is to be made available for current use. The quality of backup and recovery therefore relates only to how

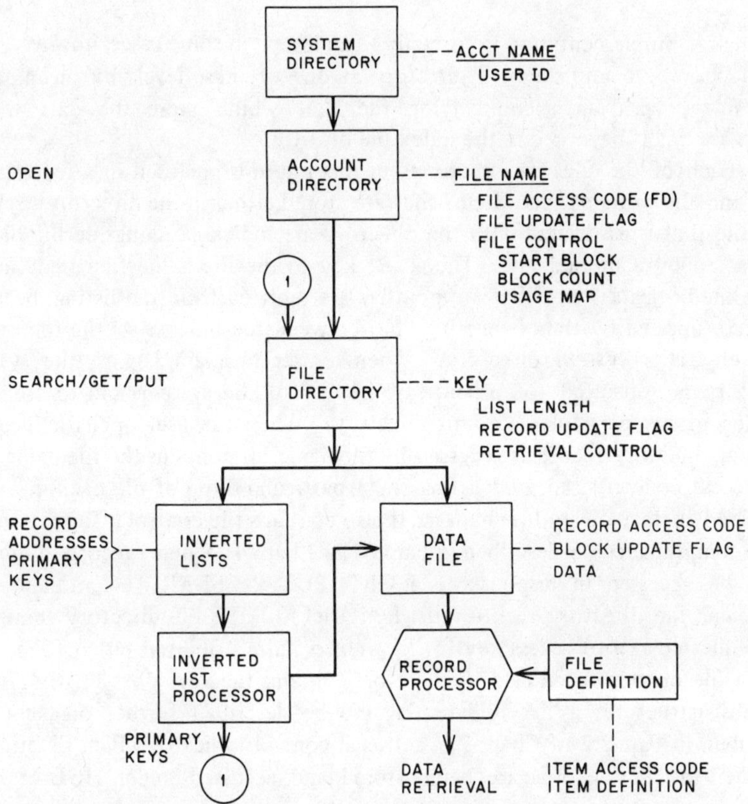

Figure 6-67 Hierarchy of system directories

much file processing work will have been lost through a recovery and not to whether the files that are ultimately made available for continued processing are at all processible. It is also the case that for some types of processing, and under certain conditions of system malfunction, it is impossible to provide adequate backup to assure recovery up to the moment of malfunction. In these cases, a methodology is introduced that checkpoints the state of the file system periodically and, if required, will roll the files back to a checkpoint after such a crash.

Before proceeding to a more detailed discussion of backup and recovery, it is of interest to review the use of the four principal record types in the data management system, namely, *file definition, index, inverted list,* and *data* records. In particular, these are viewed within the overall control framework of the data management system. As shown in Fig. 6-67, this framework appears primarily as a hierarchy of system indexes or directories, with the file definitions, inverted lists, and data files supporting the search and access functions of data management. In Fig. 6-67, the generic term, *directory,* is used instead of *index,* although its implementation is normally as an index; in some cases, however, one might choose to implement a directory at one of these levels by means of a randomizer with an accompanying file that would store the data which otherwise might be stored in the index file directly.

Each of the files or directories in this figure is enclosed in a rectangular box, and the principal data items that are stored either in the directory itself or in a file that is associated with the directory are indicated alongside the block, connected by a dashed line. The access key to the file is the first item and is underlined. Data items that are pointers are omitted from the listing, because they are implied by the connecting lines between the blocks. At the top of the hierarchy is a *system* directory. When a user program begins, the system directory is consulted to authenticate his use of the systems and to obtain a pointer to his particular account directory. When the user opens a file, the account directory record is accessed by file name. It contains the file name, the file access code if used, and a flag for a particular type of file backup, to be discussed further on in this chapter. It also contains file control information for space maintenance, as described in Par. 4.1 of Chap. 4. When a record in the file must be accessed in response to a GET, PUT, or SEARCH command, the particular file directory record must be retrieved. The file directory translates the requested record access key (or keys) into address pointers either to records of the file or to inverted lists. It therefore contains the key, a list length if it is a multilist structure, a list update flag (to be described further on), and, as described in Par. 2.2 of Chap. 2, a retrieval control indicator which determines whether the file records are being stored and accessed under HOL or EOL control.

The file directory will point either to inverted lists or to the data file, depending upon the type of file organization. The inverted lists contain sequences of record addresses or primary keys, and these are processed by the inverted list processor in accordance with data access logic presented in a search command. If record addresses are stored in the inverted lists, the output of the inverted list processor will be used directly by the file access mechanism to retrieve records from the data file; if primary keys are stored in the inverted lists, then these keys must be fed back to the file directory in order to translate them into addresses, and then to access the appropriate records from the data file. The data file record contains a record access code that is used to control selectively, on a read or write basis, access to individual records in the file; it will also contain a record update flag if a certain type of file backup is employed, which is to be described below; and, finally, it will contain the data of the record. The file definition is then used to process the data record by means of the item definitions and to qualify individual items for access by a code that is stored in the file definition record.

It is seen from this diagram that accessibility and ownership of information within the system, and particularly within the data file, is dependent upon the maintenance of these vital directories and data definition files. Should any of these files be partially or completely destroyed, the routes of access to the data will thereby be eliminated. This does not mean, however, that the data are lost but merely that they are inaccessible by the normal hierarchic and random route. Given that the prototype record formats described in Par. 2.2 of Chap. 2 have been employed , and in particular that the headers contain the appropriate information, it would be possible to reconstruct the hierarchy of directories by scanning and identifying each of the record types, and by this means to reconstruct, where data are valid, the original system.

6.4.1 Sources of File and Data Integrity Loss

Data integrity can be lost by overlapped update of a file. The general process of updating a record under any of the file organizations, as described in Par. 4.4 of Chap. 4 is to read the data block containing the record, to update the record, repack the data block, and then to write the data block back to the DASD. If two different programs are updating the same data block of the same file, and if both of these programs have concurrently read the data block into their own respective buffers, then the last program to write the data block after its update has been effected will overwrite and eliminate the update of the other program. The loss of integrity in this case is with respect to the data of a particular user of the file, and not necessarily to all users of the file. That is, the user whose update was effected first and thereby eliminated by the second update, will not see the file in a state that he thought it had been put in as a result of his update operation. Nor has the file been compromised in the sense that the index points to nonexistent records or that certain records are inaccessible. The way to control this potential loss of integrity is either to prohibit two different user programs from having the same file opened in an update mode at the same time or, in a more sophisticated approach, to interlock against access of the same data block by two different user programs, both of which have the file opened in an update mode.

If multiple users are permitted to access and update the same file concurrently, there must be a file control record maintained (in core) for each user to show the current status of the file with respect to this user. In addition to space maintenance information previously discussed, the file control record would now have to record the mode in which the file has been opened, and the address of the current data block that the file has buffered in core. Then by scanning the file control records for each user currently active in the system with one or more files open, the update interlocks can readily be introduced on either a filewide or a block basis.

A second source of integrity loss is the writing of information into the wrong data block. This would happen, for example, if during a PUT operation, an index record from the wrong user were accessed, or if any incorrect type of record were interpreted as an index record and consequently used to address a data block for the purpose of storage. Protection against this type of malfunction is via the record type and file ID in the header of every record, which is tested by each data management processor in the system to determine first whether it is processing the correct type of record and second whether it belongs to the file that is currently calling for service from the processor. As an added protection, the validity of data within the record may also be tested by means of the checksum in the header of the data block, so that if the header is valid but somehow the data in the index are destroyed, the checksum will with the highest probability detect the invalid state of the block. Of course, data can be pointed to and written incorrectly into the file from record types other than indexes. Link addresses within data records can be a source of such failure, and the same header examination principles apply to the processing of data records as to the processing of index records. If in some way data are incorrectly written to disk, despite these protections, then a back up and recovery procedure for file restoration must be used. These will be described in the next section.

A third cause of integrity loss is a system crash that causes core memory destruction. In this case, the state of the data files on disk will be as it was immediately prior to the crash, but multiple record updates (as described in Par. 4.4 of Chap. 4.4) cannot proceed if vital data in core are lost. For each of the file update types described in Chap. 4, a method was given to enable the update to be reinitiated and properly completed once the system is restarted. Some of these methods, however, particularly in the case of the chained list structure, would impose an undesirably heavy overhead on the normal system operation. In these cases, it would be more cost effective to recognize at the time of restart that file integrity had been lost, and to resort to file backup and recovery, as described in the next subparagraph. A similar problem may present itself to the user in his application program, since a particular transaction in the application environment may be composed of a series of file updates, and the interruption of service in the middle of this series, without a normal continuation after the interrupt, could make restart impossible. In this case, the user would want to employ a user-dependent recovery technique, and this will also be described subsequently.

A fourth and last cause of integrity loss is the system crash that destroys information on the DASD itself. The recourse to restoration of file integrity in this case is to use file backup or, if it is an index that is lost, to regenerate it from the data file.

6.4.2. File Backup and Recovery

File backup essentially means file redundancy. This can be achieved by copying a file or several files from disk to tape or from disk to disk, in which case a backup for the on-line file is said to exist at the time of the copy. From this point onward, the value of the backup decreases as updates are made to the on-line file. If incremental copies or snapshots of the file are taken as updates are made, or at intervals during which updates are made, then the original file copy plus the incremental copies constitute an accurate backup of the file system. Three methods of backup and recovery based upon these principles are to be discussed. In addition to file backup, it may also be useful to be able to dynamically reconstruct individual files or the entire disk file system (from data currently residing on the disk) in the event that certain vital information in the system or account directories is lost and cannot be retrieved from backup files. Or, alternatively, one may want to rely primarily upon such disk reconstruction, and upon backup in only a minimal way, in order to restore file integrity. These three methods of file backup plus reconstruction constitute system oriented or *automatic recovery* procedures from the viewpoint of the user. These, however, may be inadequate for certain kinds of applications. Such applications and a method of *user-dependent* backup and recovery will therefore also be discussed.

Method 1–Backup by Complete Journal

Step 1 Periodically, all files are transferred from the DASD to either reels of magnetic tape or, if the DASD is a pack, to another disk pack. The periodicity is a function of the total amount of data to be transferred and the availability and relative cost of the time to perform the transfer. It is also a function of the additional backup that is to be provided, and the critical nature of file loss among the users of the system, in the eventuality that the tape copy must be reinstated. In systems that utilize a tape or disk copy, it is normally performed anywhere from daily to weekly.

Step 2 Every update that is made to any file is recorded in another file, called the *journal.* This includes new records that are added, records that are modified, and records that are transferred from one list to another. The journal record is created by writing the *after-image* of every data block that is modified as a result of the update. This means that the index data block (or blocks), the inverted list data blocks, and the data file data blocks would all be stored as they appear *after* the update. File restoration is made by overlaying the new data blocks in their respective files.

Step 3   Should the file have to be recovered, the state of the complete file is first restored from the periodic copy, and then all of the journal updates to that file are restored in chronological order. This method of backup will restore integrity to the file as of the last update prior to the system malfunction. It also minimizes data loss but is operationally expensive because it adds an additional file write to every update operation, which effectively increases update time and channel loading for updates by around 50 percent for unique key files (since there are at least two accesses per update) and by something under 50 percent for list structured files, since there are multiple accesses per update.

A variant on this approach is to buffer the journal updates so as to reduce the overhead at the risk of losing a few additional updates. However, logical rather than physical records should be written in order to assure reasonable sized buffers and high blocking factors. This approach will necessitate block repacking when the file is recovered because records that may have formerly been deleted must now be reinserted. After the files have been recovered, the user is responsible for determining the state of his files vis a vis the processing that may have been going on at the time of the system failure. In the next section, some approaches to automatic recovery and restart are discussed, where a transaction oriented system is interrupted in the middle of an update series.

Method 2–Selective Dump of Updated Files

Step 1 Periodically transfer data from DASD to magnetic tape or disk packs, as in Step 1 of Method 1.

Step 2 Whenever a file is updated, the *file* update flag is set in the account directory (see Fig. 6-67).

Step 3 Periodically dump only the updated files, as indicated by the file update flag in the account directory. This dump is usually made to magnetic tape, and can either be replacement merged with the former dump tape, or a series of such tapes can be accumulated. That is, if it is desired to maintain only one cumulative tape, then any file dumped onto the most current tape would replace its appearance on a previous tape, and all files on a previous tape not appearing on the current tape would be merged into the current tape. The dumping period in Step 3 is naturally considerably shorter than the period of Step 1 and would be a function of time availability and the potential data loss liability that is to be sustained.

Step 4 If the file is lost as a result of a system malfunction, the recovery procedure is to reload the file from the dump of Step 3, if it exists on that tape, and if not (which means that it had not been updated since the dump of Step 1), to reload it from the dump of Step 1. This method of backup cannot guarantee that all updates performed against this file will be preserved, as in the journal method; the preservation is guaranteed only up to the time of the last selective file dump (Step 3). Thus, the qualify of backup by this approach is somewhat less then that by the former approach. Furthermore, the overhead of this method may be more or less than that of the journal. Since the entire file is being dumped in the latter method, whereas only one or a small number of records is being dumped per update in the former method, the number of accesses and the amount of data being transferred could be substantially higher in the second method; however, the processing activity in the second method may be carried out at a time of convenience and possibly lower system load, whereas the activity in the journal method is invariably associated with the update itself, regardless of current system load, and hence may be relatively more expensive in terms of total system performance than the second method. In addition, if the same file is being updated frequently, then as many journal entries will be required by the journal method, but by the selective file dump method, the file is dumped only once per period, regardless of how frequently it has been updated. Therefore one cannot say in advance of having knowledge about these factors which of the two methods would be operationally more expensive.

Method 3–Selective Dump of Updated Records

This method combines the approaches of the first two methods. Only the records that have been updated are dumped, but as in the second method, it is done on a deferred basis.

Step 1 Periodically all data in the DASD are transferred to magnetic tape or disk packs, as in Step 1 of Method 1.

Step 2 Whenever a record is updated, the *record* flag is set in the primary key record for the given data record in the file directory. If the file is a chained list structure and it is the case that either there is no primary key for the record or other records on the list are also affected by the update, such as the modification of forward and backward links, then an additional update flag must be set in the header of the data block within the data file for each record on the list that has been modified.

Step 3 Periodically all file directory and data file records that have been updated will be dumped to tape. As in Step 3 of the selective file dump of Method 2, the newly dumped records can replace and otherwise be merged with those of the former dump tape, so that only the latest image of any data or index block that has been updated in the given period need be retained.

Step 4 If the file is lost and must be restored, the same procedure used in Step 4 of the selective file dump method is employed. The overhead by the selective record dump method may be considerably less than that of the file dump method, especially if the files are large and relatively few records within any given file are updated within the dump period. The number of accesses to perform these dumps under the selective record dump method will be approximately the same as that required under the journal method, the major difference being the deferral of dumping, which in terms of total system utilization may be more economical. However, like the selective file dump method, this approach will also not assure file recovery up to the moment of a crash.

Method 4–Disk Reconstruction

The need for file backup and the particular methodology employed is to some extent dependent upon the hardware and software reliability of the system. If operations were such that disk file loss, which is the occasion for the requirement of a backup file, were so infrequent that the users of the system would tolerate restoration back to the all system dump (defined in Step 1 in all of the foregoing methods), then no other backup would be necessary. It may be useful, however, to be able to reconstruct a single file or account or even the system directories shown in Fig. 6-67 in the event that these are lost so as to obviate the need for a file backup. Therefore, some systems will rely only upon the periodic system dump of all files plus the ability to reconstruct from the disk any file or account directory at any given time, as the methodology for backup and recovery. The reconstruction, of course, will apply only to currently valid data. Any data that have been destroyed on the DASD will be reported as a byproduct of the reconstruction, and the user will then have to decide, based upon the type of loss, as to whether he will require restoration of a former version of the file or whether he can repair the file. It should be emphasized that the reconstruction may also be useful in conjunction with any of the above backup methods.

Figure 6-68 shows the process of on-line directory reconstruction of the entire system. An individual account or file directory would be reconstructed by entering the flow at an appropriate point within block 3 or 5, respectively. This procedure would be carried out normally when no other activity is permitted against the file system, although one could devise schemes whereby inquiry and/or update would be permitted for already reconstructed accounts and files. As indicated in the figure, reconstruction starts in block 1 by determining whether the system directory is accessible. If it is not accessible either randomly by means of the pointer to this directory or by means of a sequential scan of the file system that would pick up all of the data blocks contained in the system directory, then it would have to be reconstructed by a scan of the file system for the account directories. Via either route, the procedure continues by accessing each account directory. That is, if the system directory were accessible, it will point to all of the account directories. If the system directory is not accessible, then a serial scan of the entire file system will detect all available account directories. These will be reported, so that the operations staff can compare it with a list of accounts, whereupon the missing accounts will have to be reloaded from a backup tape. It is also possible that an account directory will be known to exist from the scan of the file system (block 2) as a result of accessing one or more valid blocks, but that the entire directory cannot be put together because some of the blocks have been destroyed. Either by way of a positive response from block 1 or a negative response from block 1 and a route through block 2, the reconstruction continues in a line, and in block 3 a determination is made whether each account directory is accessible. If a given account directory is not accessible, then a scan of the file system must again be made for all file directories belonging to the given account and the account directory will be reconstructed in the same way that the system directory was reconstructed in Block 2.

It would be more efficient, of course, to scan the file only after all missing account directories had been determined so that one scan would be made to reconstruct all of them. Again, for user notification, all file directories that are found in block 4 are reported. By way of an affirmative response from block 3 or a negative response and a route through block 4, reconstruction processing continues, and, for each file directory within a given account, the question is

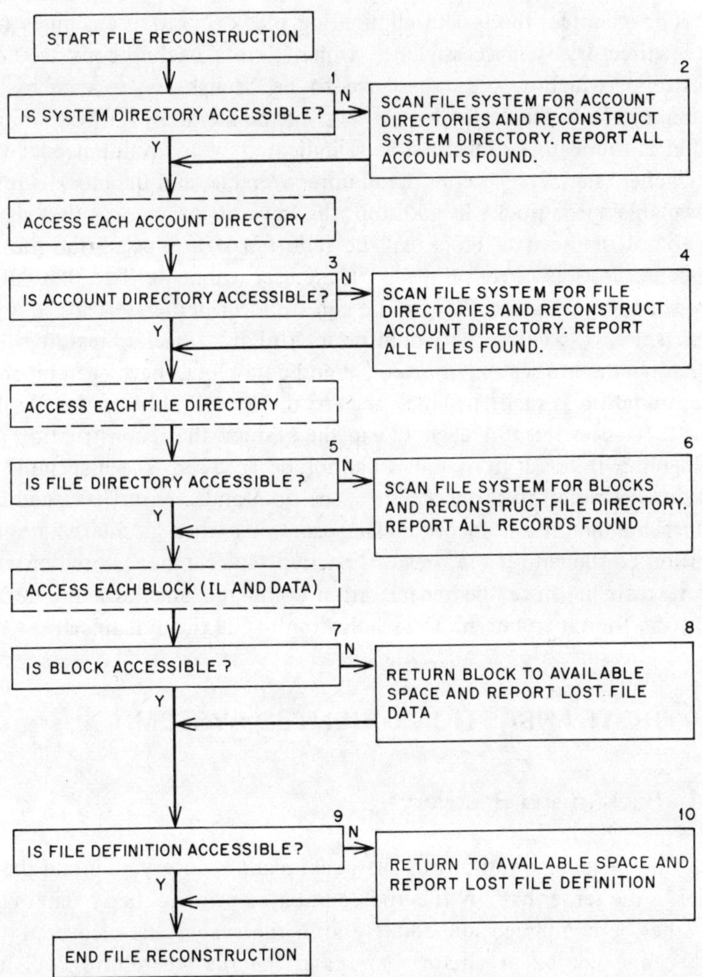

Figure 6-68 On-line file reconstruction

asked in block 5 whether the directory is accessible. If it is not, the system must be scanned for all blocks belonging to the given file and the directory thereby reconstructed. A report of all records may be made at this point, or it may be omitted and left to the user to determine the exact state of the file, and then, if desired, to request a backup. These files may either be inverted lists or data files. As one proceeds down the chart and is forced to use the total file scan alternatives represented by blocks 2, 4 and 6, the value of the yield per scan decreases significantly so that an economic cutoff may be imposed at the lower end. For example, the loss in eliminating block 6 is to lose a single file where the file directory is inaccessible, at which time a backup copy would have to be restored, which would then have to be brought up to date by the user.

Block 7 represents the lowest level of the hierarchy; any data block in the file that is found to be inaccessible as indicated by an invalid header (incorrect file ID, checksum, etc.) is considered unrecoverable, and the block is returned to the available space pool. In addition, the keys of the records that should have been found in the data block can be reported if in block 5 the file directory had been accessible. From this report, the user will be notified that data records are missing from a given file, and he can decide whether to leave the file in its present state, or whether he would prefer to have a backup restored. After the hierarchy of directories and inverted list and data blocks have been reconstructed, a determination is made in block 8 as to the accessibility of the file definition record. If accessible for each file in the system, the reconstruction process is terminated. If for a given file it cannot be accessed, the associated block or blocks are returned to the available space pool and a report is issued indicating the lost file definition record. The user must then decide whether the file definition contained on the previous backup tape can be restored or whether he must recreate it, since the redeclaration command enables a file definition to change the format and even the organization of the file dynamically.

6.5   THE TRANSACTION ORIENTED SYSTEM

6.5.1   Backup and Recovery

The preceding methods of file backup and recovery maintain the integrity of files in the sense that any file update initiated prior to the system malfunction will either be completed immediately after the system has recovered or will not have been executed at all; in some cases the files themselves will have been restored to a former state, as they exist at the time of a dump. Each of these conditions may present restart problems to user programs that will have been in process at the time of malfunction, and which because of the nature of the malfunction, would have to be restarted. Consider, for example, a user transaction which consists of a series of file updates. Such a transaction might be the processing of an invoice in an on-line accounting system, where a customer record, a series of inventory records, and a transaction file would have to be updated. If the system were to crash in the middle of processing such a transaction, and even though the file update in process were to be completed, a restart of this program would misapply the accounts if it began to update the same records over again. In general, it can be stated that where the unit of transaction activity to the user program spans two or more file updates, a simple program restart, at the beginning of transaction processing, will multiply update those records that will have been updated prior to the crash.   This situation is called a *ragged edge*, because part of the transaction has been processed and part not, and if the transaction is to proceed without multiply updating records, it must proceed precisely from the point of the ragged edge. There is no universal approach to the solution of this probelm at the level of the data management system, because the system can have no specific knowledge of what series of updates constitutes a transaction in the user program. However, guidelines can be established for the incorporation of recovery procedures into the user's program or to enable the writing of a utility program for use in the application program that will permit the data management system to effect recovery automatically for that particular user program.   Three methods will be described for this purpose.

Method 1–File Restoration to Last Complete Transaction

The *Back-up by complete journal technique* described as Method 1 in the last section is used as the basis for the file back-up, but when a transaction is complete, it is reported to the journal program which marks the journal file. The files are then recovered only up to the last complete transaction, an indication given to the operator of the last complete transaction processed, and all transactions beyond this point are re-entered and reprocessed.

Files for which writing is buffered (sequential or possibly indexed random) will lose only the buffer still in core.   Also, systems in which new disk allocation is not recorded until a file is closed will also lose all updates into the newly allocated space.   Method 1 requires a lengthy and possibly costly procedure of restoring a file dump and restoring back to a current state, not because these data have been lost, but only because of the uncertainty as to where the ragged edge is. Hence a technique that would simply be intended to find the ragged edge and would not be a more expensive procedure to operate than the file restoration itself would be worthwhile.   Methods 2 and 3 represent such an approach.

Method 2–Backup Journal but No File Restoration

Again the Backup journal technique is employed, but only the before image of the updated record is written to the backup journal.   In addition, the end of transaction is recorded, as in Method 1.   Then if the system crashes, all records that have been updated since the beginning of the transaction in process are restored to their "before image" state so that the files appear as they did just prior to this transaction.   The current transaction can then be completely reprocessed.   If it were desired to use the backup journal both as an instrument of file recovery as well as system recovery (core memory loss), then both the before and after images of updated records should be stored so that the after images could be used for file recovery, as described in Method 1, and the before images could be used for system recovery, as previously described.   It should also be noted that this technique requires that the journal be written by a common program, probably embedded within the I/O subsystem, particularly if files can simultaneously be updated by different programs. Furthermore, a provision must be made, in the case of multiple program file updates, to identify the updating program on the journal tape along with the update image and to identify the respective end of transaction markers separately.

Method 3–Record Stamping

This method eliminates the need for the backup journal and thus can sufficiently reduce the I/O overhead implied by such a technique, but it is dependent either upon the incorporation of specific recovery code into *every* application program or can be applied in only limited cases, as will be described.

Step 1   A unique stamp per transaction is defined as the concatenation of a serial transaction number and the date. This stamp is maintained in a separate control record on the DASD. A field is made available in every file record that is updated in the user system, and the user program itself or a call to the utility program will stamp each updated record with the value of the stamp (serial transaction number and date) that is currently stored in the control record. At the beginning of the day the date must be advanced and the transaction serial number reset to 0. At the beginning of each transaction the control record is read in order to determine the current value of the stamp.

Step 2   By some means the input data to the transaction must be available when the program is restarted after a crash. This can be accomplished in two ways. The first is the maintenance of a journal of transaction input images, so that if there is no file loss after the crash, the journal file will contain the input data needed to restart the transaction. If there is file loss, processing cannot continue with the present set of files, and one of the four above described backup procedures will have to be employed, in which case there would be no partial processing (ragged edge) problem, although all transactions processed since the time of the backup file would have to be reprocessed. The existence of the journal file of input images would enable all transactions entered since the time of the backup file to be automatically reprocessed if the journal file current at the time of the crash were saved. If the journal file could not be saved, and the journal file existing on the backup tape had to be used, then all transactions after that time would have to be re-entered into the system. Since the input image journal file may be sequential (and blocked), the loss is usually limited to the last in-core buffer and file processing can thus be reinstated up to within a few transactions prior to the crash. Returning to the case where files are not lost, but the program must be restarted, as would likely be the case in the event that the crash caused core destruction, the first way of regaining the input transaction is, as stated, via the input journal file. The second way is to reintroduce the transaction externally. In order to do this, the last transaction processed would have to be suitably identified so that the terminal operator would know from which transaction to begin re-entry. Further on in this discussion, various kinds of user interaction in multiple update transactions will be discussed, and the complexity of identifying the transaction to be re-entered varies according to the method of interaction.

If the input journal is used, it is stamped with the current value as Step 2 and then written to its file. If it is not used, identification of the transaction in process is a function of the particular mode of user-process interaction, to be discussed further on, and it would be unnecessary to maintain any control in Step 2.

Step 3   As each record in the transaction is updated, it is stamped.

Step 4   Most transaction systems maintain a log of completed transactions, usually for the purpose of printing a journal of all entered and processed transactions. This file plays no particular backup role in systems with an input journal, but in systems with no input journal and in which the mode of interaction allows processing to lag behind input, the transaction file must be used to identify the last completed transaction to the terminal operator. Step 4 is required for backup, therefore, only in systems that do not maintain an input journal and that interact in what is to be called the *delayed process* mode.

Step 5   When the transaction is complete, the control record must be updated either by the user program directly or by a call to the utility program, where this update simply amounts to advancing the transaction number by one. The processing of the transaction is thus bracketed by stamping the input transaction journal or the first updated record at the beginning and by incrementing the transaction number in the control record at the end.

The above five steps or procedures constitute the mechanism for backup. The following are the recovery procedures for Method 3 after a crash and a required program restart, without the loss of data files. Two procedures are to be given, one corresponding to that which would be employed if an input transaction journal were maintained; the other represents the procedure that would be followed if such a journal were not maintained and the operator were required to re-enter the transaction in process at the time of the crash. A shortcoming of the latter approach is that should the operator make an error in re-entry, such that a different record or set of records were accessed, the recovery process would not accurately restore the files.

Recovery With Input Transaction Journal

Step 1 Read the control record.

Step 2 The input transaction file may either be sequential or keyed on the transaction number part of the stamp. Read the last record on the input transaction journal if it is maintained as a sequential file; if it is maintained as a random file, the record in the input journal that is keyed with the control record transaction number is accessed. If there is no record in the input journal containing the transaction number currently in the control record, then it is either the case that the transaction has been completed (that is, the control record stamp has been incremented, but the next input journal record has not yet been written with the incremented stamp), or it is the case that the crash occurred between steps 1 and 2 of the backup procedure. In other words, the system crashed between the time that the control record was read and the time that the input journal was to be written with the current stamp. Either of these situations means that there is no ragged edge. In the first case the current transaction had been completed, and in the second case it had not yet begun, at least with respect to the updating of the input journal or any of the user data files.

Step 3   If a record *does* exist on the input journal which contains the serial transaction number and date currently in the control record, the crash occurred somewhere between steps 2 and 5 of the backup procedure, and a ragged edge exists. At this point the user must make provision in his transaction processing program to mock reprocess the transaction (that it, to access every file record that would normally be accessed under this type of transaction processing but not to actually update any of the files) for those records whose stamp equals that in the control record. With the first record that contains a stamp that is *not* equal to that in the control record, actual processing of the files can continue, becasue this is the point of the ragged edge. The mock reprocessing can be complicated by certain factors. One of these is the requirement to maintain running totals that may be based upon data in the records that are being mock reprocessed and which have already been altered as a result of the initial processing. In this situation, the mock reprocessing must reverse the value in accordance with the input data and the algorithm responsible for the modification of that data, in order to obtain an accurate processing of the running total.

The second complicating factor may be that the course and type of processing is a function of data that may have been modified. For example, a back order or purchase notice may be triggered as a result of a quantity level within the record. The result of processing these reocrds is to modify these quantity levels, say, in the inventory items; therefore, as in the former instance, the values of these fields must be reverted in accordance with the input data to their original values in order to make the same decision with respect to further processing as was made the first time through.

In the case where the processing path taken by the program is *not* a function of the data in the record, the mock reprocessing function could be centralized in the I/O routines, thus avoiding any special recovery code requirement on the part of the application programmer. To do this, a *recovery status flag* and a *stamp register* are required. When the recovery status flag is *off*, the I/O functions normally. When recovery is initiated, the stamp of the transaction in process is placed in the stamp register, the recovery status flag is turned on, and the current transaction is reprocessed. With every update operation, the I/O routine compares the record stamp with the register. If they are equal, the I/O routine does not write the record but returns control to the calling program. When the I/O routine encounters the first record that has a different stamp, it turns the recovery status flag off and continues processing normally.

Step 4 A notification of the completed record can be displayed for the operator so that he may know the last transaction to have been successfully processed by the system and, depending upon his mode of interaction, to be described, can react accordingly with the continuation of his input.

Recovery Without Input Transaction Journal

If the backup procedure does not utilize an input transaction journal but relies upon user re-entry of the transaction in process at the time of the crash, then the recovery procedure described above would have to be modified as follows:

Step 1   The control record containing the current stamp must be read.

Step 2   The input of the entire transaction in process at the time of the crash must be requested.

Step 3   The transaction as described in Step 3 of the above described recovery procedure must be mock processed with the transaction input journal.

Step 4   Same as Step 4 of *Recovery With Input Transaction Journal.*

6.5.2 User Interaction With a Transaction Oriented Application Program

Figure 6-69 indicates that there are three possible levels of process interaction with the transaction oriented application program under the control of a time-sharing system. These interactions refer specifically to on-line, interactive processing. A transaction is assumed to consist of one or more line entries, where each entry generates a series of one or more file updates.

To use the example of the invoice again, a series of lines at the beginning of the transaction, called the *header*, sets up the transaction with respect to reading certain significant data records such as the Customer record and Code records that enable the translation from code numbers to names for the translation of salesmen, shippers, terms, etc. It would also cause the control record described above to be accessed. Lines subsequent to the header are called body or detail lines, and every such line might cause an inventory record to be accessed and updated. Some detail lines could perform other functions such as recording the sales of non-inventory items, in which case there would be no corresponding inventory record to update, or recording other kinds of charges such as for freight or postage. A terminating line of the transaction would cause the customer record to be updated, a transaction record to be written, the serial transaction number in the control record to be incremented, and the control record written to disk.

INTERACTION	ADVANTAGES	DISADVANTAGES
LINE	(1) RECOVERY CAN BE MANUAL IF LINE IMPLIES SINGLE RECORD UPDATE (2) ERROR MESSAGE NEED NOT IDENTIFY LINE (3) MINIMAL INPUT BUFFERING	(1) INTERLINEAR DELAY IS A FUNCTION OF SYSTEM LOAD (2) TRANSACTION ABORT REQUIRES BACKOUT
TRANSACTION	(1) TRANSACTIONABORT DOES NOT REQUIRE BACKOUT (2) NO INTERLINEAR DELAY (3) MANUAL RECOVERY IS POSSIBLE BUT MORE TEDIOUS	(1) ERROR MESSAGES MUST BE RELATIVE TO A LINE (2) INTERTRANSACTION DELAY IS A FUNCTION OF SYSTEM LOAD (3) LARGE INPUT BUFFER REQUIRED
DELAYED PROCESS	(1) NO INPUT DELAYS (2) ALL BUFFERING IS ON DISK. PROGRAM CAN OPERATE WITH A LINE BUFFER (3) TRANSACTION ABORT DOES NOT REQUIRE BACKOUT	(1) COMPLEX PROGRAM (2) ERROR MESSAGES MUST BE RELATIVE TO A LINE WITHIN TRANSACTION (3) RECOVERY MUST BE AUTOMATIC

Figure 6-69 Three levels of process interaction

The three types of interaction indicated in Fig. 6-69 are called *line*, *transaction*, and *delayed process*. *Line interaction* requires that all transaction processing that pertains to the input of a given line must be completed before the operator can enter the next line. This means, in the case of the preceding example, that upon entry of a detail line that requires an inventory record update, the record must be accessed and updated before the next detail line may be entered. *Transaction interaction* means that all lines of a transaction must be entered before the processing of the transaction may commence and that the transaction processsing must be completed before the first line of the next transaction can be entered. *Delayed process interaction* means that the transactions are recorded or spooled on an input file (or *symbiont*, as it is sometimes called), such as the input transaction journal that was recommended for user dependent file backup and recovery. Thus, the transaction input journal can serve two purposes in the delayed process mode of interaction.

The processing of transactions out of the spool can be free running where the processor automatically removes transactions from the spool as long as there is at least one complete transaction to be processed. The input of transactions is, therefore asynchronous with the processing, and the operator can enter lines and transactions as rapidly as the input spool can record them. Alternatively, processing from the spool can be delayed and all transactions released as a batch upon specific command by the terminal or system operator.

Figure 6-69 indicates the advantages and disadvantages of each type of interaction. The advantages of line interaction are that recovery can be manual if the line implies a single record update, because the data management system will guarantee the integrity of the files in the sense that the update will either be completed or will not be effected at all. It would still be desirable to stamp each record that is updated with the transaction number, so that when the system recovers, the operator can inquire against the record that was to have been updated by the last line, such as a particular inventory record, and can have displayed the transaction stamp in the record. If it matches the current transaction number (which could be displayed for the operator), then the operator knows that the line has been processed and updated. If it does not match, the line is re-entered.

The second advantage is that errors detected in the input, such as check digit error, an incorrectly formated field, or a nonexistent record do not have to be cross-referenced to an input line, but invariably reference the last line entered. In this type of interaction, the system must acknowledge in some way the acceptance and processing of the line so that the operator can know whether to continue or whether there is a correction to be made. With half duplex terminals such as the IBM 2741, this recognition can be given by the unlocking of the keyboard. If a full duplex device such as a teletype is used, a specific signal such as line feed and carriage return or line feed carriage return and some symbol such as an asterisk can be displayed when the operator is permitted to continue with the next line, or an error message displayed if re-entry were required.

The third advantage indicated is that the program does not have to buffer very much input information. Buffering becomes a problem with transaction interaction, since a limit must be placed on the number of body lines that can be buffered. If it is desired to exceed the buffer size, then programming must be provided to write the buffer to disk and to link all the buffers for processing. The major disadvantage of line interaction is that the interlinear delay is a direct function of system load. Therefore, at times when the system is heavily loaded, the operator may be delayed for some number of seconds to possibly some tens of seconds on an overloaded and poorly designed system. What is more annoying is a time-varying change, since the operator would prefer to maintain a certain synchronism of interaction with the system. It is normally the case that interlinear delays above two or three seconds become intolerable for high volume input. Chapter 7 will discuss methods of enabling the designer to specify an expected interlinear delay given an average process time and a desired number of terminals that the system is to service. The second disadvantage of line interaction is that a transaction abort, once one or more lines have been entered, requires a backout procedure that reaccesses the updated records and reverses the processing against each one.

The first advantage given in the figure for transaction at a time interaction is that the transaction abort does not require a backout, since the entire transaction is buffered before processing begins; therefore, the operator has the opportunity to modify any line of the transaction or to abort it prior to any of the file updates. The second advantage is that there is no interlinear delay, and the third advantage is that manual recovery is still possible but somewhat more tedious than in the line interaction. In this case, the operator would have to examine every record in the transaction that was to be updated, looking for the current transaction stamp. The first record that did not contain this stamp would identify the ragged edge and would indicate the starting line for re-entry, although a special recovery processing mode must be provided to enable the transaction to begin processing in the middle. It may, therefore, be as convenient to provide automatic recovery, as described previously, by finding the ragged edge and completing the processing, based upon a re-entry of the complete transaction. The disadvantages are that the error messages must be relative to a line, the inter-transaction delay is a function of system load, and a large input buffer or chain of buffers is required. The second disadvantage is probably the most critical, since, again, for high volume input, a delay in excess of 5 or 6 seconds per transaction would normally be unacceptable.

The third method is specifically intended to solve the interlinear and inter-transaction delay problem but is more complex to program. The delay process or spooled method has the advantages of no input delays, all buffering is on the disk so that the program can operate with as little as a line buffer, and the transaction abort does not require backout. The disadvantages of spooled interaction are that a complex input spooling program is required, error messages must be relative to a line within a transaction, and recovery must be automatic (but as indicated previously, recovery can proceed from the spool itself, used as an input transaction journal). The spooled method of interaction enables the highest transaction input rate and is recommended for high volume, on-line processing systems. It is also useful to enable the operator to control the spool in two ways. One is to allow it to be free-running, so that as long as there is at least one complete transaction in the input spool, the application program will automatically process any transactions currently in the spool. The second mode of operation would be to enable the operator to release transactions for processing in batches as desired. This would enable him to edit and correct transactions while still in the input spool. The input spooling program can also be designed to check input message syntax. Chapter 8 will discuss the design of specific data management applications, one of which is the transaction system, and a method of editing syntax will be described in some detail. It might also be possible to develop certain batch control computations in the input spool itself that would enable the operator to form a gross accuracy check on the input data. For example, the sum of all numbers in a given field of input per line could be used as a control total. In the case of the invoice example, it could be the quantity ordered field of each detail line; the operator would make an independent total of all quantities on his input sheet, compare it with the control total produced by the input spool summary, and, if it checks, could then release the batch for processing.

The identification of error lines is facilitated if the spooling program responds with a line number after it has approved the syntax of a given line. If the syntax is incorrect, it returns an error message instead of the line number. Errors reported by the processing of the transaction are also identified by these line numbers.

It should also be noted that the delayed processing of transactions can be performed either as an interactive or a noninteractive process. In the former case the processor stops and injects the error message in the same way that the syntax errors are transmitted. The operator must then respond with a correction or a response to abort the transaction. In the latter case, the transaction is always aborted when an error is detected, and the error is written to a message file which is displayed at the end of the batch. The operator then re-enters all transactions with appropriate corrections.

This chapter has discussed some of the hidden aspects of data management system control. Those design factors that contribute to the mode of processing and to the protection of file integrity in situations where it can be lost as a result of a hardware or software failure. There are basically three modes of data processing. One is *interactive to on-line files,* where file inquiry or update transactions are processed immediately and on a one-at-a-time basis, that is: transaction in, transaction processed. The second mode is *small batch to off- or on-line files,* where the files are stored on a disk pack that may be off or on line, and file access is random so that the transactions can be economically processed in small batches. This type of processing can provide reasonably fast turnaround because the batches may be arbitrarily small, and the system may be far less expensive to maintain because the files can be mounted only as required. The third mode is *large batch to off-line files,* where the files are stored on magnetic tape, and the transactions are sorted and sequentially processed against the files. The second of these modes has some notable advantages; it can become mode 1 by maintaining the file on-line and by providing interactive processing responses. It also shares with the third mode the advantage that the complex on-line transaction recovery procedures of Section 6.5 are not required. A batch can be completely reprocessed by restarting with backup files, as described in Sec. 6.4.

7
System Configuration and Analysis

7.1 QUEUING MODEL OF THE PROCESSING SYSTEM

In this chapter the automatic data processing system is to be viewed as a machine for which measures of performance are to be determined. To do so, it is necessary to (1) specify a work unit that can serve as the basis for measurement, (2) specify the system performance measures, and (3) specify the machine as a design model. The primary objective of the chapter will be to present methods whereby the performance of a system can be determined from its design model. An analytic method for analysis will be presented that enables the designer to quickly approximate the performance of the system. It will also be shown that simulation techniques are applicable to design model analysis, and that by means of such techniques the analyst is freed from assumptions of statistical ideals that characterize the analytic approach.

7.1.1   The Work Unit

A practical work unit is one that relates to the application in which the machine is used, rather than to an absolute unit of machine activity like a disk access. The *transaction* is normally a unit of processing that can be meaningfully interpreted by the user of the system. For example, one could tell a user that the system can process 1,000 invoices per hour or, more specifically, that one inquiry per minute can be handled per communication line in a 100-line system and that the response time to the inquiry is 5 sec. The fundamental units of work in the framework of machine processing are the disk access and the CPU processing, but the analyst must translate from these fundamental units into an application work unit, such as the transaction, in order to make a meaningful statement of system performance to the user. The *transaction* will therefore be considered to be the work unit for the purpose of performance measurement.

7.1.2 Performance Measures and the Model

The diagram in Fig. 7-70 helps to define the performance measures and to grossly describe the model (it is further defined in the more detailed diagram of Fig. 7-72). At the left of the diagram are n input lines; a transaction appears on each of these lines at an expected arrival interval time of A_n. If a transaction arriving on one line does not depend upon the arrival of a transaction on another line, and if arrival times do not depend upon one another on a given line, then the number of transactions that arrive within a given interval of time is Poisson

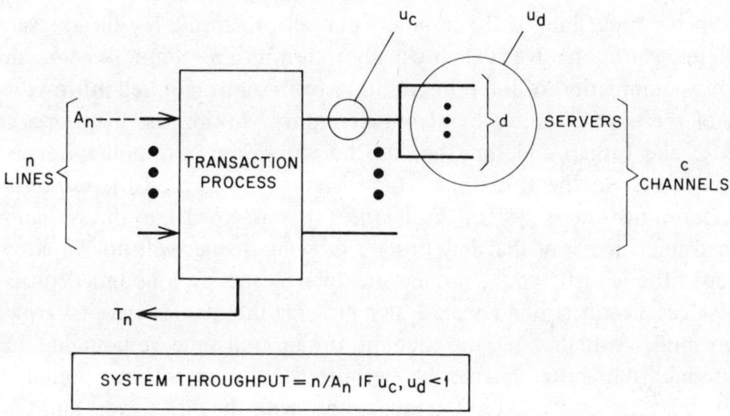

Figure 7-70 Gross model of the processing system

distributed, and the distribution of arrival intervals is exponentially distributed.[17,18] Therefore, A_n represents the expected value of an exponential distribution. The data processing system, for the purpose of these analyses, is assumed to consist of servers that provide the data for processing the transactions and channels over which the data are transmitted from the servers to the transaction processor. It is assumed that the servers require an amount of time to process a transaction that has some statistical distribution based upon the characteristic of the server and that a fixed amount of time is required to transmit the data over the channel to the central core memory of the computer system. During this transmission three facilities are engaged (refer to Fig. 6-63)—the disk unit and its controller, the channel or I/O processor, and the core memory. The core memory unit (not the specific memory words) is time shared with other processors, and if the I/O processor is a multiplexer, it is time shared with other controllers during the period of this transmission. The processing of the transaction can be associated with three specific facilities, each of which requires a certain amount of processing time that is a function of the transaction and the device characteristics. These are (1) the disk accesses, (2) the disk to core memory data transmission over the I/O processor, and (3) the transaction processing by the CPU. Since mechanical motion of the disk heads and rotation of the disk plate is involved in the first two facilities, but only electronic computation in the third, it is frequently the case that the third activity is at least an order of magnitude faster than the other two. In order to simplify the model and the subsequent discussion, the CPU processing time is to be ignored. If it were not negligible, the same principles that are to be developed with respect to the other two facilities can be applied to the CPU in order to accurately model the system.

Two performance measures are defined in the figure. One is the *turnaround* time, T_n, for a transaction arriving on one of the n lines. The turnaround time is measured from the moment that the completed transaction appears on the input line to the moment that all processing for the transaction is complete. An interactive system usually transmits a response over the same line to signify completion of the transaction or to transmit required information as a result of the transaction, such as from an inquiry. In this case the user is acutely aware of the turnaround time because he is awaiting a response; hence, in an interactive system the turnaround time is sometimes called the *response* time. The second measure is system *throughput*; it is assumed that the system will be designed in such a way that indefinitely growing queues will not be allowed to develop; otherwise it would not be possible to specify a bounded turnaround time, since the turnaround would also grow as the queues were to grow. The system model will thus require that the turnaround time be bounded and that no internal transaction queues be permitted to grow without bound. Since transit times are associated in the model only with the disk servers and the channel, it is only with respect to these two components of the system that queues can develop. In queuing theory and simulation, such components are called *facilities*, and the utilization factor is defined as the fraction of time during which the facility is active. The utilization factors for the channel and servers are labeled u_c and u_d, respectively. As will be shown later, the number of transactions that will develop as a queue against a facility with utilization u is the ration of u to 1-u. Therefore, a utilization of unity implies an infinite queue. The system model assumes that u_c and u_d are always less than 1, in which case a steady state flow of transactions can be assumed through the system at a rate of n/A_n. In summary, the performance measures are T_n, the turnaround time of an individual transaction, and n/A_n, the system throughput per unit time for all transactions input to the system.

For simplicity, it is assumed that there are c independent channels and that each channel can serve d disks. In a simulation it is easy to specify a varying number of disks per channel but in the analysis, it is more convenient to assume a uniform distribution of disks over channels, although one can analyze the performance of each channel individually. The model of the machine is crudely shown in Fig. 7-70, where utilization factors are associated only with the servers, or direct access storage devices and the channels. For the type of transactions of normal concern in a data management system, the elimination from consideration of the CPU as a facility is frequently justified; there are two cases, however, in which one would have to consider the CPU as a facility in addition to the channels and DASD's. One is the case where a significant amount of in-core processing, which is a function of the CPU, is to be associated with each server access. In this case, a processing queue could develop on the CPU. The second case for CPU facility consideration is in those systems for which there is channel/CPU interference. In these systems, the data channel and the CPU share a common memory bus and may even share logical circuitry. Then, if the channel utilization to achieve a given turnaround and throughput is high, there may be insufficient CPU availability to the core memory (and possibly shared logical circuitry) to enable it to perform even the minimal amount of processing that is necessary upon the accessed data. The following analyses of Pars. 7.2 and 7.3 assume that neither of these cases is applicable; however, techniques that are presented enable one to incorporate the CPU as a facility either into the analytic approach or into the simulation approach.

7.2 HARDWARE DEVICES AND CHARACTERISTICS

There are three types of large scale peripheral storages. All of them record data on a magnetic medium and all are electro-mechanical. The first is called a fixed head disk or drum, in which there is mechanical motion associated only with the rotation of the disk or drum. The access time to data stored on this device is a function of its rotational speed. On the average it will take one-half rotation to reach any data item stored on the device. This half rotation is called the *latency* period. The second type of electro-mechanical peripheral storage is the moveable head disk or drum. There is one motion associated with positioning of the recording heads over the appropriate tracks of the disk or drum and a second motion associated with the rotation of the disk or drum. The time to position the heads is called the *seek* time. The third type of peripherial storage is generically called the *magnetic card* or *strip memory*. It stores information on relatively small magnetic cards or strips that are held in cartridges or cannisters, and a single memory device of this type will contain a number of such cartridges or cells, as they are sometimes called. There are four mechanical motions associated with the access of data from this memory. First is the access of an indicated cartridge; second is the picking of a card or strip from the cartridge and its placement upon a rotating drum; third is positioning of the recording heads over the appropriate tracks of the card or strip; and fourth is the rotation of the drum under the heads.

The data are addressed on the track in two ways depending upon the construction of the machine. One is hardware addressable, wherein each track is divided into sectors of fixed length data blocks. The block has a fixed address given by track and sector number and is transferred to and from core memory as a fixed-length physical record. The other type of addressing is logical, where only the track has a fixed hardware address. Within the track the data blocks may vary in size and are logically identified by a symbolic, program–generated key that is stored in a separate record in front of its data block. The key record also contains the length of the data block. The I/O processor scans these control records for a match with the key of the block to be accessed or for a relation such as greater than, less than. Thus, the channel or I/O processor is occupied, after the end of seek, from the time an index or start search point on the disk is reached until the required data block is reached and transmitted. The sector or hardware addressable disk will require the attention of the channel for set-up only a few milliseconds before the sector is reached.

In order to model and simulate a system properly it is necessary to incorporate a statistical characterization of these motions under the particular file organization that is to be implemented for a given device. In Fig. 7-70 it is assumed that one or possibly several of these peripheral storage devices has been selected as a server, and that d devices are connected to the central core memory and processing unit via a single data channel. Fig. 6-63 illustrates this same configurational concept, where it is shown that a series of disks is connected to a single disk controller, which in turn is connected to a selector I/O channel.

In some systems, as was discussed in Chap. 6, a disk controller can be attached to a multiplexing I/O channel. The disk controller is designed to accommodate a fixed number of disks. For example, the controller that is associated with the IBM 2311 disk pack can handle eight disk drives. If more than eight drives were needed, another controller would have to be added to the system. If two disk controllers are attached to a selector I/O channel, then all of the disks attached to these controllers must share the same channel path to memory; hence, if there were two controllers on one channel and 16 disks on these controllers, then d in Fig. 6-63 would be 16. If, however, the controllers were attached to a multiplexing I/O channel, the data streams from each of the controllers would be multiplexed into core memory and each stream effectively flows in parallel. This means that two independent channel paths to memory have been provided, and two controllers with eight disks each, both attached to a multiplexing I/O channel, would be represented in Fig. 6-63 by a value of c equal to 2 and of d equal to 8. It is important, therefore, to distinguish in the configuration between multiplexing and selector I/O channels.

Some computer systems, like the Burroughs B6500 do not require a controller to be fixed to a specific I/O processor but can automatically attach a controller to one of several I/O processors, depending upon availability. This increases the actual channel utilization since all channel queues are dynamically equalized, whereas in the fixed channel system it is possible to have a queue on one channel while another is idle. This can be accounted for in a simulation but the analysis assumes the load always to be equalized.

In order to derive the statistical model for a particular direct access storage device, the device specification must be obtained from the manufacturer. A critical part of this specification for the second and third DASD types is the seek time characteristic. An example of such a characteristic for the IBM 2311 disk pack system is shown in Fig. 7-71. Table 7-1 presents a summary of various devices and the pertinent characteristics in the IBM equipment line. All three of the DASD classes described above are represented in the table. The two drums are fixed-head devices, the four disk packs are movable-head devices, and the data cell is the magnetic strip type. After indicating the type and model of the device, the third column specifies the average seek time, assuming that the storage is filled and the data randomly accessed. In the case of the fixed-head devices, seek time is zero, and the random access of data invariably implies only rotational latency; in the moveable-head devices, however, it is not always the case that the average seek time is to be sustained.

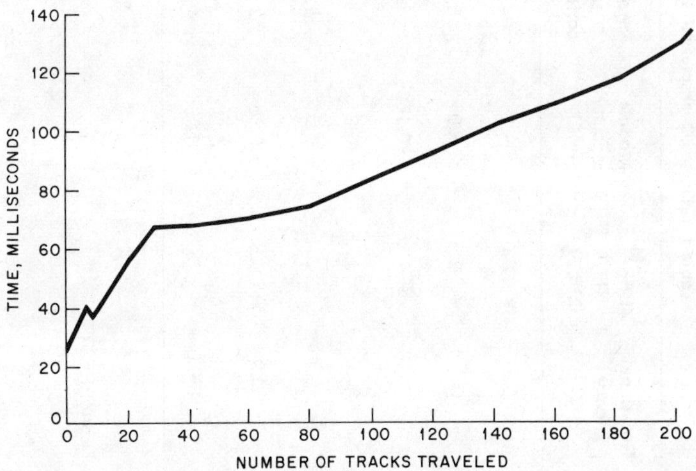

Figure 7-71 Seek time characteristic of the IBM 2311 disk pack

If, for example, a given data file were to be arranged in cylinders such that the seek time were minimized, and the processing of transactions were arranged such that all file accesses and updates to a particular file would be completed before the disk were released for another user's file, then the average seek time would be considerably less than that given in the table. In the multiprogramming environment, this condition of reserving a device for a particular user's transaction, where the transaction extends over more than one record access, cannot normally be satisfied. What can be achieved in order to effectively reduce seek time, however, is to distribute the files of the various users of the system over the d disks (or drums) that are attached to a given channel and to overlap

Table 7-1 Device Characteristics

Device		Seek	Rotational latency	XFER[1] RT	Module capacity	Modules per controller		Module cost	Controller cost
Type	Model	(MS)	(MS)	(MB/S)	(MB)			($/MO)	($/MO)
DRUM	2301	0	8.6	1.2	4	4		2,185	2,300
DRUM	2305-1	0	2.5	3.0	5.4	2		3,900	2,500
PACK	2311	75.0	12.5	0.156	7.25	8		570	525
PACK	2314	60.0	12.5	0.31	$29^{(2)}$	8		$535^{(3)}$	1,480
PACK	2319	60.0	12.5	0.31	$87^{(4)}$	3		1,000	1,480
PACK	3330	30.0	8.3	0.80	200	4		$3,700^{(5)}$	Included in first mod 700
DATA CELL	2321	400.0	25.0	0.055	400	1		2,800	

(1) X = RECORD SIZE IN BYTES/XFER RT
(2) SINGLE DRIVE
(3) DOUBLE DRIVE COSTS $920
(4) TRIPLE DRIVE
(5) 2 MODS—$5,000; 3 MODS—$6,300; 4 MODS—$7,600

the head positionings so that the effective seek time on a single disk is approximately factored by d. The power of simulation provides the ability to determine the effective seek time for a given set of devices and channels, taking into consideration the data transmission interference that the d devices will encounter as they contend for the single channel, and also to determine how this interference acts to increase the overall access time. That is, the transaction throughput, which is assumed in a data management oriented system to be primarily a function of disk access rates, will be somewhat less than that which would be simplistically predicated upon a fully overlapped seek time. The fourth column presents the rotational latency of each device. It is one half the rotation time of the disk or drum. The fifth column of the table presents the transfer rate in megabytes per second of each device. The footnote indicates that the parameter X, which is to be used in subsequent analyses, is calculated as the record size in bytes divided by the transfer rate. The parameter X is the data transfer time and represents the time, exclusive of track search time, to which the channel is dedicated for data transfer to a particular disk or drum access. The sixth column indicates the capacity in megabytes of a single module of the device, and the seventh column indicates how many modules can be attached to a single controller. The last two columns indicate approximate costs of a module and a controller. These, however, must be regarded as indicative and not precise because of the way in which module multiples are sometimes priced differently than individual modules. Also, as in the case of the 2314, the controller is an integral part of the device, and is normally not priced separately.

7.3 THROUGHPUT ANALYSIS

The purpose of the throughput analysis is to enable the designer to determine approximately the parameters needed to achieve a given level of system performance. In some cases, the performance is given, and certain system parameters are to be determined. In others, it is just the opposite; a system is configured, and it is required to determine what the performance will be. In terms of Fig. 7-70, it is normally the case that a transaction arrival interval A_n, a number of input lines n, and a required turnaround time per input transaction, T_n, will be given. It is then required to determine how many servers, d, of a given type and how many channels are required. Some additional constraints on the number of servers may also be imposed because of the size of the data base. That is, minimum number of disk or drum modules may be specified in order to satisfy the storage requirement of the data base. The class of equipment or price may also impose constraints on the number of servers and channels. As indicated previously, certain machines, such as IBM 360 models 30, 40 and 50, are designed so that heavy channel utilization will interfere with CPU utilization. This, at a certain point, may also have to be taken into consideration in the design analysis or simulation.

Figure 7-72 enlarges the model of Fig. 7-70 in order to place in evidence the disk and channel queues, which represent the basis of both the throughput analysis to be presented in this section, and the simulation to be presented in the next section. The n lines enter at the left of the figure and are connected by the data communications controller (DDC) into the multiplexer, as was also indicated in Fig. 6-63. If the arrival interval on a single line is designated as A_n, the aggregate arrival interval for all n lines into the multiplexer is A_n/n. Other peripheral lines are also shown coming into the multiplexer. If one of these should be attached to another DCC with, say, n lines, then the aggregate arrival interval through the multiplexer would be $A_n/2n$. It is assumed that all the data files are uniformly distributed over the c channels so that c independent transaction queues are established for processing against the data management system.* Since each of the channel system is independent, it is necessary only to focus attention upon the queue against one of these systems, as indicated by a dashed rectangle enclosing the middle path between the multiplexer and the memory. The effective transaction arrival interval to this disk system is $A_n c/n$, where c is the number of channels. Because of the finite processing time of a transaction through a disk, there is a utilization factor, u_d, associated with each disk system, and therefore, a queue of transactions to be processed can develop against the disk system. The queue of transactions would be physically stored either in the main memory or in an input spool on another DASD. The analysis of an actual system, therefore, might be multistaged in the event that the physical queue of transactions were also to involve disk processing.

It is further assumed, in the model, that the processing of a particular transaction (which may involve a series of disk reads and writes) can be interspersed with that of other transactions that are also addressed to data bases on the same disk module. The turnaround time for a given input transaction consists of the sum of the actual process time in the disk and channel plus the time spent in waiting for the availability of the disk and channel. In the diagram the process time is labeled P and the disk wait time is labeled DW. The time DW may be distributed between an initial wait time, while the transaction is in an input queue waiting to start processing, and an interspersed wait time, while the disk module is in the service of another transaction in the multiprogramming mix. All this time is consolidated as DW and is represented in the diagram as a wait time within the queue.

In the upper right-hand corner of the diagram, it is indicated that the process time is the sum of the disk access and data transmission time (P_o) and the channel wait time (CW), since, as shown in the diagram, there will be a series of

---

*It may occur that a given data base for which the analysis is to be performed is distributed only over a part of the disk and channel system, in which case the analysis is applied only to the indicated subsystem. In some cases a series of analyses may have to be made for various transaction types and data bases. Simulation provides a more effective tool for performing this type of analysis.

disks on one or more disk controllers (DC) that will contend for the same channel. Therefore, a queue can develop for the channel, and a channel utilization factor u_c exists. The assumption of the model in Fig. 7-70 is that the channel and disk utilization factors u_c and u_d must both be less than one in order for the system throughput to achieve a steady state value of n/A_n. If in the course of the design, either of these utilization factors should exceed unity, it would be required to expand the facility. In the case of u_c another channel must be added; in the case of u_d additional or faster disks must be added.

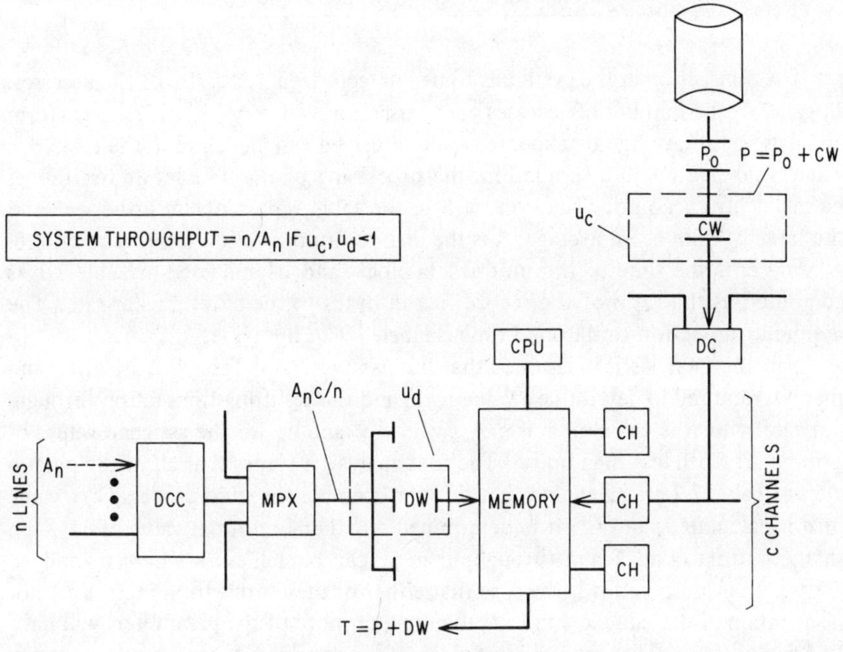

Figure 7-72 Detailed model of the processing system

Table 7-2 enumerates the parameters that are normally given at the beginning of the design process. Some of these have already been mentioned. The arrival interval per transaction per line and the number of lines are normally given, but sometimes only A_n is given, and it is required to determine the number of lines that can be supported. The size of the data base is normally a known factor, and given the type of device, the minimum number of disks required to satisfy this storage requirement, d_m, will be known. At least an initial estimate of the number of channels can be given, and if the desired throughput cannot be achieved, then this is one of the factors that can be manipulated in order to modify the design appropriately.

Table 7-2   Table of Given Parameters

A_n = Arrival interval per transaction per line
n = Number of lines
d_m = Minimum number of disks required to satisfy storage requirement
c = Number of channels
a = Number of accesses per transaction
S = Seek time plus latency time (average)
R = Disk or drum rotation time
X = Block transmit time (average)
T = Required transaction turnaround time

A transaction in the system is to be characterized as a series of file accesses. In general, the number of accesses per transaction will vary. In order to perform an analysis, an average or expected value must be assigned, and in the table this value is labeled a. In a simulation, the processing of the transaction itself must be taken into account. The symbol S in the table represents both the seek and the latency time as an average; R is the disk or drum rotation time. The symbol X represents the time to transmit a data block, and, as indicated in Table 7-1, is computed as the ratio of the record size in bytes to the byte transfer rate. The required transaction turnaround time is labeled T in the table.

In the analysis it is assumed that the parameters of Table 7-2 are given and that it is required to determine a value for d and the resulting transaction throughput rate, which is calculated as n/A_n, where u_c and u_d for the assigned values of c and d are both less than unity. The first analysis assumes that all of the parameters of Table 7-2 are given and that through a simple iteration process (1) a value of d is calculated, and (2) it is determined whether the initial value of c is such that the turnaround T and throughput n/A_n can be achieved, where u_c and u_d are less than unity. If it is the case that either of these utilization factors cannot be maintained at a value less than 1, then one or more of the parameters will have to be modified. This modification will, of course, be a function of the design constraints. It may be within the designers prerogative to alter the throughput requirements in terms of either A_n or n; it may be his prerogative to modify the number of channels, c; it may be his prerogative to modify the device itself, in which case the characteristics S, X and R may change; or it may be his prerogative to alter the required transaction turnaround time T.

In summary, the analytic procedure is to start with a given set of parameters, as designated in Table 7-2, and to follow the steps outlined in the subsequent analysis, which will indicate algorithmically the consistency of these parameters with a calculated value of d and a level of disk and channel utilization that is less than unity. If the algorithm indicates an inconsistency, the designer must appropriately modify one or more of the input parameter and/or decide to increase d in order to achieve total design consistency. The analysis is then modified to show how the number of lines, n, is made a dependent rather than an independent variable.

7.3.1 Derivation of an Analytic Design Procedure

Compute the effective transaction arrival time per channel, A, and the minimum disk storage per channel, d_s, as

$$A = A_n c/n \qquad\qquad (7\text{-}1)$$

$$d_s = d_m /c \qquad\qquad (7\text{-}2)$$

Compute the transaction process time with no channel delay as

$$P_o = a(S + X) \qquad\qquad (7\text{-}3)$$

The disk system utilization per channel, based upon P_o, is

$$u_d = P_o/Ad \qquad\qquad (7\text{-}4)$$

where d is the number of disks serviced by the channel.

Queing theory has found that the number of transactions that will arrive for processing within a given time period is Poisson distributed if there is no dependence upon the arrival of one transaction by any other. Furthermore, the arrival time is exponentially distributed. It is shown below that given an expected process time of P_o and an expected arrival interval per disk of Ad, the turnaround time, T, is given by

$$T = P_o \left[\, 1 + \frac{u_d}{(1 - u_d)} \, \right] \qquad\qquad (7\text{-}5)$$

where u_d is given by Eq. 7-4 and must be less than unity.

Equation 7-5 may be derived by assuming that the interval of arrival time is exponentially distributed with mean value $Ad = \alpha$, and that the process time is exponentially distributed with mean value $P_o = \pi$.

Let p_n be the probability that there are n transactions waiting to be processed by the disk system. According to the Poisson hypothesis, the probability of an arrival within a time dt is $(1/\alpha)dt$, and the probability of completing service is $(1/\pi)dt$. Consider now the quantity dp_n, which is the differential or change in probability of there being n transactions waiting for process. If it is assumed that no more than one transaction arrives within the time dt or that one transaction completes processing within time dt,* then an increase of p_n is proportional to $+ (1/\alpha) \, p_{n-1}$ and $+ (1/\pi) \, p_{n+1}$; it will be decreased if there are n transactions waiting and there is an arrival or completion; hence, it is also proportional to $- (1/\alpha) \, p_n$ and $- (1/\pi) \, p_n$. The differential probability, according to Poisson assumptions, is then

---

*This assumption is valid because dt can be made arbitrarily small.

$$dp_n = [(1/\alpha)p_{n-1} + (1/\pi)p_{n+1} - (1/\alpha)p_n - (1/\pi)p_n] \, dt, \text{ for } n \geqslant 1$$

$$dp_o = (1/\pi)p_1 - (1/\alpha)p_o, \text{ for } n = 0 \tag{7-6}$$

This represents an infinite set of differential equations, which can be solved for a steady state solution by setting

$$dp_n/dt = 0 \text{ for all } n \tag{7-7}$$

Then,

$$(1/\pi)p_1 - (1/\alpha)p_o = 0 \text{ for } n = 0$$

$$(1/\alpha)p_{n-1} + (1/\pi)p_{n+1} - [(1/\alpha) + (1/\pi)] \, p_n = 0 \text{ for } n \geqslant 1 \tag{7-8}$$

Solving this equation, successively for values of n gives:

$$p_1 = (\pi/\alpha)p_o$$

$$p_2 = (\pi^2/\alpha^2)p_o$$

$$\vdots$$

$$\tag{7-9}$$

$$p_n = (\pi^n/\alpha^n)p_o$$

According to probability theory, the sum of the left side of these equations must be unity; therefore,

$$\sum_{n=0}^{\infty} p_n = 1 = p_o[1 + (\pi/\alpha) + (\pi/\alpha)^2 + \cdots + (\pi^n/\alpha^n) + \cdots] \tag{7-10}$$

from which it follows that

$$1 + (\pi/\alpha) + (\pi^2/\alpha^2) + \ldots + (\pi^n/\alpha^n) = 1/p_o \tag{7-11}$$

Let $u = \pi/\alpha$ and evaluate $\sum_{n=0}^{\infty} u^n$ for $u < 1$.

$$Z = \sum_{n=0}^{\infty} u^n = 1 + u + u^2 + u^3 + \ldots + u^N$$

$$uZ = u + u^2 + u^3 + u^4 + \ldots + u^{N+1}$$

$$Z - uZ = 1 - u^{N+1}$$

$$Z = (1 - u^{N+1}) / (1 - u) \tag{7-12}$$

As N approaches infinity, Z approaches $1/(1 - u)$ since $u < 1$.   Therefore,

$$\sum_{n=0}^{\infty} u^n = 1/(1 - u) \tag{7-13}$$

From Equations 7-11 and 7-13,

$$p_o = 1 - u \tag{7-14}$$

Substituting in the last equation of 7-9,

$$p_n = u^n(1 - u) \tag{7-15}$$

Since p_n is the probability that n transactions are in the queue, the expected number of transactions in the queue is

$$E = \sum_{n=0}^{\infty} np_n = (1 - u) \sum_{n=0}^{\infty} nu^n \tag{7-16}$$

$$\sum_{n=0}^{\infty} nu^n = u \sum_{n=0}^{\infty} nu^{n-1} = u \sum_{n=0}^{\infty} du^n/du$$

$$= u(d/du) (\sum_{n=0}^{\infty} u^n) = u(d/du) [1/(1 - u)]$$

$$= u/(1 - u)^2 \tag{7-17}$$

From Equation 7-16,

$$E = u/(1 - u) \tag{7-18}$$

The turnaround is defined as the time to process the transaction, P_o, plus the waiting time to process as many transactions as are in the process queue; therefore,

$$T = P_o + (\frac{u}{1 - u}) P_o = P_o (1 + \frac{u}{1 - u}) \tag{7-19}$$

From Equation 7-4,

$$u_d = P_o/Ad = \pi/\alpha = u \tag{7-20}$$

Therefore,

$$T = P_o \left(1 + \frac{u_d}{1 - u_d}\right) \qquad (7\text{-}21)$$

Substituting Equation 7-4 into Equation 7-21 and solving for d yields

$$d = TP_o / A(T - P_o) \qquad (7\text{-}22)$$

If $d \geqslant d_s$, the minimum storage requirement is satisfied and the procedure continues; otherwise, set d equal to d_s. If $u_d < 1$, the disk system is unsaturated and the procedure continues; otherwise either increase d until $u_d < 1$, or increase c by 1 and recalculate from Equation 7-2.

At this point a first estimate of the number of disks, d, that is required to yield a turnaround T has been computed. An assumption has been made, however, that the process time is given by Equation 7-3, which does not allow for the delays caused by channel utilization. That is, although it may require a time S to position the read/write head to the beginning of the block and a time X to transmit the block, it is nonetheless possible that the channel may be busy at the moment that the disk is ready to transmit, in which case the disk will fly by without transmission and without using the channel for the duration of the rotation time R. It is difficult, however, to statistically describe the distribution and mean of process time extension as a result of these flybys because the flyby does not cause a continuous time extension, but rather a discrete extension of time R per flyby. A method will be described for estimating the average number of flybys per disk.

Assume that a queue can develop for use of the channel. From Equation 7-18, the average length of this queue will be $u_c/(1 - u_c)$ if u_c is the fractional channel utilization. The queue per disk is then given as

$$u_c / d\,(1 - u_c) \qquad (7\text{-}23)$$

Since each unit of delay is X time units, the channel wait time per disk, CW, caused by channel interference is in principle

$$CW = u_c\, X / d\,(1 - u_c) \qquad (7\text{-}24)$$

But the delay is not in fact continuous; when the disk flies by because the channel is busy, the time extension is not X but a full rotation R. Therefore, the delay per disk is more accurately given as

$$CW = u_c\, R / d\,(1 - u_c) \qquad (7\text{-}25)$$

The procedure for estimating the channel wait time, CW, that should be added to the disk access time, $S + X$, is as follows. First, empirically estimate u_c, the maximum channel utilization for d disks, as

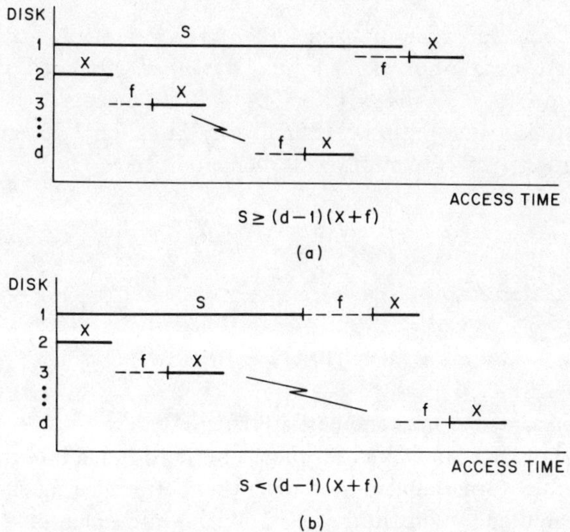

Figure 7-73 Channel utilization and disk overlap

$$u_c = \begin{cases} dX/(S + X) & \text{if } S \geqslant (d-1)X \\ \\ 0.95 & \text{if } S < (d-1)X \end{cases} \tag{7-26}$$

This formula is based upon certain assumptions that are illustrated in Fig. 7-73. Channel utilization is defined as the ratio of the total time used to search or transmit data by the d disks (dX) to the turnaround time for all disk transmissions. This gives rise to the two cases shown in Fig. 7-73. The first, shown in Fig. 7-73a, is the case, $S \geqslant (d-1)(X+f)$, where f is the average time that a disk is prevented from transmitting because of channel interference *and* during which time nothing is transmitted. As an example, assume that disk 2 is ready to transmit at time $t - e$ but cannot do so because disk 1 is transmitting through to time t; as a result, disk 2 flies by. At time t the channel is free and unused. Assume further that disk 3 is ready to transmit at time $t + 1/2\,R$ so that the unused channel time is only $1/2\,R$ instead of R. In this case, f for disk 2 would be said to be $1/2\,R$, and averaged over the three disks, it would be $1/6\,R$.

The other case, shown in Fig. 7-73b, is $S < (d-1)(X + f)$. The maximum disk utilization for these two cases is then

$$u_c = \begin{cases} \dfrac{dX}{S + X} & \text{for } S \geqslant (d-1)(X + f) \\ \\ \dfrac{dX}{d(X + f) - f} & \text{for } S < (d-1)(X + f) \end{cases} \tag{7-27}$$

Note that the boundary conditions, $S = (d - 1)(X + f)$ is satisfied by these two expressions. An assumption is made that f is small compared with X so that u_c is given by $dX/(S + X)$ if $S \geqslant (d - 1)X$ and that u_c approaches unity if $S < (d - 1)X$. In this way, u_c can be estimated by Equation 7-26, and the delay is given by Equation 7-25. Equation 7-3 is then modified as

$$P = a(S + X + CW) \tag{7-28}$$

and d is recalculated as

$$d = TP/A(T - P) \tag{7-29}$$

This represents the final and best estimate of d.

Since d must be integral and is therefore transformed into the next higher integer, the actual turnaround will be somewhat better than the design value (T) and can be computed by substituting Equation 7-4 into Equation 7-5 as

$$T_{actual} = P(1 + \frac{P}{Ad - P}) \tag{7-30}$$

The entire procedure for calculating d, the number of disks per channel, the validity of c, and the number of channels, given all of the parameters indicated in Table 7-2, can be summarized algorithmically in the following way:

STEP 1   Compute

$$A = A_n c/n$$
$$P_o = a(S + X)$$
$$d_s = d_m/c$$

STEP 2   If $T > P_o$, continue; otherwise, increase T or change device characteristics S and X and return to STEP 1.

$$d = INT^+ [TP_o/A(T - P_o)] *$$

STEP 3   If $d \geqslant d_s$, continue; otherwise, $d = d_s$

STEP 4   If $u_d = P_o/Ad < 1$, continue; otherwise, either (1) increase d until $P_o/Ad < 1$, or (2) increase c by 1 and return to STEP 1.

STEP 5   If $S \geqslant X(d - 1)$,

$$u_c = dX/(S + X)$$

---

*INT$^+$ [x] means the next higher integer value of x if there is a remainder; otherwise, it means the integer value of x.

If $S < X(d - 1)$, either (1) increase c by 1 and return to STEP 1, or (2) let $u_c = 0.95$.

STEP 6   Compute

$$CW = u_c R/d(1 - u_c)$$

STEP 7 $P = a(S + X + CW)$

STEP 8   If $T > P$, continue; otherwise, increase T or change device characteristics S and X and return to STEP 1.

$$d = INT^+ [TP/A(T - P)]$$

STEP 9   If $d \geqslant d_s$ continue; otherwise, $d = d_s$.

STEP 10
$$T_{actual} = P (1 + \frac{P}{Ad - P})$$

The final design parameters will then be d, as calculated from STEP 8 or 9, c as determined either by the input or one of the choices made in STEP 4 or 5 and T_{actual} as calculated in STEP 10.

Four examples are given to illustrate the application of the throughput analysis.

Example 1 Consider a transaction queuing system in which each user of the system has a table that interprets his input transactions. Since there are a large number of users, these tables are stored in a disk file. A transaction consists of several typed lines of input. Each line is a record; ten records are blocked and then written to disk; however, since there are many data communication lines, each with a different user, it is not possible to retain the transaction interpretation table in core for all users. Therefore, it is assumed that a disk read for the table is required for every typed input line, and for every tenth message line a block is written to disk, giving 1.1 accesses per typed input line. Given that a disk pack system with two disks is dedicated to the message queuing function as well as to the users' data bases, how many disks must be used in order to achieve a turnaround of 1 sec per typed line on a single channel, with an arrival interval per typed line of 10 sec and 200 input communication lines? The given parameters for the problem are as follows:

$$A_n = 10 \text{ sec} \qquad\qquad S = 78 \text{ msec}$$
$$n = 200 \qquad\qquad R = 25 \text{ msec}$$
$$d_m = 2 \qquad\qquad X = 8 \text{ msec}$$
$$c = 1 \qquad\qquad T = 1 \text{ sec}$$
$$a = 1.1$$

STEP 1 $A = 50$ msec $d_s = 2$

$P_o = 94.6$ msec

STEP 2 $T = 1,000$ msec $> P_o = 94.6$ msec

$d = INT^+ [2.1] = 3$

STEP 3 $d = 3 > d_s = 2$

$d = 3$

STEP 4 $u_d = P_o/Ad = .63$

STEP 5 $S = 78 > X(d-1) = 16$

$u_c = .28$

STEP 6 $CW = 3.2$ msec

STEP 7 $P = 98$ msec

STEP 8 $T = 1,000$ msec $> P = 98$ msec

$d = INT^+ [2.2] = 3$

STEP 9 $d = 3 > d_s = 2$

$d = 3$

STEP 10 $T_{actual} = 0.283$ sec

Final Design Parameters

$d = 3$ $T_{actual} = 0.283$ sec
$c = 1$

Example 2 The average transaction in an on-line invoice processing system requires the following schedule of file accesses for an invoice with five body (detail) lines:

File	*No. of Accesses*	*Access Type (Read/Write)*
Customer	1	R
Control record	1	R
Inventory file	5	R
	5	W
Customer	1	W
Transaction	1	W
Control record	1	W
TOTAL	15	

Consider the following set of parameters:

$$A_n = 60 \text{ sec} \qquad S = 78 \text{ msec}$$
$$n = 200 \qquad R = 25 \text{ msec}$$
$$d_m = 3 \qquad X = 8 \text{ msec}$$
$$c = 1 \qquad T = 5 \text{ sec}$$
$$a = 15$$

What is the number of disks that must be overlapped?

STEP 1 $A = 300$ msec

$P_o = 1300$ msec

$d_s = 3$

STEP 2 $T = 5{,}000$ msec $> P = 1{,}300$ msec

$d = \text{INT}^+ [5.9] = 6$

STEP 3 $d = 6 > d_s = 3$

$d = 6$

STEP 4 $u_d = 0.72$

STEP 5 $S = 78 > X(d-1) = 40$

$u_c = 0.56$

STEP 6 $CW = 5.3$ msec

STEP 7 $P = 1{,}370$ msec

STEP 8 $T = 5{,}000 > P = 1{,}370$

$d = \text{INT}^+ [6.3] = 7$

STEP 9 $d = 7 > d_s = 3$

$d = 7$

STEP 10 $T_{actual} = 3.95$ sec

Final Design

$$d = 7 \qquad T_{actual} = 3.95 \text{ sec}$$
$$c = 1$$

Example 3 In Example 2 can an additional channel reduce the number of disk drives required for overlap?

STEP 1 $A = 600$ msec

$P = 1{,}300$ msec

$d_s = 1.5$

STEP 2 $d = \text{INT}^+ [2.9] = 3$

STEP 3 $d = 3 > d_s = 15$

$d = 3$

STEP 4 $u_d = 0.72$

STEP 5 $S = 78 > X(d - 1) = 16$

$u_c = .28$

STEP 6 $CW = 3.2$

STEP 7 $P = 1,340$ msec

STEP 8 $T = 5,000 > P = 1,340$ msec
$d = INT^+ [3.06] = 4$

Two channels would require eight disks to achieve a turnaround of less than 5 sec and therefore the number of drives cannot be reduced by the addition of another channel. It should be noted, however, that the calculation of STEP 8 yields a remainder of only 0.06, which means that if the system were to be implemented with six drives and two channels, the turnaround would be only slightly greater than 5 sec. Application of STEP 10 for $d = 3$ and $c = 2$ yields a turnaround of 5.2 sec.

Example 4 A multilist file serves as the data base for an information storage and retrieval system. The following schedule of file operations and their relative frequency is known to exist for the anticipated users of the system.

File operation	*No. of accesses*	*Relative frequency*
Single record keyed access	2 (1 index read and 1 data file read)	0.5
Record update	3 (Record access plus 1 data file write)	0.3
Record addition	4 (Record access plus 1 index write plus 1 data file write)	0.15
Multilist search	2 to 100 uniformly distributed	0.05

If the number of disks to be used in the system can be no more than four and the number of channels cannot exceed one, how many terminals can the system service with an expected arrival interval of 60 sec and a turnaround of 3 sec? The given parameters of the system are as follows:

$$A_n = 60 \text{ sec} \qquad d_m = d = 4$$
$$n = ? \qquad\qquad c = 1$$

$$a = (2 \times 0.5) + (3 \times 0.3) + (4 \times 0.15) + (50 \times 0.05)$$
$$= 5$$
$$S = 200 \text{ msec}$$
$$R = 50 \text{ msec}$$
$$X = 16 \text{ msec}$$
$$T = 3 \text{ sec}$$

In order to solve the problem for n, given d and the other parameters, we start with

STEP 5 $S = 200 > X(d - 1) = 48$

$u_c = 0.3$

STEP 6 $CW = 5.3 \text{ msec}$

STEP 7 $P = 1,106 \text{ msec}$

At this point, Equation 7-5 must be solved for u_d, yielding

$$u_d = (T - P)/T = 0.63$$

From Equation 7-4

$$A = P/u_d d = 440 \text{ msec}$$

From Equation 7-1

$$n = A_n c/A = 136$$

Final Design

$$n = 136$$
$$d = 4$$
$$c = 1$$
$$T = 3 \text{ sec}$$

7.4 SIMULATION OF SYSTEM THROUGHPUT

The analytic approach to the throughput analysis discussed in the previous section has two shortcomings. First, it requires an expert knowledge of queuing theory and statistics on the part of the analyst and designer to make the major modifications in the outlined procedures that would become necessary if the underlying assumptions of the analysis were to change as a result of system configuration and usage. The second disadvantage is that the actual behavior of the system is in many respects not statistically parametric and hence is most simply described through a simulation model.[19]

The simulation also enables the designer to fine tune the system by modifying a variety of operational parameters that are under his direct control either through hardware selection, system software design, or file structure.. The effect of changing these parameters is immediately seen through a re-run of the simulation. In the analytic approach, the effect of the parameter change would have to be related to the basic statistical assumptions. For example, if the channel is busy when a disk is ready to transmit, the disk must fly by, extending the process time by one rotation. If at the end of this rotation the channel is still busy, the disk must fly by again. A high channel-utilization factor could thus cause a considerable process time extension, such that turnaround would be increased and over-all disk utilization reduced. The disk I/O scheduling algorithm could be designed so that after a specified number of flybys the channel is reserved for a given disk, but it is difficult to represent such an algorithm in a queuing model like that used in the analysis of the preceding section. The adjustment of the flyby limit will fine-tune the system throughput for high channel utilization.

Since simulation represents activity in the real world, it must be capable of parallel processing, which is incompatible with the operational capabilities of the digital computer. Continuous simulation, as implemented by an analog computer, achieves parallel processing by the simultaneous operation of individual simulation circuit components (called operational amplifiers). Discrete event simulation, which is the type to be used here, is programmed for operation on a digital computer and achieves parallelism in the following way. Consider two time clocks—one called *machine time* and the other *simulation time*. Machine time is governed by the computer clock and other logic circuitry of the computer, and all operations (including those that comprise the simulation program) are performed sequentially in machine time. Simulation time is asynchronous with respect to machine time and represents the actual or real world time of the simulation problem.

There are two basic techniques of computer simulation. One is oriented toward the description of *transactions* or processes that can be executed in simulated parallelism under the control of a simulation clock. The transactions interact through common data storages, queues on single service facilities (on either a first-come, first-served or priority-interrupt basis), and global system variables such as time and the length of queues. Simulation languages utilizing this technique are GPSS[20] and SOL[21]. Parallelism or overlap of simulation time activity is obtained by virtue of the fact that a transaction occurs in nonzero simulation time, which may overlap the start of another transaction. In machine time, the transaction duration is only as long as the time required for the simulation program to execute it, which may be greater or less than the simulation time corresponding to the start-up of the next transaction. The next transaction will not start in machine time until the machine execution of the current transaction is complete, but the simulation time duration of the first transaction may cause it to overlap the simulation time duration of the second.

The other approach is oriented toward the description of *events* that occur sequentially and in zero simulation time. The simulation time duration *between* events is the time during which processes, which have either their beginning or end at an event, occur, and any number of these (implied) processes may be ongoing at one time simply because their starting and termination times (events) overlap. Any event can reschedule itself or can schedule another event, and hence the simulation is perpetuated until some precondition set upon a simulation variable or upon simulation time is met. Two commonly used languages utilizing the *events* approach are SIMSCRIPT[22] and GASP.[18]

GPSS and SIMSCRIPT employ their own self-contained languages and as such can be regarded as packages. They are fairly easy to use, but one must have a version of the simulator written specifically for a given machine because the system package is not written in a high-level language like FORTRAN. SOL is in a similar class, although its statements are ALGOL-like constructs and in any of its implementations it enables the simulation program to be embedded into a host ALGOL program.

GASP is the most portable or transferable of the four since it is written entirely as a set of FORTRAN subroutines* and hence can be compiled for almost any computer; however, it requires FORTRAN programming capability to code the user-designed *event* programs.

The functional capabilities of each of these languages is similar, although the packages facilitate the use of certain functions such as determining the state of scarce (one-user-at-a-time) facilities.

It has been decided to use GASP to illustrate simulation in this book because it is readily accessible to the reader at virtually no cost and is usable on any general-purpose computer. A limitation in simulation capability is imposed on any of these simulators by machine core size and speed. For example, simulations with indefinitely expanding queues will overflow machine storage capacity and must either be self-limiting within the simulation or must be recognized as an abnormal condition that will cause the simulation to stop.

Given a basic working knowledge of FORTRAN (FORTRAN II is adequate), GASP simulations are easy to set up and run, although, as is the case in any simulation, great care must be exercised in both the model and the program design, particularly because parallel processing, though common in one's everyday life experience, is conceptually alien to normal computer programming principles. And it is, after all, a computer program that is being written.

The following is a brief course in the methodology of computer simulation based upon use of the GASP simulator and the *events* approach, but since it will be presented as *principles*, it could readily be applied to any of the other available simulators. The objective is to apply simulation technique to the model of Figs. 7-70 and 7-72.

---

*A listing of the FORTRAN programs comprising the *complete* system is contained in Reference 18.

A number of definitions are necessary as a starting point for an understanding of computer simulation technique.

1. An *entity* is a unit of activity or description in the simulation. Examples are a person waiting in a queue, a completion of service, and an inventory stock receipt.

2. An *attribute* is the most basic unit of description of an entity. Examples are the arrival time of the person to the queue, the type of queue, and the priority or position of the entity in the queue (if other than by arrival in time).

3. The *queue* (or, as it is called in GASP, the file) is an ordered list of entities.

4. The *rank* of a queue is a single (usually initially specified) attribute type of the queue upon which the queue is ordered.

5. The *rank order* is ascending or descending by rank value. The simulator is responsible for maintaining the rank order of all queues at all times. For duplicate rank values, the order of entities on the queue is by ascending arrival time to the queue.

6. An *event* is a special entity and, in GASP, is always assigned to queue 1. Furthermore, in GASP, its first two attributes are *schedule time* and *event type*, respectively, and the queue is always ranked by increasing schedule time.

7. The *schedule time* of an event is the simulation time at which the event is to occur. All the different event types are serial-numbered in GASP. Examples of events are arrival of a man to the (simulated) system, end of service, end of a delay, completion of a task, or start of a task. The simulation is thus driven by the simple act of accessing events from the event queue in schedule time sequence. The simulator is responsible for this accession and the subsequent transfer of control to the user written subprogram that describes the action subsequent to the particular event. These events then generate other entities, including more events, and file them into the appropriate queues, thus perpetuating the simulation in simulation time.

8. In addition to accessing events from the event queue, the simulator provides a number of *functions* for performing a variety of housekeeping and computational tasks.

Figure 7-74 illustrates the control of a simulation program by the simulation executive. There are four classes of subprograms involved in a complete simulation program. First is a user-written main program (block 1) which initializes all of the user variables. These are variables that the user assigns either for the purpose of his own internal control within his event subroutines or for the purpose of communication between subroutines. After initialization, the main program transfers control to the simulation executive (block 2), which is the second class of subprogram. It is not written by the user but is provided as part of the simulator software. In GASP, it is a subroutine called GASP plus a few other subroutines that perform certain data acquisition and file (queue) initialization services for it. The simulation executive performs four functions:

(1) It reads user-provided parameters of the simulation such as initial queue contents, statistical parameters, report specifications, and initial assignments of user variables where it is preferred to enter these as run time data rather than as compiled data in the main program; (2) it accesses the next event to be executed from the event queue, using a file access subrouting in block 4 for this purpose; (3) it transfers control to a user-written event program, according to the event accessed from the event queue; and (4) it terminates the simulation run based upon a specified stop time (given in the parameters) or upon a signal given by one of the event programs. At the end of a run the executive calls upon a report generator (block 4) to display in a standard format the mean, deviation, and, if

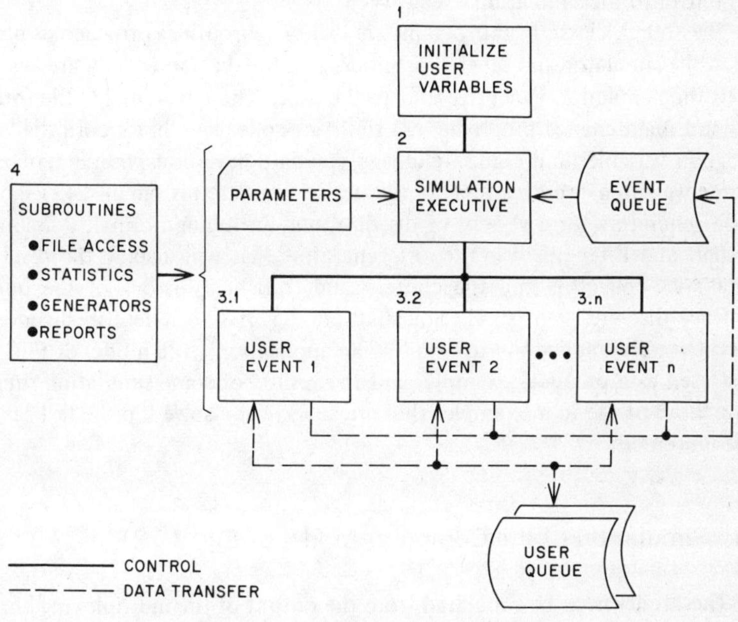

Figure 7-74 Flow chart of simulation control

desired, histogram of various simulation variables. The input parameters are again read and may indicate that another run should be initiated with a new set of parameters. The simulation executive will then reset the entire system and start processing again, but will not return to the main program. GASP returns to the main program only when all simulation runs are complete, whereupon the user is again in control. The user may then (1) perform final analysis and print his own reports, (2) initialize and restart the simulation, or (3) terminate it.

The third class of subprogram in the simulation is the user written event, labeled as the series 3.1 through 3.n in the diagram. An example of an event is "the arrival of a transaction on the line for service." The user must decide what processing and other activities are triggered by such an event. The description of all n events represents the *model* of the simulation. In the case of the transaction arrival event, it may (1) schedule the next arrival, as indicated in the diagram by the dashed line from a user event to the event queue, and (2) find out if there is a disk available for service. If a disk is available, it may schedule a disk access event, as also indicated by the dashed line from a user event to the event queue, and if a disk is not, it may queue a request for service when the disk is available, as indicated by the dashed line from a user event to a user queue. It will then be the task of another event, such as the "end of Channel service" event to process this user queue. When an event program run is complete, it returns control to the simulation executive.

The fourth class of subprograms are utility subroutines provided as part of the (GASP) simulator and labeled as block 4 in the diagram. They are available both to the simulation executive and to the user. These include (1) file (queue) access and maintenance programs; (2) statistics collectors that record the values of program variables and compute means, standard deviations, minima, maxima, and time-weighted averages and that can also generate histograms; (3) random variable generators for a variety of distributions, including normal, Poisson, exponential, and Erlang; and (4) report generators that will display the results of the statistics collectors and the content and statistical history of the queues.

Once discrete event simulation methodology has been described generally, it is most readily understood in detail by an application. The model of Fig. 7-72 will be used as a practical example, and the results of some simulation runs, including those of the four examples that are analytically solved in the last section, will be presented.

7.4.1 Simulation of the Computer Model of Fig. 7-72

The model is to be simulated from the output of the multiplexing channel (MPX) through a single channel to the set of all disks and controllers attached to the channel. The aggregate transaction input flow is known to be $A_n c/n$ before the queue DW, and the effects of multiple channels are linear, assuming negligible CPU interference or negligible CPU utilization.

The hardware (sector) addressable disk is to be simulated where the following sequence of disk operations and states is assumed to exist:

1. Seek—The heads are positioned to the cylinder address. The channel is required momentarily in order to transmit the seek order.
2. Latency—The disk rotates until the heads are a few degrees in front of the sector address.
3. Ready—Between end of latency and sector read, the channel must be attached for transmission.
4. Transmit—The sector is transmitted through the channel.

Table 7-3   Events in the Simulation Model of Fig. 7-72

Event No.	Event program name	Event description
1	TRAVL	Arrival of a transaction to the system (that is, to the queue DW in Fig. 7-72).
2	ENDSK	End of seek.
3	ENDLAT	End of disk latency.
4	ENDRED	End of disk ready for transmission. There is a small period of time immediately preceding the appearance of the data block under the recording heads during which the channel is reserved for data transfer, if the channel is free. During this time the disk is in a ready-to-transmit state. If the channel does not become available during this time, the disk must fly by. ENDRED is the event that signals the end of this period and sets up the fly by.
5	ENDCHSV	End of channel service. This event signals the end of data transmission for a given disk access and frees the disk for another access and the channel for another transmission.
6	ENDSM	End of simulation. This event re-initializes the user variables (since the main program does not gain control between runs), sets the end of simulation indicator (MSTOP = -1), and returns control to the executive.

5. End of Transmit—The sector transmission is complete and both the channel and disk are free.

It is also assumed that a single user's data base is contained on one disk module and that the operating system is multiprogrammed so that the chain of disk accesses required to execute a single transaction may be interrupted for the service of another transaction. The simulation could readily be modified to suit other assumptions, such as allowing a given data base to be distributed over a number of disks or requiring that a disk be dedicated to a single transaction until complete, which would considerably simplify the simulation.

The events in the model are given in Table 7-3.

The queues (GASP files) in the simulation are given in Table 7-4. Queue number 1 in the simulation is the GASP event queue. Number 2 is a user queue that stores each transaction for the duration of its processing. When the trans-

Table 7-4   Queues in the Simulation Model

Queue No.	Queue name	Attribute	Content	Rank	Order
1	EVENT	1	Scheduled time of event	X	LVF*
		2	Event code		
		3	Transaction number		
		4	Disk number to which transaction is assigned		
2	TRANS	1	Time transaction entered system	X	LVF
		2	Number of disk accesses remaining to complete transaction		
		3	Transaction number		
		4	Disk number to which transaction is assigned		
3-10	DISK	1	Time of disk access request	X	LVF
		2	Unused		
		3	Transaction number		
		4	Unused		

*Least value first.

action arrives, it is assigned its disk access parameter a (attribute 2) and serial transaction number (attribute 3) and is then assigned to a disk (attribute 4). This information is recorded along with its arrival time and stored as an entity on the TRANS queue (number 2). When all accesses have been made, the transaction is considered complete, a turnaround statistic is taken, and the transaction entity is deleted from the queue. Each of up to eight disks is also assigned a queue, numbered 3 to 10, on which the accesses to the disk are stacked. Each access is identified by its transaction serial number in attribute 3 of the DISK queue entity.

Five transaction types are defined. For types 1 to 4 the parameter a is a constant. That is, the number of disk accesses required to execute the transaction is a constant. In Example 2 of the previous section an invoice required 15 accesses; therefore, a for this transaction type would be 15. The relative frequency of the transaction types 1 to 4 and the four respective values of the parameter a are specified via parameter cards at run time (block 2 of Fig. 7-74). Transaction type 5 has a uniformly distributed value for the a parameter. The relative frequency and the upper-lower cutoff of the uniform distribution for the type 5 transaction are also given as run time parameters. The relative frequencies of the five transaction types are expressed in the parameter table as a 4 valued density function, the last value assumed, of course, to be 1.

The seek characteristic of the disk is assumed to be linear between minimum and maximum values, like that of Fig. 7-71. Many current disks approxi-

Table 7-5   Run Time Parameters for the Simulation

PARAM		Content
J	K	
1	1	Disk rotation time (R)
1	2	Ready to transmit period
1	3	Record transmit time (X)
1	4	Maximum No. of flybys before channel reservation
2	1	Number of disks (d)
2	2	Minimum disk seek time
2	3	Maximum disk seek time
2	4	Mean transaction arrival interval ($A_n c/n$)
3	1	Number of disk accesses for Trans Type 1
3	2	Number of disk accesses for Trans Type 2
3	3	Number of disk accesses for Trans Type 3
3	4	Number of disk accesses for Trans Type 4
4	1	Density function value of Trans Type 1
4	2	Density function value of Trans Type 2
4	3	Density function value of Trans Type 3
4	4	Density function value of Trans Type 4
5	1	Minimum number of access/Trans Type 5
5	2	Maximum number of access/Trans Type 5
5	3-4	Unused

mate such a characteristic. Others, like the IBM 1301, have discrete access times as a function of the number of cylinders traversed. This characteristic would be simulated by randomly generating the number of cylinders traversed and then using a table look up to derive the access time.

The user parameters read by the simulation executive are contained in a two-dimensional array named PARAM. Table 7-5 gives these parameters.

The user variables (or non-GASP variables as they are called in Reference 18) are given in Table 7-6.

Figure 7-75 presents a gross flow chart of a GASP simulation program for the model illustrated in Fig. 7-72 and analyzed in the previous section. The simulation starts in the main program, which initializes the program variables of Table 7-6 and then transfers control to the GASP executive. The executive reads the data cards, which include run control information, the parameters of Table 7-5, and two events that are stored in the event queue. The specification of the entire data card input deck for GASP is given in Appendix A. The two events that are initially stored are a transaction arrival (TRAVL) and a terminal event that ends the simulation (ENDSM). The GASP executive then reads the first event from the queue, which in this case will be a transaction arrival (TRAVL) at simulation time 0 and transfers control to the events subroutine (EVNTS), which in turn will call whatever event subroutine has just been accessed from the event queue by the GASP executive. The simulation has six events, as indicated in Table 7-3.

Table 7-6   User Assigned Variables of the Simulation

Variable name	Use	Value	Meaning
KDBS (I)	Disk I busy Indicator	0	Not busy
		1	Busy
KRED (I)	Disk I ready for transmission	0	Not ready
		1	Ready
KFB (I)	No. of flybys on disk I for a given access	Max is PARAM (1,4)	
KTR (I)	Transaction number being serviced by disk I		
KCBS	Channel busy	0	Not busy
		1	Busy
KTRN	Transaction No. counter		
KRES	Channel reservation flag	0	Not reserved
		1	Reserved

Figure 7-76 presents a more detailed flowchart of the transaction arrival subroutine, TRAVL. Appendix B contains a FORTRAN micro flowchart of subroutine TRAVL in order to illustrate how the actual program is written. The numbers in the upper left-hand corner of each flowchart box of Fig. 7-76 have corresponding box numbers in the microchart of Appendix B. TRAVL first assigns the number of disk accesses to the transaction upon its arrival. The algorithm for assignment in this program was described above; there are four trans-

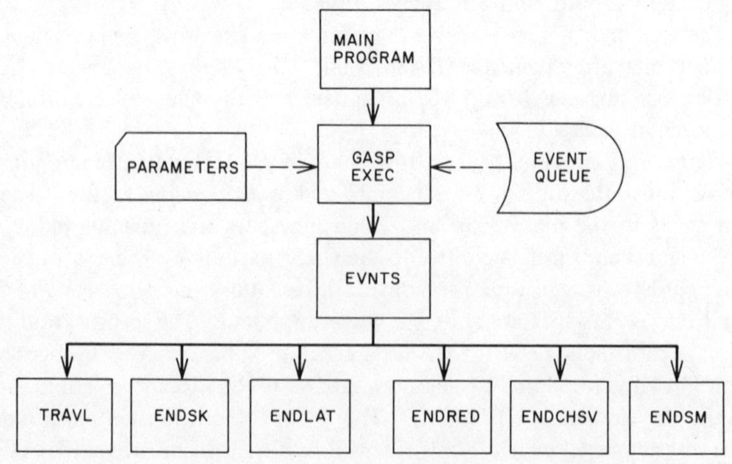

Figure 7-75   Simulation flow chart for the model of Fig. 7-72

action types, each with a fixed number of accesses (a), each of which occurs according to a given set of relative frequencies. The fifth transaction type is assigned a number of accesses according to a uniform distribution between two limits given as parameters, PARAM (5, 1) and PARAM (5, 2). The occurrence of the fifth transaction type is also included in the relative frequency schedule. The

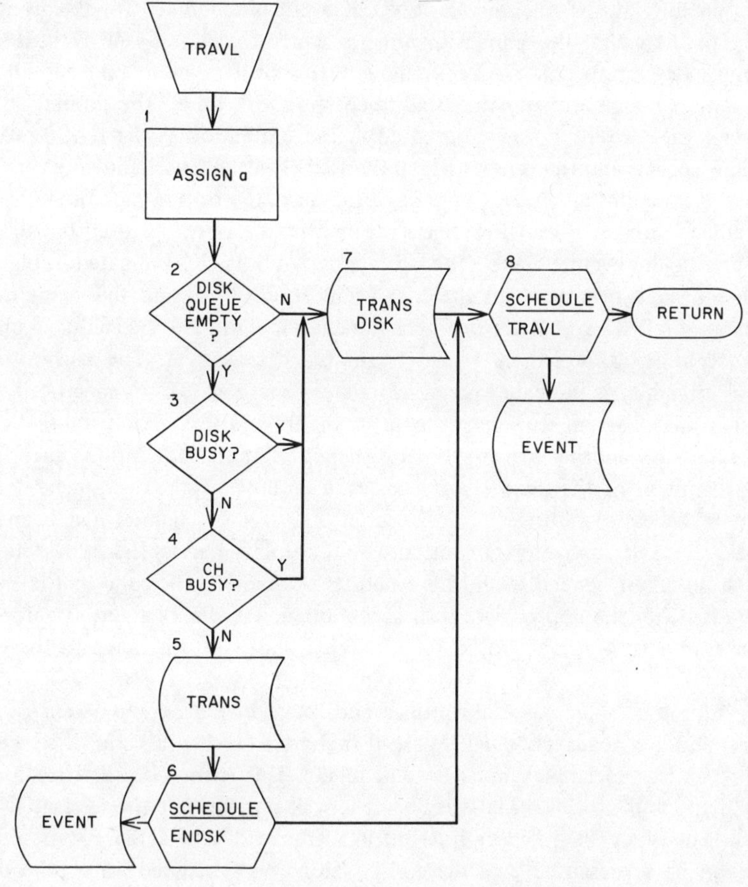

Figure 7-76   Event subroutine TRAVL

relative frequencies as well as the number of accesses associated with each transaction type are given as data parameters, PARAM (3, K) and PARAM (4, K). It is assumed in the simulation that all accesses for a given transaction are against the same disk drive. That is, the data base for a particular user (for whom the transaction is being executed) is on the same disk or drum. After assigning the number of accesses, the program inquires as to whether there are currently any accesses queued against the disk to which the current transaction has been assigned (block 2). If not, it inquires as to whether the disk is busy, since it may be the case that no accesses are waiting, but one is currently in process. If the disk is not busy, the channel is tested because the seek order to the disk utilizes the channel. If the channel is not busy, attribute 2 of the transaction (see Table 7-4), which counts the remaining accesses, is decremented, the transaction is stored in the TRANS file and an ENDSK event is scheduled for the given disk.

It is here that the simulation time at which the end of seek event is to occur must be computed. The seek characteristic of the device and a suitable random variable generator must be used to compute this time. The simulation time between the current time, represented in the simulation as the GASP program variable TNOW, and the time at which the ENDSK event is scheduled, is assumed to be the time during which the heads of the disk are positioning. The hexagonal "schedule" box in these flowcharts means that an event is stored by an event program in the event queue. This storage is symbolically indicated in Fig. 7-74 by the dashed line between the user event subroutines and the event queue. After an ENDSK event has been scheduled, the simulation schedules another transaction arrival and then returns to the GASP executive. The distribution of arrival intervals, as indicated previously, is exponential. This is specifically indicated in the program flowchart block 8A in Appendix B. Each transaction arrival schedules another arrival, thereby perpetuating the simulation run. If after the assignment of the number of accesses, a, in block 1, the disk queue had one or more accesses waiting (block 2), or if the disk or channel had been busy (blocks 3, 4), the current transaction would not have had its first access serviced by the disk, but instead would have had its transaction filed and its first record access filed on the appropriate disk access queue (block 7); then, as before, another transaction arrival would be scheduled and a return made to the GASP executive.

In Figure 7-77, the subroutines end seek (ENDSK), end latency (ENDLAT), and end ready (ENDRED) are flowcharted. When an end of seek event occurs, an end of latency must be scheduled. This is the only activity that occurs at the end of seek. Statistically, it is well known that the average disk latency is one-half the disk rotation, but in a simulation, the actual rotation of the disk can be represented, and the end of latency is scheduled for a time that is uniformly distributed from 0 to the rotation time of the disk.

At the end of latency, the record can be transmitted if the channel is available. If it is not available, a period of ready to transmit is entered, during which the disk can still be conditioned to transmit if the channel should become free. Therefore, the ENDLAT subroutine first inquires as to whether the channel is busy. If not, it inquires as to whether the channel is reserved. The channel can be reserved for a given disk if it has sustained more than a predetermined number of flybys. If the channel is not reserved, then an end of channel service for this disk can be scheduled, or, in other words, the record can be transmitted. If the channel had not been busy in block 10 but had been reserved (block 11), the question is asked whether the reservation is for this disk; if it is, then again the end of channel service can be scheduled. If the reservation were for another disk, then the channel is regarded as being busy. If the channel is busy either in actu-

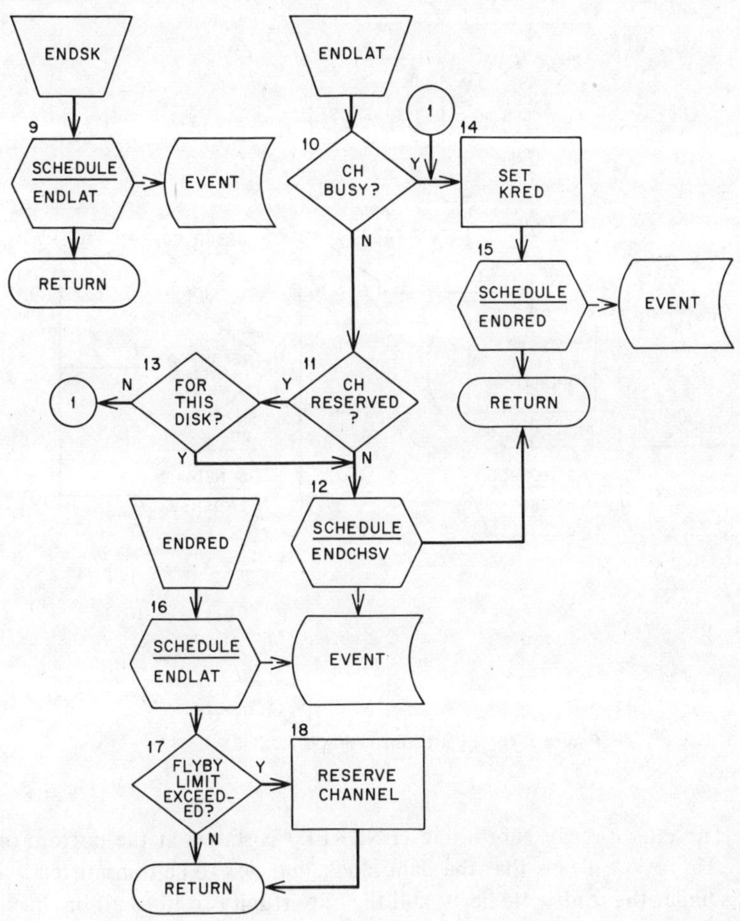

Figure 7-77 Event subroutines ENDSK, ENDLAT, and ENDRED

ality or by virtue of reservation, a ready to transmit flag is set in block 14 for this disk and an end-of-ready event is scheduled. If subsequently the channel should become free and the ready-to-transmit flag is set for a given disk, the channel service will immediately be given to this disk.

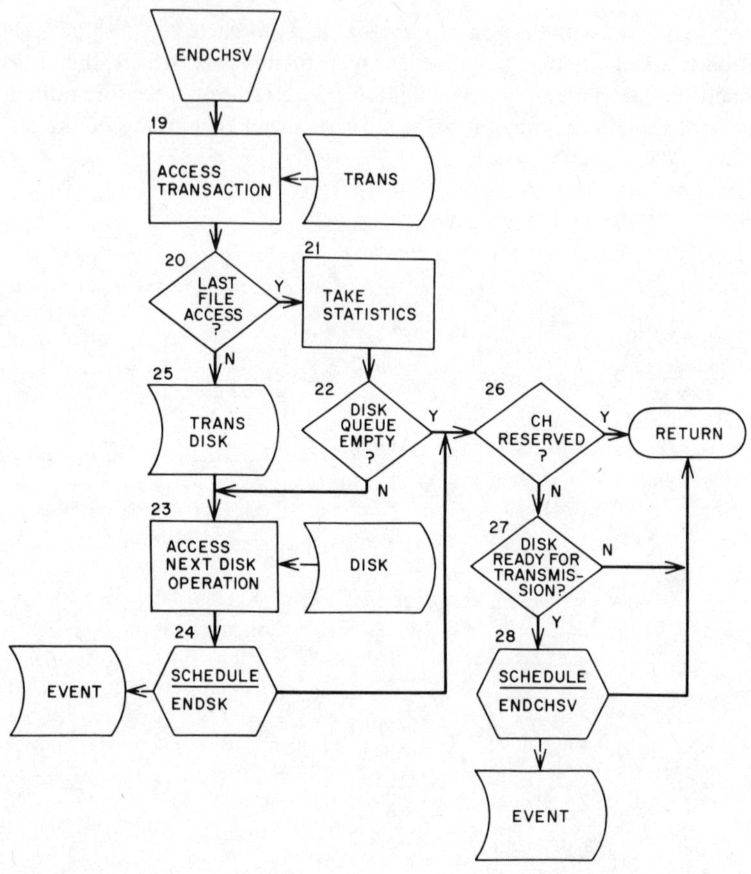

Figure 7-78 Event subroutine ENDCHSV

The end-of-ready subroutine (ENDRED) is shown at the bottom of Fig. 7-77. This event means that the data block that was to be transmitted is about to pass under the read/write heads and the opportunity to transmit has been lost. The disk must flyby with one complete rotation before there will again be the opportunity to transmit the record. An end of latency, which in this case is one complete rotation, is first scheduled. Then a test is made to determine whether the flyby limit has been exceeded. If it has not, return is made to the GASP executive; if it has been exceeded, a channel-reservation flag for this disk is set.

Figure 7-78 presents the end-of-channel-service (ENDCHSV) event flow-chart. First, the transaction that has just been serviced by the channel is accessed from the TRANS queue. It is then determined whether the last file access (a) has just been made. If so, statistics are taken in block 21. In particular, the turnaround time can at this time be sampled, since it is at this moment that the transaction has been completely processed. As indicated in Table 7-4, the time at which the transaction entered the system was logged in attribute 1 of the transaction file entity. After the statistics have been taken, it is determined whether another access has been queued against this disk (block 22). If it has, the disk queue will be greater than 0 and, as indicated in the flowchart, the next disk operation will be accessed from the DISK queue in block 23. It should be noted that this disk request may or may not be from the same transaction, since all transaction processes are being multiprogrammed.* An end of seek is then scheduled for the next disk operation. If, in block 20, more accesses were required on the current transaction, statistics would not be taken, but attribute 2 of the TRANS entity would be decremented, the entity would be refiled on the TRANS queue, and a disk access to the same disk would also be filed. This disk would now be considered free for another assignment, which is made in block 23. After the disk has either been reassigned via block 23 or has been idled by a Y exit from block 22, a determination is made in block 26 as to whether another disk is ready for channel service or whether the channel must be idled. First the question is asked as to whether the channel is reserved (from an ENDRED event) or not. If it is so reserved, it cannot be reassigned and a return is made to the GASP executive. If it is not reserved, then it is asked in block 27 whether any of the disks is ready for transmission. If none is ready, then control again returns to the executive; if a disk is ready for transmission, an end of channel service is scheduled.

7.5 COMPARISON OF ANALYSIS AND SIMULATION

Table 7-7 compares the turnaround time for these three examples as calculated analytically, according to the procedure of the preceding section, with the values obtained by means of the simulation program. Two different simulation

Table 7-7   Turnaround Times for Examples 1, 2, and 4: Analysis vs. Simulation

Example	Analysis value (sec)	Simulation			
		$f = 1$		$f = \infty$	
		Value	Max flybys	Value	Max flybys
1	0.283	0.248	1	0.215	4
2	3.93	9.56	1	4.8	16
4	3.0	3.34	1	2.48	4

---

*One could develop another processing algorithm and thereby another simulation by requiring that all files accesses for a given transaction be completed before another transaction on the same disk can begin.

runs were made for each of the three examples. In the first, the number of disk flybys (f) before channel reservation was limited to 1; in the second, the number of flybys was unlimited. In Example 1, the design called for a transaction per line every 10 sec with an expected processing turnaround of 1 sec. The minimum number of disks required was two, but in order to achieve the 1-sec turnaround, three disks had to be used, resulting in a calculated actual turnaround time of 0.283 sec instead of 1 sec. The simulation with a flyby limit of one yielded 0.248 sec, and with an unlimited number of flybys, 0.215 sec, where the actual maximum number of flybys in the latter run was four. In the second example, however, the analysis yields a turnaround time of 3.93 sec for a design specification that called for 5 sec, and the simulation indicated 9.56 sec for $f = 1$ and 4.8 sec for an unlimited f.

In this case, there is a significant difference in the values of the parameter that controls the number of flybys. Hence, one may conclude that if the design specification of 5-sec turnaround is to be achieved, the maximum number of flybys before channel reservation must be allowed to be unlimited. The maximum number of actual flybys in the simulation run turned out to be 16. In Example 4, the analysis was constrained to yield a turnaround time of exactly 3 sec, the objective of which is to determine the number of lines that can be serviced. Using the number of lines that were calculated in the analysis, namely 136, the simulation was again run for the two flyby conditions. For $f = 1$, the turnaround time was computed as 3.34, which exceeds the allowance in the specification, but for unlimited f, the turnaround 2.48, which meets the specification.

In Table 7-8, the other critical design parameter, transaction throughput, is examined for the three examples. The correspondence here between the analysis and the simulation, particularly for the case where f is unlimited is seen to be very high, and there is a good reason for this. The throughput is not a direct function of the model or its statistical description. It is based entirely upon the state of nonsaturation of the two facilities in the model, namely the disk system facility (u_d) and the channel facility (u_c). If u_d and u_c are both less than unity, the throughput is analytically given by nc/A_n, as shown in Fig. 7-72. If there are no indefinitely growing queues associated with the disk system or the channel in the simulation, the throughput will be governed entirely by the arrival-time intervals of transactions to the system. Hence, dissimilarities in the statistical models are not directly relevant to the determination of transaction throughput, as long as the assumed facilities do not saturate in either of the models under the given set of operational parameters.

Although the analysis and the simulation produced close results in the specification of T_n for Example 1, the divergence in Example 2 of the value with limited flybys leads one to suspect the actual correspondence in the statistical models that are being described by the two techniques. It was recognized at the outset that the analysis can only represent a gross approximation to the model and that it should be used only for purposes of approximation. By performing a statistical test upon the means obtained from the three examples, it

Table 7-8
Transaction Throughput for Examples 1, 2, and 4
Analysis vs. Simulation

Example	Analysis (transactions/sec)	Simulation	
		$f = 1$	$f = \infty$
1	20.0	20.5	19.1
2	3.33	3.05	3.28
4	2.27	2.30	2.24

was found that in none of the three cases could the hypothesis that the two methods were describing identical statistical phenomena be accepted. Further tests indicated that statistical correspondence was directly related to loading (that is, to the values of u_d and u_c) and that although above 50-percent loading, the correspondence was poor, below 50 percent it became good enough to indicate statistical identity.

In conclusion, the analysis has considerable value in producing a fast approximation of system performance; however, given that one is confident in the fact that his model accurately portrays the actual configuration of hardware and software, and given that one is confident that he has properly constructed a simulation program to represent that model, the methodology of simulation would appear to be superior to that of analysis, since certain approximations and assumptions of analysis (for example, loading) can be completely discounted. The simulation program will give the true results regardless of these assumptions, and the parameters of the simulation can continuously be modified in order to achieve any desired design objective.

8
Applications of
Data Management

There are two broad areas of endeavor that occupy a central position in the life of modern man, *commerce* and *communications.* A large number of people, if not the majority, earn their living either directly or indirectly in these fields, and the impact of technology is felt by all of us most directly through them. *Commerce* means the transfer or exchange of goods and services; *communications*, or as it can more descriptively be stated, *information collection and dissemination*, covers media communication, libraries, telephone service, education, social and economic planning, government policy, military intelligence, and so forth. Both of these activities obviously depend heavily upon information and data flow, and it is therefore not surprising that the most extensive use of computers for data processing has been in commercial transaction systems and in information storage and retrieval systems.

A model of an information system is described in Chapter 1 of Reference 1, wherein it is stated that such a system represents a bilateral relationship between two types of people called the *generator* and the *user*, who communicate through an exchange medium called a *file*; A commercial transaction usually implies the existence of two correlated transactions, both of which engage a generator and a user (or donor and receptor) in bilateral relationship. One is the *real* transaction and the other, a *virtual* transaction. The former is the actual exchange of goods or services, whereas the latter is an image or abstraction of the exchange that is retained for a variety of reconciliation and reporting purposes at a later time. The *virtual* transaction is pure information, and the amount of data that is retained as the image of a real transaction is normally very small; but it must be processed with an exceedingly high (one might say infinite) precision and at a low cost relative to the *real* transaction or its value will be nil.

In contrast, an information storage and retrieval system, such as a newspaper, television, library, or school, must abstract, convert, store, and dispense enormous volumes of data, though there is considerable latitude for interpretation. Hence, these two system types, upon which most data processing attention today is focused, represent extremes in basic requirements and certainly approach the five facets of data with a different emphasis. Representation and the denotative meaning are more important to the IS&R system. Syntax in the commercial system is a relatively simple set of well-defined accounting algorithms, whereas in the IS&R system, as will be seen, syntax is neither well-structured nor well-understood at this point in time in any but its simplest and most primitive contexts.

The purpose of this chapter is to model and describe these two diverse applications and to frame the range of techniques, from basic to advanced, that are currently employed in their design and implementation.

8.1 COMMERCIAL TRANSACTION SYSTEMS

8.1.1 Model of the System

A generalized conceptual model of the transaction oriented information system is illustrated in Fig. 8-79. Units of input activity, called *transactions*, are defined for processing against predefined and preorganized data files. Usually, the transactions themselves are recorded either before processing or after processing, or both. The preprocessing transaction file is called an input transaction or input message file. The postprocessing transaction file is called the transaction or journal file. The transaction processor combines information from the data files in accordance with specific transaction algorithms. A third type of file in the system is an intermediate; it is used either to hold and communicate intermediate processing results within a processor or between processors, or to report exceptional conditions that may transpire during the course of processing transactions. These may be input errors that prevent processing of the transactions or specific conditions that are generated as a result of the transaction processing and which should be brought to the attention of the system operators or managers. The only output from the system in a series of reports that is generated from the transaction, intermediate, and data files.

Reports produced from transaction files are called *registers* or *journals*. The intermediate files generate error and exception reports and are used to maintain transaction generated data that are printed periodically in reports called *analyses*. The data files generate a variety of reports individually and in combination that essentially show the current *status* of these files. They are sometimes used also to provide fixed information such as headers, labels, and descriptions for the registers and analyses. The transaction and intermediate files are transient in as much as the current version will be deleted or backed up in a grandfather, father, son series as soon as their reports have been generated. They may also be accumulated and saved for cumulative report generation. The data files, on the other hand, are normally permanent, although certain kinds of data files may periodically undergo purge or even a complete deletion, as will be shown later. A specific kind of report that is drawn from the data file is an *inquiry* or *search* for a specific record of a particular file or for a series of such records. Within the model of Fig. 8-79 an inquiry is regarded as a report that is generated directly from a data file. In summary, the only inputs that are visible to the users of the system are transactions, and the only visible outputs to the same or possibly other users are reports. Subsidiary inputs and outputs are, of course, the backup and cumulative archival files drawn from all three of the above mentioned data bases.

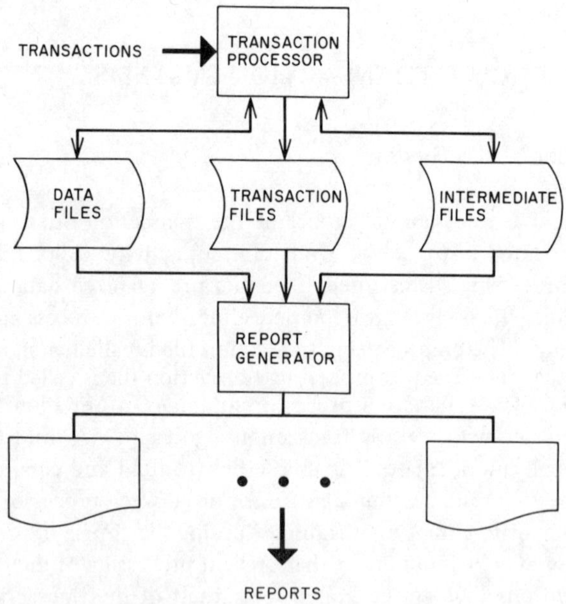

Figure 8-79   General concept of the transaction-oriented information system

Traditionally, the three file types have been implemented using magnetic tapes, since the volumes of data are normally very large, and the turnaround requirement for transaction processing is usually consistent with a mode of operation that would batch a number of transactions and sort them into a sequence suitable for efficient updating of the data files. More recently, however, with increasing demand for immediate response to transaction input, for on-line or interactive inquiry capability of data files, and as a consequence of the decreasing cost of large-scale secondary storage, systems of this type have been implemented using randomly organized disk files for the data, transaction, and intermediate files. There is, nonetheless, a high cost associated with the control and execution of such processing, as well as the relatively high cost of data storage, at least as compared with magnetic-tape costs. Furthermore, there are costs associated with the preparation and maintenance of backup files and specific programming involved in recovery, where a transaction is in process at the time of a system failure. These considerations have been discussed in Chapters 4 and 6.

A very useful compromise configuration has therefore evolved for the implementation of transaction-oriented information systems using randomly organized files. This configuration permits direct interaction with files via on-line terminals and also the processing of small batches as economically as large ones, so that any desired turnaround can be achieved for a transaction entry without imposing penalties for small batches. A block diagram is shown in Fig. 8-80. At the top of the diagram is shown a remote terminal that communicates interactively with a program called the *editor*.

Three kinds of input and output are distinguished. On-line inquires and updates directly to the data files bypass the normal transaction controls, such as batching, journaling, and generation of batch control totals, although certain limited controls may be imposed, such as passwords, and sometimes in the case of updates, journaling. Because of this lack of control, only those data fields are permitted to be updated that are not maintained and used as controls in transaction processing. For example, in a customer record, the name and address may be updated by such direct file interaction but not the customer balance, which must always be under transaction control (such as invoicing or cash posting) so that control totals and auditable journals are systematically maintained and produced.

The second system input is the transaction, which, after editing, is stored in an input transaction file (ITF), and the third input is a system control transaction that is not directed to the data files, but which is used to control the flow of transactions to the processors.

The editor performs syntax checks upon all of the input and formats all response messages to the remote terminal. The most general way to implement this program is as an interpreter of a table in which the syntax for each input message type can be stored. The edited message can flow to the processor in one of two ways. The first is the interactive route and requires that the processor be loaded for execution concurrently with the editor. This would be most useful for the inquiry and search program, for non-transaction-oriented updates, and for transaction types that require immediate turnaround. The second and normal route for most of the transactions is via a file called the input transaction file, which is actually an input symbiont or spool. The input message queueing system that follows the editor can be so constructed as to separate the transactions by type into various files or can store all transactions in a single file, which is subsequently sorted or distributed into separate batches. Throughout a given period, such as a normal working day, the edited transactions are collected in the input transaction file or files. At the end of this period, the temporary collection file is added to a cumulative input transaction file, and the current status of each cumulative ITF is reported by a program called *transaction control.*

The *transaction report* will indicate, for each processor, the number of transactions by subtype or mode within the processor, along with the earliest date and time of arrival and the most critical completion date of any transaction in the queue. This report can either be used by a system manager or automatically processed through a predefined control algorithm in order to determine when to run the cumulative ITF into the processor. When it is decided to release this ITF for processing, a job is scheduled in the normal batched job stream of the computer system, and an input journal may be generated, which lists every transaction on the ITF. This journal is used only for control purposes and is compared with the output journal, which is a product of the processor. Usually, the input journal is retained on a disk file and is not printed unless there is a discrepancy in control totals, which can readily be obtained from the transaction report and the output journal.

The processor in Fig. 8-80 is the same transaction processor shown in Fig. 8-79 and communicates with three file types. The data and output transaction (OTF) files are as shown in Fig. 8-79. But three kinds of intermediate files are shown in the second diagram, one is the exception file, which as described above, is used to report exceptional or specific error conditions; the second is a process transfer intermediate, which is used to transfer data that are generated to serve as input from one processor to another processor or analysis report program; the third intermediate is called a control file. It reports on the completion status of the processing of each particular batch that is submitted to the processor. It may be as simple a report as "batch number X has completed processing at a given time and date," or it may itemize the processing status of each transaction in the batch. In either case, a control report is also generated for use by the system manager or by the automatic control program in order to determine a schedule of subsequent processing. In this way the flow of transactions to a particular processor or through a chain of processors can readily be controlled.

Another interesting aspect of the control file, when it itemizes the processing completion status of each transaction, including its time and date, is that it can examine the entire control file in order to determine which transactions should be at which processing stations according to a pretabulated schedule. That is, if a transaction enters the system at a particular time and if the transit time through each of the processes, which may include manual as well as automated operations, is known in advance, then the data flow can be automatically tracked through the control file, and if the unit of activity associated with the input transaction has not arrived at a given station in time, it can be so noted on the control report. Thus the information system with multistation processing can be

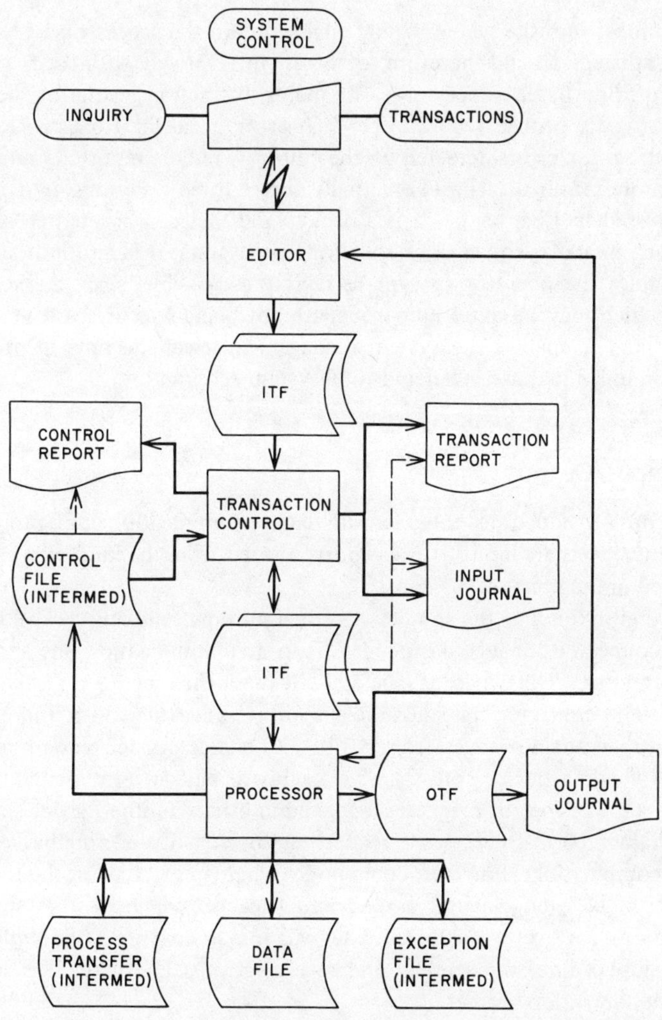

Figure 8-80   Organization of a random file transaction system

compared with a multi-stage processing plant, and the flow of data and transactions through this plant can be readily controlled through the transaction and control reports by relatively few people no matter how complex the data flow routes may be or how great the volume.

The system manager issues commands to the transaction control program by means of transaction control statements shown as the third type of input to the remote terminal at the top of the diagram.

The most versatile system would enable any of the processors to be loaded either with the editor, and therefore to operate interactively with the file system, or as an off-line batch processor. The major distinction insofar as the user is concerned would probably be the fact that errors resulting from processing, as opposed to syntax errors detected by the editor, would be reported immediately to the remote terminal. The ITF actually serves three functions, two of which were discussed in Chapter 6. It is a backup file that can be used to reprocess transactions in the event of a crash during processing; it is an input symbiont which enables the operator to type as rapidly as possible, since the actual file updates, which may be quite numerous, are not being executed as the operator is typing; and it enables the system managers to select the time of processing based upon individual user need and total system economy.

8.1.2 Input/Output

Figure 8-81 illustrates three remote data communication configurations by which transactions are input to and reports printed from the kind of system that is described in the previous diagram.

Configuration 1 is the simplest. A dual purpose send-and-receive terminal device is connected through a modem (M) to a communication line and thence to the computer. This device is labeled KSR (keyboard send and receive) in the diagram. The character transmission and print speeds at which these devices are currently available ranges from 10 to 120 characters per second. In some cases, the sending device consists of a keyboard and an intermediate storage medium such as paper or magnetic tape, and in others another device such as an optical character or a mark sense reader may be substituted for the keyboard. All these combinations, however, come under what is portrayed in the figure as a Class I terminal arrangement: a send and a receive unit both communicating through a modem over a single data line, which may be half or full duplex. If it is a half-duplex line, the sending and receiving must alternate; if it is a full-duplex line, they may overlap.

The second configuration needs a full duplex line and will utilize it more fully than the first configuration. It is the optimum low-cost configuration for high-volume input and a steady but not ultra-high volume output. A KSR or a keyboard and a character-display tube serve as the data input and interactive data receiver; this combination communicates through a program-activated switch to the modem and communication line. The keyboard is always connected to the modem and can transmit through half of the duplex at any time. The receipt of data over the other half of the duplex is gated either to the KSR printer (or display) or to a receive-only-serial (ROS) printer depending upon the position of the program-operated switch.

An example of the use of the configuration is an invoice transaction system in which the transaction input that is used to create invoices is entered on the

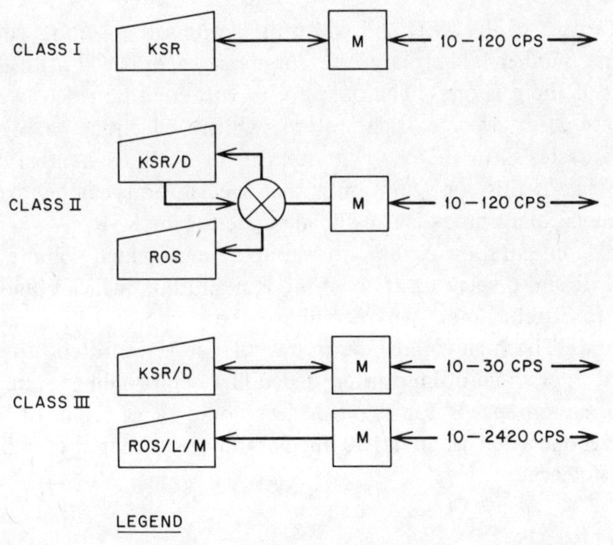

LEGEND

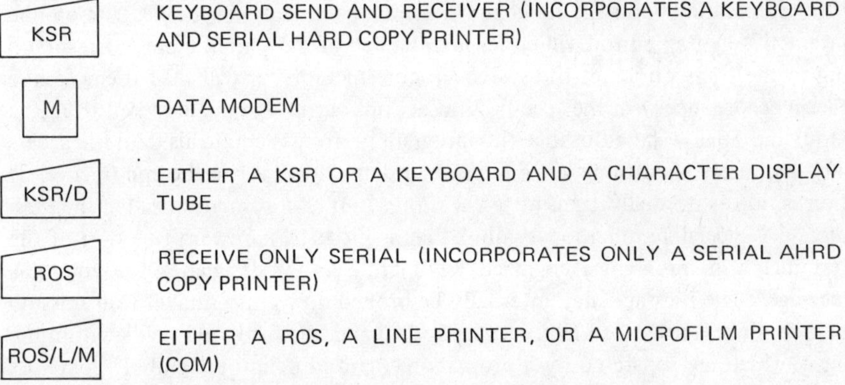

Figure 8-81 Input/output configurations

keyboard and transmitted to the computer while finished invoices (from prior transactions) are simultaneously being printed on the ROS. If there is a syntax or processing error that is to be communicated immediately to the operator, the output program switches the data flow from the ROS to the printer or display of the KSR, transmits the message, and then reverses the switch in order to continue typing invoices.

The interruption of the KSR is readily synchronized with the input in the following simple way. With every carriage return the output program switches the output data flow to the KSR and will print a prompting symbol such as an asterisk or a line number if there are no error messages, or it will print the error message instead if there is one. The operator is thus conditioned to wait for a positive response after every carriage return, which will either be a go-ahead signal such as an asterisk or the next line number or it will be an error message. Another advantage of this configuration is that special forms can be maintained is the ROS, whereas blank stock is usually adequate for the KSR.

The third configuration is the only suitable one for high volume output. It places the KSR and display on its own modem and line, which could readily operate at 10 to 30 characters per second for the purpose of input and error message reaction. The high-volume output would be transmitted either to an ROS, a line printer, or a microfilm printer, depending upon volume requirements, and data transmission speeds for these devices could range from 10 to 2,400 characters per second (that is, an 1,100-line-per-minute printer at the upper end of the transmission scale).

8.1.3 The Syntax Editor

Depending upon the number of different transaction syntaxes, the on-line interactive syntax editor will either maintain all of the syntax tables corresponding to the transactions of the system in core memory or will read them from a file in accordance with the specific transactions currently being entered from the input terminal. The edits that this program performs require no data file access and are purely algorithmic once the appropriate table has been placed in core. A transaction is normally transmitted within a unit of information called the *message*. A special termination symbol that is either a hardware function of the terminal or a program recognized keyboard symbol designates the end of a message. The message may internally be broken down into smaller transmission units as lines (terminated by a carriage return and line feed) and fields within the lines, which are separated by a program-recognized delimiter symbol. A syntax check may therefore be made upon individual fields, the number and type of fields within a line, and the number and type of lines in a message.

Table 8-1 presents the items that can be checked in the edit of the individual data field plus certain other information that is useful to provide as a part of the interactive function of the editor. Nine items of information are provided for the edit interaction of each field. A syntax table is therefore composed of a ninetuple description for every field of each line type in a message. Some transaction types require that another layer of control be superimposed upon the simple field-to-field line to line scan. In these, the transaction syntax is subdivided into two parts, one called the *header* and the other the *body*. The header lines are scanned once, field by field and line by line. The body either consists of a single line that is repetitively scanned until the message termination symbol is encountered, or it consists of a variety of line types each specifically identified by a typed symbol as the first field. Such lines can be intermixed and repeated as many times as desired until, again, the message termination symbol is en-

Table 8-1   Input Syntax Checks

Syntax Check	Check Types	Interpretation
MODE	A	Alphanumeric
	I, IP	Integer. A P appended to any item means that it must be unsigned; otherwise it may be signed or unsigned.
	n, nP	Has exactly n decimal places and may or may not have an integral part.
	D, DP	Has any number of decimal places, including none.
	C	Calendar in the format (m)m/(d)d/yy.
CHECK DIGIT	C	Perform check digit test.
	N	Do not perform check digit test.
TYPE	F	Fixed length field.
	V	Variable length field.
LENGTH	n	If TYPE = F, n is the exact field length; if TYPE = V, n is the maximum length.
REQUIRED	Y	Field is required.
	N	Field is not required.
ACCUMULATE	n	If n is 0, no accumulation is made; if n is an integer, 1, 2, 3 . . . , the value of the field is added into accumulator n.
NAME	Name	The field is named for the purpose of communicating errors to the terminal.
ID	Identification number	The field is uniquely numbered in order to communicate an ID to the program.
CONVERT	L, R	Left or right alphanumeric justification
	PD	Packed decimal
	$\pm n$	A binary integer scaled by $10^{\pm n}$
	f	A floating point number
	C	Calendar display format (m)m/(d)d/yy
	J	Julian date.

countered. Consider now the individual items of field test, as indicated in Table 8-1. All data fields are seen by the editor as a stream of characters delimited fore and aft by the field terminator symbols, by a terminator symbol and carriage return in the case of the last field, or by a line feed (or other initiating symbol) and field terminating symbol in the case of the first field. Two consecutive field delimiter symbols indicate a null or default field entry. Programmatically, therefore, the mode of all data in the input stream is alphanumeric, but editorially any field can be assigned a variety of modal interpretations. The most useful of these are indicated in the first entry of Table 8-1, associated with the syntax check labeled MODE. Mode check A is interpreted as alphanumeric, which means no check at all, because the data, as stated above, are already interpreted as alphanumeric. The second check type is I, which is interpreted as an integer. This means that the data field must be purely numeric and may have no decimal point. If a P is appended to check type I, then the integer must be unsigned or positive; otherwise it may be unsigned, positive, or negative. The third check type is n, which means that the input must again be purely numeric and must have exactly n decimal places. It may or may not have an integer part. Again, the appended P means that the number must be purely positive or unsigned. The fourth and less restrictive numeric check type is D, which means that the input field is interpreted as a number and may or may not have a decimal point. The last check type is a C, which interprets the input field as a month/day/year calendar format. One could also include a consistency check within the C format to assure that the value of the month is between 1 and 12 and the value of the day is between 1 and 31.

The second syntax check indicated in the table is called a *check digit*. It is a number appended to certain data items or identification keys for which a high degree of transcription accuracy is imperative. These keys may be customer account numbers, inventory item numbers, invoice numbers, or the like. The appended number, which is the check digit, it computed by an algorithm that operates upon the individual digits or characters of the key itself; its purpose is to detect digit or character omissions, alterations, and transpositions in the original key. A simple algorithm that accomplishes this almost invariably (it is impossible to design a check digit that will detect all possible errors, such as multiple transpositions or alterations) is the following: number the character positions from left to right as 1, 2, 3, . . . , Multiply the first digit by 1, the second digit by 2, the third digit by 3, the fourth digit by 4, the fifth digit by 1, the sixth digit by 2, the seventh digit by 3, and so forth. If the key contains a mixture of alphabetics and numerics, all of the letters could be replaced by a single number, say 3. The units digit of the sum of these weighted products would then be the check digit. The assignment of the check digit to the key is normally made at the time the key is generated, which, of course, is not the function of the editor; the editor, using the same algorithm, will only check to make sure that all the digits belonging to the original key, as they appear in the transmitted data field, do in fact generate the check digit, which is now also a part of the key and normally appears as the last digit of the key. It is sometimes separated upon input or output from the original key by a hyphen or a space, so that persons using the key can recognize the original, which may have some coded or serial significance apart from the check digit. The editor, when it detects a hyphen in a check digit field, will ignore it as a nonedit character in the field.

The third syntax check is called the *field type*; it designates the field as being fixed (F) or variable (V). The *length check* is interpreted as an exact length if the type is *fixed* and as a maximum length if the type is *variable*. The fifth check is simply to determine whether the indicated field is required or not. A nonrequired, defaulted field appearing in the middle of a line must be replaced by a field delimiter, as indicated above. One or more defaulted fields at the end of a line can be eliminated simply by the carriage return.

The next syntax check is not intended for individual field edits but rather is used as an overall or global check on the accuracy of the input of certain critical data fields across all transactions within a batch. It is called a *control total* and is the accumulation or total of the values contained in all appearances of a specified data field. For example, the body line of an invoice may consist of an inventory item number and a quantity. It may be desired to compute a control on the quantities, in which case all quantity values in all invoice transactions that are entered in a given batch will be accumulated and displayed at the end of the batch entry. The operator would independently total the quantities from the input data sheet and would compare the external to the machine-produced control total. A mismatch will clearly indicate an error either in data entry or in the external control, whereupon an examination of the data entries either from the hard copy or from a replay of the ITF should readily locate the error. It might also be desirable, in the above example, to generate a control total on the item numbers themselves; this is sometimes referred to as a *hash total* and is useful for detecting multiple or totally omitted line entries. The syntax table indicates whether a control total is to be generated for a given field by the appearance of an *accumulate* numeral. A zero would indicate that no accumulation is to be made, and an integer n would indicate that an accumulation is to be made into accumulator number n, where the system is presumed to supply some fixed number of accumulators for this purpose.

Frequency counts (that is, the number of times a given data field appears), rather than an accumulation of the values within the field, is another useful control. A convention can be established such that certain accumulators are used for frequency counts and others for accumulation. For example, a 10-accumulator editor may allocate 1 to 7 for one function and 8 to 10 for the other. The program can associate a given accumulator with the *name* of the field, which is also indicated in the syntax table, so that the final readout of control totals will be labeled by the assigned names rather than accumulator numbers. The name also serves the purpose of communicating errors by field name to the operator. That is, if a particular field does not pass any of the above described syntax checks, the operator will be informed of the error by line, field name within line, and error type. He may then be requested to re-enter the field or the entire line.

The next syntax item in the table is an identification number that serves to uniquely identify the field to the process program. The ID is passed along with the converted data item through the ITF to the processor. This facilitates the writing of the processing code, since the program can be set up to simply transfer control to specific routines depending upon the field identification number instead of locking it into a specific field sequence. In this way the same processor could be used with a variety of field and line sequences.

The last syntax item again involves communication between the editor and the processor. It is the conversion from alphanumeric input to a desired working storage format in the program. The *convert* is specified here as part of the syntax table but may be processed either by the editor before it places the data in the ITF or by a preprocessor as the data are transmitted from the ITF to the processor. The latter is the normal approach, and therefore the editor transmits only the value of the data and the identification number. The most useful set of conversions, though by no means the only possible ones, is indicated in the table.

There are, of course, some conversions that are impractical, such as alphanumeric to numeric. The A mode is converted to either a left or right justification in working storage. A numeric mode may be converted to a packed decimal, to a scaled binary integer, or to a floating point number. The second of these is rather useful in commercial systems, since the scale n could be zero for integer quantities and two for money, which is to say that the money is stored as cents and arithmetically manipulated as cents. This is the most efficient way to process numbers in a computer, and a thirty-two bit machine would provide for the expression of approximately 100 million dollars. The calendar input mode C could be converted either to a calendar display mode which would simply be eight left-justified alphanumeric characters or to a Julian date that would be represented as a five-digit integer, the first two digits being the year and the last three being the Julian day within the year. The latter format is more useful for computation and the former for display.

8.1.4   A Functional Flowchart

After one has provided for the validation of input data, as discussed in the preceding section, there remain three major functional components of the business or commercially oriented transaction system. One is the set of processors that update the various data files of the system from the input transactions; the second is a report generator that provides the management information for which the system is primarily intended, and this is usually done either by printing all or certain parts of data files in a suitable display format or by subjecting these data files to some subsequent processing, such as sorting and merging with the data of other files. The third component is an inquiry/update system by which any data item within any of the files can be immediately interrogated, and by which certain data that are not normally under the control of transaction processing can be subject to update on an ad hoc basis. These updates normally pertain to descriptive elements of data such as names and addresses, prices, tables for taxes, salesmen, shippers, and the like.

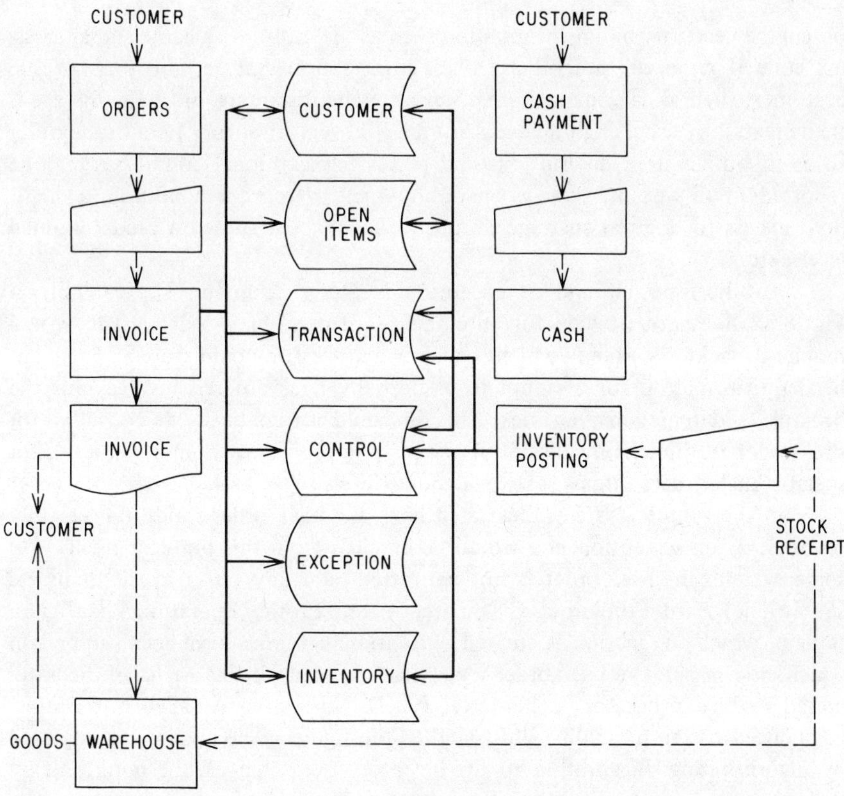

Figure 8-82   Flow chart of a commercial transaction system

8.1.5 Processors

Figure 8-82 presents a flow chart of a commercial transaction system with three processors. This system will generate invoices, post cash receipts and adjustments, and post inventory receipts and adjustments. The system will therefore perform the functions of billing, inventory control, and the maintenance of accounts receivable. This type of system would be characteristic of the wholesale distribution industry, manufacturer distributors, and certain types of retail business.

When an order arrives from a customer, an invoice transaction is submitted to the system.* The invoice processor reads the customer record, as indicated by the leftward pointing arrow emanating from the customer file, in order to

---

*Sometimes the order is entered and held for invoicing pending shipment or production. This represents a variant on the above example called *post billing* and would normally include an order entry processor.

obtain the necessary billing information such as the customer's name and address, tax code if required, and other variable information that pertains to a specific customer, such as salesman, shipper, terms, trade discounts, etc. The invoice is then created by accessing the inventory file for every inventory item in the order so as to obtain item descriptions and prices. Exceptional conditions may be reported at this point, such as an out-of-stock or reorder condition, a credit limit excess for a given customer, a profit that is above or below predetermined levels, etc.

Another special kind of exception is the back-order. The example in Fig. 8-82 does not provide for automatic control of back-orders. This would require a back-order file in which the invoice processor would store all pertinent header information for a complete or partially back-ordered invoice plus the back-ordered items and quantities. This file could automatically be consulted for back-order fulfillment by the inventory posting processor when stock levels for specific back-ordered items rose to adequate levels.

In the simpler system, illustrated here, the back-order condition is simply reported as an exception and would be handled from this point manually. In some systems the back-order is not permitted, and any out-of-stock items are simply deleted from the order. There are, of course, other operational configurations in which the invoice is created only after the goods have been shipped, in which case, again, the back-order identification need not be a part of the automated invoice processor. This latter type of operation is called *post-billing,* as opposed to the pre-billing illustrated in the figure. The invoice is completed by incorporating, in addition to the inventory item charges, the noninventory item charges, freight or postage, taxes, and the netting of trade discounts. The balance that is due from the invoice is then used to update the customer record balance. It is also possible and quite useful to store in the customer record the individual aging period balances in addition to the total balance so that all of the information needed to display the aging of a given account is contained within the same record. The customer record might also contain such information as year-to-date sales, which would be updated at this point as well.

A control record is maintained that contains system global parameters such as the current total accounts receivable, daily sales totals, daily cash receipts, and adjustments and total inventory value. This file is updated with every transaction and enables the users of the system to make daily control total checks between the contents of the control record and the control totals that have been developed through use of the syntax editor and adding machine tapes prepared from their original data input. The system also uses the accounts receivable control when preparing an aged accounts receivable report which will be described later.

Each inventory record is also updated, as indicated by the inward pointing arrow to the inventory file, by decrementing the quantity on hand and incrementing sales data. The invoice is entered as a new open item in the open item file. This file can be keyed by customer number/invoice number or by customer number/date/invoice number, or it may be chained from the customer record. This organization of the open item file enables a customer statement to be immediately produced and is a useful mode of account status interrogation. If the file has an indexed sequential organization and one of the two above mentioned keys is used, then the total set of customer statements can immediately be produced by reading the open item file sequentially. If the file is indexed random, the statements can be produced by reading the file sequentially via the index, but the data file will be accessed randomly for each item. A decision would have to be made in this case, therefore, as to whether it would be more economical to sort the file first into the appropriate sequence for producing the statements or to access each item randomly. The tradeoff would involve two factors. One is the size of the file and the number of statements to be produced, and the other is the manner of print distribution. Normally reports of this type are most economically produced on a high-speed line printer, but in a time-sharing environment, where a number of systems like the one illustrated in Fig. 8-82 are concurrently in operation, it may be more desirable, and even more economical, to require each individual statement-generating program to print on a remote terminal; thus, rather than centralizing the print function at the computer site using a high-speed line printer, the printing of many sets of statements would be performed simultaneously using communication lines and lower-speed printers at remote sites. The advantages are that the various clients (that is, the people requiring the statements for transmittal to their customers) can have them printed on their own premises and at their own convenience and can in fact select their own report cycle.

With regard to the maintenance of the open items, there are two general methods of accounting; one is called the *balance forward* method, whereby at the end of the month, all its items, including invoices, cash receipts, adjustments, and memos against the invoices are reported on a customer statement. At this point all current outstanding invoices in the open item file are deleted, and only the unpaid balance of these invoices is retained. This balance is then carried forward as the current receivable amount for this customer into the next aging period, and the existing period balances are carried forward or "rolled" into the next period. Such a system has a finite number of such aging periods (usually three to five) and the oldest accumulates all monies owed beyond this period. A typical balance-forward system may have a current (meaning 1- to 30-day-old) period, plus periods of 30 to 60 days, 60 to 90 days, and over 90 days. Cash payments in the balance-forward system are therefore not normally made against specific invoices but rather on account, although they may be applied to specific aging periods, particularly when interest charges are levied for balances that go beyond a given age. A device for enabling a cash payment to be automatically assigned to the period of a specific invoice for which the payment is being made, even though the invoices themselves have been deleted at the end of the month, is as follows. Assume that all invoice numbers are assigned sequentially; at the end of the month, when the current open item file is deleted, the last invoice number is stored in the control file and is called a *global* or *range* for that particular period. At a later time, if the invoice number accompanies a payment, it can be directed to the appropriate period by determining which invoice globals bracket the given invoice number.

The other type of accounting system is called an *open item* system, in which all items are maintained perpetually until specifically deleted by a payment that references the given invoice in full or by a series of payments which cumulatively pay off the invoice. Of course, the invoice can also be removed by an adjustment of the invoice amount or by writing off the invoice entirely, in which case the difference between any amount already paid and the net amount of the invoice would appear as a discount. Automatic terms calculations can readily be performed in the open item system since all parameters of the term discount are at hand when the cash payment is made, namely, the term, discount, net invoice amount and data (from the open item record on file), invoice number, amount paid, and payment date (from the cash receipt transaction input).

Finally, the invoice processor will write a record to a sequential transaction file that is used at the end of the day or process cycle to print a hard copy register of every transaction, after which the transaction file can be deleted. The invoice processor generates the invoice as a printed document that is sent to the customer as his bill, and which can also be transmitted to the warehouse (possibly with pricing suppressed) for inventory picking and shipping. This completes the order-billing-shipping cycle and includes the updating of the customer and inventory files, the generation of an open item record, the generation of exception messages, the updating of the control record, and the generation of a transaction record.

Cash receipts can be applied either to a specific invoice or on account. In the balance-forward system, a payment to an invoice will result only in the application of the payment to the period in which the invoice was issued. In the open item system the payment will be applied specifically to the invoice. A cash receipt to a particular invoice will first cause the invoice to be accessed from the open item file and then rewritten with an indication of the amount of payment and the current status of the invoice, whether it is partially paid, paid off, or written off. It is at this time that terms discounts must also be computed. If the invoice is paid or written off, tax, freight and postage collections are appropriately registered in the control file. The total system accounts receivable amount is also updated in the control file, as are the total and period balances in the customer record. Finally, a transaction record for the end of day cash register is generated.

When stock items are issued from inventory, the quantity on hand in the particular inventory record is appropriately reduced by the invoice processor. When stock items are put back into inventory through stock receipt, as shown at the right-hand side of the diagram, the quantity and cost of the items received are entered as transactions into the inventory posting processor, which updates the inventory file and also updates a control on the total current valuation of inventory. It may also generate a transaction record, if an inventory transaction register is to be produced.

8.1.6   Report Generator

The flow chart of Fig. 8-82 represents an example of a system of transaction processors in the sense of the model shown in Fig. 8-79. The purpose of these processors, as shown in that diagram, is to update data (customer, inventory) transaction and intermediate (open items, control, exception) files based upon input transactions. The other block shown in Fig. 8-79 is a report generator, the purpose of which is to draw reports periodically or upon demand from these same files. Figure 8-83 illustrates some of the reports that may be produced from the files in the example of Fig. 8-82. From the customer and open item files are produced the customer statements, which are sent directly to the customer. In the balance forward system, the generator itemizes his current invoices and payments, presents the current period starting and ending balance, and may also show an aged breakdown of his total balance. In the open item system, the statement will normally show the unpaid balance of the outstanding invoices and the payments made against invoices during the current month, or alternatively, only the outstanding invoice balances.

The counterpart report to the statements, which is used for accounting and credit management, is the aged trial balance, which is also produced from the customer and the open item files. This report program performs two balance checks to test the accuracy of each customer account and to test global accuracy of the system. First it compares the customer balance with the summary of all open item balances*; second, it compares the summary of all open items in the system (that is, the report total) with the total system accounts-receivable value maintained in the control record. If any customer record is indicated as being out of balance by this process, an investigation must be made into each of the transactions posted for this customer during the current period. This can most readily be done through the registers, which represent a hard copy audit of all transactions entered into the system. The cause of such an imbalance may be records that are somehow lost from the open item file, perhaps as the result of a crash that was not suitably recovered.

The customer statements and aged trial balance are the principal reports used for the management of accounts receivable. They are customarily produced on a monthly cycle, but in an on-line system either of these reports can be generated whenever and as frequently as desired. After the pair of reports has been produced, the individual period balances in the accounts are rolled into the

---

*In the balance forward system, it compares the balance less the beginning of month balance with the open item summary, since these are only the current period items.

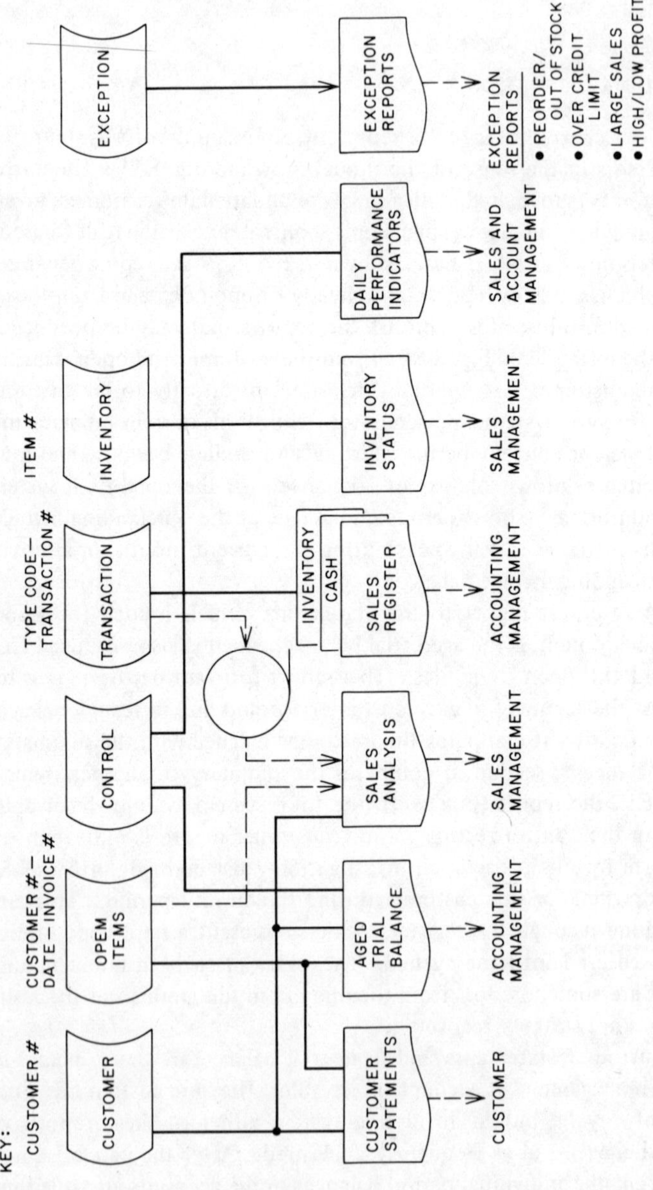

Figure 8-83 Report generation

next period, month to date figures are reset, and globals, whether in the form of invoice numbers or dates, are also rolled. The other accounting management tool is the register, which is produced directly from the transaction file on a more frequent schedule, such as daily or several times weekly. The register is normally used only for audit and error analysis.

Analyses of sales and inventory status are produced specifically for sales management. The former report is generated either from the customer and open item file or from the customer and transaction file. An invoice by customer sales analysis can most readily be produced by a sequential scan of the open item file, omitting cash payments, and incorporating such information from the customer file as the customer's name, dollar sales year to date, report period to date, salesman, and possibly current balance and gross profit. If, on the other hand, the analysis were required to detail each inventory item by customer, a more elaborate system would have to be established in which the transaction file, which contains the invoice including its line items, would be dumped and cumulated through the month, say to magnetic tape. The report is produced by sorting the cumulative sales transaction file into customer sequence and then reading it, along with the customer file, in order to show the customer number and name, sales for the period and year to date, account balance, and gross profit; for each item, the quantity and total value sold to this customer is shown for the report period.

The other sales management report is the status of inventory, which is produced simply by a sequential scan and display of the inventory file. The data of interest in this report would be the current quantity on hand, quantity sold during the report period and year to date, the turnover, the current quantity on order and on backorder, and the gross profit per item. The sales management reports may be produced on an extended cycle, such as biweekly or monthly, since longer term management reaction to this information is normally accepted. However, one of the greatest benefits of the on-line, up-to-the-moment computer system is the ability to identify on an exception basis a variety of potentially critical situations. Hence, as was indicated in the flowchart of Fig. 8-82, exceptions are immediately transmitted to a file that can be printed at the end of the day or whenever required. Exceptions that both sales and accounting management might be interested in are out-of-stock and reorder conditions, customer accounts that exceed a predefined credit limit, individual sales that are greater than a predetermined size, and profit margins on individual sales that are either above or below predefined levels.

Another type of routine daily report that may be of general interest to management is generated directly from the control register and consists of a series of daily performance indicators. These may include the daily cash receipts, adjustments and discounts, and postage, freight and taxes collected; the daily indicators would also include sales statistics, such as the number and volume of sales on account, cash sales, credit memos, returns and reshipments, and the net change to accounts receivable as a result of all sales and cash activity. Following this type of breakdown, the current accounts-receivable value can be displayed. Other information such as the average sale of the day, the average profit per sale of the day, the minimum profit sale, and the maximum profit sale can also be displayed. The daily performance indicators and the exception reports enable managers to formulate and adjust policy in credit management, sales, and promotion and inventory management on a day-to-day basis with accurate statistical information at their instant disposal.

It is sometimes desirable to be able to generate the same type of report in a variety of layouts and formats. For example, although all invoices produced by a particular system may generate for display the same or nearly the same set of data elements, it may be required to print on different forms. It may also be the case that variants of the same invoice processor are used to generate somewhat different data for display. One user may require terms and another not; one may require shipping instructions and another not. Figure 8-84 illustrates on the right-hand side a typical invoice display. This diagram illustrates how a program that is driven from a table can be used to interface between the invoice processor output and the actual display of the invoice. In the upper part of the table, four sections of the report (in this case the invoice) are identified. These four sections are normally referred to as the *header*, *body*, *bottom* or *balance line*, and *footer*.

The absolute starting and ending lines are indicated in the table for each section, enabling one to coordinate the display for any size form. The fourth column of the upper part of the table contains a type code, where type A means that all line references given in the item section of the table below are absolute vertical-displacement references within the given start-end region. The R type means that the line reference is repeatable and is displayed on the next blank line within the same section. For example, Section 2, the body, is of type R, which means that each body line is placed after the preceding body line, and the table itself cannot absolutely position any of them in the vertical dimension, because this is a function of the number of body lines on each particular invoice. However, it may be the case that one would want to define a multiple-line body entry, such as a two-line entry, where the first might contain the quantity ordered, the item number, price, extended amount, and the first of two lines of description, and the second line would contain the second line of description. This would be indicated in the table by designating a relative line position of 1 for the quantity, item number, price, amount, and first description line, and a relative line position of 2 for the second line of description.

The fifth column in the upper part of the table contains a page control code. Code R, which is assigned to Section 1, means that the section is repeated on each succeeding page of a multiple page report; thus, if a particular invoice were to exceed a single page, the header information would all be repeated on the second page. If it were desired to repeat only certain parts of this information, the header section would have to be broken into two sections in order to indicate the repeatable and nonrepeatable portions. An alternative is to place page control on each item, in the lower portion of the table, if this degree of repetition control is desired.

The lower section of the table contains the individual item control. There are three types of line item control. The first, D, indicates a *display* item, which means that there will be an item found in the processor output file with the same name (but not necessarily in the same order) as that appearing in the item column; for example, there will be an item in the output file called INVNO, and if the table type is D, the content of this data item is to be displayed in the report according to the display format appearing in the last column in the table (DSPLY). The second item type is a *conditional,* C, which means that a specific data item with a name appearing in the item column will also appear in the output file, but in addition to data there will also be a control field associated with the data item in the output file that is set to ON or OFF, depending upon whether the appearance of this particular data item in this record is or is not to be displayed. If the control field is set to ON, the data item is displayed as though the type were D; if it is OFF, the line in the display table is disregarded. The third type of line item is a *literal*, L, which means that the characters appearing in the item column are to be displayed exactly as given, and that there will be no correspondence in the output display file.

In the example of Fig. 8-84, all items in Section 1 are of the D type since they always represent data to be extracted from the display file. Some of the items in Section 2, the body, are of the D type, such as quantity, item number, item, price and amount; others are conditionals such as a blank line that would be placed beneath the citation of all of the inventory items in order to separate it from other line items such as discounts, freight charged, postage charged, taxes, etc. The example further shows the conditional display of a discount literal, which would be, in this case, a literal stored within the display file, such as "DISCOUNT," and the amount of the discount itself, which is also a conditional item. An example of a literal is shown in Section 3, the balance line, in which the word REMARKS is printed exactly as it appears in the item list of the table itself.

The third column of the table indicates the section in which the data item is to appear. The fourth column specifies the relative vertical line position starting from the beginning of the section, as indicated in the upper part of the table. This relative line, as discussed above, is interpreted as a line count from the start of the section in case of an A type section, and as a relative line within a repeatable set in an R type section. The fifth column of the table contains the starting horizontal character position of the field to be displayed within the line, and the length column indicates the maximum number of characters to be displayed. The last column of the table contains a display format code similar to the mode interpretation code for the input syntax.

Table 8-2 contains an interpretation of these display codes. For alphanumeric displays there is a left and right justification. For numeric displays there is an integer that may be displayed with or without commas; there may be a

SECTION	LINE		TYPE	PG CTRL
	START	END		
1	10	25	A	R
2	26	55	R	N
3	56	56	A	N
4	57	66	A	F

ITEM	TYPE	SECTION	REL LINE	POSN	LENGTH	DSPLY
INVCNO	D	1	1	3	6	IK
DATE	D	1	1	12	8	C
CUSTNO	D	1	1	35	6	L
CUSTNAME	D	1	3	5	20	L
ADDRESS 1	D	1	4	5	20	L
·						
·						
·						
QUANTITY	D	2	1	3	6	IK
ITEMNO	D	2	1	11	8	L
ITEM	D	2	1	22	20	L
PRICE	D	2	1	45	10	2
AMOUNT	D	2	1	57	10	2
BLANK	C	2	1	1	1	L
DISCOUNTLIT	C	2	1	24	20	L
DISCOUNT	C	2	1	57	10	2
·						
·						
·						
REMARKS	L	3	1	3	7	L
BALANCE	D	3	1	57	10	2
REM 1	D	4	1	4	14	L
·						
·						

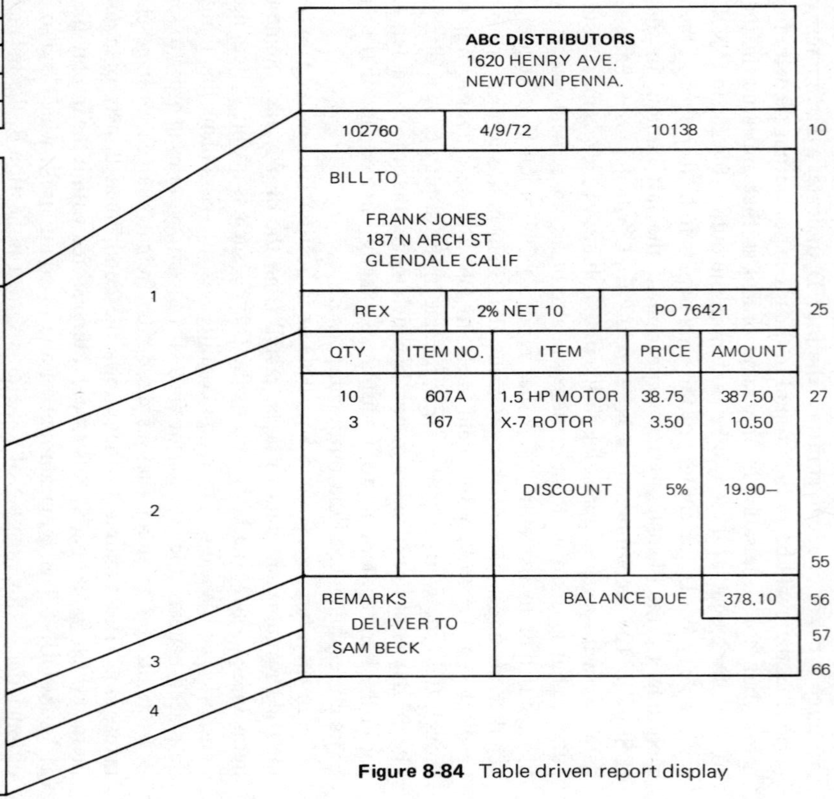

Figure 8-84 Table driven report display

Table 8-2   Display Syntax

Display type	Interpretation
L	Left justified alphanumeric
R	Right justified alphanumeric
I, IK	Integer. A K appended means that no commas are to be inserted at thousands.
n, nk	Exactly n decimal places
C	Calendar (m) m/(d) d/yy

requirement to display exactly n decimal places, such as for money, and there may be a requirement to display in a standard calendar format.

8.1.7   File Inquiry and Update

It is also useful to design an interactive inquiry and a generalized, non-processor oriented update program to be driven from a table, since this will enable a single program to interrogate and update any of the files, and suitable protection can be built in to inhibit update of specific fields within files that should only be modified by processors. An example of such a table and its application to the customer file is given in Fig. 8-85. On the right side of the figure is shown a COBOL defined data division of a customer record. On the left side is shown the inquiry/update table with parameters that would correspond to the illustrated customer record. The first column of the table contains an item name, which does not have to correspond with the name of the data item in the file definition. It is used only for display when a record is interrogated or to identify a particular field for update. It is assigned by the users of the system, who are responsible for filling out these tables.

The order of the items in the table must correspond with the order given in the file definition. This order, in combination with the information contained in the second and third columns, is used to locate the field within the data record. The second column indicates whether the item named occurs more than once in the record and the third column indicates the length of each occurrence. The fourth column contains a display format code, which is interpreted as shown in Table 8-2.

A special display code, X, is used in this table in order to designate a non-displayable item, such as a program control field which is of no particular interest to the user, or a field that is specifically excluded from display for security reasons. The fifth column contains the record ADD prompt sequence. When a new record is added to the file, the user is prompted by the items that have a

ITEM NAME	OCCUR	LENGTH	DSPLY	AAA	UPD	COMBINATIONS				
						1		2		3
CUSTNO		8	L	1	K	1		1		1
NAME		20	L	2	R	2		2		2
ADDRESS	3	20	L	3	Y					3
CREDLIM		4	2	4	Y	3				4
$SLSYTD		4	2		Y	4				
BALANCE		4	2		N	5		3		
CURRENT		4	2		N			4		
30-60		4	2		N			5		
60-90		4	2		N			6		
OVER 90		4	2		N			7		
TRANS CTRL		2	X							

INQUIRY SYNTAX

ENTER key, combination, file

01   CUSTOMER RECORD
    02   CUSTOMER-NUMBER PICTURE X (8)
    02   CUSTOMER-NAME PICTURE X (20)
    02   ADDRESS-LINE OCCURS 3 TIMES PICTURE X (20)
    02   CREDIT-LIMIT PICTURE 9(5)V99
    02    $SALES-YTD PICTURE 9(5)V99
    02   ACCOUNT-BALANCE PICTURE 9(5)V99
    02   PERIOD-BALANCES PICTURE 9(5) V99
            03   CURRENT
            03   30-60
            03   60-90
            03   OVER-90
    02   TRANS-CTRL PICTURE XX

Figure 8-85   Table driven inquiry update

number appearing in the ADD column, and they are prompted in the sequence indicated by these numbers. In the example a new record would be prompted for customer number, name, three lines of address, and credit limit. All other data are not appropriate entries for the establishment of a new record and therefore do not have a prompt number appearing in the ADD column.

The sixth column contains update control. A record key is designated as K. Depending upon the file structure, there may be unique or multiple K appearances, and K may or may not be an updatable field, depending again upon the file structure and design of the update program. If an item cannot be updated, an N is cited; if it may be updated, an R or Y is cited. An assumption is made here that any field cited in the ADD sequence is permitted to be updated, but any field that is permitted to be updated does not necessarily have to appear in the ADD sequence. In the illustration, $SLSYTD is not inserted at the time of adding a new record but may be updated at a later time through the update program. The $SLSYTD would normally be modified by the invoice processor automatically, but since it may not be considered to be critical accounting information, can also be adjusted through the update program. In contrast, the customer and period balances are specifically excluded from update. An update item with an R code is interpreted in the ADD sequence as a required field of entry, while an update item with a Y code is interpreted as an optional entry in the ADD sequence.

The last three columns of the table specify display options expressed as three combinations. The user may designate by means of the table which data items are to be grouped for specific display combinations. For example, combination 1 will display the basic sales information, which is the customer number, name, credit limit, sales, and account balance. Combination 2 will display the aging information, which is the customer number, name, account balance, and period balances, whereas combination 3 displays the static descriptive information of customer number, name, address and credit limit. The ability to display all of the record would also be provided within the syntax of the command statement, an example of which is shown at the bottom of the figure. The *key* is the value of a key field (K) of the desired record; the *combination* is 1, 2 3, or ALL; and the *file* is the name of the file from which the record is to be accessed.

8.2 INFORMATION RETRIEVAL SYSTEMS

8.2.1 Concept Coordination

In the first chapter of Reference 1 there appears a diagram titled "Model of an Information System." It is indicated in this diagram that there are two distinct types of people who interact with a mechanized information system, *generators* and *users*. The generators produce documents that are introduced into the system via two paths. Through one of these paths the documents undergo data reduction, and some distillant of the original document becomes what is called in the diagram a *reference file*. Along the other path, documents themselves or microfilm copies are stored in document depositories. The user interacts with both the reference and the document files. The chapter goes on to discuss the construction of various components of the reference file.

8.2.2 The Coordinate Index

The most basic reference file construction is the *coordinate index*. As shown in Fig. 8-86 it consists of a term directory, implemented either as a tree or a randomized mapping, which points to either an inverted document list or to a multilist. A coordinate indexed reference file of this type enables one to cross or to coordinate two or more terms using AND, OR, and NOT logic.

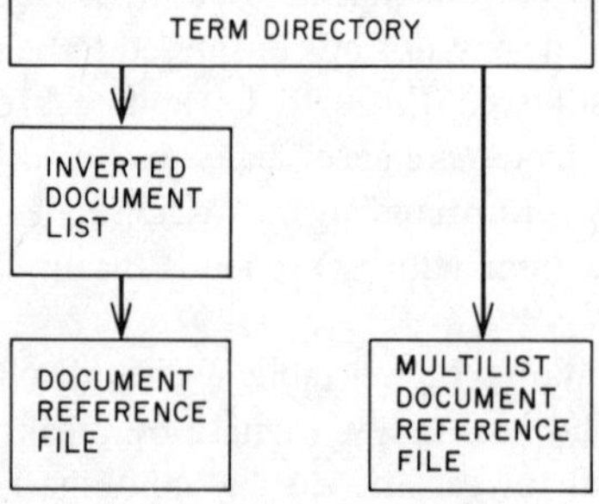

Figure 8-86 Coordinate index systems

The major purpose of the reference file is the location of documents in the depository by means of the index. Information retrieval systems use a variety of indexing techniques in order to achieve specific kinds of interaction between the user and the document file; however, since it is in fact the generator who is responsible for having placed the document in the depository, the interaction is *actually* one between the user and the generator, the files and indexes serving simply as a medium for this communication.

The coordinate index, though precise and efficient in its ability to subdivide or partition the total file for effective access, frequently falls short of providing adequate communication between the generators of information and the users. The coordinate index conveys very little information about the nature of the total collection and is therefore of little help to the user who wants to browse or who wants to adapt a question or series of questions to the specific characteristics of the file. Also, it does not reveal interrelations or equivalent terms within the general vocabulary of index terms and can actually obstruct or inhibit recall.

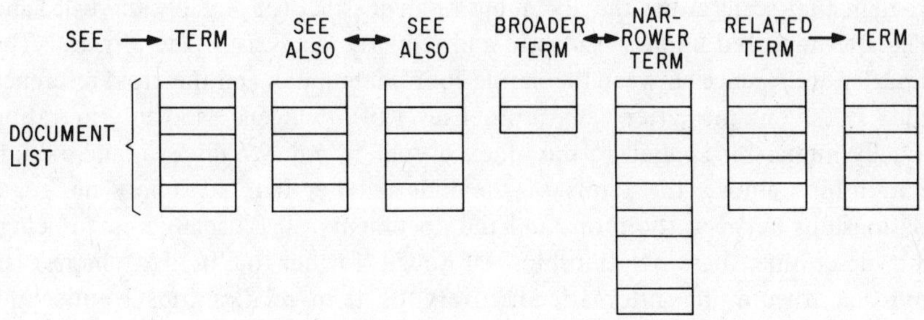

Figure 8-87   Cross reference index.

8.2.3   The Cross Reference Index

Figure 8-87 shows one of the techniques that can be overlayed upon the simple coordinate index. This technique is normally called a *cross reference index* and is familiar to all who use a library. Certain terms may appear in the index solely for synonymic or cross reference value. They are included in the index term vocabulary but do not appear at all in any of the document reference file records or surrogates. These terms point specifically to counterpart terms that are members of the coordinate indexing system and therefore have associated a list in the document reference file. They are called *SEE* terms and mean "see the other term instead of this one in order to enter the coordinate index system." This is illustrated in the upper left of Fig. 8-87. Some terms in the coordinate index are synonyms or have, in some sense, equivalent meaning to other terms in the index. This bilateral relationship is called *SEE ALSO.* A third type of cross reference is that of broader and narrower terms. A term that has a narrow or more specific meaning may coexist in the index system with other terms that have a more general meaning or are categorically inclusive of the given term. For example, the term *microwave circuits* might reference as a broader term, *electronic circuitry.* These two relations are also bilateral, but,unlike the SEE ALSO, are assymetric. A fourth mode of cross reference is the *RELATED* term, wherein a given term is not considered to be equivalent or interchangeable as in the case of SEE ALSO but is related in some way to another term; this relationship may be unilateral or bilateral. One should therefore not consider one term as a substitute for the other, nor should it necessarily be expected that the related term will draw down information that is actually pertinent to a request. (A related term to *microwave circuits* might be *radar.*)

The indexing of documents for the purpose of creating a simple, coordinated index, as shown in Fig. 8-86, can be exclusively performed by individually examining each document that is to be indexed. This examination and the subsequent indexing of the document can be performed by the author of the document, by a trained indexer who either selects from a controlled vocabulary of terms or can assign terms in an uncontrolled way, or even automatically by a program that scans either the document or an abstract (or possibly the title) and selects terms based upon a syntactic and semantic analysis of the phrases. The important difference between the simple coordinate index and the cross reference index is that in the latter case another level of intelligence and interpretation (usually human) is applied to the index overall, in order to discover and exhibit relationships among the terms of the index rather than to simply designate relationships between the terms and the documents. It is usually human beings who determine these relationships, although further on in this chapter an approach toward the automatic discovery of term relationships by machine processes is to be discussed.

8.2.4   Links and Roles

The coordinate and cross reference index systems treat only semantics of information in the file structure, leaving the syntax or associations that can be made among terms of processing at inquiry time. Furthermore, the syntax

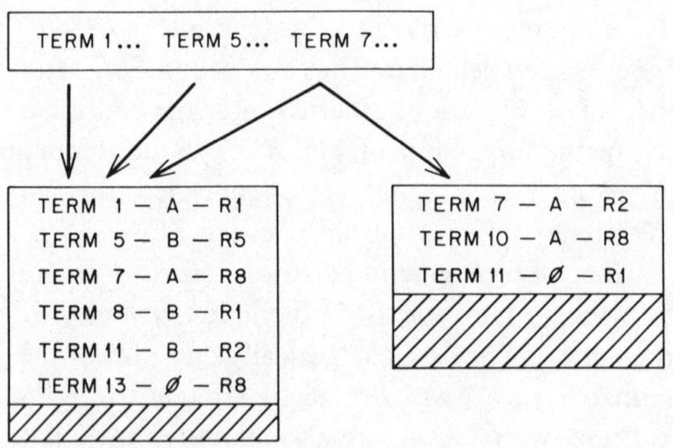

Figure 8-88   Links and roles

is limited to the three logical processes discussed in Chapter 4: Boolean, weighted, and relational logic. However, the syntactic facet of the information structure can be enhanced through the file organization itself by two techniques called *links* and *roles*; these can be used independently but are frequently applied together. The link is a formal association among two or more terms within the same record. In Fig. 8-88 the links are identified as letters; in the first record, terms 1 and 7 are considered to be linked by A, and terms 5 and 5, 8 and 11 are linked by B. Term 13 is linked to no other term. The role is a classification device, used to indicate functional differences in the usage of like index terms throughout the system. The set of roles is always defined manually and prior to the establishment of the file system. The role itself may appear either in the file or in the index. In Fig. 8-88 it is shown in the file.

Consider as an example of roles *manufacturing* and *sales*. In the figure, term 7, which appears in both records, has role R8 in the first and R2 in the second. If one were to assume that R8 represented *manufacturing* and R2, *sales* and term 7 represented, say, *alcohol*, then it would be the case that the first record pertained to the manufacture of alcohol, whereas the second pertained to the sale of alcohol. Someone who is entering the index with the term alcohol may not be interested in both of these connotations, and hence could limit his inquiry according to the desired role. Note also that the appearance of term 7 in each of these records is also associated with link A; this is coincidental, because the links are operative only within the record, not across record boundaries. When the links and the roles appear in the data file, the access of records via the term index is based only upon the term, and the individual records that are so accessed are then qualified according to whether a link among a given subset of terms has been requested in the inquiry and according to the desired role of the term.

Note that the link letters need have no particular significance; merely the fact that they are linked or associated according to some criterion of linkage established at the time the record was created is significant. An inquiry may thus be of the following form: To retreive all records that have terms 1 and 7 and 8 linked, where term 7 must assume role R8. This inquiry would retreive neither of the records shown in Fig. 8-88, because term 8 is not linked to terms 1 and 7. If the inquiry were to retreive all records that have terms 1 and 7 and 8, where terms 1 and 7 are linked, and where term 7 has role R8, then the first record would be retrieved. This method of linkage is called an *undifferentiated* link. It is desirable in some applications to establish specific categories or types of linkage, whereupon the linkage letters A, B, and the like are significant and represent certain pre-established categories. The inquiry will then state the category along with the fact of linkage. This is called a *differentiated* link system. In summary, the linkages enhance the syntactic facet of the information structure, whereas the roles enhanced the connotative semantic facet. As indicated above, the links can be implemented only within the data record itself, but the role could be either in the data record or the index.

8.2.5 The Articulated Index

An example of the usage of roles in an index is shown in Fig. 8-89. It is commonly called the *articulated* index. The most practical format for this index is graphic and has generally not been applied in automated, magnetic storage. The indentations correspond to levels of a tree. The index terms are cited at the first (leftmost) level of the tree, and the roles, which may be nested, are cited below (to the right). Three levels are shown in the articulated index of Fig. 8-89. The articulation or sentence structure relating to a given term is algorithmically

ALCOHOL

> APPLICATIONS OF_____
>
> > COMMERCIAL ____
> >
> > INDUSTRIAL ____
> >
> > ____ IN THE PRODUCTION OF WHISKEY
>
> MANUFACTURE OF____
>
> MEDICAL USES OF____
>
> ____ICS ANONYMOUS
>
> ____SALES IN THE U.S.

AUTOMOBILES

> PRODUCTION OF____
>
> STYLING OF____
>
> THE RELATION OF SOCIAL MOBILITY TO___
>
> ____IN THE DECADE 1960 TO 1970
>
> ____FOR PROFITABILITY

Figure 8-89 Articulated index

interpreted as follows: One may enter at any level of the tree. A sentence is formed by scanning the phrase at a given level, and whenever a hyphen is encountered, the entire phrase at the next higher level is inserted in place of the hyphen. The process is recursive or nested in the sense that a hyphen encountered in the next higher level is itself treated in a like manner. For example, entering Fig. 8-89 at the second level, one can define "applications of alcohol, manufacture of alcohol, medical uses of alcohol, Alcoholics Anonymous, and alcohol sales in the U.S." As another example, entering at the first level, one can define the phrase, "automobiles." As a third example, entering at the third level, one can define the phrases, "industrial applications of alcohol" and "applications of alcohol in the production of whiskey."

Note that in the second level example, "applications of alcohol," one would be led to all of the records dealing with (1) the commercial applications of alcohol, (2) the industrial applications of alcohol, and (3) applications of alcohol in the production of whiskey. The documents referenced by "manufacture of alcohol" would not be indexed under "applications of alcohol," because "manufacture of—" and "applications of—" both appear under "alcohol." Note also the complex syntactic phrase structures that can be developed through this algorithm, as illustrated by "the relation of social mobility to the styling of automobiles."

8.2.6 The Classified Index

A schema whereby conceptual relationships among terms are formulated is called a *classification*. The concept of classification is further refined beyond that of the cross reference index of Fig. 8-87 or the roles of Figs. 8-88 and 8-89 in the *hierarchic index*, or as it is sometimes called, the *thesaurus,* of Fig. 8-90.

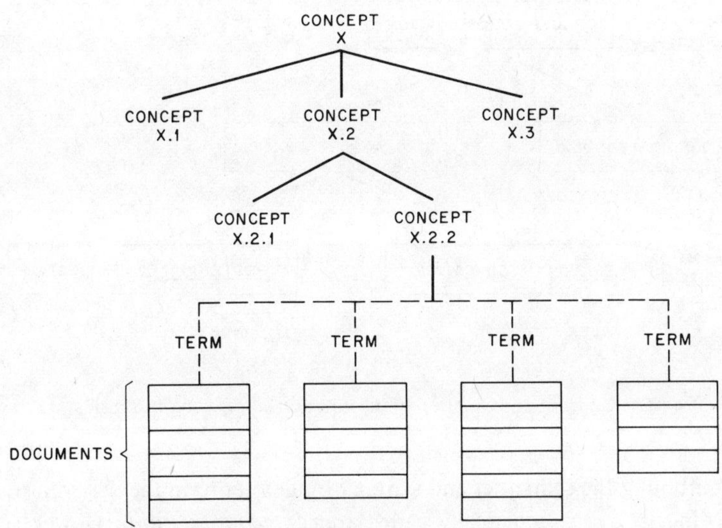

Figure 8-90 Hierarchic index (thesaurus)

Here the notion of broader term/narrower term is extended in a treelike fashion to multiple levels. At the top one may find a very broad concept, denoted in the figure as X. This concept relates to a number of more narrowly defined but nonetheless inclusive concepts identified in the figure as X.1, X.2, and X.3, as an example. Concept X.2, in turn, relates to the more specific, but inclusively related, concepts labeled X.2.1 and X.2.2. None of these concepts is assumed to be an index term that coordinates documents in the reference file; they are thought of only as entries in a classified index, the thesaurus, leading one to another as a progression is made from the top of the tree downward. At a terminating point in the tree, as illustrated at concept X.2.2, all index terms appear that might be subsumed under a given concept. Some of these terms may also appear under other concepts. The concept portion of this index, or what has been called a thesaurus, is prepared and maintained manually, since it is the experts in the particular field for which the information retreival system is being designed who must decide upon the conceptual hierarchy. The bottom of the hierarchy, where the terms are cited, is normally a coordinate, cross reference, or articulated index possibly with links and roles. One can use the thesaurus-index combination either by direct entry to the automated term index appearing at the bottom of the hierarchy, or by entry into one of the upper levels of the classification schedule that has been prepared for the index. The latter mode of usage is not unlike any of the standard library classification systems, Dewey Decimal, UDC, or Library of Congress.

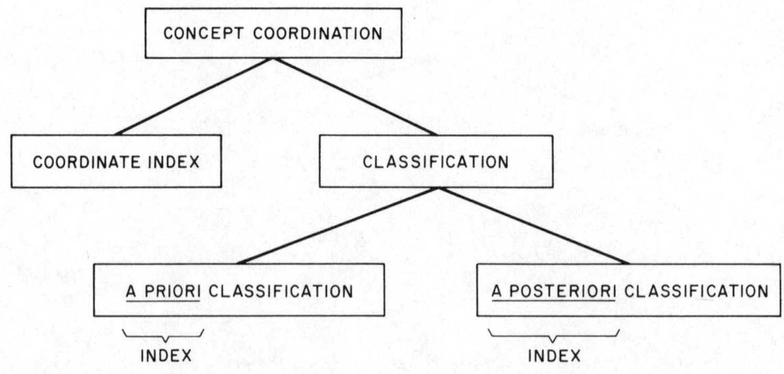

Figure 8-91 Concept coordination in information storage and retrieval systems

Combining the semantics and syntax of index terms in the ways illustrated in preceding figures is generically called *concept coordination.* However, one can broadly divide the methods of concept coordination into two groups, the *classified* and unclassified systems. Figure 8-91 illustrates the general schema for concept coordination. The unclassified systems are the pure coordinate indexes, as modeled in Fig. 8-86. Various kinds of classification ranging from the cross reference to roles to the more formal thesaurus depicted in the hierarchy of Fig. 8-90 can be visualized. There comes, however, a notable distinction that can be introduced directly as the result of computer technology *within* the classified systems. This one may call the *a priori* versus the *a posteriori*, classification systems. Traditionally, bodies of knowledge have been classified and a thesaurus or classification schedule has been drafted before or in the very early stages of document accumulation. The documents, as they were generated, could then be assigned index terms and a position in the classification system according to the predetermined thesaurus. Systems like the Dewey and Universal

Decimal systems and the Library of Congress system fall into this category. Later systems that have been automated for information retrieval like the DDC[23] (formerly known as ASTIA) and the NASA[24] systems have also had thesauri prepared in a hard copy book form to be used by the searcher as a manual aid in selecting terms prior to performing his machine search of the file. He enters the thesaurus by class and is led downward through the tree of the thesaurus to increasingly specific classes and at the terminus will find a list of index terms that can be used as the basis for logical search in the automated coordinate indexed file.

The major shortcomings of *a priori* classification are that it fails to provide satisfactory cross referencing from one node of the classification tree to another, except at the terminus of the tree, where the index terms are cited and the cross-referencing techniques illustrated in Figs. 8-87 through 8-89 can be employed. Second, the tree can only be modified in time at its terminal points unless a completely new classification is generated. Thus, if the document collection is a rapidly growing one and reflects changing patterns of knowledge and technology, the upper, more generic levels may only reflect the true classification of the earlier documents in the collection, and possibly the minority of them. It is obviously very expensive to produce a new classification manually, particularly if one must examine every document in the collection in order to make the judgments necessary to portray them accurately in the classification schedule. However, this procedure may become feasible though the use of computer algorithms that would be designed to examine the index terms of a document and to suggest through their concurrent usage among the manifold of all documents in the collection what a new classification schedule should be. Thus, an *a posteriori* generation of a classification schedule can be considered as a viable alternative to the traditional *a priori* methodology, where the *a posteriori* classification is continually updated and periodically regenerated as documents are added to the collection.

In Chapter 1, a three-step analogy was drawn between the development of information system technology and the development of the vacuum tube. It was indicated there that the third step in information system development is characterized by the use of the computer as a human intellect amplifier. Certainly the automatic classification of documents can be looked upon as falling into this category of activity. By means of the *a posteriori* or automatic classification of documents one is reorganizing a data base, not so much for the purpose of increasing the efficiency of the automated retrieval mechanisms, as would be characteristic of Step 2 in the analogy, but rather for the purpose of presenting a view of the data base, or document collection, to the user of the system in such a way that he could not possibly have viewed it himself without this assistance. He may therefore see *intensive* meaning, in the sense of facet 1 of Chapter 1, in the total collection of data that is not *extensively* or explicitly apparent or stated through the simple coordinate index, and, therefore, will have truly been provided with an amplifier of his own intellectual powers.

It is not the intent of this book to examine in any detail the current state of the art in automatic classification, but in order to make some of these ideas a little more concrete, a brief description of one such approach to the subject will be given, and Reference 26 can be consulted by those who have further interest in the subject. This reference also contains a very extensive bibliography.

Consider first that each document within a collection that is to be classified has been assigned indexed terms. Retrieval capability in the system, both with respect to relevance of material accessed and comprehensiveness of recall is, of course, related to the quality of index term assignment, but the process of *a posteriori* classification, as it is to be described here, begins *after* the assignment of index terms to the individual documents. Naturally, the quality of the classification in terms of its partitioning and cross-referencing capabilities will also be affected by the relevance of the indexing.

The purpose of classification is to find relationships for cross, sub, and super references among the various documents in the collection. This is achieved in *a priori* classification by devising a tree of *classification terms,* which may or may not appear as specific index terms to the documents. There appears in this tree one classification term at each node in the tree. Thus, for example, the classification term "physical science" may represent a particular high level node of a tree, which branches to lower level nodes such as "physics" and chemistry." These nodes in turn will branch to further subdivisions, such as "nuclear physics," "mechanics," etc. At the bottom of the classification tree, where the most specific terms appear, are enumerated the various documents falling within the specific partition implied by the path leading from the top of the tree to the given terminal node. Cross referencing is achieved by denoting all of the terminal nodes, and thus a total collection of documents, subsumed under a given higher level node. Thus, all of the documents falling under the node "physics" are, in a sense, a family and hence are implicitly cross referenced.

This type of classification has a weakness, however, in that specific cross referencing from one terminal node to another that can only be linked through a higher level node common to both of them in inefficient, because a very large family of documents may be included in the total cross reference family. For example a document under "physics" and a document under "chemistry" may share one or more of their index terms in common, and thus there is an implied cross reference, but in terms of the classification the cross reference will include all documents under the family "physical science." An inversion technique called the "key to node translation mapping," to be described later, is a device that can be used to improve the precision of cross referencing in a classification tree.

The *a posteriori* classification has a similar construction, but with two basic differences. One is that the index originally assigned to the documents become the descriptive entities appearing *within* the classification tree, and second, a node of a classification tree may be characterized by or contain more than one classification or index term.

The classification process is to be described as a top-down breakdown set of three telescoping principles or algorithms. The first and highest level of description defines the gross functional properties of the classification that will result. The second level of description is presented as a model of an automatic *a posteriori* classification system. It is a framework or broad algorithmic statement within which computer programs can be written to effect the classification whose properties are defined in the first level description. The third level description contains a specific algorithm for generating classes. One such algorithm is given in Reference 25, and Reference 26 discusses others.

The properties of the *a posteriori* classification are as follows:

1. The nodes of the classification tree are populated by index terms of the documents.

2. Every document contained in the classification is described by a set of terms that is wholly contained within a set of nodes that form a path within the tree.

3. Each term will appear only once within the set of nodes of the path described in Property 2.

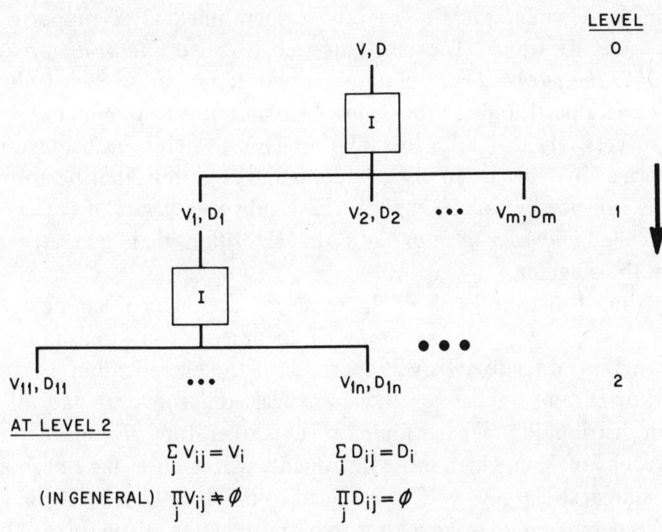

Figure 8-92 Model of an *a posteriori* classification, Step I: Creation of inclusive groups

An algorithmic model of an *a posteriori* classification is illustrated in Figs. 8-92 and 8-93. The inputs, shown in Fig. 8-93, are (1) the vocabulary, V, of the index terms and (2) the set of documents, D, that is currently indexed by these terms. The elements of the set V are index terms or integers representing

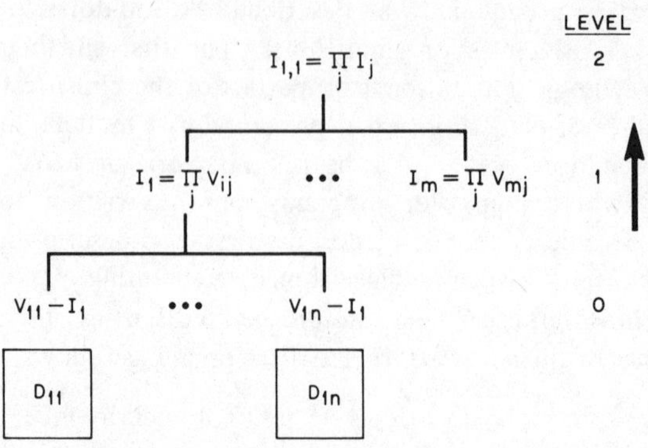

Figure 8-93 Automatic classification, Step 2: Creation of a term hierarchy

index terms; an element in the set D is a set of index terms (or integers representing index terms) that has been assigned to the given document, along with a unique reference number to the document. The output or resultant of the classification model, shown in Fig. 8-93, is a tree, the nodes of which contain index terms and which satisfies the above mentioned three properties of an *a posteriori* classification. The resultant tree is called a *term hierarchy* or, in library terms, a *thesaurus.* It is generated in a two-step process. Step 1, illustrated in Fig. 8-92, is a partitioning process in which all terms contained in vocabulary set V are successively divided into subvocabularies, wherein each subvocabulary contains terms that are as closely related as the algorithm that performs these subdivisions can possibly make them. These subvocabularies of closely related terms are called *inclusive groups,* and the algorithm that generates them is labeled I in the diagram.

Algorithm I distributes all of the terms in vocabulary V among m inclusive groups, $V_1, V_2, \ldots V_m$, by examining all document descriptions in D. A rule of algorithm I, in order to satisfy Property 2 of the classification, is that every description of D must appear together in at least one subvocabulary of V after V has been distributed. A partitioning of D is, therefore, also made along with the subdivisions of V in which those documents whose terms have been assigned to a given subvocabulary V_i will be assigned to the document partition D_i. The algorithm I is permitted to assign a term to more than one of the subvocabularies, although it should attempt to assign a given term to as few as possible, but a document description must be uniquely placed in one partition D_i of D. The nodes of the tree of inclusive groups, shown in Fig. 8-92, have been canonically numbered. At level 0 exists one node with the pair of sets V and D, without subscripts; at level 1 each node consists of a V, D pair with a single subscript; at level 2 each node consists of a V, D pair with double subscripts, and so forth. The partition constraints on I stated above are formally expressed at level 2, as shown at the bottom of the diagram.

Thus, the objective of I is to divide the terms of V in such a way as to create groups of closely related terms that have minimal overlap and where the descriptions of documents that were composed of these terms are exclusively distributed among these groups. This statement contains the inherent characteristics of any classification system and in addition assures the satisfaction of the properties given to an *a posteriori* classification above. The number of groups into which I distributes the sets V and D at a given level of the tree and the number of levels and balance of the tree are purely functions of the strategy employed in algorithm I. One example of such an algorithm is given in Appendix B of Reference 1. Others are given in Reference 26.

The classification is completed in Step 2 (Fig. 8-93) by a process that starts at the bottom of the tree of inclusive groups, generated from Step 1. The document partition $D_{i,j,k,\ldots}$ appearing at the terminal node of the tree is called a *cell* or classification set of documents. It corresponds approximately to a "shelf" in an *a priori* classification system, that is, a collection of documents within a lowest level class of the classification system. In an automated system, it may be worthwhile to take particular advantage of this "shelving" arrangement by storing these documents in some contiguous way, such as on the same cylinder of a movable head disk or on a section of magnetic tape. Chapter 7 of Reference 1 presents an example of the utility of such a storage strategy in the case of batch searching on magnetic tape and multiple inquiry processing from a disk.

In Step 2 the classification or term hierarchy is created by intersecting the vocabulary sets appearing under a given subnode of the tree. For example, numbering the levels now in reverse as 0, 1 and 2, a node at the second level (level 1) is created by intersecting all V sets under it at the 0th level. Thus node I_1 equals the intersection of the sets V_{ij}. The resulting tree consists of nodes that are occupied only by index terms, since only the original index term vocabulary V and subvocabularies were used to generate them, and all documents reside in their respective cells at the terminating points of the tree. Note also that as a result of the partitioning algorithm I, a document is guaranteed to appear in one and only one cell, and every document in the original collection, D, is so represented.

Appendix B of Reference 1 contains an illustration of this process and also contains a description of how one would organize cross referencing indexes in order to enable maximum utilization of the classification. For this purpose an index called the *key to node* table is generated, where key is the equivalent of an index term in this discussion. It is an alphabetic arrangement of the keys or index terms which points to all nodes in the classification tree that contain the given key. One can then approach the file system in a variety of ways. The thesaurus or tree can be used directly as an instrument of classification obtaining terms to be used in the construction of inquiries. One can broaden or narrow an inquiry by moving upward or downward, respectively, in the tree. Or one can combine terms selected freely, or from the alphabetically organized vocabulary V, with Boolean logic, and by examining a key to node table can determine whether there are indeed paths through the tree which, based upon the logic, would lead to documents existing in the cells at the terminals of the tree. A number of problems are given in the problem listing for this chapter that relate to the properties and utilization of *a posteriori* classification. The interested reader is invited to explore the subject further through these problems, through Appendix B and Chapter 7 of Reference 1, and through Reference 26 and its bibliography.

8.2.7 Text Search

The subject of file structures and of indexes, as emphasized in the preceding discussion, is largely one of access to units of information at the record level within the hierarchy of data aggregates. The application of information retrieval, however, must also be concerned with the processing of data *within* a record. This processing may be relatively simple, such as the formating of specific data fields for display, or it may be complex, such as the examination of textual information for symbol string matches, for Boolean or other syntactic relations among the symbol strings, or for even more complex linguistic analyses that may involve syntax, semantics, and even translation. Other types of analyses may include numerical and statistical computations and heuristic data processing.

Text search is one of the more common types of intrarecord processing in IS & R systems. The input or inquiry to the search is a set of symbol strings, usually words or partial words that are to be found imbedded within the record text either as a set or according to some syntactic relation. The relation may be a Boolean logic relation or it may be a concatenation or "followed by" relation. The general approach to this problem is to determine first whether each of the required inquiry words is imbedded in the record text, and if so, to qualify the record based upon the required syntactic relation, if one is given. This procedure, however, can be very expensive in terms of machine (that is, CPU) time, particularly where the record text is long. It is certainly desirable to devise an efficient indexing scheme so as to call out as few records for this type of examination as possible, but the number of records searched is always going to be a function of the file size, the file organization, and the inquiry characteristics.

Since quite a number of systems have been developed that make heavy use of text search, and it has become a significant economic factor in the operation of these systems, some attention has been given to maximizing the efficiency of text-searching processes. One of the most efficient that this author has encountered was developed at the Illinois Institute of Technology Research Institute (IITRI) and is described fully in Reference 27. The approach taken by the IITRI group is shown in Fig. 8-94. Consider, as shown at the top of the diagram, that the inquiry contains three parts, the record access logic, the text search strings, and the text search syntax. The first part is transmitted to the

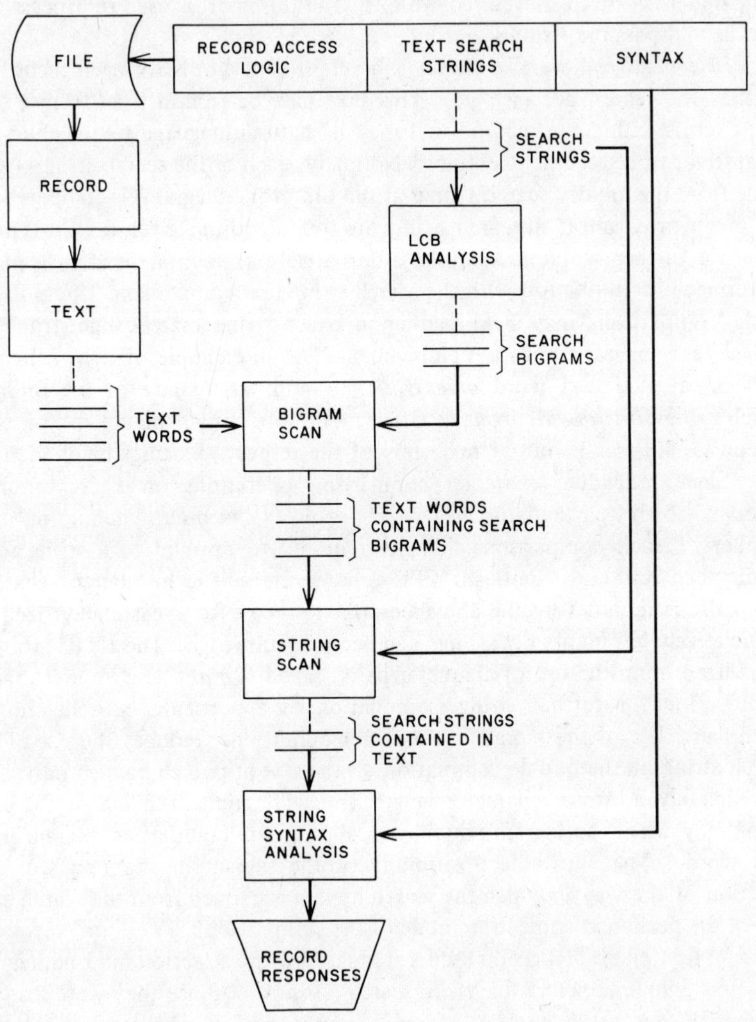

Figure 8-94   The text search

file and index system, which, as indicated, produces the records to be searched. The second part transmits the strings for a preprocessing analysis and is then compared with the retrieved record text. The third part is used to process those records that pass the string search.

The result of the file search is a set of text words for each record that satisfies the record access logic. This text may be from a title, from a set of index terms within the record, or it may be natural language text such as from an abstract or a document extract. Normally, each of the search strings (which come from the inquiry search strings at the top of the diagram) is compared with the text words, and if all search strings are found within a given text, it is passed along for further syntactic analysis. Alternatively, the syntactic analysis may be performed in combination with the search string-text comparison. The individual string comparisons may be based upon exact string match, right-truncation embedment, or left-truncation embedment. As an example of right-truncation embedment, the text word *organization* would satisfy any of the following search strings: *org*, *organ*, *organiz*. Other modes of comparison are also possible, of course, such as n out of m letters of the respective strings being identical.

Since individual character comparison operations on a computer are generally costly, particularly in a word-organized machine, a reduction in the number of such comparisons that are required to respond to a string search inquiry can result in significant CPU time savings. The number of character comparisons required by the above described process for a reasonably sized text and relatively few number of strings, can become quite high. The IITRI group has capitalized upon the use of character pairs, called *bigrams**, as a conditioner or qualification for further string examination of a particular search string-text word pair. Use of the bigram as the search conditioner reduces the size of each search string, in the initial examination, to the size of two characters rather than a completely arbitrary character length and will require the use of the entire string only when the bigram matches an appropriate counterpart bigram in the text word. The allowable positioning of the bigram in the text word is a function of the way in which the search bigram is derived from the search string and of the particular truncation mode of the comparison.

At first, the IITRI group used a standard bigram selection method, namely, the first two characters of each search string. Since they were searching sequential files for a current awareness application in which every record in rather large files had to be examined, however, they found that there were still a fairly large number of text words that passed this bigram screen and thus necessitated full search string comparison, although there was a very substantial cost reduction over not using bigrams at all. They then conceived a technique of bigram analysis that generated a far superior screen in terms of search string-text

---

*Other character combinations such as triples and quadruples (trigrams and quadra-grams) could also be used, and the particular use of trigrams as opposed to bigrams is discussed in Reference 27.

word selectivity. This was to generate all possible bigrams in the search string, and then to select the least commonly occurring bigram, based upon a predetermined table of bigram occurrence within the existing data base to date.

As an example, the search string *organ* would be found to contain the bigrams *or*, *rg*, *ga*, and *an*. It is obvious that the bigram *rg* is likely to be far less common in a given file than either of the bigrams *or* or *an*. Thus, as shown in the diagram, a least common bigram (LCB) analysis is first performed on each search string, which then produces the actual search bigram for the string. These are used in the bigram scan against the text words in conjunction with the particular comparison mode specification (left truncation, right truncation, etc.) for each search bigram and each text word. The output of the bigram scan is all text words containing the search bigrams. As shown in the diagram, all of the search strings must then be compared with these text words, and those search strings that are contained within the text are submitted to the string syntax analyzer in order to determine whether the record is a true response to the original three part inquiry.

The investment in LCB analysis appears to have a pay-off, according to the experience at IITRI, when the file is to be searched sequentially and all records are to be scanned. Whether this analysis is justified in the case of a list-structured, random-access file would be a function of the average number of records to be searched per inquiry and the length of text within these records.

8.2.8   Model of the IS & R System

Having discussed in the previous two sections the indexing of data files and text analysis of data within records, as functional requirements of an information storage and retrieval system, it will be useful at this point to summarize the discussion by presenting a model of an IS & R system. This is illustrated in Fig. 8-95. In accordance with the concept of the information system illustrated in Fig. 1, Chapter 1 of Reference 1, there are the *generators* of information who feed documents into the system, and there are the *users* of the data base who feed inquiries into the system. At the top of Fig. 8-95, data are entered by the *generator*, normally in the form of data base documents. These undergo a data selection and encoding process. First, the data base documents that are to be processed into the system undergo a screening, and then certain specific items of data extracted from the document, formated and encoded for data conversion, whereupon a data file record will be established. After data conversion, or in the case of manual indexing, concurrent with conversion, the documents are indexed.

Manual indexing can be an expensive process, because it requires human intellectual effort that must be devoted to each incoming document. If this process is not properly performed, it can result in extraneous, and therefore expensive, retrievals; it can also result in a failure to retrieve relevant documents and thereby degrade the general performance of the system. In some systems

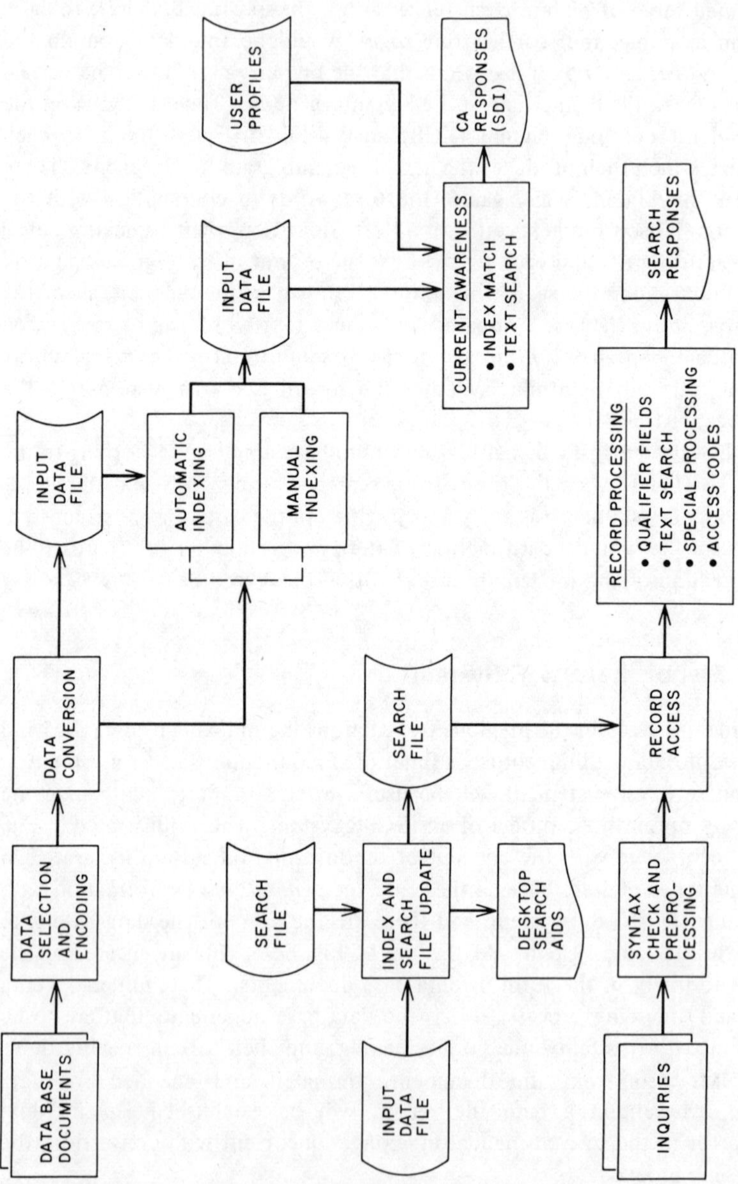

Figure 8-95 Model of an information storage and retrieval system

there is sufficient control exercised over the generators of information, so that they are required to index the documents that they are submitting. This significantly reduces the cost of indexing because the conceptual effort of understanding the material of the document does not have to be repeated.

In systems where such control cannot be exercised, and where the volume of documents is very high, automatic indexing techniques have been attempted.[28] The simplest approach to automatic indexing makes use of the text scan. A ceratin part of the converted data, such as the title, an abstract of the document, extracts of the document, or possibly the entire document itself is examined. Certain rules for word exclusion and word modification are built into the scan in order to derive a meaningful and economic set of index terms. The exclusions normally come from a stop list of words that includes prepositions, conjunctions, articles, and a number of commonly used verbs and nouns. Word modifications may include the truncation of suffixes and plurals.

A manual index, on the other hand, can be created in diverse ways, as indicated by the illustrations in Figs. 8-86 through 8-90. At this point, whether indexing is manual or automatic, the input data file will contain both the converted data base document extracts and the indexing necessary for the generation of a random search file.

Sometimes an IS & R system must serve two requirements. One, called *current awareness*, alerts users spontaneously to new incoming material in which they may possibly be interested. The other, *retrospective search*, provides search of the total accumulated data base or certain selected subsets of it. *Current awareness* is implemented by developing user profiles much in the same way one develops an inquiry and submitting them regularly to each new data base increment.

The user profile may contain the index terms as well as textual search strings. If the number of profiles is large, it may be more economical to perform the current awareness search sequentially on the input data file rather than submitting it to the indexed random file. The resultant product of current awareness, which is sometimes called *selective dissemination of information* (SDI), is a set of document references compiled for each user profile. For user convenience, these responses can be printed on cards with a perforated attachment that contains check-off boxes and document numbers so that the recipient can simply tear off and return the attachment, indicating the documents that he would like to receive, and then file the citation card itself.

The input data file containing both the converted document and the indexing information is processed by the index and search file update program. These files are updated in the manner described in Chapter 4. An auxiliary output of this process may be a printed desktop search aid. One form of such an aid is called the KWIC index, which means Keyword in Context. The KWIC index is basically a multiple entry index, usually based upon the document title words. Each significant title word is an entry point to the index. The significance of a word is normally denoted by its nonexistence on a stop list, similar to the type of stop list alluded to in the preceding discussion. Each entry of the KWIC index contains a citation of the complete title along with the document reference number. The title is entered once into the index for each significant word in it, and its position in the index is designated by the alphabetic position of the word corresponding to its entry. Furthermore, the entry word is prominently displayed in order to facilitate its visual location. This can be achieved in a number of ways. One frequently used method is to print all of the entry words in a single column down the middle of the page, with the title itself being shifted to the right or to the left in order to accommodate such an alignment. Another approach is to print the entry word in its own column, say at the left hand edge of the page, followed by the complete title.*

Another type of desktop search aid would be the thesaurus that results from either an *a priori* or *a posteriori* classification, as illustrated in Figs. 8-90 and 8-93. In some systems, inverted lists are even printed as search aids in addition to indexes, so that for certain types of questions, where the logic is simple and the lists to be manipulated relatively short, an entire search can be performed without the use of a computer.

The processing of an inquiry is illustrated at the bottom of Fig. 8-95. Normally there is a syntax check of the input and preprocessing of the inquiry logic. The records are then accessed from the search file based upon the output of the preprocessing, and the individual records are processed using any data fields within the record that may be required to qualify the ultimate retrieval. Such intra-record qualification may be based upon text search or upon other special processing requiring algorithms to pass upon a portion of the data content. For example, there are chemical structure search systems[29,30] that store within a record a connection table which describes precisely all of the atom connections within the molecule. The index terms of such a record are structural fragments that represent characteristic or topological substructures of the chemical molecule. The inquiry is a substructure for which all structures in which it is embedded are to be searched. The fragments contained in the inquiry are the search keys, and once a record has been accessed, an iterative atom-by-atom search is performed upon the connection table of the structure to determine whether the inquiry substructure is definitely embedded within it.

This type of special processing would therefore act as the final qualifier for access of the record, in addition, possibly, to any of the other types of record processing cited. The output is a set of search responses per inquiry. In the case of the chemical search system, the output may include a structural diagram. Furthermore, it may be desirable to provide graphic input capability as well in order to enable the inquirer to draw the substructure using a light pen or electronic tablet as an input device. Figure 8-95 characterizes, at a broad

---

*This arrangement is sometimes referred to as a KWOC–keyword out of context.

functional level, the majority of IS & R systems, although some of them may not contain all of the indicated components.

The two general applications discussed in this chapter, transaction oriented business data processing and document oriented information storage and retrieval, represent the principal usage of digital computers today for symbolic data processing, and it is largely from these applications, with perhaps one exception, that the techniques and the systematization of data management, as organized, defined, classified, and described in this book have come. The other application, though not as extensively used, which has contributed to the development of data management technique, is artifical intelligence. In fact the techniques employed in the applications of artificial intelligence are usually more advanced than is normally required to solve the problems of transaction and document data processing; the hierarchic and network structures described in Chapters 2, 3 and 4 are frequently employed with unending variation by the programmers of artificial intelligence applications.[31,32,33]

EPILOGUE

In Chapter 1 it was indicated that one purpose of the book would be to move the body of knowledge referred to as *data processing* a step closer to being an organized and properly structured science. It is hoped, as a result, that when one says *data management*, he can think in, at least, definitional terms and perhaps also operational terms in a way that can be readily communicated from one investigator to another. Furthermore, it is hoped that the operational or technique oriented aspects of this book, which in a science would be considered as postulates and theorems (though no such presumptions can as yet be made with respect to this science) may serve to standardize, and relieve duplication of effort in, the conceptualization of the algorithms and procedures associated with data management.

Data, as indicated in this first chapter, have five facets. Throughout the book we have approached this multifaceted object from each of its pentagonal sides. But, perhaps there is a sixth facet that cannot so aptly be defined or even presently discussed. This is man's interaction with and reaction to the data and all the processing and manipulative aspectsof their relationship. What is the role of data and data processing in the human cognitive and decision making process? What is the relation of the human brain, its physiological and logical structure, to the external environment that these data and data manipulations represent?

It is certainly enough for us to understand the first five facets of data in order to accomplish the myriad of practical assignments given to us, but the significant challenge of the future, also referred to in the first chapter as the third stage of technological development of information systems, is the use of the computer, and more particularly the data processing system, as a human thought amplifier. At some not too far distant time it will become necessary to gain significantly greater insight into and to arrive at an adequate understanding of the sixth facet of data—*interaction.*

Bibliography

CITED REFERENCES

1. Lefkovitz, D., *File Structures for On-Line Systems,* Spartan Books, New York, 1969.
2. Yovitz, M. C., "Information Science: Toward the Development of a True Scientific Discipline," *American Documentation*, vol. 20, 4, Oct. 1969, pp. 369-376.
3. "IBM System/360 Operating System COBOL Language (E and F)," No. C28-6516-8, IBM Corporation.
4. "IBM System/360 Operating System PL/I(F) Language Reference Manual," No. GC28-8201-3, IBM Corporation.
5. Metaxides, A., *et al*, CODASYL Data Base Task Group Report, April 1971.
6. Johnson, L. R., "An Indirect Chaining Method for Addressing on Secondary Keys," *Communications of the ACM*, vol. IV, No. 5, May 1961.
7. "Introduction to IBM System/360 Direct Access Storage-Devices and Organization Methods," No. GC20-1649-4, IBM Corporation, 1969.
8. Prywes, N. S., and Gray, H. J., *et al*, "The Multi-List Type Associative Memory," *Proceedings of Symposium on Gigacycle Computing Systems*, AIEE Publication, No. S-136, Jan. 1962, pp. 87-107.
9. Meadow, Charles T., *The Analysis of Information Systems*, Wiley, New York, 1967.
10. Landauer, W. I., "The Balanced Tree and Its Utilization in Information Retrieval," *Transactions on Electronic Computer of the IEEE*, vol. EC-XII, No. 5, Dec. 1963.
11. Patt, Y. N., "Variable Length Tree Structures Having Minimum Average Search Time," *Communications of the ACM,* 12, 2, Feb. 1969, pp. 72-76.
12. Susenguth, E., "Use of Tree Structures for Processing Files," *Communications of the ACM*, 6, 5, May 1963, pp. 272-279.
13. Kain, R. Y., "Block Structures, Indirect Addressing, and Garbage Collection," *Communications of the ACM,* 12, 7, July 1969, pp. 395-398.
14. Castleman, P. A., *et al*, "The Prophet System," Bolt Beranek and Newman, A Report produced under Contract No. NIH 70-4113, May 1970.
15. "IDS/COBOL General Electric Information System," CPB-144, August 1966.
16. Hsiao, D. K., "A File System for a Problem Solving Facility," Ph.D. Dissertation, U. of Penna., 1968.
17. Wadsworth and Bryan, *Introduction to Probability and Random Variables*, McGraw-Hill, 1960.
18. Pritsker, A., and Kiviat, P., *Simulation with GASP II, A FORTRAN Based Simulation Language,* Prentice Hall, 1969.

19. Baker, N. R., and Nance, R. E., "The Use of Simulation in Studying Information Storage and Retrieval Systems," American Documentation, 19, 4, Oct. 1968, pp. 363-370.

20. "General Purpose Simulation System/360 OS, Version 2, User's Manual," No. SH20-0694, IBM Corporation, 1969.

21. Knuth, D. E., and McNeley, J. L., "SOL, A Symbol Language for General-Purpose Systems Simulation," *IEEE Transactions on Electronic Computers*, vol. EC-13, No. 4., Aug. 1964.

22. Kiviat, P. J., and Villanuava, H. M., *SIMSCRIPT II Programming Language Reference Manual*, Prentice Hall, 1968.

23. "Technical Abstracts Bulletin," Defense Documentation Center, Cameron Station, Alexandria, Va., 22314.

24. "Index of NASA Technical Publications with Abstracts," July 1960-December 1961, NASA SP-9.

25. Needham, R. M., and Sparck Jones, K., "Keywords and Clumps—Recent Work on Information Retrieval at the Cambridge Language Research Unit," *Journal of Documentation*, vol. XX, No. 1, Mar. 1964.

26. Jardine, N., and Sibson, R., *Mathematical Taxonomy*, Wiley, New York, 1971.

27. Ondirisin, E. M., "The Least Common Bigram: A Dictionary Arrangement Technique for Computerized Natural-Language Text Searching, An Internal Report," IIT Research Institute, Chicago, Ill.

28. Rush, J. E., et al, "Automatic Abstracting and Indexing Production of Indiccative Abstracts by Application of Contextual Inference and Syntactic Coherency Criteria," Journal of the American Society for Information Science, 22, No. 4, 1971, pp. 60-274.

29. Lefkovitz, D., and Van Meter, C., "An Experimental Real Time Chemical Information System," *Journal of Chem. Doc.*, 6, 173, 1966.

30. Milne, M., Lefkovitz, D., Hill, H., and Powers, R., "Search of CA Registry (1.25 Million Compounds) with the Topological Screens System," *Journal of Chem. Doc.*, 12, 183, 1972.

31. Newell, A., and Simon, H. A., "The Logic Theory Machine," IRE *Transactions*, vol. IT-2, No. 3, Sept. 1956, pp. 61-79.

32. Newell, A., *Human Problem Solving*, Prentice Hall, 1972.

33. Newell, A., *Information Processing Language V Manual*, Prentice Hall, 1961.

GENERAL REFERENCES

Chapter 1

Dodd, G. G., "Elements of Data Management Systems," *Computing Surveys*, 1, 2 June 1969, pp. 117-133.

Chapter 3

Arora, S. R., "Randomized Binary Search Techniques," *Communications of the ACM,* 12, 2, Feb. 1969, pp. 77-80.

Chapter 4

Lowe, T. C., "The Influence of Data Base Characteristics and Usage on Direct Access File Organization," *Journal of the ACM,* vol. 15, No. 4, Oct. 1968.

Crick, M. F., and Lorie, R. A., "A Data-Base System for Interactive Applications," IBM Data Processing Division, Cambridge Scientific Center, G320-2058, July 1970.

Hsaio, D. K., and Harary, F., "A Formal System for Information Retrieval from Files," *Communications of the ACM,* vol. 13, Feb. 1970, pp. 67-73.

Shaffner, R. M., "The Organization, Maintenance and Search of Machine Files," *Annual Review of Information Science and Technology,* vol. 3, pp. 137-167.

Bayes, A. J., "Retrieval Times for a Packed Direct Access Inverted File," *Communications of the ACM,* 12, 10, Oct. 1969, pp. 582-583.

McGee, W. C., "Generalized File Processing," *Annual Review in Automatic Programming,* vol. 5, 1969, pp. 77-149.

McGee, W. C., "File Structures for Generalized Data Management," *Proceedings of the IFIP Congress,* 1969, Applications 1, Booklet F, pp. 68-73.

Pan, G. S., "Generalized Structure and Optimum File Design Considerations," *Proc. 5th National Conf. of the Comp. Soc. of Canada,* 1966, pp. 309-322.

Chapter 5

"COBOL Extension to Handle Data Bases," Data Base Task Group, Clearinghouse, U.S. Dept. of Commerce, Springfield, Va., PB177 682, Jan. 1968.

Chapter 6

Kleinrock, L., "A Continuum of Time-Sharing Scheduling Algorithms," *Proceedings of the AFIPS,* SJCC, 1970, pp. 453-458.

Denning, Peter J., "Third Generation Computer Systems," *ACM Computing Surveys,* vol. 3, 1971.

Chapter 7

Stimler, S., *Real-Time Data Processing Systems,* McGraw-Hill, 1965.

Martin, J., *Design of Real Time Computer Systems,* Prentice Hall, 1967.

Appendix A

GASP Data Cards

Card type	Columns	Field name	Format	Use
1	1-12	NAME	6A2	Name or problem ID
	13-16	NPROJ	14	Project number
	17-18	MON	12	Month
	19-20	NDAY	12	Day
	21-24	NYR	14	Year
	25-28	NRUNS	14	Number of simulation runs
2	1-5	NPRMS	15	Number of parameter sets
	6-10	NHIST	15	Number of histograms
	11-15	NCLCT	15	Number of random variables to be tracked by COLCT
	16-20	NSTAT	15	Number of random variables to be tracked by TMST
	21-25	ID	15	Maximum number of entries in all queues
	26-30	IM	15	Maximum number of attributes in an entry
	31-35	NOQ	15	Number of queues
	36-40	MXC	15	Maximum number of cells to be used in any histogram
	41-50	SCALE	F10.4	Scale factor
3	1-5	NCELS(1)	15	Number of cells in histogram 1
	.			.
	.			.
	.			.
	20-25	NCELS(5)	15	Number of cells in histogram 5
4	1-5	KRANK(1)	15	The attribute number that ranks queue 1.
	.			
	.			
	.			
	45-50	KRANK(10)	15	The attribute number that ranks queue 10

Card Type	Column	Field name	Format	Use
5	1-5	INN(1)	I5	Designation of whether queue 1 is accessed LVF or HVF. INN = 1 for LVF; INN = 2 for HVF
		.		
		.		
		.		
	45-50	INN(10)	I5	Queue 10 access
6	1-10	PARAM(I,1)	F10.4	Parameter I, 1
		.		
		.		
		.		
	30-40	PARAM (I, 4)	F10.4	Parameter I, 4 (One card is entered for every parameter set; the total number of parameter sets is indicated by NPRMS on card 2).
7	1-5	MSTOP	I5	Method of stopping the simulation MSTOP = 0 means that a particular event has been provided by the user MSTOP = + 1 means that the simulation is to end when $TNOW \geqslant TFIN$ MSTOP = − 1 means that the simulation is to end immediately. The user program sets MSTOP to this value
	6-10	JCLR	I5	JCLR = 0 means that statistics are not to be reset JCLR = 1 means that statistics are to be reset
	11-15	NORPT	I5	NORPT = 0 means that a final summary report is to be automatically printed NORPT = 1 means that a final report is not to be printed
	16-20	NEP	I5	NEP indicates the data card type at which the *next* run is to begin reading
	21-30	TBEG	F10.3	Initial simulation time (TNOW)

Card type	Column	Field name	Format	Use
	31-40	TFIN	F10.3	Final simulation time if MSTOP = + 1
	41-43	JSEED	I4	JSEED = 0 means that the random number generator and simulation time are *not* to be reinitiated JSEED ≠ 0 means that the random number generator is to be seeded with JSEED and TNOW is set equal to TBEG
8.0	1-10	JQ	I10	JQ = − 1
8.1	1-10	JQ	I10	JQ is the queue number into which the attributes on the card are to be stored
	11-20	ATRIB (1)	F10.4	Attribute 1 in queue JQ
	41-50	ATRIB (4)	F10.4	Attribute 4 in queue JQ
8.2	1-10	JQ	I10	JQ = 0 (a blank card may be entered); this card signals the end of the Card Type 8 series
9				4 Blank Cards

Appendix B

TRAVL
1A
CALL
DRAND
(ISEED, R)
1B
DO 1
I = 1, 4
1C
R — PARAM
(4, I)
0, +
1D
CONTINUE
1F
AT (2) = PARAM (3, I)
1E
AT (2) = INT (UNFRM
(PARAM (5, 1),
PARAM (5, 2) + .999))
2
NQ (AT
(4) + 2)
+
3
KDBS
(AT (4))
0, −
−, +
4
KCBS
0
−, +
0
2
7
CALL FILEM (AT (4) + 2)
CALL FILEM (2)
FILE
TRANS
DISK
1
8A
CALL DRAND (ISEED, R)
AT (1) = TNOW — PARAM (5, 1)
* ALOG (R)
8B
AT (2) = 1
AT (3) = KTRN
AT (4) = INT (UNFRM
(1.0, PARAM (2, 3) + .999))
KTRN = KTRN + 1
8C
CALL
FILEM (1)
FILE
EVENT
TRAVL
RETURN
1

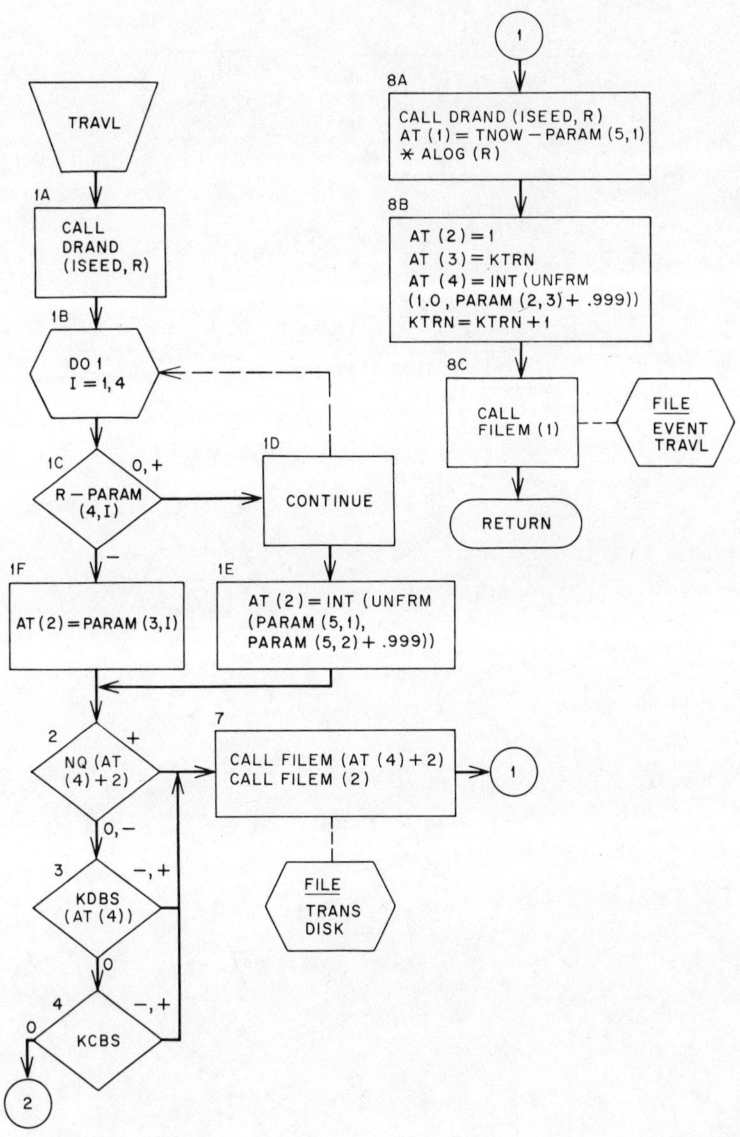

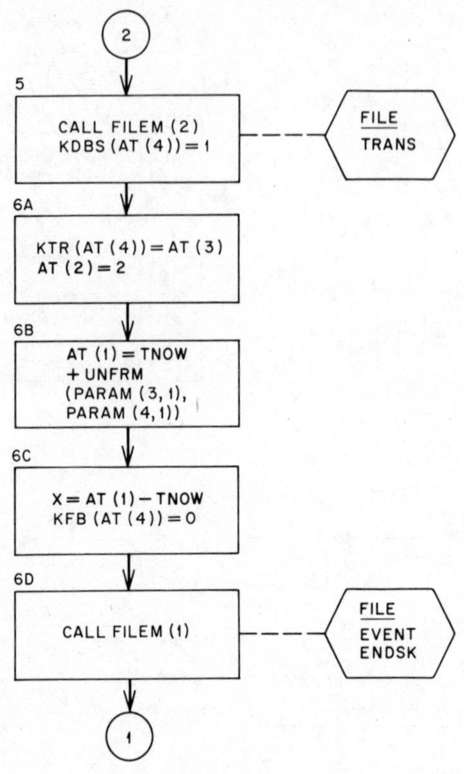
2
5
CALL FILEM (2)
KDBS (AT (4)) = 1
FILE
TRANS
6A
KTR (AT (4)) = AT (3)
AT (2) = 2
6B
AT (1) = TNOW
+ UNFRM
(PARAM (3, 1),
PARAM (4, 1))
6C
X = AT (1) − TNOW
KFB (AT (4)) = 0
6D
CALL FILEM (1)
FILE
EVENT
ENDSK
1

Problems and Exercises

1-1. Describe the relative importance and respective roles of the five facets of data in the following information or information transfer systems:
   (1) A telephone system
   (2) An inventory system
   (3) A conversation between two adults
   (4) A conversation between an adult and an 8 year-old child.

1-2. Present day computer technology feeds from three wellsprings: (1) Numerology (number systems), (2) algorithms, and (3) mechanization. Trace the origin and significant developmental milestones of each, culminating in 1944 with the ENIAC.

1-3. Elaborate upon the concept of a computer as a human thought amplifier. What should be the characteristics and functional capabilities of such a machine? What significant problems lay in the path of its realization?

2-1. What are the trade-offs between an FD that is compiled into a program and an FD that is interpreted from a record in a file?

2-2. What alternative storage methodologies are there for handling variable length keys in indexes to the methodology shown in Fig. 2-11?

2-3. It is possible to implement both a forward and backward link with a *single* link address on the assumption that the list is to be used only for beginning-to-end or end-to-beginning traversal. How is this done?

2-4. (a) Write the file definition and index record formats (Figs. 2-10, 2-11) and a graphical description like that of Fig. 2-23 for the following information structure:
   1. Citizen
       1.1 Account number
       1.2 Name
       1.3 Debits
             1.3.1   Date
             1.3.2   Amt
             1.3.3   Account number

      1.4 Credits
          1.4.1 Date
          1.4.2 Amt
          1.4.3 Account number
      1.5 Administration
          1.5.1 Legal
              1.5.1.1 Type
              1.5.1.2 Penalty
              1.5.1.3 Status
          1.5.2 Employment
              1.5.2.1 Job type
              1.5.2.2 Salary
              1.5.2.3 Performing rating
              1.5.2.4 Vacation accumulation
              1.5.2.5 Sick leave accumulation

Assume that the following items are keys:

1.1	1.5.1.3
1.2	1.5.2.1
1.5.1.1 (also FIFO)	1.5.2.3
1.5.1.2	

Assume that 1.3, 1.4, and 1.5.1 are dimensioned, and state all assumptions made, such as record type.

(b) What implicit data can be derived from this information structure?

2-5. The statement is made in this chapter that ". . . data processing independence comes down to a differentiation between that part of data description or those data facets that the programmer or user . . . is expected to control himself and that part which he does not have to control." Comment on this division and give your interpretation of the concept of *data processing independence.*

2-6. Devise a canonical numbering system for a graph.

CHAPTER 3

3-1. Flow chart the generation, update, and decoding of one of the tree indexes.

3-2. Devise some other storage strategies for handling variable length keys.

3-3. Extend the example of Problem 2-4 by defining first a hierarchic multiple file structure, then an associative (network) multiple file structure.

3-4. For Problem 2-4, show a trade-off between record and file structure with respect to data items 1.3, 1.4, and 1.5.1. Assume that 1.3 and 1.4 are frequently updated and that 1.5.1 is infrequently updated.

3-5. What is the memory requirement and decoding speed of a tree index of the type shown in Fig. 3-38 for a file with:

  50,000 records
  4 keys/records

Average list length $= 1.5$
Average key length $= 8$ bytes
Data block $= 2,000$ bytes

3-6. Formulate timing for the inverted list Boolean search via address (or key) lists versus the bit map. Would a hybrid system be feasible, in which all lists for which $p > 1/B$ are stored as bit maps, with the rest stored as address lists? Describe how such a system would work.

3-7. Develop another example of an associative multiple file structure.

CHAPTER 4

4-1. Compare the following two space allocation methods:
    (1) A logical record address is by block plus record sequence number; there is no file control level, and files may share blocks.
    (2) A logical record address is by block plus record sequence number; there is a file control level, and a block is exclusively assigned to one file.

4-2. Describe a process of sweeping empty space into contiguous blocks on a dynamic basis, that is, the process can start and stop (as a background job of low priority) as often as required, but when it stops, the file system must still be usable.

4-3. Flowchart the generation of a mapped random file structure.

4-4. Flowchart the recovery procedure for Fig. 4-44 when the index has a multiple access update, and also for Figs. 4-46, 4-48, 4-50, 4-51, and 4-52.

4-5. If the *value* in a relational logic condition (Fig. 4-53) were to be a computed value of a function, such as AVERAGE (X), comment on the possible definitions of the range of X and its implications for interactive search.

4-6. Flowchart an infix to postfix converter.

4-7. Flowchart a pushdown list processor.

4-8. Formulate the file access and update times of chained and inverted list processors.

4-9. Discuss and give examples of the trade-offs between file and intrarecord data structures.

CHAPTER 6

6-1. Compute the maximum response time of a Class 1 time sharing system, where response time is defined as the time between the transmission of an end-of-message character (such as carriage return) to the time sharing system from the terminal and the earliest possible response of the user program to the terminal.

6-2. Flowchart the three file back-up and recovery methods.

6-3. Formulate the cost in terms of DASD accesses as a function of file size and update frequency of back-up and recovery methods 1, 2, and 3.

6-4. Devise pricing algorithms for the three classes of time sharing systems of Fig. 6-66. Assign a symbolic cost to each of the resources shown in Fig. 6-63 and combine them into a charge formula.

6-5. The reconstruction process of Fig. 6-68 may require multiple passes of the file. Can you devise another strategy that would pass the file once? What disadvantages does such a method have compared with that of Fig. 6-68?

CHAPTER 7

7-1. Modify the simulation to process all a transactions of a given transaction in a sequence.

7-2. In this chapter a 10-step algorithm is developed for computing d, the number of disks to be overlapped per channel, and T $_{actual}$, the actual turnaround time, given the parameters A_n, n, d_m, c, a, S, R, X, and T. Develop similar algorithms for the following cases:

Case	Given Parameters	Computer Design Parameters
1	A_n, d, c, a, S, R, X, T	n
		Throughout $= n/A_n$
2	n, d, c, a, S, R, x	T
		Min A_n
		Max throughput $= n/A_n$

7-3. Show that the maximum system throughput is dc/P, if $DX/(S + X) \leqslant 1$.

7-4. How does one determine in the simulation when steady state has been achieved? Modify the simulation program to achieve this.

7-5. Adapt the simulation program to the IBM 2314, taking into consideration the use of channel for seek command and track search.

7-6. What will the best turnaround time be for a transaction system with the following parameters:

(1) Records/block $= 5$

(2) Record size $= 400$ bytes

(3) DASD transfer speed $= 200,000$ bytes per sec

(4) DASD seek time (avg) $= 90$ msec

(5) DASD rotation time $= 40$ msec

(6) Transaction description: one data record is read from a one-disk level indexed random file; one record is written to a sequential file

(7) Recovery is via selective file dump method

(8) $d_m = 3$

(9) $c = 1$

    (a) Neglecting channel delay, what is the theoretical minimum transaction arrival interval per line for a 500 line-system? What is the turnaround for this arrival interval?

    (b) Answer part (a) if channel delay is not neglected.

    (c) What are A_n and T if $u_d = 0.8$ for a 500-line system? (Do not neglect channel delay).

7-7. Micro flowchart (as shown in Appendix B) and program in FORTRAN the entire simulation fo Figs. 7-75 through 7-78.

CHAPTER 8

8-1. Diagram the tree of Fig. 8-89.

8-2. Produce an example of an articulated index that is a network but not a tree.

8-3. The second (telescoped) level of description of a *posteriori* classification is the two-step process illustrated in Figs. 8-92 and 8-93. Can you devise another procedure, at this level of description, for an *a posteriori* classification? Do the above, maintaining the three properties given as the first level description, and then devise another second level procedure for some other set of properties. State the properties.

8-4. Describe another I algorithm.

8-5. Prove that the properties of *a posteriori* classification are satisfied by the algorithm of Figs. 8-92 and 8-93 and by the algorithm I.

8-6. Define a file structure for the key-to-node table that will facilitate finding paths from a conjunction.

8-7. Define records for the files of Fig. 8-82, and file update algorithms for each processor.

8-8. Add a backorder file to Fig. 8-82, and update the figure. Then perform the appropriate tasks indicated in Problem 8-7.

8-9. In Par. 8.1.1 it is indicated that the control file can be used to report delay arrivals of a transaction to a designated processor by pretabulating all of the transit times and paths of a transaction through the system processors. Design this table, the report that would be issued, and describe how the speed of transaction flow can be controlled in this way.

LONGER TERM DESIGN PROJECTS AND PROBLEMS

P-1. Consider the automation of a blood bank inventory. Units of blood are inventoried with a shelf life of 21 days. A patient must be assigned n units of blood per doctor's request, to be ready for use at time t. The following transaction cycle must be carried out:

    (1) B units of blood type T are received into inventory or removed from inventory.

    (2) A request for n units of blood for patient P is made, to be used at time t. The record for patient P must be created if not already existing.

    (3) A sample of blood from patient P is received and sent to the lab for type analysis.

(4) The lab results on type analysis on patient P is complete. The type is S.

(5) n units of blood of type S are reserved for use by patient P at time t. The bottle numbers of the blood are B_1, B_2, B_3 ... B_n. The n units are sent to the lab for compatibility tests with the sample of patient P. A given bottle number, B_i, may be reserved for more than one patient, and when one of the patients uses it, another must be taken from inventory and put on reserve.

(6) Compatibility tests between the reserved blood in bottles B_1, ... B_n and the sample from patient P are completed and a report produced for the doctor. If there are any incompatibilities, more blood is reserved from transaction 4.

(7) The doctor calls for x of the n units for patient P to be dispensed. The bottles are delivered and withdrawn permanently from inventory.

(8) The doctor returns y units for patient P to reserve or to inventory or releases y units from reserve.

(9) A bill is generated for patient P with item charges for lab tests and blood units used.

(10) Patient P is deleted from the system.

(11) Inquiries can be made on:

(a) Patient P blood request status

(b) Total amount of a given type of blood in inventory and on reserve

(c) Number of units waiting for a given test. Assume that three tests are performed for typing and three for compatibility.

(d) A patient's current bill

(e) Bottle numbers in inventory that are d days old.

Questions:

1. Define a data and file structure for on-line implementation of this system such that the *minimum* explicit data representation exists.

2. Define same for *maximum* explicit data representation.

3. Indicate for question 1 or 2 some of the trade-offs that can be made between data (record) structure and file structure. Represent the data structures as graphs.

4. Flowchart this system using the data structure of question 1 or 2.

5. Program a part of this system using the DMS language of Chap. 5.

P-2. Design a questionaire that might be used by a systems analyst in order to obtain from a potential user the initial, salient facts needed to begin a data management system design. For example, one must obtain the information needed for data and file structure, processing, storage, response time, and the like.

P-3. (a) Catalog all system design trade-offs that you can think of, both in hardware and software, in the following format:

Class
  Components
For example:

  File Medium
    Tape
    Disk
    Data cell
  DASD Type
    Fixed head
    Moveable head
    Magnetic strip
  File Structure
    Sequential
    Indexed sequential
    Etc.

(b) Indicate in either a diagrammatic, tabular, or expository way a number of the constraints and interrelations among the usage of components within each *class*. At least twelve classes should be defined.

P-4. Design a file structure to handle HOL, EOL, FIFO, LIFO retrieval control with multiply keyed records, where any list can have its control changed at any time by a REDECLARE statement.

Index

Index